Insurgency and War in Nigeria

Insurgency and War in Nigeria

Regional Fracture and the Fight Against Boko Haram

Akali Omeni

I.B. TAURIS
LONDON • NEW YORK • OXFORD • NEW DELHI • SYDNEY

I.B. TAURIS
Bloomsbury Publishing Plc
50 Bedford Square, London, WC1B 3DP, UK
1385 Broadway, New York, NY 10018, USA
29 Earlsfort Terrace, Dublin 2, Ireland

BLOOMSBURY, I.B. TAURIS and the I.B. Tauris logo
are trademarks of Bloomsbury Publishing Plc

First published in Great Britain 2020
Paperback edition first published 2021

Cover image: Ruin of the Government Girls Secondary School Chibok in Borno State
north-eastern Nigeria on March 25, 2016. (© STEFAN HEUNIS/AFP/Getty Images)

A catalogue record for this book is available from the British Library.

A catalogue record for this book is available from the Library of Congress.

ISBN: HB: 978-1-7883-1128-1
PB: 978-0-7556-3684-6
ePDF: 978-1-7883-1724-5
eBook: 978-1-7883-1725-2

Typeset by Integra Software Services Pvt. Ltd.

To find out more about our authors and books visit
www.bloomsbury.com and sign up for our newsletters.

To Sharan, mere saathee and to Piglet, my trusty French Bulldog and sturdy companion.

Contents

List of Figures

List of Tables

Preface

This volume aims to explain and deconstruct, in clear and accessible language, four broad themes. First, the emergence, organization and militarization of Boko Haram. Second, how Boko Haram's resilient military threat drives both its overt and its covert conflictual strategies. Third, the theory and practicalities of insurgent warfare and why defeating insurgents poses a challenge for government forces. This analysis will be situated within the frame of Boko Haram as an archetypical insurgent. Finally, the book critiques counter-insurgency (COIN) theory and employs case studies within an analysis of why the Nigerian military has struggled in its war against Boko Haram.

As much as the Federal Government of Nigeria (FGN) refrains from using the word 'war' to describe Boko Haram's insurgency in the country's north-east, the conflict has features that elevate it above the average internal security disturbance. The high incidence of military fighting, the human and material cost, the scale of refugee displacement and the ungoverned spaces where Boko Haram challenges state writ – all lend this insurgency features typically associated with the civil war archetype that historically has troubled African nations, Nigeria included. This conflict, moreover, is one with markers of jihadist insurgencies elsewhere: in Syria, Iraq, Somalia and Mali. Indeed, with Boko Haram establishing operational connections to jihadists in Somalia and Mali, and with Daesh (the Islamic State of Iraq and the Levant) declaring Boko Haram as its West Africa province in 2016, there are linkages between Boko Haram's threat and the jihadist military challenge as it exists elsewhere.

Boko Haram's threat manifests on two fronts. In its covert front, the group employs suicide bombings and irregular tactics, operates in small cells and demonstrates a doctrine of war avoidance: that is, it refuses to engage state forces and instead employs guerrilla-style warfare. In its overt front, by contrast – essentially its standing army – Boko Haram employs military fighting and motorized infantry elements in surprise offensives that engage, and sometimes even defeat or force tactical retreats from, Nigeria's military forces. Within this front, fighters live and train together in large camps. The sheer size and military capabilities of this standing army have led Boko Haram to acquire and hold territory.

Much of the existing literature on Boko Haram fails to interrogate the unmistakably military footprint of both fronts, however. And with the north-east Nigeria conflict now nearing a decade long without an end in sight, questions, therefore, remain: around Boko Haram's resilience, around the nature of its insurgency, around the sophistication of its military threat, and around the apparent failure of Nigerian military and security forces tasked with countering the insurgency.

Part national study of insurgency as political conflict and part military treatise, this book aims to evaluate such questions within a meditation on civil conflict as a continuation of inter-ethnic and sometimes religiously charged political intercourse in

Nigeria. The book draws from fieldwork with military units and domestic intelligence in north-east Nigeria as well as from war theory, international relations (IR) theory and sociological studies. The aim is to comprehensively examine what a complex conflict, prosecuted by a terrorist organization with a complex structure, complex ideology, complex operations and complex beginnings.

This volume's opening part sheds new light and corrects existing assumptions on Boko Haram's beginnings, evolution, leadership and organizational structure. An equally vital contribution to the existing literature lies in the book's threading of Boko Haram as a military actor, throughout its narrative. Even aside from this central theme of Boko Haram's military threat, the volume also dedicates an entire part – two chapters – to dissecting Boko Haram's military campaign, and how its overt and covert fronts drive that campaign. Preceding this analysis will be a breakdown of how the environment has force-multiplied Boko Haram's threat at both the tactical and operational levels of war. Likewise, the book's breakdown of the Islamic State's West Africa Province (ISWAP) adds a much-needed perspective on what is still an embryonic area of research around group infighting within Boko Haram and its implications for the north-east Nigeria conflict. The theory and practical concerns around why superior Nigerian military forces have struggled to contain Boko Haram's threat, even into 2019, are evaluated within the final part of the book.

The nature and scope of its analysis will make this volume a particularly useful text to war theory scholars, especially those interested in insurgency and the COIN challenge against modern jihadist perpetrator groups. The volume, however, is also relevant to a broader audience including political scientists, International Relations scholars interested in the emergence of domestic level threats, contemporary African conflict students, military personnel, and security practitioners. Moreover, for senior and mid-level military personnel in Nigeria interested in understanding Boko Haram and its military threat, this text is an essential read. Additionally, the updates from September 2019 make this volume one of the most complete currently available publications on Boko Haram and its military campaign.

Introduction

Since 1960 when it became an independent political entity, Nigeria has faced threats to its sovereignty. Compared to the Francophone countries that border it except at its southern coast, however, Nigeria historically has possessed considerably better military capabilities, whether in force structure, combat readiness or sustainable capabilities. Nigeria's main security threats, therefore, have not been from these countries, especially since the signing of strategic West African alliance treaties in the early 1980s. Instead, the most notable security threats have been endogenous, localized within the country: in its east, deep south and far north-east. Continuing this storied history of internal conflict and violent rebellion that spans decades, Nigeria today still struggles against insurgency. More to this point, whereas armed militias in Nigeria's oil-rich yet socio-economically fragile Niger Delta had been the main internal security threat since the turn of the century, a more violent rebellion in the country's north-east and its frontier has supplanted them.

In July 2009, Islamist militant group, Jamā'at Ahl as-Sunnah lid-Da'wah wa'l-Jihād, widely referred to as Boko Haram, gained mainstream notoriety. In a bloody rampage within series of widespread riots that claimed hundreds of lives, Boko Haram demonstrated its intent to disregard police authority and violently contest the rule of law in the north of Nigeria. Eventually called in to support the civil power, the Nigerian Army (NA) contained Boko Haram's violence after only a few days of operations. For Boko Haram, the cost of its violent rampage had been high. Muhammad Yusuf, its leader, was killed; his followers scattered, with many dead or detained. The group's congregations were banned shortly after. In yet another instance of kinetics employed against a smaller, weaker enemy, the results seemed to affirm the utility of force for the Nigerian military in operations against an armed threat. Indeed, 'mission accomplished', said the Army at the time; but was it?

Such optimism, in hindsight, proved short-lived. In September 2010, Boko Haram resurfaced with a new leader to wage an insurgency from its base in the north-east of Nigeria. Sophisticated, better prepared and more calculated than in its opening gambit from 2009, Boko Haram fought a war whereby the tactical fulcrum was not powerful field units as in conventional warfare. Instead, the population became the centre of gravity as Boko Haram dispersed and became a highly irregular threat. Over time, Boko Haram gained sufficient capabilities, and local fighters, to engage in military fighting, but this was not what made the group so dangerous.

Boko Haram was such a danger because its use of guerrilla warfare and suicide bombings gave war avoidance a new meaning in Nigeria. However, this enemy was increasingly sophisticating also as the conflict matured – able to field an army of thousands, with light forces, motorized infantry and, in some cases, heavy armour deployed for the engagement. Added to this were diverse methods of funding including bank robberies and kidnappings. Use of new media and social media, exploitation of ethnocultural linkages across three borders and a central reference to Salafi-Jihadist ideology were all additional ways by which Boko Haram further hybridized its threat. Against such an enemy, the NA's traditional military advantages, such as superior firepower and an ability to deploy its manoeuvre divisions at scale, were rendered far less effective, even irrelevant in some instances.

As its operations sophisticated, moreover, Boko Haram's orbit of terror extended beyond north-east Nigeria. Parts of northern Cameroon, Chad and Niger, Nigeria's closest neighbours within the Lake Chad Basin Commission subregion, were now impacted by the conflict. Furthermore, insofar as some of the affected cross-border areas share ethnic identity with Nigeria's north-east, this has further influenced the people-centred nature of the conflict. Such socio-ethnic considerations further frustrate the possibility of a military determination in a war form wherein the battleground has shifted to the population itself.

Driving its military threat and further complicating the response by Nigeria's forces is Boko Haram's ability to operate on two fronts. Boko Haram's covert front emphasizes guerrilla warfare and terrorist tactics such as bombings, kidnappings and early-dawn raids. Conversely, Boko Haram's overt front – its standing army, operational since 2013 – emphasizes strategic objectives including territoriality and counter-denial of the NA's localized presence.

Using this mix of acquired conventional military assets, lightning-fast offensives, suicide bombings and exploitation of the local environment, Boko Haram has been successful at protracting conflict while minimizing its operational footprint. Ergo, Boko Haram's doctrine of war avoidance and its role as a generator of asymmetric attacks have served Boko Haram best as a military actor. Aside from guerrilla tactics, however, Boko Haram also has maintained a conventional threat. Using unarmoured technicals, scores of fighters and armoured vehicles, Boko Haram, as an example, has been able to capture and hold territory and even overrun some Nigerian military formations in the north-east.

Against this shape-shifting threat, and combined with the characteristically complex and multifaceted nature of insurgency, the Nigerian military has struggled, or at the least has performed below the expectations of many. On paper, after all, Nigeria's forces hold a conspicuous experiential and capabilities advantage over Boko Haram. On paper, a battlefield decision in favour of Nigeria's forces appears almost a foregone conclusion. Indeed, the picture of Boko Haram's forces on the move – an impedimenta of moribund trucks and armoured fighting vehicles supported by unkempt irregular fighters, some no more than boys – can be described as a ragtag army. The Nigerian military, by contrast, is better equipped, better trained and has the numbers. Nigeria, furthermore, consistently for decades, has remained one of sub-Saharan Africa's most significant defence spenders. This strategic superiority, most expect, should reflect in Nigeria's campaign against Boko Haram.

Additionally, the Nigerian military has a storied history of fighting 'irregulars': ragtag armies of non-state actors employing improvised capabilities; even in instances such irregulars were semi-professionalized. This operational experience goes back decades. Aside from its peacekeeping adventures in West Africa, which came later in the 1990s, Nigeria's military also fought a civil war at home against separatist Biafra forces, between 1967 and 1970. The Civil War of Nigeria marked a turning point in the NA's ability to plan and conduct combat operations that required manoeuvre activity at scale. Moreover, additional experience against local irregulars came as the military conducted counter-insurgency (COIN) operations in Nigeria's restive Niger Delta region decades later.

Why then, despite its combat operations pedigree and strategic advantage, has the Nigerian military struggled against Boko Haram's insurgency? In trying to come up with an answer, some points are noteworthy. First, an examination of the NA institution gives the lie to the notion that it is purpose-built to counter insurgency, despite its past operational experience and conventional military capabilities. Second, insurgencies tend to deny government forces their traditional military advantages. Moreover, in further examining this second point, we see that Nigeria's unremarkable experience against Boko Haram insurgents – its COIN challenge – in many ways mirrors that of government forces fighting insurgents elsewhere.

It is, nevertheless, important not to run away with this idea that the intractability of Boko Haram's insurgency is entirely due to incompetence within the Nigerian military as a counter-insurgent. The enduring challenge in Nigeria's COIN is very much about Boko Haram as an armed threat that emerged from innocuous beginnings to repeatedly defy the odds and exploit the environment in ways a conventional army would not. Insofar as this is not just about Nigeria's military shortcomings, therefore, much of the interrogative analysis on the north-east insurgency should fall on Boko Haram itself. Moreover, to understand insurgency and war in Nigeria as a phenomenon that is bigger than even Boko Haram's threat, we must likewise expand our examination.

Consequently, this volume's thesis features four broad themes. The first of these revisits Boko Haram's origins, with a particular focus on the group's ideology, its leaders, the events that led to its transition into a violent perpetrator group and the aftermath of those events. Next, the text evaluates the interaction between Boko Haram and the environment in which it wages its insurgency. The emphasis here is on specific features of this environment that have force-multiplied Boko Haram's threat. Moreover, this environment extends beyond north-east Nigeria to northern Cameroon, Chad and Niger. As its third major theme, the book examines the underpinnings and particular features of Boko Haram's military and organizational sophistication and why Nigeria's forces do not, in practice, hold certain COIN advantages that seem apparent on paper. In its final part, the volume takes a theoretical lens towards its investigation of Nigeria's COIN challenge. The book summary theorizes reasons for which the Nigerian military has struggled in its COIN. A breakdown of the book's chapters follows.

Book structure

Part I of the book is made up of two chapters that together evaluate Boko Haram's emergence as a military threat. Chapter 1 acts as background discussion to Boko Haram and the northern Nigeria religious climate from which the group emerged. The chapter evaluates Boko Haram's formative years and highlights the tell-tale signs that the group was on a collision course of violent confrontation with Nigeria's government and the established Islamic order in northern Nigeria. The chapter's analysis discusses Boko Haram across three phases: before it became a military actor, as Boko Haram began crossing lines and tending towards violent confrontation, and at the point where the group effectively becomes a violent non-state actor if not yet a credible threat *per se*. A focal point of Chapter 1 is an examination of Boko Haram's ideology from an Islamic jurisprudence perspective. This analysis, which draws from a wide range of sources and accounts relevant to unpacking Boko Haram's claims, aims to provide one of the most substantive yet accessible breakdowns of Boko Haram's idea system. Part of this meditation also reflects on the innovative nature of Boko Haram's interpretation of the Qur'an and how, across phases of the sect's radicalization, this led to violent confrontation against the Islamic establishment and Nigerian government authorities (what the group refers to as 'jihad'). Other themes discussed in Chapter 1 include Boko Haram leaders' personalities, their influence, the group's ideological clashes with notable clerics in the Islamic establishment and, finally, the problems with the police that climaxed in the Battle of Maiduguri, in July 2009.

Using first-hand interview accounts from the police, military and Department of State Services (the primary domestic intelligence agency of Nigeria) and drawing also from earlier research from the author's PhD project on COIN in Nigeria, Chapter 2 details the backdrop, events and aftermath of the Battle of Maiduguri. This incident and the related violence, which spread across northern Nigeria at the time, acted as a flashpoint in Boko Haram's history. These events transformed the group's religious and political identity and led to a changing of the guard, so to speak: from Yusuf's era, which had once seen Boko Haram as part of the northern Nigerian (ummah) Muslim body, to that of Shekau, within which Boko Haram had become a discredited and disowned fringe movement. Now violent and entirely rogue, Boko Haram was determined to make the Nigerian government and the Islamic establishment pay for its downfall; its use of suicide bombings since 2011 completed that radical transitioning into a perpetrator group. This transitioning in the post-Yusuf era was seemingly championed single-handedly by one individual: Abu Shekau, a man as ever-present in Boko Haram's propaganda videos as the group came to be in Borno and its environs.

Interrogating his background and idea system, the final section of Chapter 2 discusses Abu Shekau himself; the man who emerged, circa 2010, as de facto leader of Boko Haram. This part of the chapter, however, shows that Shekau was far from alone as an influential figure within Boko Haram. Indeed, as far as operations, planning and transnational outlook were concerned, Shekau's vision was possibly eclipsed by that of another more shadowy figure in the group, Boko Haram's operational mastermind, Mamman Nur.

Retaining a strong focus of unit-level analysis (analysis of individuals) within Boko Haram, Chapter 3 examines the origins of Abu Mus'ab al-Barnawi's faction, including its endorsement by Daesh (the Islamic State) to head its Islamic State West Africa Province (ISWAP). This faction would repeatedly clash with Boko Haram since 2016, conducting separate operations and undermining the leadership of erstwhile Boko Haram leader, Abubakar Shekau. Insofar as al-Barnawi is central to ISWAP's narrative, questions and discrepancies exist within this individual's background including details of his lineage, formative years, age, knowledge of Islamic law and operational experience. The purpose of this part of the chapter, in exploring such themes, is not to challenge what already exists on the subject. Nor is the aim to discredit the research body on the subject (much of which is excellent). Instead, the chapter's analysis aims to contribute to the still-emerging literature on ISWAP and Abu Mus'ab al-Barnawi.

Chapter 3 also introduces the reader to influential Boko Haram figure, Mamman Nur, who supposedly orchestrated the breakaway of the al-Barnawi faction; becoming the leader of the group while Habib (al-Barnawi) remained as little more than a figurehead due to his connection to the Yusuf bloodline. Finally, an update to Chapter 3, written in the Spring of 2019, further discusses ISWAP's role and features as well as the Dapchi Girls Kidnapping in February 2018, and how the controversy surrounding their release by ISWAP in March 2018 likely contributed to the assassination of Nur in August of that year. Furthermore, this updated section of Chapter 3 explores Boko Haram's continuing struggle with the Abu Mus'ab al-Barnawi faction (ISWAP) and discusses notable incidents within the timelines of both groups. The NA response over this period and the implications of the interactions of all three actors (Boko Haram, ISWAP and the NA) shall also be examined. The chapter's conclusion reflects on the current security implications of ISWAP's emergence.

In summary, therefore, by providing fresh details of the processes that contributed to Boko Haram's transitioning, Part I of this text aims to contribute to the research-based literature body on Boko Haram's shift towards militarization from its innocuous but non-violent beginnings in north-east Nigeria. Moreover, in taking a closer look at ISWAP's leadership, ideology, military operations, and current threat implications, Chapter 3's full-spectrum analysis is uniquely positioned as a fresh addition to this fledging area of research on what has emerged as a significant Boko Haram faction.

Chapter 4 examines Boko Haram's interaction with its immediate environment, exploiting certain features of the latter to recruit and conscript fighters and suicide bombers from both municipalities and rural areas. 'Environment', however, is not just the socio-economic milieu, which typically has been the emphasis within the literature. Rather, the context here includes the physical environment: the geographic features of north-east Nigeria and the areas it shares with Chad, Niger and Cameroon that connive to sustain Boko Haram's military threat. 'Environment', as it relates to these three countries, neighbouring to Nigeria and also affected by Boko Haram's violence, shall be Chapter 5's focus.

The literature on Boko Haram remains embryonic with regard to field-based studies around specific environmental features that have directly influenced Boko Haram's ability to field a standing army and pose an enduring military threat. How, for instance, does the environment – socio-economic, political but also *geographic* – enduringly enable the insurgent's operational resilience and force-multiply its threat? Certainly, ideology and leadership, discussed in Chapter 1, play their roles. Indeed, in the case of Boko Haram, the pivot towards a military campaign arguably built on preceding shifts within the movement's leadership and ideology over time. However – and this is central to Part II's overarching narrative – 'environment' is also required by the insurgent if he is to both attract an audience to participate in the insurgency and then initiate and sustain a military campaign.

At the core of Part II's analysis, therefore, are three factors that underpin the effectiveness of Boko Haram's people-centred military campaign. More than merely driving the insurgent's military campaign, these factors explain the emergence and resilience of Boko Haram's military threat in north-east Nigeria. The factors, in examination order, are (1) features of the geographical environment, which connive to force-multiply Boko Haram's threat beyond its borders and into the near region: Chad, Niger and Cameroon. Boko Haram has come to exploit physical features such as mountainous areas, open plains, wetlands and forest terrain to tactical advantage. This part of the volume shall evaluate how. (2) use of extremist ideology as soft power by Boko Haram, to exploit social and political inequalities with an ethnocultural and religious character. Using modified economics marketplace rules of supply and demand, I present a relationship between what Boko Haram offers and the population that 'buys' this proposition. Furthermore, I evaluate how Boko Haram employs not just 'sticks', but also 'carrots', to seduce and incentivize fighters, who also come from across the border in many instances.

The third and final factor discussed in Part II of the volume builds on this 'carrot' and 'stick' thesis, and develops it into a spectrum of participation within Boko Haram's insurgency. Within this spectrum, coercion (including strong-arm tactics and conscription) dominates one end, whereas persuasion and soft incentives (including food, shelter, camaraderie, abuse of substances such as tramadol, but also relatively unique benefits such as access to Apple devices) feature at the other, within fighter camps. Boko Haram makes full use of this spectrum in its recruitment calculus. Moreover, the range of recruitment tools identifiable here is employed neither indeliberately nor without method. On the contrary, Boko Haram has demonstrated a surprisingly calculated approach to creating and maintaining control mechanisms for its recruits.

The factors highlighted above contribute to the north-east Nigeria conflict. The first of these factors, the geographical environment, is discussed in Chapter 4. Chapter 5 builds on this idea of 'environment', relating it to Cameroon, Chad and Niger as Nigeria's closest neighbours who also have been affected by the conflict. The ethnocultural links between Nigeria and Cameroon are an example of a local feature, aside from the terrestrial environment, also exploited by Boko Haram in its transnational activity. Chapter 6's discussion of 'environment' is more consistent with the term's common connotations within the social sciences. More to this point, Chapter 6 discusses the social, economic and political connotations of 'environment' and how this has been exploited by Boko Haram to swell its ranks and to popularize, in the past at least, its agitation against the Nigerian authorities.

Part III of this volume shifts the insurgency and war meditation towards Boko Haram as a military actor prosecuting both overt and covert conflictual strategies. Chapter 7 initiates this analytical shift by focusing on Boko Haram's military fighting and how, against the odds of far superior Nigerian forces, the insurgent has demonstrated an organizational resilience. This organizational resilience has meant that Boko Haram so far has been able to recover from government offensives and targeted killings of its leadership and commanders that may have crippled some smaller, younger, perpetrator groups. Rather than merely survive, moreover, Boko Haram, in some periods of its insurgency, has thrived as a military actor now almost a decade old as of 2019. Along these lines, Chapter 7 argues that the sophistication of Boko Haram's overt front, and this standing army's capabilities, have underpinned Boko Haram's ability to contest territory via military fighting eventually.

Chapter 7 also discusses the Nigerian military's attempt at dismantling and degrading Boko Haram's organizational structure. The former, in dismantlement, is an intelligence-driven strategy for network building and influence operations by military and security forces within communities at the grassroots. The mechanism is one of networking and trust-building within vulnerable communities. Stakeholders are from the government, religious establishment, the military, and security and intelligence agencies. Degradation, on the other hand, is via physical destruction of Boko Haram's military assets such as its motorized infantry vehicles, via the destruction of its camps and the elimination of its fighters in battle, as well as via 'decapitation', whereby senior leaders, commanders and influential figures within Boko Haram (such as bombmakers) have either been eliminated or captured. Even though such decapitation strategies have been successful for the Nigerian military, however, Boko Haram has remained resilient. More to this point, Chapter 7's analysis finds no substantive correlation between successful decapitation and reduced violence by Boko Haram, within proximate periods of its insurgency. This reflects Boko Haram's resilience. However, this enemy shows resilience in other ways, too.

As an example, even in aspects of warfighting where Nigeria's forces, on paper, should dominate, they have failed to force a capitulation of Boko Haram's standing army. Resilience against the Nigerian Air Force's airpower is one such aspect, evaluated within the chapter, of where Boko Haram has exceeded battlefield expectations. The chapter's analysis of the air-land threat and the surface-to-air counter helps explain why. The airpower analysis here is essential: virtually no substantive analysis of this area of Boko Haram's threat exists within the literature.

Chapter 7 also investigates the idea within the discourses that Boko Haram poses a 'hybrid threat'. The chapter concludes that such assessments should be more measured but acknowledges that Boko Haram's threat is indeed diffused and highly irregular, taking different forms across phases of its insurgency. Insurgent warfare theories, specifically Maoism and post-Maoism, are used within this analysis to explore these phases and map them within a table in the chapter. These insurgency concepts also assist with the definition of Boko Haram's threat as one that mimics different theoretical insurgency archetypes, without necessarily conforming to a single identity over time.

One last point on Chapter 7 is that it appears here as a revised version of a paper initially published as 'Boko Haram's Increasingly Sophisticated Military Threat', *Small Wars and Insurgencies*, Volume 29, 2018, Issue 5–6, edited by Paul B. Rich. The revised version, exclusive to this volume, includes a rewritten introduction as well as four substantive chapter subsections. These are (1) 'Understanding Boko Haram's organisational network and command structure', (2) 'Decapitation: Target-based weakening of Boko Haram's command structure in Nigeria', (3) 'Is decapitation degrading Boko Haram's organisational network?' and (4) 'Grassroots intelligence operations: Another approach to dismantling Boko Haram's network'. Minor changes have also been made to the sections on airpower within this chapter. These revisions contribute to Chapter 7's uniqueness, insofar as the chapter's narrative now discusses not just Boko Haram's military sophistication (as its parent paper does) but also how resilient to military degradation, in general, Boko Haram has become over time.

For all its military capabilities, however – including its capacity to assemble an operational motorized infantry force – it is Boko Haram's use of a range of irregular tactics, across a vast operational theatre, that has frustrated the NA's traditional military advantages. It is this irregular threat, and more specifically the tactic of suicide bombing, that is Chapter 8's focus.

Boko Haram's use and sophistication of suicide bombings have force-multiplied and projected its orbit: from the north-east of Nigeria further inwards and into metropolitan areas of the Federal Capital Territory (FCT), Abuja. Part III nonetheless ends with a summary caution that whereas Boko Haram's covert activity increasingly has featured *istishhadiya* (martyrdom operations), there is much more to Boko Haram as a guerrilla threat than its demonstrated technical proficiency in suicide bombings. Moreover, what is telling about Boko Haram's covert and overt fronts is not their absolute threat *per se*, but their relative threat and the fact that the group deploys both fronts in ways that negate the Nigerian military's superior firepower as well as its other traditional battlefield advantages. As a final note, Chapter 8 is an updated and much-revised version of a research paper published in 2018 as Omeni, Akali (2018) 'Boko Haram's Covert Front', *Journal of African Conflicts and Peace Studies*, Vol. 4: Iss. 1.

Part IV of the volume shifts the text's focus within the domain of military scholarship: from insurgent warfare and the insurgent to COIN and the counter-insurgent. Chapter 9 of the book opens with a brief primer on international relations and war theory to provide some context to the central theme of the chapter: counter-insurgency (COIN) theory and the COIN challenge for government forces. More to this point, Chapter 9 discusses the theory and contemporary debate on COIN and examines why insurgency, in departing from the 'saw-saw model' of military warfare as victory or defeat, considerably complicates the nature of a government's COIN response. The chapter's critique begins with classic COIN theory and employs contemporary cases to test the heuristic utility of COIN's so-called best practices within the conduct of operations today.

The chapter's analysis suggests that for smaller armies especially, the scope of activity that COIN entails, makes it a well-discussed yet rarely achieved operational approach. Add to this the fact that the insurgent tends to be better at 'bottom-up' warfare than state militaries (which tend to be traditional, 'top-heavy' organizations) and the practical outcomes of COIN become even more sobering. Considering such viewpoints, Chapter 9's critique of the COIN debate identifies three common themes within the discourses that make the so-called best practices and popular theory recommendations within this war form problematic for the traditional military institution. The chapter's analysis is not just about COIN theory and general practice, however. Rather, the frame is within the specific challenges of the NA in countering Boko Haram's threat.

On another note, changes to this volume's publication schedule mean that beyond Chapter 9, a September 2019 update to this book bridges that chapter and the volume's conclusion. This update discusses some developments within the NA's COIN campaign between 2017 and 2019. Within this update, there is some reflection on Army operations in the north-east, within the past two years. Next, the human security dimension of the crisis is discussed. Finally, after criticisms and a pessimistic view of the NA's COIN conduct is taken, the most significant adaptations made by the Army, as its campaign has matured, are examined. Particular emphasis is on adaptations within the Army's combat function, and, in particular, to the Army's Mobile Strike Teams (MSTs) initiative (2017 onwards).

The volume's Conclusion reflects on the COIN challenge, why it exists and how militaries come to experience it. Drawing on external case studies, the Conclusion explains why the NA, much like counter-insurgents in modern operations, has struggled in its operations against Boko Haram. Important themes emergent from the discussed cases are then used to test against COIN theory. The chapter, however, keeps the Nigeria case firmly within the analytical frame; this is not a standalone COIN critique by any means. What it is, is a summary of the COIN challenge in Nigeria that draws from previously discussed 'broad ideas' from the literature and practice of this war form.

As a final note on this volume, where the Nigerian military in COIN constitutes the debate focus, my now-published PhD research study, *Counter-Insurgency in Nigeria*, is emphasized. The aim here is not to unduly self-reference; however, the limited extent of research-based studies on Nigerian military COIN operations, during certain periods of the insurgency, made such self-referencing, in certain instances, a necessary recourse.

Part One

The Insurgent

Boko Haram's Formative Years, Ideology and Transitioning to Violence

Introduction

Boko Haram is a complex group waging a complex insurgency predominantly in Nigeria's north-east. Thus, although this book's narrative of insurgency and war in Nigeria ends with the Nigerian Army; it begins with, and places considerable emphasis on, Boko Haram. Without assuming reader familiarity with Boko Haram and the environment of its insurgency in north-east Nigeria, this chapter serves as an introduction to both. The theoretical hook and thread of this chapter are, respectively, a thematic and chronological analysis of Boko Haram's radicalization process, and the contributing factors that unsystematically and haphazardly translated that radicalization into a violent military threat.

Existing theoretical frames on Boko Haram focus on such themes as the group's leadership succession, the history of Islam in northern Nigeria, the contemporary religious 'marketplace' of northern Nigeria, the conflict's impact and use of sociological theories, such as relative deprivation, to explain support for the insurgency (Forest 2012, Umar 2012, Agbiboa 2013, Comolli 2015, Varin 2016). Such frames provide useful background information but fail to account for the perspective on Boko Haram provided by this chapter. This chapter's discussion advances the debate in three ways that existing narratives fail to. First, it evaluates questions around the nature of Boko Haram's idea system and local appeal. Second, this chapter provides, from ground zero in north-east Nigeria, first-hand police and security services accounts of Boko Haram's emerging threat in the years up to its 2009 rampage. Third, Chapter 1 gives the reader insight into the mindset of Boko Haram as an emerging military actor from a period when the group's militaristic ambitions were, as yet, embryonic. A specific aim of the chapter is the avoidance of the current dialogue's tendency to provide too much background information on northern Nigeria and too little substance about Boko Haram itself.

The interrogation conducted in the pages that follow is explicitly thematic: this chapter is subdivided into sections, each of which occupies a space in the overall discussion. However, the chapter's analysis is also implicitly chronological: whereas the chapter subsections mention dates but try to de-emphasize period overall, the first themes evaluated are relevant to Boko Haram's formative years. The topics discussed by the end of the chapter, conversely, shed some light on how Boko Haram crossed a line and in so doing became a violent perpetrator group. The chapter, however, does not use sequentiality to establish causality; rather, in warning against such assumptions, the chapter crisscrosses through the years between 1995 and 2010, to extract and connect themes relevant to its theoretical hook and thread. For its data, the chapter uses the author's interviews conducted in Maiduguri, interviews conducted elsewhere in northern Nigeria, the author's research since 2011, and the existing body of research-based literature on Boko Haram and the environment of north-east Nigeria.

Boko Haram: An introduction

Jama'atu Ahlis Sunna Lidda'awati wal-Jihad, translated from Arabic as 'People Committed to the Propagation of the Prophet's Teachings and Jihad' and widely known as Boko Haram, is a violent radical Salafi-Jihadist movement in Nigeria. The name itself is a compound of the Hausa language and Arabic. 'Boko' is Western education but also suggests Westernization in the broader sense. In its literal translation, however, the term is a reference to Western books (literature). 'Haram' is Arabic for something (often, a practice) that is non-permissible.

The name, 'Boko Haram', therefore, references the group's fundamentalist millenarian position that pre-Westernized and strict Muslim society was more puritanical than the present secular nature of governance and indeed society. Later in this chapter, the theology around Boko Haram's position shall be interrogated. Suffice to say for now, that due to this stance, western education and its influence are, therefore, to Boko Haram, viewed as un-Islamic and so, non-permissible (*haram*). Boko Haram itself has tried to clarify what its name connotes, noting in a statement a decade ago (translated from the Hausa language) that:

> 'Boko Haram' does not in any way mean 'Western education is a sin' as the infidel media continue to portray us. Boko Haram actually means Western civilisation is forbidden. The difference is that while the first gives the impression that we are opposed to formal education coming from the West, that is Europe, which is not true, the second affirms our belief in the supremacy of Islamic culture (not education) for culture is broader, it includes education but not determined by Western education. (Vanguard 2009)

For Boko Haram, several, though not necessarily all, forms of Western influence, therefore, are non-permissible. Democracy, pluralistic society (including co-existence with *Kāfir* – infidels or disbelievers), non-Islamic law, and a general departure from fundamentalist Islamic conservative norms, all appear to be areas that Boko Haram has taken issue with and blames the government for permitting and the Islamic establishing for compromising on. Where strict Islamic customs are relaxed to be tolerant of non-Muslim practices, which arguably has to be the case in Nigeria due to the pluralistic nature of society, Boko Haram interprets such doctrinal concessions and social practices as *Bid'ah*. This Arabic term connotes innovation or heresy, with reference to doctrines and practices that contravene, or that lie potentially in opposition to, the teachings of the Qur'an and the *Sunnah*.[1]

Still, Boko Haram appears to make exceptions for itself. For instance, the group is highly dependent on Western weapons and technology, insofar as these same Western technologies provide an advantage, whether on or off the battlefield, for its campaign. In the same way, Boko Haram also uses Western media platforms, such as YouTube and Twitter, to propagate its ideas and broadcast messages. Adherents to Boko Haram's ideas would, in the group's early years, adopt a name: *Yusufiyya* – followers of Yusuf – after Muhammad Yusuf, Boko Haram's firebrand lead preacher.

As this chapter's analysis would demonstrate, Yusuf and his followers emerged at an opportune period in northern Nigeria (see Figure 1.1 for Nigeria map). There was a robust and longstanding struggle between upstart religious movements and the establishment in northern Nigeria at the time. Still, the radical chatter that Boko Haram generated, and the doctrines the sect espoused, were precisely the sort of approach to enable it to cut through the part-theological, part-political debate and get noticed. Just as the environment, wherein Boko Haram generated this chatter, was ripe for its audience: the poor, the downtrodden, mostly youth, mostly male. Northern Nigerian society has a name for this social caste: the *talakawa*, or the commoners. Their numbers make them a politically relevant demographic and a powerful one, within a part of Nigeria where, as much as any other, religion, culture, social castes and politics are often linked. Therefore, some background is essential to situating Yusuf's emergence within this environment of northern Nigeria, which was going through notable changes at the time.

Figure 1.1 Map of Nigeria, Showing Parts of Niger, Chad and Cameroon

1970s–1990s: Competing theologies of Sufism and Salafism in Northern Nigeria

Hailing from the Kanamma area of Yobe State in Nigeria's north-east (Umar 2012, 127), Muhammad Yusuf was a one of an emerging class of radical clerics who, shortly after the turn of the century, looked to establish themselves within a new generation of Salafist thought in the profoundly religious society of northern Nigeria. Main characteristics of this new school of doctrine were that (1) it was stricter and less accommodating of modernization and syncretic doctrines; moreover, (2) it was particularly critical of the Islamic establishment (typified by the Sufi Brotherhoods), which they accused bid'ah (innovation in religious matters), dilution of matters concerning fundamentalist interpretation of Islamic law, and syncretism.

As some background to the doctrine's emergence, conservative Salafi and Wahhabi ideology originally formed the religious identity of the older generation of northern Nigerian Muslim scholars under the banner of Shaykh Gumi's religious organization. Shaykh Gumi's movement established in the late 1970s as the '*Jamā 'at 'izālat al-bid 'a wa iqāmat al-sunna* (the group for removing religious innovation and establishing Sunna, i.e. the normative model of Prophet Muhammad)' (Umar 2012, 120–121). This broad school of Sunni adherents is known as *Izala* for short. Shaykh Abubakar Gumi is a notable religious figure in this conversation. He was Grand qadi of northern Nigeria during the country's First Republic (the brief period of Nigerian, rather than British, constitutional rule between 1963 and 1966). A highly regarded theologian, eloquent speaker, *Qur'anic* scholar and expert on Islamic jurisprudence, Shaykh Gumi is widely considered a pioneer of post-colonial Islamic reforms in northern Nigeria. At his peak from the 1960s, Shaykh Gumi was even somewhat a radio and television star, having popularised the format of media-broadcast preaching, debates and dialogues (Oxford Islamic Studies Online n.d., Loimeier 1997, J. N. Hill 2010, 22).

Shaykh Gumi's idea system called for ' … a return to the *Quran* and hadith [and] criticised traditional Sufi orders, local religious practices, and modernising secularism' (Oxford Islamic Studies Online n.d.). Gumi was also highly critical of the Islamic establishment and the Sultan of Sokoto as its spiritual head, as well as major Muslim syncretic movements such as the Sufi Brotherhoods, particularly the *Tijaniya* and Qadiriyya (Loimeier 1997). Moreover, whereas 'Gummi did not embrace Wahhabism in its entirety, many of its values chimed with those he held' (J. N. Hill 2010, 21). Indeed, this fact is vital in understanding the fundamentalist nature of the early Izala movement, represented by 'Gumi and the generation that supported his idea system, circa the late 1970s and into the 1990s.

In the decades since its formation, Shaykh Gumi's movement greatly expanded and the *Izala* became a significant force within the Muslim society of northern Nigeria. Perhaps due to this expansion, schismatic tensions emerged, by the 1990s, between practitioner schools of Gumi's core Salafist/Wahhabi doctrines initially associated with the 'Yan *Izala* religious identity. Such tensions came about as the Islamic doctrines were softened to be more tolerant, particularly in the area of modernizing secularism, by the younger generation that followed (Umar 2012, 120–121). In a sense, therefore, the early syncretic and modernizing influences of traditionalist Sufism in northern Nigeria were again being warmed to by the *Izala* B, the younger generation of *Izala*, who at the least were less critical of the influential Brotherhoods than radicals like Yusuf who emerged from this very school.

Indeed, such has been the ideological differences involving the established Sufi order, newer movements like *Izala* A and (even more recent) upstart movements like Boko Haram, that Jon Hill once questioned whether Sufism, as a modernizing movement could counter-balance radical groups like *Izala* (J. N. Hill 2010)? This may well be a rhetorical question, however. The mere existence of Sufi practices suggests that Salafist opponents such as the *Izala* A and indeed Boko Haram's own idea system, which also is Salafist although much further along the radical spectrum, would always be at odds with the syncretic and modernizing doctrines associated with Sufism. This 'suspicion and hostility that exists between Sufis and Salafists throughout the Islamic world and in Nigeria specifically' (J. N. Hill 2010, v–vi) may well be, for all intents and purposes, irreconcilable. At its heart, the main quarrel here is that many of Sufism's practices, such as the 'rejection of scriptural and legal specificity [and the] veneration of saints [...] to many Salafists, verges on the heretical.' The latter practice is particularly problematic, moreover, 'as it seems to undermine or contradict the Oneness of *Allah*' (J. N. Hill 2010, 19).

Now, insofar as *Izala* B seeks to soften the core Salafi/Wahhabi doctrines fundamental to *Izala* as a religious identity, tensions between them and the older generation's adherents, *Izala* A, are inevitable. However, differences between the *Izala* collective and the Sufis are consistent with historical Salafist–Sufi animosity and suspicion. Therefore, the differences between the *Izala* collective and the Sufis tend to be more pronounced than intra-movement differences within *Izala*, both schools of which fall under the general umbrella of Salafist–Wahhabi doctrines. Indeed, as Jon Hill observes, '*Izala* members have not shied away from confronting their rivals in the *Qadiriyya* and *Tijaniyya* [Sufi Brotherhoods] head on. Numerous times throughout its existence, its [*Izala's*] young men have clashed with the Sufis on the streets' (J. N. Hill 2010, 22).

Nevertheless, clashes, mostly ideological but sometimes violent, *have* also occurred between both *Izala* schools in northern Nigeria, with *Izala* A representing the older generation, and *Izala* B, the younger (Loimeier 1997, Umar 2012). Especially within the 1990s, such clashes were not unusual as the religious environment of the *Izala* became increasingly crowded with new actors, and ever so slight shifts in its core doctrine (Loimeier 1997, Umar 2012, 120–121). Clashes of this nature nevertheless subsided by the turn of the century as Nigeria returned to Christian civilian rule 'and Muslims began to feel politically marginalised' (Umar 2012, 121).

Even so, such tensions never entirely went away. For instance, with *Izala* B becoming increasingly crowded and with little room for individuals impatient to wait their turn, upstart movements that shifted away from the softened core of *Izala* B threatened the reignition of ideological but also violent tensions. The tensions have been identifiable within *Izala* B, between *Izala* A and *Izala* B, and against the Sufis as a separate body of Islamic identity.

It was within this school, the *Izala* B, which Yusuf and his movement were initially situated in, but later splintered. This breakaway came about because Boko Haram chose to pursue the 'attractive short-cut [which] was to start a new religious discourse that would be distinctively different from the established doctrines of *Izala* A as well as the softened doctrines of *Izala* B' (Umar 2012, 122). Before further examining the splintering of Yusuf and his group away from Izala B, however, it is worth providing some background to Yusuf himself, a man who long was Boko Haram's spiritual leader and face.

The formative years of Muhammad Yusuf (Abu Yusuf al-Barnawi)

Muhammad Yusuf, whose full names and description are 'Muhammad bin Yusuf bin Muhammad bin Ahmad al-Dagheri by origin, al-Maiduguri by residence, al-Jakusi by birth, and al-Barnawi by tribe and ancestry [...] was born on 20 Dhu al-Q'ida 1389 AH in Jakusko in the northern countryside of Yobe in north-east Nigeria' (Al-Tamimi 2018). As a child, Yusuf was born to 'a family with deep roots, and to two religious parents who embraced the religion [of Islam]' (Al-Tamimi 2018). Yusuf's year of birth would have made him between thirty-nine and forty years of age around the time he died in July 2009.

As some background to his childhood years, Muhammad Yusuf was said to have been ' ... raised among two noble parents. His father was among the 'ulama of the Sufi Zawaya, who teach the young the Qur'an. Sayyid Yusuf [Muhammad Yusuf's father] was known for hostility to the Western colonialists and their ideas, which made him migrate with his son Muhammad from the state of Yobe after pressure from the apostate dogs against him to put his son in their school. And so, he moved to the city of Maiduguri' (Al-Tamimi 2018). Yusuf was already a regular at the Muhammadu Indimi Mosque in Maiduguri as far back as 1995 or 1996, according to the statements by Muslim convert and notorious Niger Delta militant warlord, Mujahid Asari Dokubo. Asari Dokubo claimed to have met Yusuf and his group there, during the former's Islamic studies (2012).

Moreover, whereas it may be tempting to dismiss Yusuf's pedigree as an Islamic scholar, based on some seemingly ill-informed exchanges Yusuf had with the Ulama in Maiduguri after he had radicalized (discussed later in this chapter), it nonetheless should be pointed out that Yusuf spent much of his life within Islamic scholarship at various levels. With regard to his formative years, as an example, Yusuf:

> ... Grew up in a religious environment in Maiduguri, and he mastered the Qur'an in the Qur'an school his father ran, and he studied the sciences of Arabic and the sciences of Qur'an, hadith and jurisprudence at the hands of the 'ulama of al-Zawaya in the states of Borno and Yobe in particular and the north of Nigeria in general, and he joined the night course classes in the al-Kanemi institute, and the period of his study in it was one year. (Al-Tamimi 2018)

Yusuf's 'organizational and da'wa beginning', that is, his first serious forays into going beyond just Qur'anic studies and into conveying the message of Islam as a teacher, 'was with the Muslim Brotherhood group in Nigeria led by the Rafidite apostate

Ibrahim al-Zakzaki who presented himself under the guise of reform and Sunnism, and kept secret his Shi'i tendency to the heretic Majous Rafidites' (Al-Tamimi 2018). This account of Yusuf's association with al-Zakzaki, written by two of his sons in 2018 under the banner of the Islamic State of West Africa Province (ISWAP) appears negative, with Yusuf said to have split with the group in his mid-twenties. Specifically, it is said that the Sheikh (Muhammad Yusuf), 'noticed the first signs of Rafidism and Iranian Shi'ism, which began to expand in 1994 CE, he separated from them and became an enemy against them, declaring them to be a danger and exposing their dark faces. And likewise, a great portion of those who had been deceived in the beginning by the [al-Zakzaki] group defected' (Al-Tamimi 2018).

By 2002, now in his thirties and through years of Islamic law understudy, some of which he spent as protégé and 'favourite student' of highly respected *Izala B* cleric Ja'afar Adam (Umar 2012, 122), Yusuf had himself had eventually been afforded some preaching duties at the Muhammad Indimi Mosque in Maiduguri and subsequently began amassing followers. Moreover, increasing numbers of these supporters came not only from outside Maiduguri but even outside of northern Nigeria (Abubakar 2012). Things took a turn for the worse, however, as Yusuf's professed views were increasingly radical, much to the disappointment of his mentor, Ja'afar Adam. Specifically, Yusuf's views and declarations were evidence of this emerging idea that the Islamic establishment and the 'Yan Boko – the political elite – were complicit with the Nigerian secular government and authorities. For Yusuf, these actors together tolerated or outright encouraged the dilution of Islamic doctrines to accommodate pluralistic society in ways that were incompatible with fundamentalist interpretations of Islamic law in northern Nigeria. These fundamentalist interpretations, such as the idea that Western education was 'haram', were what Yusuf seemed to prefer as he increasingly refused to moderate his rhetoric.

Yusuf's departure from *Izala* B's softened core doctrines and his fiery anti-establishment rhetoric, however, cut through the rest of the theological chatter and provided a powerful shortcut to amassing followership numbers. Indeed, as shall be discussed in more detail later in the chapter, this was a significant difference between Yusuf and his mentor, Ja'afar Adam. The former was a fundamentalist that interpreted Salafi/Wahabi doctrine in its strictest form, whereas the latter had a more tolerant worldview, which formed a more progressive, modernizing shift within the already softened *Izala* B core (Mohammed 2010, Umar 2012, 122). Yusuf, however, was not just a radical; he was an extremist that wished to forge an entirely new movement with little tolerance for a Westernized northern Nigerian established, even if that meant a clean break from *Izala*.

Perhaps sensing the trouble brewing from Yusuf's combination of poorly informed radical views and the large congregations of *talakawa* (ordinary folk) being fed anti-establishment ideologies, the Indimi Mosque leadership will eventually ask Yusuf and his group of troublesome and increasingly bellicose young men, to leave (Mohammed 2010, Walker 2012). A section of the group will indeed leave Maiduguri and head north-west towards the Nigerian border with Niger. There they will form an isolated community at Kanamma, in neighbouring Yobe State (Abubakar 2012, Walker 2012). This event, a *hijra* (migration) of sorts by the group, took Boko Haram's first members away from the perceived evils of an 'intolerably corrupt and irredeemable' urban centre, in Maiduguri (Walker 2012).

Yusuf and his group, having left Maiduguri and the Indimi Mosque, resurfaced in Kanamma, his ancestral home, later in 2003. They came to be known by locals as the 'Yobe Taliban' after a brief period of residence in the town (Abubakar 2012). This moniker relates to their troublemaking in Yobe. Also, the group's unusually fundamentalist practices as well as its strict dress code and sense, ostensibly modelled after the Afghan Taliban, likely contributed to the infamous reference (Abubakar 2012). Other sources also point out that they were known by a more general name – the Nigerian Taliban – for similar reasons outlined above (Umar 2012, 127–128).

December 2003: Early troublemaking

At Kanamma, from December 2003, during Yusuf's withdrawal from public life, skirmishes with authorities and disagreements with locals punctuated his group's residence (Loimeier 2012, Umar 2012). In the most serious of these later that month, the group raided a local police station at Kanamma and carted away small arms and ammunition from its armoury, before burning it down. According to the interview sources within the Department of State Services, there was, at the time, some confusion around exactly who these men were (Ahmed 2012, Bello 2012). The first suggestion within security forces was that they were robbers, as it was not unusual for police officers to be ambushed for their weapons and ammunition by criminal gangs. There was little to point to the fact that this was a radical religious sect, enacting one of its core doctrines that espoused enmity with the police and security forces. Indeed, 'Yusuf's role became public knowledge only in 2006 after his falling out with his fellow Salafists within *Izala B* [the younger generation of a major Muslim movement in northern Nigeria, which followed Salafi/Wahhabi doctrines]' (Umar 2012, 128).

It is worth pointing out that, within the December 2003 skirmish, there are conflicting narratives around the number of 'Yobe/Nigerian Taliban' casualties, comparative to those of local security forces.[2] There exists, however, a virtual consensus on three points. First, that the confrontation with security forces at Kanamma involved Muhammad Yusuf. Second, that Yusuf's involvement was not immediately clear, even after his return to Maiduguri in 2004. Third, that after the events at Kanamma, Yusuf emerged as Boko Haram's *de facto* leader.

2004: Exile and return to Maiduguri

Possibly in his mid-thirties at the time and having first escaped to Saudi Arabia via Sudan before returning to Nigeria, Yusuf resettled in Maiduguri (Loimeier 2012, Rice 2012). This was after Kanamma's events. The intervening period meant Yusuf was no longer viewed as the security threat that he and his original band, many of whom were now dead, previously posed as the 'Yobe Taliban' (Abubakar 2012).

Secondary sources tend to be non-specific on this resettlement, but primary field findings put Yusuf's return to Maiduguri within the calendar year of 2004 (Abubakar 2012). If Yusuf indeed spent time in Saudi Arabia, he appeared restless there and was not away for long. Moreover, upon his return to Maiduguri, Yusuf showed no signs of ideological repentance or diminished radical thinking. If anything, he appeared emboldened in his determination for a strict Sharia state in Nigeria. Gradually amassing a broader support base, Yusuf continued to espouse Boko Haram's central ideology that 'evil in the society is as a result of the embrace of Western civilisation and to curb such evil an Islamic society must be entrenched by destroying modern state institutions' (Danjibo 2010, 7).

While he was at Indimi Mosque, Maiduguri, before the move to Kanamma, Yusuf's followership and local popularity will increase quite substantially (Mohammed 2010, Walker 2012). Here, he had the title of *Amirul Shabaab* or 'leader of young people' (Mohammed 2010, Abubakar 2012). Many young men, some against the will of their parents, were drawn to Yusuf's preaching. Some of these men eventually had to be rescued and physically relocated away from Yusuf's sphere of influence, years later when Boko Haram began showing signs of becoming the violent extremist group it is today (Abubakar 2012). For substantial numbers of *Yusufiyya*, however, there was more to Boko Haram's unusual attraction than just narrative.

Indeed, local sources suggest that economic incentives were a draw for 'riffraff' often 'hanging around' the group's gatherings (Ahmed 2012, Bello 2012). The prospect of hot food, small amounts of Naira as payment for odd jobs and, night shelter, held an undeniable appeal for the underprivileged, including many *almajiri* as well as a range of lower caste youth demographics, who formed Yusuf courted (Omeni 2015).

Yusuf's wealth and economic influence on the socially disadvantaged

Yusuf was adept at communicating his message; he was, after all, described as a 'brilliant orator' who attracted fervent new followers in the hundreds (Rice 2012). Sermons were likewise widely distributed via cassette tape, an accessible medium, which Boko Haram exploited in extending its reach beyond those who physically attended its gatherings in Maiduguri, Borno (Mohammed 2010, Abubakar 2012, Loimeier 2012, 149).

Yusuf did more than merely spread his idea system through preaching, however. There also were economic incentives he provided for his supporters, which significantly augmented the faith-based soft power influence he wielded over them (Ahmed 2012, Bello 2012). Such soft-influence mechanisms contributed to a situation wherein by 2008, Yusuf had a large following, was a personal benefactor to many and was, increasingly, seen as a firebrand cleric who could no longer be ignored as merely a rabble-rouser and little more. Yusuf cared directly, or indirectly through funds arrangements, for his support base. Furthermore, loans were provided to purchase motorcycles for many, as the *achaba*, an entire social caste of motorcycle riders formed a central part of Yusuf's audience. There were other forms of social support, too. Provision of hot meals and the prospect of night-time shelter, in particular, was more than many of the *Yan Boko*, the educated political elite, could boast of providing for the *talakawa* (Ahmed 2012). Even beyond helping with their most basic needs of food and shelter, ' … Yusuf, in amassing this following, also helped his followers with economic assistance and even some forms of microfinance' (Comolli 2015, 30). Such seeming acts of social benevolence lent Yusuf and Boko Haram a form of soft power that coercion may not bring.

The reasons for such provision may, however, have been disingenuous insofar as they were, effectively, a control mechanism for the *Yusufiyya*. Simply put, there was a calculated return for Ustaz Yusuf, in making this human investment. Large numbers of supporters, after all, historically have been, and even today remain, a form of political currency within the religiously charged climate of northern Nigeria. For instance, as has been robustly debated in the literature on northern Nigerian faith and politics concerning the link between both, the growth and political relevance of the powerful Sufi Brotherhoods, since the 1970s form a case in point (Loimeier 1997, J. Paden 2002, J. N. Paden 2008, J. N. Hill 2010). This strategy, moreover, has been emulated by smaller groups aside from the Brotherhoods (J. N. Paden 2008, Umar 2012). The larger the group, after all – measured in its most primitive sense, by the size of those who attend its gatherings – the more relevant its voice within the religious conversation. Moreover, as the lines between religious and political numbers blur, the higher the political stock of such religious movements which can lay claim to large followership.

For an upstart religious entity like Boko Haram, therefore, it was vital that the group could amass the numbers to at least stay relevant in the 'crowded religious marketplace' of northern Nigeria (Umar 2012). There was, moreover, a side benefit to these numbers. Large numbers also meant that, for Boko Haram, 'mobilisation and indoctrination arguably became easier' (Comolli 2015, 30). The former because the numbers made Boko Haram a military threat, as the riots of July 2009 demonstrated, the latter because crowd behaviour invariably influences that of the individual. In this way, Boko Haram found ways to attract crowds by giving them something – socio-economic incentives, radical ideas as explanations for the lower castes' challenges or both – in return for their support (Ahmed 2012, Bello 2012).

That Boko Haram could provide loans to members, or potential members, to begin with, may have been possible because Yusuf was relatively wealthy, with high-class accommodation, possession of 'exotic cars including expensive jeeps' and access to private healthcare (Danjibo 2010, 11, Abubakar 2012). Yusuf's wealth came with some assistance from his father-in-law, Baba Fugu Muhammad on whose land in north-central Maiduguri *Ibn Taymiyya Masjid* was built (Walker 2012, 3). Buji Foi, a former Commissioner of Religious Affairs and an open Boko Haram supporter and 'financier' also contributed. Additionally, 'Salafist contacts in Saudi Arabia' funded Yusuf (Danjibo 2010, 13, Walker 2012, 3). Yusuf's wealth, however, contrasted that of his desperately poor congregation. Yusuf's was a life of deception in which he criticized the political elite and identified with the common folk, and yet himself had a relatively lavish lifestyle (Danjibo 2010, 11). Nevertheless, what is of more import to this particular analysis is not the distinction between Yusuf's life and those of his followers and the hypocrisy that it entailed. Rather, it is that Yusuf's ability to use his economic resources, as a vehicle to amass local support, played a role in the soft power wielded by Boko Haram (Ahmed 2012, Bello 2012).

Whether by soft incentives, charisma, narrative or ideology, Boko Haram's numbers were increasing. To some established Muslim scholars and Imams, Yusuf's continued radical posturing was already unacceptable. The speed at which this radical movement was attracting supporters also alarmed many notable figures within the *Izala B* generation, and added urgency to the need to address Boko Haram's emerging threat (Umar 2012). Influential individuals within the establishment began taking steps to correct Yusuf's thinking or otherwise check Boko Haram's religiously misplaced momentum.

Contrasting idea systems of Muhammad Yusuf and Sheikh Ja'afar Adam

Perhaps the most notable personality from the *Izala B*, with whom Yusuf had an open and acrimonious falling out, was the renowned Qura'nic scholar and cleric, Sheikh Ja'afar Adam. Sheikh Ja'afar Adam preached at Maiduguri's Indimi mosque and later relocated to Kano where he began preaching as Imam at some local mosques. These included the Gadon Kaya mosque (as his Da'awah centre), the Al-Muntada mosque at Dorayi quarters in Kano – another major Da'awah centre for Sheikh Ja'afar (he also was the chief Friday Prayer Imam here),[3] and a small mosque along Ungogo road, opposite to Daula hotel in Kano (Isa 2009). Before his activities in Kano, 'Mallam Ja'afar', as his followers fondly called him, had been prominent at the Ndimi mosque in Maiduguri. It was at here where Adam and Yusuf crossed paths, ideologically, although it is unclear if this is where both individuals first met. The ideological differences between the two would worsen over the years, leading to more pointed confrontations as the sections below shall show.

Sheikh Ja'afar was one of the most respected Islamic scholars and Imams of guidance in northern Nigeria, despite being relatively young (in his forties) for his accomplishments. Sheikh Ja'afar had known Yusuf for a while and at a time was Yusuf's mentor at Indimi mosque, during the period when the latter was *Amirul Shabaab*. As early as 2002, however, there were falling outs, some public, between the pair at Indimi Mosque (Mohammed 2010, Umar 2012). However, even when Yusuf eventually separated from his mentor in Sheikh Ja'afar in 2002, the split did not appear to be acrimonious *per se*. Specifically, whereas Yusuf 'separated from them in 2002 CE … he did not resign by himself, nor was he hostile to them. He was pleasant with them and called on them not to be allies of and enter into the democratic government, for it is a greater evil than your becoming feverish with scabies, and you cannot be treated by entering into it' (Al-Tamimi 2018).

Nevertheless, Yusuf, by that time, despite this conciliatory tone, had increasingly deviated from his mentor's preaching around Islam in a pluralistic society (Mohammed 2010). To Sheikh Ja'afar, the now-estranged Yusuf was little more than a novice attempting to use fervour as a substitute for the rational thought, scholarship and the evidence relevant to Islamic jurisprudence. By the mid-2000s, Adam (Sheikh Ja'afar) saw Yusuf as:

Lacking sufficient knowledge of Islam; his religious views should thus not be accepted. He also lacked the moral integrity of abiding by his own religious views and the foresight to identify the best interests of Muslims and how to protect them rather than gravely endangering them. Additionally, Adam claimed that Yusuf was serving the cause of a conspiracy against Muslims. (Umar 2012, 132)

Criticism of Yusuf and his followers by Ja'afar Adam was not just about Yusuf's poor grasp of the ideologies he espoused. To Ja'afar Adam and indeed many other clerics and jurists who had become aware of Yusuf's preaching, the situation was especially problematic because Boko Haram was cutting corners in rapidly amassing followers. These followers did not have the grounding in Islamic jurisprudence to filter fact from fiction, and Yusuf was a persuasive orator and benefactor. The combination was a powder keg: a fast-growing movement of zealots, led by a firebrand who knew how to whip the crowds into a frenzy, without the need for theological and Qur'an grounding to his thesis.

Additionally, Ja'afar Adam, in particular, voiced his concerns that Yusuf was too inexperienced, knew too little and had been studying and preaching for too short a time. Yusuf, to Adam, had not been sufficiently exposed to the broad range of scholarly ideas around Sharia and its place in pluralistic society. Yusuf had too narrow an interpretation of Islamic jurisprudence, and limited an understanding of Qur'anic exegesis, for him to claim the sort of authority he did, around the reform of Muslim society in northern Nigeria (Umar 2012, 135–136). Sheikh Ja'afar, however, was not only critical of Yusuf and his followership, but he also tried to clarify the Muslim's duty in northern Nigeria. Secular education, for Ja'afar, was not just to be accommodated by northern society, it was to be embraced. In this sense, Ja'afar Adam:

Advocated the importance of Western and secular education for Muslims – for instance, in a taped sermon entitled *Boko da aikin gwamnati ba haramun ba ne* (Hausa: 'Western education and work for the government are not forbidden'). [Adam argued that] only the conscious adoption of Western and secular *boko* education would eventually enable Muslims to fight the Western enemy effectively. Ja'afar Mahmud Adam also defended the long-term strategy of slowly Islamising these institutions. The militant struggle against the Nigerian state was seen as counterproductive. (Loimeier 2012, 149)

Fundamentally, therefore, Sheikh Ja'afar Mahmud Adam and Muhammad Yusuf had different ideologies. Whereas both men were from the *Izala* B, the Salafist/Wahhabi worldview adopted by each highlighted the doctrinal differences even within *Izala* B. Localized to the contest between Ja'afar Adam and Yusuf, these differences also showed how individuals even within the same theological strain, can (choose to) interpret doctrine in unique ways. Therefore, 'the differences between Adam and Yusuf demonstrate that Salafism/Wahhabism should not be understood as a monolithic set of radical Islamic doctrines irreconcilably opposed to Sufism and also implacably dedicated to violence' (Umar 2012, 140).

The distinctions between Boko Haram's idea system and that of the *Izala* B from which it broke away, are, indeed, mostly an upscaled differentiation between the ideology of Yusuf and the theological arguments by Ja'afar Adam. Such differences suggest an essential point: that Salafism and Wahhabism doctrines should not be erroneously linked to the incitement of violence or even the incidence of radicalism. Instead, the reasons for which an extremist movement adopts anti-establishment confrontation are a great deal more nuanced, as this chapter's interrogation of Boko Haram's emergence seeks to demonstrate.

The critical difference between the two men was that Ja'afar Adam rejected the misguided notion, subscribed to by Yusuf and his followers: that the government had to be overthrown, by force if necessary, so that universal Sharia law and Islamic rule could take its place in northern Nigeria. 'Who are you to say you can implement the Islamic system of government?', Ja'afar Adam once rebuked Yusuf (without referring to him by name) (Umar 2012, 136).

Indeed, whereas Yusuf urged 'Muslims to remove their oppressors forcefully', Ja'afar Adam, on the other hand, cautions 'Muslims against confrontation with Nigerian government because they could not hope to win' (Umar 2012, 136). Scholarship, Islamic knowledge but also *Western* knowledge were, for Ja'afar, important tools by which the Muslim could problem-solve and self-empower. Consequently, for Ja'afar Adam, rather than 'judge Muslims as unbelievers because they have Western education or because they work for the government', it was important to understand why both were necessary for the Muslim body in northern Nigeria to thrive (Umar 2012, 136). Such scholarly debates punctuated Ja'afar's rhetoric.

Yusuf, on the other hand, did not encourage this sort of scholarship amongst his followers but rather was prone to substituting scholarly debate and Qur'anic exegesis with fiery rhetoric and extremist fervour, both of which he often linked to political thought.

Now, it nevertheless is problematic to assume that Yusuf had no understanding of the Qur'an and hadiths, which he used to justify his confrontational thesis. Indeed, as had been pointed out, the notion that even the most extremist Muslim groups do not understand the Qur'an or that they are 'misguided' may not be entirely true. Such groups simply may have chosen to interpret it differently. Even groups that go on to employ terrorism in the name of Islam do not necessarily represent 'deviant sects' but are often guided by a radical interpretation of the religion (Schmid 2011, 25).

So, it was in the case of Boko Haram that, as the group's radical interpretations of the Qur'an continued, Yusuf grew more incalcitrant. As for his religious challengers, as Yusuf's audience and political voice grew over time, he treated them with increasing disdain, acting as an authority unto himself. Indeed, within his sermons, Yusuf began to 'ridicule his opponents with sarcasm and disgust' to 'repeated applause of his disciples who [would] shout '*Allahu akbar*' each time' (Umar 2012, 124). Ustaz Yusuf's sermons, therefore, increasingly came across as part rambling, part polemical and part provocation against the established Islamic order and the government.

Not surprisingly then, and consistent with Boko Haram's increasingly anti-establishment trajectory, Yusuf over time would eventually begin to encourage violence as a vehicle for the realization of his anti-*boko* ideas. That is, the backroom differences in opinion between himself and the likes of Ja'afar Adam, would not only gradually escalate to open rhetorical confrontations, but they would also embolden Yusuf's unrepentance (Mohammed 2010). The pointed criticism was not always one way, however.

For instance, 'in his sermons and pamphlets, Ja'afar Mahmud Adam criticized Muhammad Yusuf's theological positions as 'ignorant' and 'stupid' and as dangerous for the political ambitions of Muslims in Nigeria' (Loimeier 2012, 149). Such sharply differing views meant Yusuf and his idea system could not coexist within the mainstream. Eventually, an unrepentant Yusuf left Indimi Mosque, forced away in 2003 (Loimeier 2012, 148).

2005–2007: Boko Haram establishes in Maiduguri

By 2005 when he resurfaced in Maiduguri after his Hajj (pilgrimage to Mecca, Saudi Arabia), Yusuf's refusal to go away suggested that he and his movement had outlasted the damage caused by the Kanamma incident years back. Indeed, as his popularity grew, Yusuf even adopted the title 'Ustaz', to denote the fact that he was now a recognized teacher (Mohammed 2010). Around this time, Yusuf significantly increased his preaching activity and his movement's numbers grew. With regard to the specific details of these teaching and educational activities, which by now had spread beyond just Maiduguri:

> The sheikh [Mohammed Yusuf] and his students had centres in Bauchi state, Kano state, Gombe and other places from the towns of north[ern] Nigeria, in so far as Borno state was the base and the directorate house for the brothers. In most of its local governorates they had centres and agents, and in the capital of Maiduguri alone they had different schools and centres, and at the top of them were five councils for teaching, and they were:
>
> 1. Ibn Taymiyya centre: Sheikh Abu Yusuf would give in it the sermon every Friday, and teach on Saturdays and Sundays the tafsir of Ibn Kathir, and Rahiq al-Makhtum. And he would teach Sahih al-Bukhari on Wednesday, after finishing Riyadh al-Saliheen. And the mashayakh would give general lectures in it. 2. The Ta'ifa Mansura mosque in the Unguwan Doki neighbourhood. In it he set up a council for tafsir of the Qur'an every Friday night. 3. Millionaire's Quarter: in which he would give tafsir of the Qur'an every Thursday in the Kanuri language. But he transferred the lesson to the Ibn Taymiyya mosque for security reasons. 4. Fezzan mosque: he would give some lessons, and appoint some preachers on his behalf in his absence. 5. Lawan Bor neighbourhood: he used to teach in Riyadh al-Saliheen on Saturday evening in Kanuri language, which is spoken by the majority in the states of Borno and Yobe. 6. Abu Hurairah mosque in Gomari Iyabut neighbourhood: da'wa meeting and gathering for the brothers who were distant from the centre and they would advise each other for purifying the souls, and sometimes the mashayakh would visit them for the same purpose. (Al-Tamimi 2018)

With a large membership and the funding to run his mosque (Ibn Taymiyya centre) and the other preaching initiatives such as those highlighted above, Yusuf and his movement had become much more than just a small band of troublemakers. Practically now a sworn enemy of the Islamic establishment and authorities, and confident that he had the numbers to support his position, Yusuf would begin launching four-pronged polemics. Yusuf quarrelled against the established Islamic schools, against the Nigerian government and what it represented; against the 'corrupt' Nigerian police; and against individuals, particularly the trio of Sheikh Ja'afar Mahmud Adam, Sheik Abba Aji and Yahaya Jingir (Danjibo 2010, 6). By now, of course, the break from Sheikh Ja'afar's orbit was complete.

2007: Ja'afar Adam's assassination and a point of no return

In 2007, events appeared to take a turn for the worse in the disagreements between the two, after Sheikh Ja'afar's assassination in Kano, in the morning of Friday 13 April, 'while performing the Subhi (Dawn) prayer' (Isa 2009). There have been theories around whether Yusuf was involved and many have been careful to not to assume knowledge of the assassins (Mohammed 2010). Some have been less cautious here, Andrew Walker, for instance, alleges that 'it is now acknowledged that it [the killing] was carried out on the orders of Muhammad Yusuf' (Walker 2012, 4). Few others, however, even those close to Sheikh Ja'afar Mahmud Adam and who knew him personally, have made such pointed accusations. For instance, neither Garba Isa (2009) in his eulogy to the late Sheikh nor Yakubu Muhammad Rigasa (2008), in questioning the killing of Adam, mention either Boko Haram or Yusuf. Although this silence on the perpetrators may have been out of concern for repercussions.

For Walker, nonetheless, Adam's assassination effectively pushed Boko Haram beyond the point of no return insofar as such an act meant 'there was no longer the possibility of turning Yusuf and his followers back to the mainstream of the northern Islamic establishment' (2012, 4). Whereas there is no evidence that Yusuf personally ordered Adam's murder, there have been allegations. In reality, however, Boko Haram's involvement in Ja'afar's murder, a shooting by assailants riding by on *Okada* (motorcycles), was never established. What is a less speculative is that by the time of Sheikh Ja'afar's assassination, Yusuf and his followers had reached a point where they were edging closer to a violent confrontation. This seeming collision course with the authorities underscores the idea that 'radical discourses challenging the Islamic legitimacy of modern government have the potential to end in catastrophic violence … ' (Umar 2012, 139–140). Indeed, this theme of violence, a constant challenge to the Islamic establishment and a refusal to recognize authority is critical to understanding Boko Haram's radical departure and its foray into armed confrontation.

More to the above point, as Boko Haram's violent campaign escalated over the years, the term Khawarij have been used by ISWAP to refer to Shekau and his faction of the movement (Al-Tamimi 2018). However, it is also a term that many interview sources repeatedly used to refer to Boko Haram, even as far back as 2012. Why has Boko

Haram been referred to by this term by rival splinter factions? The next section of the chapter aims to briefly evaluate the term and its applicability to Boko Haram as a now-mature perpetrator group that seemed to quarrel with virtually everyone who was not part of its insurgency.

Boko Haram as 'Khawarij'

'Khawarij: Kharijites (Arabic Khawārij خوارج, literally "Those who Went Out"; singular, Khariji) is a general term embracing various Muslims who, while initially supporting the caliphate of the fourth and final "Rightly Guided" caliph Ali ibn Abi Talib, later rejected them' (Diintayda, Dadkayga & Dalkayga (Somalia) 2010). Generations after the death of the Prophet Muhammad in 632 AD, by which time a significant portion of the rightly guided Islamic rulership of the period had passed,

Religious innovations regarding takfeer [excommunication doctrine] began to appear, particularly in the caliphate of 'Alee, the Companion and fourth caliph of Islaam. A group of religious extremists called the Khawaarij appeared, and they established innovated principles regarding the serious issue of when a person is or is not a Muslim. They expelled people from the fold of Islam for being sinful, and they put much stress on the faults of rulers, thus making it permissible to set out against them in a violent manner' (Oliver 2005, 16).

As Abdul-Azim Ahmed writes, 'many Muslims use the term "Khawarij" as a pejorative term to describe the Islamic State and many other modern terrorists'. Making comparisons between modern jihadist movements like Daesh, and the historical Khawarij, Ahmed observes that 'The Khawarij intended to destabilise the early Islamic empire and its culprits had no intention of walking away from it alive' (A.-A. Ahmed 2017). There are also some comparisons here to Boko Haram, some of which I attempt to highlight below.

As time went by, Yusuf and his followers were increasingly fanatical in their exhortations, yet also intransigent when confronted. This led them to be viewed by many as 'Khawarij': religious extremists who use 'textual evidences, but fall short in understanding them' and so distorted the meaning of the Qur'an (Oliver 2005, 16). Such groups are quick to make accusations of apostasy, put out fatwas[4] without the right authority, and, without the appropriate consultations, expel 'people from the fold of Islam on the basis of poor use of takfeer and innovated principles (Oliver 2005, 16). A feature of movements viewed as Khawarij is their violent approach to resolving ideological differences such as where they 'hold that a majority of the leaders of the Muslims lands are disbelievers and must be killed by any means' (A.-A. Ahmed 2017). Moreover, because of their incalcitrant disposition around theological issues, Khawarij 'do not hold the scholars and people of knowledge in high esteem if their opinions do not conform with theirs' (A.-A. Ahmed 2017). Such intransigence often acts as a catalyst for more radical interpretations of the Qur'an and, eventually, violent action against the establishment and authorities, based on these problematic interpretations.

Consequently, 'Khawarij accuse of apostasy the people who oppose their opinion and stance, and consider it legal (halal) to kill them' (A.-A. Ahmed 2017). Other characteristics of Khawarij are that they are, in general, young in age and immature in their actions and in particular to the reactions to attempts by established and older scholars and theologians to correct their errant ways (A.-A. Ahmed 2017). By way of what they professed and, crucially, their actions, there were indications that even before Yusuf died (which further led his remaining followers down an even more fanatical path), Boko Haram already demonstrated such traits.

Moreover, because of all these features and the fact that radical interpretations of the Qur'an fail to be corrected, differing positions around such interpretations, even within the movement, emerge. Consequently, Khawarij tend to eventually 'disagree amongst each other to the point of dividing into several sects and attacking each other' (A.-A. Ahmed 2017). Accusations of apostasy within these groups will increasingly deepen ideological rifts, fuel suspicions and then lead to irreconcilable doctrines and different viewpoints, even though factions all began from the same ideological base. Perhaps the most prominent example of such ideological rifts within Boko Haram over the years is evidenced by the emergence of the Islamic State West Africa Province (ISWAP) faction of Boko Haram under Abu Mus'ab al-Barnawi. Chapter 3 shall discuss this idea of splintering and factionalization, within Boko Haram, in more detail.

Yusuf's ideological influencers

Boko Haram's actions consolidated the movement's extremist identity and departure from the Islamic fold in northern Nigeria. Further, Yusuf's radical exhortations and the retaliatory attacks against authorities in 2009 as a consequence of such views, suggest that the idea of holy war ('jihad', with its military connotations) long held some fascination for him (Mohammed 2010, Abubakar 2012, Umar 2012). In this context, the theological influencers on Boko Haram's early thought processes served as a marker for the movement's violent path. It is, therefore, worth taking a closer look at some of these individuals, whose ideas arguably helped radicalize Yusuf.

To begin with, Yusuf's 'heavy reliance' on the theology of controversial thirteenth-century Cleric, Ibn Taymiyya, as an example, influenced his mindedness towards violent confrontation against the established order and the state (Umar 2012, 122). Specifically, Yusuf's Ibn Taymiyya-influenced worldview, on ' … how Muslims should establish the desired government, led Yusuf toward radicalism and violent confrontation with the Nigerian government, a vastly more powerful adversary' (Umar 2012, 139).

Ibn Taymiyya (1263–1328) was himself known for polemic activity, anti-establishment thinking and the encouragement of jihad against non-believers. Whereas he remains revered by the global Wahhabi movement and is central to the theology and political thought of Salafi groups, Ibn Taymiyya's writings have, nevertheless, 'been a source of inspiration for radical groups to justice acts of violence and armed struggle' (Rapoport and Ahmed 2010). A fundamentalist, Ibn Taymiyya believed 'in the strict adherence to the Koran and principles of the Prophet Muhammad and was devoted to the concept of holy war' (Rice 2012). It was along this line of thinking that Yusuf based his anti-*boko* ideology. As an example, Yusuf 'invoked the authority of Ibn Taymiyya in insisting that the Qur'anic interdictions against polytheism and apostasy – both of which Yusuf deemed applicable to obedience to *tāghūt* government – were so absolute that they must be obeyed without exception, no matter the circumstances' (Umar 2012, 127).

So fascinated was Yusuf by Ibn Taymiyya's ideologies that, when forced out of Indimi Mosque, he founded his mosque in Maiduguri (Mohammed 2010). Situated close to the railway station (Bayan Quarters), the mosque was named *Ibn Taymiyya Masjid*; Masjid meaning 'mosque', in Arabic.

Not unlike Ibn Taymiyya in his time (Rapoport and Ahmed 2010), Yusuf too was vocal against the influential Sufi Brotherhoods, but also the dominant Islamic Schools in general. In northern Nigeria, this included new schools like the *Izala*. Yusuf accused both of deviating from strict forms of Islam and of encouraging bid'ah ('innovation', or, in this context, dilution of fundamentalist Islamic views, to accommodate secularism). It is worth explaining, however, that such ideological dilution of Salafist/Wahhabi doctrine, to accommodate other faiths, Westernization and indeed aspects of secularism, cannot merely be rejected as innovation; such compromise is necessary for northern Nigeria. Nigeria is a secular, pluralistic state, not an Islamic republic where adherence to Islamic law could be expected and would be accepted as the norm, throughout the state.[5]

Moreover, Ibn Taymiyya's thinking was not as much the issue here as was Yusuf's temperament in dealing with modern-day implications of fundamentalist Wahhabi ideologies which, even in their day, were problematic (Rapoport and Ahmed 2010). Yusuf's views gradually betrayed the fact that whereas he was possibly better schooled in Islamic law than his critics would admit – he was not, necessarily, the idiot they made him out to be – neither he nor his followers had the temperament to avert fundamentalist agitation in a pluralistic and Western-influenced[6] society like Nigeria. Alternatively, perhaps Yusuf and his followers simply chose to ignore the implications of such agitations.

Other classical scholars and jurists other than Ibn Taymiyya also influenced Yusuf's worldview. Individually, the anti-secular and anti-establishment thinking of Ibn Kathir, Abdul A'la Maududi and Sayyid Qutb are relevant to understanding the sort of influences on Boko Haram's ideology (Wiktorowicz 2005). Yusuf also followed the teachings within *al-madaris al-'alamiyya al-ajnabiyya al-isti'mariyya: ta'rikhuha wa-makhatiruha* (*The Secular, Foreign and Colonialist Schools: Their History and Dangers*). Abubakar b. 'Abdallah Abū Zayd, 'a prominent Wahhabi scholar and prolific author who held several positions in academic, religious, and judicial institutions in Saudi Arabia', authored this text (Umar 2012, 123–124). Abū Zayd's anti-colonial and anti-colonial thesis was not only 'gleefully highlighted' severally by Yusuf (Umar 2012, 124), it 'served as the theological basis for his [Yusuf's] rejection of a natural science-based (Western and secular) view of the world' (Loimeier 2012, 149).

From an Islamic jurisprudence perspective, is 'Boko' truly haram?

Yusuf was so adamant about the veracity of his anti-Westernization views, and so infuriated that his mentor, Ja'afar Adam, was dismissive of his anti-*Boko* ideas, that he put a *fatwa* on those perceived by the sect to have adopted a pro-*Boko* stance (Mohammed 2010). This event was significant in Boko Haram's timeline. Yusuf had now attempted to justify, through Islamic law, military violence as an outcome of his ideology. However, did Boko Haram have any right, from the perspective of Islamic Jurisprudence, to issue out a *fatwa*? This question relates closely to whether Boko Haram's ideology, and thus its armed campaign, has its basis in the Qur'an and is supported by Islamic jurisprudence?

In answering such questions, we must first recognize the doctrinal clash between Boko Haram's 'ideology of opposing Western education' and 'the scholars of Islamic jurisprudence' (Mohammed 2010, 45). In this ideological clash, Yusuf and 'the Boko Haram proponents' always had 'an uphill task in explaining their position to the rest of the Muslim *ummah*' (Mohammed 2010, 45). At best, the deduction to be taken, regarding the question of whether Western education is indeed forbidden and 'from the Islamic jurisprudence point of view, is that *Boko* is *halal* (permissible) except what may be explicitly identified as *haram* (non-permissible) within it' (Mohammed 2010, 45).

The premise for this argument is consistent with that of the Da'awah Coordination Council of Nigeria (DCNN), a coalition of Islamic organizations and scholarship bodies that help with the monitoring of Islamic proselytizing and preaching (Amoda 2011). After Boko Haram's violence of 2009, the DCNN[7] issued a report. The report read that 'if anything in the contents and method of *Boko* does not contradict the clear teachings of the Qur'an and Sunnah or the objectives (maqasid) of Shari'ah, then it cannot be regarded as haram from an Islamic perspective' (DCCN 2009).

The DCCN's position on the matter, therefore, indicates a 'clear difference of misconception' between Boko Haram's interpretation of western education and influence, and that of other Muslim scholars (2009, 60). Moreover, that Yusuf and his followers were treading a dangerous path was not a situation lost on senior religious leaders within the *Ulama*. Indeed, several attempts were made to reach out to Yusuf and his network to make two points. The first point to be made to Yusuf was that he was wrong to issue a fatwa on behalf of the Muslim *ummah*. Yusuf did not follow due process, rigorous research and consultation associated with such a declaration. The second point to be made to Yusuf was that his reason for the *fatwa* – that Western education was *haram* – did not have grounds in Islamic jurisprudence (and also based on the findings and conclusions of the DCNN).

Conclusion

Boko Haram's claims to have a central view grounded in Islamic theology was always dubious; however, the environment may have enabled the sect's ideology to take root within its audience nevertheless. Muhammad Yusuf's charisma and personality, as well as the economic incentives that came with being his adherent, also played a role in convincing his followers. As the previous section's analysis indicates, however, the Islamic establishment was unconvinced.

However, even where 'security agencies, governments, and the *Ulama* were fully aware of the trend', attempts to dissuade Yusuf and his network from their activities were 'not effective enough' (Mohammed 2010, 58). Ja'afar Adam, Malam Abdul Wahab and Muhammad Sani (then a student at Medina University) were amongst Muslim scholars and clerics who tried convincing Yusuf that his ideology had no basis in the Qur'an. Others who likewise tried, included some members of the *Ulama* at Maiduguri University, some scholars in Zaria, and some pilgrims during the 2004 Hajj (Mohammed 2010). These attempts to reach out to Yusuf, therefore, appear inconsistent with his allegations that the establishment ignored both him and his movement. There are indications that Yusuf was indeed theologically engaged (and without provocation). Indeed, Yusuf, during at least one of these closed-door sessions, admitted that, so far as Boko Haram's Islamic legality was concerned, he was in the wrong (Mohammed 2010, 62–64). Sheik Ja'afar observed that he and others 'discussed the issue with Muhammad Yusuf [...] He acknowledged to me that he was wrong on his *fatwa*. So, I said to him that it had become a responsibility upon him to intimate to his disciples on the new disposition' (Mohammed 2010, 61–64).

After much pressure on Yusuf to communicate with his followers and recant his views, he made specific assurances. For instance, Yusuf agreed that he would 'disown association with any of his disciples that remain a proponent of Boko Haram ideology; and that such a person has been declared an "infidel"; and he is not with them' (Mohammed 2010, 64). This confession, however, was but a false show of repentance. Despite his apparent contriteness, Yusuf did not honour the assurances he made to Sheik Ja'afar. Even though he knew and had accepted his faulty logic, Yusuf failed to publicize the fact that, from an Islamic jurisprudence perspective, Boko Haram's ideology had no basis – as he insisted it did – in the Qur'an and the Hadiths. To carry on preaching, as he did, was therefore to perpetuate an exposed deception.

Even worse, Yusuf and his movement became more outspoken against Western education. This increasingly fiery anti-*boko* posture was the opposite of what Yusuf openly admitted to behind closed doors. Moreover, with Sheik Ja'afar Adam later murdered, there was one less voice of reason to counter Boko Haram's fanaticism. There also was virtually no one left who could call Yusuf to order.

The 2009 Troubles in North-East Nigeria and Abu Shekau's Emergence

June 2009: Skirmish with Operation Flush operatives

Yusuf's strong anti-establishment views meant that he was arrested several times over the years and came to have a problematic relationship with the police. Animosity between Yusuf and the Nigerian police in Maiduguri worsened with the state's introduction of Operation Flush, a police anti-robbery squad that also helped enforce other road laws as part of basic policing. Locals, however, accused Operation Flush operatives of using this security initiative as a pretext for extortion and coercion. Such accusations, and indeed police behaviour in Nigeria, which historically displays a pattern of coercion against citizens (Omeni 2017), presented an opportunity which was seized by Yusuf. Operation Flush consequently soon became a talking point in his sermons (Umar 2012). This development was a matter of concern to the police, who by June 2009, sent operatives to listen in and report on Yusuf's sermons. Such back-and-forth accusations continued the problematic relationship between Yusuf and the police, which he was convinced was a political tool: a coercive appendage of corrupt authorities used to intimidate locals.

On 11 June 2009, as tensions simmered, things came to a headway between both sides. That afternoon, Boko Haram members going to bury one of their dead rode their *Okada* (motorcycles)[1] without crash helmets. Riding without crash helmets, however, contravened recently implemented local road safety laws. As it happened, these Boko Haram members encountered an Operation Flush police patrol, while running afoul of this law. When stopped by the policemen, the members in question refused to remove their turbans and put on crash helmets. The ceremonial process meant they had to wear turbans – or at least some of them did, they argued (Adeoye 2012). The procession, consequently, refused to yield.

With the sect adherents adamant about putting on crash helmets *in situ*, the police thus declined to allow the procession to continue. A standoff ensued. As the police later stated in interview material for this chapter,[2] the *Yusufiyya* procession got off easy by being refused road access. Breaking that road transport law should instantly have led to an on-the-spot fine, confiscation of the *Okada*, detainment of the riders, or the latter two.

Escalating the standoff, the *Yusufiyya* 'began advancing on the guard location of the soldiers' (Adeoye 2012). This decision, inevitably, provoked a response by the police: some of the Boko Haram members were fired upon and injured. One viewpoint on this event is that Boko Haram's refusal to adhere to the law ' … Was perceived by the police as open defiance of authority, reflecting a continuing pattern of behaviour by Boko Haram that had to be dealt with' (Forest 2012, 63). The *Yusufiyya*, rather than the police, were the likely agitators and the instigators of the violence. Indeed, during the standoff, 'a member of the group is reported to have fired at the police, injuring several officers' (Walker 2012, 4).

Now it is unlikely that the Boko Haram procession members preemptively fired on police. It was and remains a criminal offence to possess much less openly carry unlicensed firearms. Moreover, Yusuf, at least at this point, had not openly encouraged Boko Haram members to flaunt this law and openly carry firearms. Indeed, Yusuf had a dramatically different version of events on that day. In his own words, the injured *Yusufiyya*, 'did nothing wrong, did not insult anyone, and did not commit any offence'. Instead, the attack on the procession was unprovoked, an injustice consistent with police behaviour towards Boko Haram (Umar 2012, 129).

Yusuf's in-sermon account, therefore, was that the police wounded members of the procession, without provocation, just because they were his followers (Umar 2012, 128–129). In any event, the *Yusufiyya* rushed their injured members to the University of Maiduguri Teaching Hospital. Yusuf around this time seemed more interested in avenging the attack and using it as a pretext for widespread mayhem, than drawing public attention to police injustice and brutality. This antagonism can be inferred from his instruction to his followers, stating that they should:

(1) Prepare to donate money and blood because both would be required to treat the injured, (2) strictly follow any orders even if they will die in obeying, and (3) do not do anything unless they have been told to do it, even if they will die. Remarkably, [in issuing these instructions] Yusuf invoke[d] the story of how Prophet Muhammad instructed his men before the Battle of Uhud and how their disregard of the prophetic order brought a disastrous outcome. Thereby staking his claim to following Prophet Muhammad's authority that must be obeyed. (Umar 2012, 130)

As for the injured Boko Haram members, no deaths were recorded amongst them (Forest 2012, 63–64, Higazi 2013a, 13). Existing accounts within the literature corroborate Maiduguri police statements, given for this study, and used to put together this chapter's account. At the hospital, however, was an additional standoff. Very few news reports and virtually no academic sources, discuss this second incident (probably since there were no casualties or even injuries). As put by Chief Superintendent of Police (CSP) Aderemi Adeoye, who took ownership of the police reports and was interviewed in Maiduguri for this study:

Those [*Yusufiyya*] who were injured were rushed to the hospital. Then they [the remaining *Yusufiyya*] mobilised again to go to the hospital; they said they were going to donate blood. Then the police stated that only those who wish to donate blood would be allowed inside the hospital. Others were too riotous to be allowed in. They [*Yusufiyya*] stated that they either were all going [into the Hospital] or there will be chaos. The police used tear gas on them and dispersed them. (2012)

Incensed by these incidents and perhaps even prodded on by the more radical individuals within the sect such as Abu Shekau (Ahmed 2012), Yusuf proceeded to make a declaration of war essentially. His polemics took a more sinister tone in a particularly incendiary sermon on 19 June. This was eight days after the initial confrontation. However, even before his first open sermon on the following Friday, Yusuf had previously declared on Sunday 14 June, that recent events now meant the *Yusufiyya* must begin 'Jihad' (Mohammed 2010, 71). In a recording, Yusuf is heard saying, about Operation Flush's harsh response to his members' civil disobedience, that the Borno State government formed 'Operation Flush to create obstacles for our brothers or our preaching and to humiliate ordinary people. That is the purpose of setting up the Operation Flush security patrols. As we have said before, Operation Flush was created specifically to oppose our preaching. The truth is now out' (Umar 2012, 129).

Just over a week after the first confrontation, 'On 19 June 2009, Muhammad Yusuf delivered a sermon on jihad and impressed upon his followers the need to acquire weapons of any size and type' (Higazi 2013b, 14). The Chief Superintendent of Police in Maiduguri corroborates this account in interview:

The following Friday [19 June] Muhammad Yusuf held a public sermon and said: [Translated from the Hausa language] How will an alcohol drinking soldier open fire on them [*Yusufiyya*] and go back to his tent and say that I will kill all of you [and] nothing will happen? How will they want to donate blood to save their members and the police will disperse them with tear gas? That these were injustices and they were going to fight it. The way and how they would do it, nobody would know; but that let nobody underestimate their capability.

In a public sermon! It was recorded! I read the report when I got to this state. Criminal Intelligence Bureau, they have operatives who attended the sermon; and they wrote a report. I read that report. Now, that was at a time when Yusuf was still alive – he had not been killed! (Adeoye 2012)

This police account is similar to another which notes that in his sermon, which lasted seventy-six minutes:

Yusuf complained bitterly about the humiliations he has personally experienced at the hands of security agencies in the forms of repeated arrests, detentions, interrogations, restrictions on his movements and so on. He also accused the then ruling governor of Borno State [Ali Modu Sheriff] of being responsible for all the harassment that security forces have inflicted on Yusuf and his followers, as well as all Muslims in Borno State. Proclaiming an eternal enmity between Muslims and non-Muslims, Yusuf declared that the non-Muslims in the security forces are drunk, crazy and arrogant infidels who are totally dedicated to killing and humiliating Muslims. He also stated that the time for patient endurance has passed and the time for action has arrived. (Umar 2012, 129)[3]

The first phase of the 'action' suggested by Yusuf was a mass mobilization of *Yusufiyya* adherents for a massive confrontation with the state. Insofar as the corrupt police institution epitomized the Nigerian state for Boko Haram, this, therefore, was very much a war against the police. Boko Haram began to prosecute its war against local police on the streets, against sleeping police officers in their barracks, on parade grounds and at police stations (Adeoye 2012). There was a mass mobilization of Boko Haram supporters. The police account of this mobilization holds that 'trailer loads, lorry loads of adherents from other states, started pouring into Maiduguri – and they came with their wives and children; ostensibly, to attend a religious programme. Moreover, they were camping them at the headquarters of the sect, Bayan Quarters; near the railway terminus' (Adeoye 2012).

If Yusuf's incendiary sermon and the polemics over the six weeks leading into late July 2009 were indeed a call to arms, it seemed his adherents had answered in numbers. Yusuf, moreover, had a large following[4] that 'stretched far beyond Maiduguri and Borno State, across northern Nigeria, as well as into neighbouring Niger, Cameroon and Chad' (Rice 2012). This extent of orbit likely influenced the scale of the violent confrontations, following Yusuf's call to arms. In Maiduguri, scenes were especially chaotic:

> They [the Yusufiyya] left the women and children in that headquarters [Bayan HQ, near the railway terminus]; and armed all the men. Then they trooped into town – attacking police stations, police headquarters, mobile police barracks and other government institutions. They [Boko Haram] killed the second-in-command [2iC] to the squadron commander in MOPOL 6, in Maiduguri here. He was murdered on the parade ground; unarmed.
>
> They [Boko Haram] petrol-bombed some of the barracks buildings. They killed some policemen at their duty posts – everything. They were about setting the police headquarters ablaze, when a unit from Yobe arriving in Maiduguri for special duties, not related to the sect, just arrived and saw people in mufti – with guns, firing – then they [the police unit] engaged them [Boko Haram]. That was what saved the police headquarters from been razed that night. (Adeoye 2012)

Indeed, this recurring role of the police confrontation with Boko Haram between June and August 2009 is central to the series of events that occurred around the time. On Tuesday, 21 July, the police arrested nine of Yusuf's followers in Biu, southern Borno State. These Boko Haram members, led by one Inusa Ibrahim Sabo, told reporters at the time that they were under instruction by Yusuf to arm themselves. That is, in the weeks before violence broke out in June 2009, Boko Haram's leadership had come to believe that police attacks were impending and so the movement had to be ready. Operation Flush elements especially, in Yusuf's view, would like nothing more than to silence his movement by force. For Muhammad Yusuf, this was as part of an agenda by the Borno State governor, Ali Modu Sheriff,[5] whom Yusuf felt had it out for him. The

Boko Haram members arrested were put on display at the police headquarters, near the stadium in the central area of Maiduguri, on 24 July 2009. However, these arrests barely scratched the surface of the stressful week that Borno residents were about to experience.

The same day, 24 July, an IED went off at the residence of Hassan Sani Badami in Maiduguri – further heightening tensions surrounding the impending threat of a Boko Haram rebellion in the city. By the end of July, those tensions had boiled over (Adeoye 2012).

July 2009: Major escalation of hostilities

Boko Haram's open violence against the police incidentally began in Bauchi, not Maiduguri where it had the highest numbers. On 26 July, dozens of *Yusufiyya* congregated on the local police station at Dutsen Tenshin, a small district of Bauchi city, the state capital of Bauchi. Poorly armed, but with the numbers, Boko Haram would overrun the police unit and gain access to its armoury – an act that would greatly embolden the sect against the local police. Indeed, it appears that word of this feat quickly filtered back to Maiduguri as Boko Haram's mobilization in the Maiduguri axis began shortly after the Bauchi attacks.

There were, nevertheless, police reinforcements (include bomb squads) in Bauchi the same day. This response suggests that security forces recognized something more significant was amiss. Counter-offensives and arrests swiftly followed, moreover. The attack on the police in Bauchi not only set a new precedent, after all, but there also were fears after Badami's earlier-highlighted premature IED detonation, that Boko Haram – in Borno and also in Bauchi – now possessed bomb-making capabilities. Despite police reinforcements, violence nevertheless spread quickly: to neighbouring Kano to the west and eastwards – to Yobe and Borno. In Kano, violence was mostly against other civilians and was highly riotous. In Yobe and Borno states, however, violence was more geared towards the police (police stations, police living quarters) and disrupting the function of the state, via attacks on its parastatals (Adeoye 2012).

July–August 2009: Controversy around the capture and killing of Ustaz Yusuf

When Boko Haram's riots erupted at the end of July 2009, Yusuf initially was at large, orchestrating events from the compound of his father-in-law, Baga Fugu Muhammad in Maiduguri around (Adeoye 2012). It was at Baga Fugu's compound that Nigerian Army troops, mounting a massive counter-offensive, finally cornered and captured Yusuf – alive. Amidst the military confrontation between Boko Haram adherents and Nigerian security forces in July 2009, hundreds were killed, or taken into police custody (Forest 2012). Yusuf was one of those captured by the Army and held at HQ, 21 Brigade (Giwa Barracks, Maiduguri) but was later handed over to police custody. It was while in police custody, on 31 July 2009, that Yusuf was murdered, possibly by his captors (The BBC 2009).

Benjamin Ahanotu, at the time a Nigerian Army colonel, pointed out that he handed Yusuf over to the police (D. Smith 2009b). According to Colonel Ahanotu's BBC interview transcript on the subject, he ' … Was able to pick him [Yusuf] up from his hideout and hand him over to police,' […] I asked him why he did what he has done and he responded that he would explain to me later. However, he was OK. As I got him alive, I handed him over to the authorities' (The BBC 2009).

Since 2010 when Boko Haram re-emerged, the extra-judicial killing of Muhammad Yusuf in July 2009 has served as a rallying point for the group's insurgency. Yusuf's murder meant that Boko Haram's objective was not only just ideological or political anymore; it also was vengeful. Moreover, the nature of his death may well have contributed to the problem here.

Yusuf's bullet-ridden body was shown to the public at the police headquarters in Maiduguri, despite the fact he was captured alive; the macabre image, seemingly an ironic warning of the fate that awaited those who surrendered to Nigerian forces. Nevertheless, 'few Nigerians will be surprised that their police force killed renegade Islamic sect leader Muhammad Yusuf'. The police motto, after all, 'used to be "Fire for Fire"' (Walker 2009). Human Rights Watch referred to the incident as an 'extrajudicial killing' (The BBC 2009).

The government response to Yusuf's killing was, however, somewhat ambiguous. The Information Minister at the time, Dora Akunyili, was criticized for her initial reaction to Yusuf's killing. Akinyuli noted on the BBC's Network Africa programme that, 'what is important is that he [Yusuf] has been taken out of the way, to stop him using people to cause mayhem' (Walker 2009). Akinyuli nevertheless did later say that extrajudicial killings were not acceptable and that Yusuf's death would be investigated (Walker 2009). However, the information minister stood by her comments 'that the death of Mr Yusuf – whom she described as being a leader 'in the mode of Osama Bin Laden' – demise was 'positive' for Nigeria' (The BBC 2009). Overall, therefore, both the Nigerian government and the police, who were most likely culpable for his death, refused to take responsibility for it. This issue of responsibility for Yusuf's murder in government custody remained a sticking point for some time afterwards.

In December 2010 at an Abuja Federal High Court, Colonel Benjamin Ahanotu gave testimony against five police officers indicted in the extra-judicial murder of the Boko Haram leader, reaffirming the above account of events (Ogundele 2011). This version of events is consistent with police accounts in Maiduguri, regarding the circumstances around Yusuf's death. Addressing the issue in-interview, the local police chief in Maiduguri described the heated scenes that occurred shortly before Yusuf's death:

> Yusuf was eventually arrested; interrogated by the military – which was documented – and handed over to the police. In police custody, because of that attack on the mobile squadron; the killing of the second-in-command; the murder of some [police officers'] family members in their sleep and everything; tempers were out of control. In fact, arrangements were being made to fly him [Yusuf] to

Abuja. Policemen were saying: if that helicopter took off, they would fire it down. So, in between there, I was not serving in the state then, I did not witness it, but in that confusion, Yusuf was gunned down, and he died and the sect scattered. They [*Yusufiyya*] started regrouping during the one-year anniversary of the death. [By] now, Shekau had now assumed command. He [Shekau] had always been an apostle of armed confrontation. (Adeoye 2012)

So, it would appear that disgruntled police officers murdered Yusuf while he was in custody of authorities. It would never be clear or revealed who pulled the trigger, however. In any event, Muhammad Yusuf's corpse was last seen photographed at the Police Headquarters in Maiduguri on the evening of 31 July 2009. Reporters 'were told that the man had been 'executed' at the police headquarters, at about 1900' even as Yusuf's 'bullet-ridden body was shown to journalists hours after police announced they had captured him alive' (The BBC 2009).

August 2009–September 2010: Aftermath of Ustaz Yusuf's murder

With Yusuf dead and with hundreds of alleged *Yusufiyya* killed or in custody, Boko Haram disappeared from the public eye for a while. Although not before the group released a statement with an ominous warning in August 2009, 'that we [Boko Haram] have started a Jihad in Nigeria which no force on earth can stop. The aim is to Islamize Nigeria and ensure the rule of the majority Muslims in the country. We will teach Nigeria a lesson, a very bitter one' (Vanguard 2009). With this warning, the group dispersed and over the next year, with no activity from Boko Haram, there was an uneasy sense of calm in Maiduguri. Most Nigerians thought of it as a one-off set of intra-faith riots, which were not, *per se*, unusual in northern Nigeria. The media moved on, even as Boko Haram became an illegal movement.

Several extrajudicial killings by the police are alleged to have occurred in Maiduguri around this time, however, in the aftermath of Yusuf's murder. Suspected Boko Haram's supporters may have been targeted this way perhaps in retribution for the way the group came after the police specifically, at the start of its rampage. Yusuf's death, it would appear, was insufficient for the angered police force, which began a crackdown on anyone suspected to be a Boko Haram member. As the crackdown commenced, those killed or arrested by the police, in the aftermath of the Battle of Maiduguri, is alleged to number in the hundreds. This crackdown is a well-documented subject within the literature (Forest 2012, Walker 2012, 4, Comolli 2015).

That at least some civilians were killed extrajudicially by local police forces or paramilitary forces, is undeniable; widely available video footage exists showing these killings and has been widely viewed (Al Jazeera 2010). It is unclear whether the guilty policemen in these videos were held accountable for such incidents. There have, however, been trials – with military personnel giving witness against the police, in what is an unusual state of security affairs in Nigeria (Vanguard 2011). What is clear is that Yusuf's death at the hands of the police effectively ended, abruptly and violently, the first phase of Boko Haram's violent civil disobedience. Even so, Yusuf appears to have left behind a long enduring legacy. Some Boko Haram members, for instance, remain loyal to Yusuf personally and to his bloodlines, not just to the idea he represented, *per se.*

For example, circa August 2016 there was media chatter around the emergence of a Boko Haram faction, supported by Daesh[6] and with an active membership base, led by one Abu Mus'ab al-Barnawi, who supposedly is the son of Yusuf. This development has since moved beyond mere chatter to the formation of an operational jihadist rival to Boko Haram, in the Islamic State West Africa Province (ISWAP). The emergent in-fighting as had a significant impact on the identity, operations and territorial footprint of Boko Haram in Borno, with the faction (ISWAP) occupying the northern axis of the state holding separate loyalties to the faction strongest in Central and Southern Borno, including Sambisa Forest.

Yusuf's death, in itself and also the nature of it, therefore, and the leadership vacuum that left, has had significant implications on the direction taken by Boko Haram's leaders. Indeed, it is believed by many, even today, that if events had not escalated so quickly in June and July of 2009, Boko Haram might not have become the metastasized threat it is now.

Splintering and leadership disputes within Boko Haram, along with the key figures within the emergent factions, shall be the focus of Chapter 3. However, not discounting such leadership disputes within the timeline of the movement, which eventually spilled into the public domain (The BBC 2016d), Boko Haram has had a central figurehead since its emergence after Yusuf's demise: Abubakar Shekau.

September 2010 onwards: The Shekau era

On 8 September 2010, 700 detainees from a prison in Bauchi, a city in northern Nigeria, were jailbroken (The Guardian 2010). The incident was the most massive orchestrated jailbreak in the history of the reformed Nigerian Prisons Service (NPS). Such spectacular displays of military tactics, moreover, would become the signature of Abu Shekau, Yusuf's successor, who since 2010 shaped Boko Haram's increasingly bolder military ambitions.

Just as Ustaz Yusuf's role is vital to understanding the ideology of Boko Haram in its formative years, Abu Shekau, whose 'nom de guerre is Imam Abu Muhammad Abubakar bin Muhammed Shekau' (International Crisis Group 2014, 19), is the most significant figure in the military emergence of Boko Haram. Indeed, whereas Yusuf was Boko Haram's spiritual leader, Shekau has become its military leader: a tactician who, through a bush war, has protracted Boko Haram's armed contest for nine years. By 2014, this individual would become near larger than life, wearing military fatigues, flanked by armed fighters and infantry vehicles, with a Qur'an in full view, while making animated broadcasts in a mix of ethnic Kanuri, Hausa, fluent Arabic and, occasionally, English.

Rewind to Boko Haram's formative years around a decade earlier, however, and Shekau's portrayal is that of a bookish Qur'anic scholar, a withdrawn radical who hitherto was hardly seen and heard even less often. Shekau, before 2009's Battle of

Maiduguri, was not at the forefront of the group's activity. Rather, it was Ustaz Yusuf, the firebrand preacher, the 'mischief-maker', whose sermons and movements were the focus of police and Department of State Services (DSS) intelligence in Maiduguri (Adeoye 2012, Ahmed 2012). Indeed, one of the sources for this study, an Islamic scholar who visited Yusuf at the time when Boko Haram was but a local nuisance that drew large crowds and preached without local permissions in Maiduguri, made no mention of Shekau's presence (Abubakar 2012). The literature that focuses primarily on Boko Haram's formative years, moreover, stays on Yusuf, with virtually no discussion of Shekau.[7]

Shekau is a Kanuri from Shekau village, Tarmuwa local government of Yobe State (International Crisis Group 2014, 19). He was one of Boko Haram's earliest and most influential figures but remained a quiet and understated individual early in the group's early history. Shekau first moved to Maiduguri in 1990, settling down in the Mafoni area; he would later enrol at the higher Islamic studies at the Borno State College of Legal and Islamic Studies (BOCOLIS). It also was at BOCOLIS where Shekau first met Mamman Nur, a Shuwa Arab born and raised in Maiduguri by Chadian parents (International Crisis Group 2014, 19). Mamman Nur, Abu Shekau, Muhammad Yusuf and Abu Mus'ab al-Barnawi are the four key actors within this part of the book's narrative on Boko Haram. It was Nur, for instance, who introduced Shekau to Yusuf. According to Virginia Comolli, this introduction took place 'possibly in the late 1990s' (2015, 61). Other sources on the same supposed introduction, however, do not give an exact year (International Crisis Group 2014, 19).

Moreover, interviews conducted for this book project indicate that Shekau was not always part of Yusuf's inner circle by the early 2000s (Abubakar 2012). Additional information on Shekau within those formative years suggests that he was 'devoted [to Qur'anic studies]', yet 'more feared than Yusuf' despite not having the latter's oratory skills or charisma (Rice 2012). In this sense, Shekau's emergence and his transformation from background scholar to foreground violent actor, both constituted a changing of the guard and mirrored 'the changing face of Boko Haram' (Rice 2012).

In these early days of Boko Haram, Shekau is said to have spent his time 'studying and writing' but paid attention to Yusuf's sermons and noted how little impact they seemed to be having. Moreover, unlike Yusuf who lived relatively lavishly, Shekau 'would only wear cheap clothes and did not accept even to drive a car, preferring a motorbike' (Rice 2012). Such behaviour was, in some ways, practicalizing Yusuf's criticisms around Western influence. However, although both men undoubtedly shared this viewpoint, there was a marked difference in the approach they adopted in enacting. Yusuf, for instance, was not a military tactician; he was a cleric and an aspiring Qur'anic theologian, albeit one whose understanding of Salafist/Wahhabi doctrines – or at the least, his interpretations of their innovation within a pluralistic society like Nigeria's – was too fundamentalist not to cause conflict. Shekau, on the other hand, was altogether more militaristic and violent in trying to attain Boko Haram's original goals. These goals include a stricter form of Sharia; the expulsion of the 'corrupt' Nigerian police and the replacement of the above with *hisbah* (Islamic religious law enforcers); the abolishment of *makarantun boko* (Western schools), with *madrassas* and other forms of Islamic learning as the replacement.

The goals above stayed consistent across the regime of both leaders; indeed, there is little to indicate Boko Haram has strayed, even marginally, from these broad goals. What differs drastically between both leadership eras, is (1) that Shekau's military calculations starkly contrasts Yusuf's and (2) that Shekau harbours, and at times during this insurgency (including as recently as 2019), has indeed realized, Boko Haram's territorial ambitions. The distinction is useful insofar as military action was the only feasible way through which Boko Haram could try to impose its ultra-conservative Salafist/Wahhabi vision on a democratic, pluralistic northern Nigerian society.

We must remember that Boko Haram's central thesis, as this chapter has earlier shown, has no theological ground, no Qur'anic basis. Ergo, faith and theology-based persuasion alone could not bring about such unreasonable goals. Further, the *Izala*, the Sufi Brotherhoods, the rest of the Sufi establishment, not to mention the massive Shi'ite body under Ibrahim Yaqoub El Zakzaky's Islamic Movement in Nigeria (IMN), are all opposed to Boko Haram. Without a faith-based support base, and indeed with these other movements actively repudiating everything Boko Haram claimed to stand for, military force was the only other alternative. Shekau, arguably, understood this a great deal better than Yusuf.

This military option, however, was far from viable given the strength of Nigeria's armed forces and the weakness of Boko Haram's followers at the time. Nevertheless, Boko Haram over the years has sophisticated and has surprised many of its sceptics within the military space by demonstrating a grasp of both bush war tactics and conventional warfighting tactics (Omeni 2018, Omeni 2018b).

Yusuf and Shekau – Two men, one ideology, different tactics

For Boko Haram, in the period post-Yusuf's era, therefore, any pathway to total militarization required a complete break not just from the Islamic establishment in northern Nigeria but from the Nigerian state itself. Gone would be the days where Yusuf employed preaching and grassroots influence as the primary vehicles for influence. Gone too were the days when Boko Haram's leadership, represented by Yusuf in the movement's formative years, could be called to order by the Islamic establishment and, on occasion, even made to see reason.[8] In June 2009, a line was crossed; there was now no turning back. This point of no return meant a more violent group, and this group had a new face, albeit one known within its circles for many years now. That face was Abu Shekau's and unlike Yusuf who seemed to bide his time for several years, and who and for extended periods attempted to use faith-based arguments rather than military force to enact Boko Haram's goals, Shekau wanted the escalation of an armed contest against government forces, sooner rather than later (Ahmed 2012). He indeed was a radical, quite possibly the most radical of Boko Haram influential figures around the period when the group gained notoriety in 2009. It is believed, for instance, that Shekau, led 'the more militant wing of the group [Boko Haram]' in the years following his introduction to Yusuf by the Cameroonian jihadist and influential Boko Haram figure, Mamman Nur (The BBC 2014), whose own narrative will be discussed in Chapter 3.

As of 2009, Yusuf was the head of Boko Haram, Abu Shekau and Mamman Nur were both deputies. When the group resurfaced in 2010, however, it was Shekau who was both its new face and leader. Certainly, Nur subsequently demonstrated a pedigree in kidnapping operations. Moreover, Nur too would prove his skill as a military tactician that drove Boko Haram's campaign between 2010 and 2012. Despite these leadership traits, however, it is likely that his Cameroonian background made Nur less suited than Shekau, an ethnic Kanuri, to lead an insurgency based in Borno, which has a majority Kanuri population. If Nur had led Boko Haram, this might well have made for a tactical expedient for the group. On the other hand, it could have cost the insurgency its grassroots support within its Kanuri base.

Nevertheless, what Shekau lacked in operational experience at the time he became Boko Haram leader, he seemed to make up for in terms of his radical ideologies and his doggedness to raise an army and prosecute a full-blown military campaign. This contrasted with Yusuf, who seemed indecisive between theology and armed force as a way to press Boko Haram's ideological case. Shekau's approach also saw some distinction with Nur's, which was more covert and more internationalized, with bombings, kidnappings and international affiliations with the likes of Al-Qaeda in the Islamic Maghreb (AQIM) part of his modus operandi. One reports notes that 'Shekau has neither the charismatic streak nor the oratorical skills of his predecessor – but he has an intense ideological commitment and ruthlessness' (The BBC 2014). This is consistent with what Comolli writes, that:

> Among the three [Yusuf, Nur and Shekau] he [Shekau] was no doubt the one holding the most radical beliefs to the point that he even criticised Yusuf for being too 'liberal'. Moreover, his religious drive was such that it won him the nickname of Darul Tahweed, i.e. specialist in Tawheed, or Islamic doctrine. His extreme views were reflected in some of his messages. In one of the most infamous ones, following the death of over 180 people in Kanu in January 2012 he confessed, 'I enjoy killing anyone that God commands me to kill the way I enjoy killing chickens and rams'. (2015, 61)

Shekau, therefore, was, in a sense, part-theologian, part-gangster: a ruthless rambler with contempt for Nigerian authorities. However, as Boko Haram's tactical improvisations have demonstrated for years, he also possesses resourcefulness that makes him a dangerous jihadist military leader. Shekau's authoritarian style and the respect he commands as *Amir* (leader) of Boko Haram reflects in the fact that despite breakaway attempts by factions (by Ansaru, *c.* 2012) and some in-fighting (by the Abu Mus'ab al-Barnawi faction, *c.* 2016), Boko Haram's insurgency, on the whole, has not derailed. As for the impact of his so-called 'jihad' – holy war within the military context – Shekau has entirely dismissed the impact of such a conflict on Muslims living in affected areas. Shekau's stated view on the matter is that 'one cannot stay in the domain of the infidels without showing his opposition to the prevailing system [...] it is not possible for a Muslim to profess his faith without kicking against an infidel system' (Premium Times 2016b). 'Kicking', of course, is figurative language for the duty of locals to do *any* and *everything* possible, to fight the compromised Islamic establishment, the corrupt Nigerian authorities and their security apparatus: the 'infidel system'.

Simply put, Shekau's doctrine suggests that by their failure to violently oppose *boko*, secularism, Sufism and its innovation, opposing Muslim movements, Christianity, the Nigerian government, and the police and security forces that acted as coercive appendages of the secular state, local Muslims were effectively apostates (*kāfir*). In some ways, this fundamentalist view is consistent with the tenants of Ibn Taymiyya, earlier touched upon in this chapter (Rapoport and Ahmed 2010). The ideology which Taqi al-Din Ibn Taymiyya first promulgated, inspired not just Yusuf but also Wahhabis and other revivalist movements globally, for centuries. Specifically, the tenets of the Ibn Taymiyya viewpoint were as follows: (1) The *Ummah*'s 'suffering' was often due to leaders' failure to adhere to the tenets of pure Islam (Forest 2012, 62). (2) Jihad was the duty, within the lifetime, of a true Muslim; this obligation, moreover, was not just to 'defend the *ummah*' but also was for Islamization – that is, the spread and proselytization of Islam (Forest 2012, 62). (3) The 'leader who does not enforce Shari'a law completely and [who fails to] wage active jihad against infidels, is unfit to rule' (Forest 2012, 62). These three tenets of the Taqi al-Din Ibn Taymiyya view certainly influenced Yusuf and, by implication, the *Yusufiyya* as his followers. It is clear that current leader Abubakar Shekau, like Yusuf, is a strict adherent of the Taqi al-Din Ibn Taymiyya viewpoint: Boko Haram's declarations and actions consistently demonstrate such thinking. It also is likely that Shekau is a scholar of other Salafi-Jihadist doctrines as well (hence the moniker, *Darul Tahweed*, said to apply to him), possibly even such radical doctrines that also influenced Yusuf, since Shekau would have been present during much of the deceased spiritual leader's preachings and teaching sessions.

Again, however, it was the haste and willingness of Shekau to enact such radical ideologies by force, which set apart his leadership from that of Yusuf. Consequently, with Shekau leading Boko Haram, and with the group now a proscribed terrorist organization, the price of being associated with or being a member of Boko Haram was now extremely high. Shekau demands action from his followers and supporters: it was their duty to wage jihad. There is no middle ground and the time for preaching and inactive membership, such as was seen during the *Yusufiyya* era, has long passed. Boko Haram members now fight on the battlefield, blow themselves up and conduct unspeakable acts of violence. Such risk to personal safety is now the price for being 'Boko Haram', regardless of whether recruits paid this price voluntarily or whether they are coerced. In any event, this high price point for Boko Haram's ideology under Shekau has proved quite a departure from what membership meant, for many members and many years, under Ustaz Yusuf.

There are other differences between the styles of both men. Yusuf welcomed locals and tried to persuade them, through Qur'anic theology and economic incentives, to accept his ideas and join his movement. For Shekau those same people are effectively deserving of any harm that comes their way because they choose to coexist with the 'prevailing system' rather than oppose it. Yes, also, Yusuf made some outlandish claims that scholars and jurists in the Islamic establishment felt were absurd. Yusuf, as an example, rejected Darwinism and taught his followers that the earth was flat. However, this, in itself, did not make Yusuf, for most of his adult life at least, a threat in the same vein as Shekau. Yusuf may have pushed an idea system that made violence inevitable, but it is the perpetration of such violence, under Abu Shekau, which has now defined Boko Haram.

Therefore, as the Borno State Department of Security Service (DSS) tsar pointed out to me, unbeknownst to the various actors involved in the events of 2009, those events took Boko Haram from the hands of a demagogue, in Muhammad Yusuf, to those of a 'madman', in Abu Shekau (Ahmed 2012). Moreover, with Shekau – a Yusuf disciple – assuming the movement's leadership mantle, Boko Haram finally possessed the deadly mix of radical ideology and military intent required to pursue its original goals. However, as Parts II and III of this volume will show, to successfully wage war against the Nigerian military, a lot more was required by Boko Haram.

Conclusion

Boko Haram's insurgency began in earnest with the Bauchi Prison break in September 2010. This period was about a year on from the crackdown by Nigerian authorities in July 2009. Up until that point, the group's members were the *Yusufiyya*, followers loyal to Yusuf. Transcripts of his statements, police accounts from Maiduguri and documentary records assist for a better understanding of this individual.

Ustaz Yusuf was an anti-establishment radical and rabble-rouser who had several run-ins with the police over the years. He had expressed admiration for Osama bin Laden and Al-Qaeda,[9] and there was little question that he very much planned to wage war against the Islamic establishment and Nigerian authorities. Even so, until close to his demise, Yusuf for years drew the line at violent confrontation against the armed forces of Nigeria. This apparent non-violent posture was not because Yusuf, at heart, was a pacifist. Instead, it might have been due to Yusuf's experience at Kanamma, where Boko Haram reportedly lost members years earlier. Yusuf's reluctance for 'jihad' also might have been due to his conviction not to begin an unwinnable military campaign; better to bide time and strike when his movement was ready: militarized, with the numbers and with a plan of action. In any event, the rampage of July 2009 was unlikely to have been premeditated. Rather, Yusuf miscalculated Boko Haram's ability to confront Nigeria's military and security forces directly. He sealed his fate, and that of hundreds of his supporters, with his call to arms. With such open, disorganized violence in heed of that call to arms, there was but one outcome against the poorly armed *Yusufiyya* if the Nigerian Army mobilized to protect the civil power (which it did, in force).

Ustaz Yusuf's death was a blow to Boko Haram, but it emerged under the leadership of Abu Shekau in 2010 undoubtedly wiser about engaging military forces. The group, initially, was but a small guerrilla outfit with little combat experience and virtually no military capabilities. Moreover, the limited Army response in 2011 appeared consistent with this expectation that Boko Haram's ragtag forces would fight a bush war: harassing government forces, retreating to Sambisa Forest after contact, and sticking with diversionary guerrilla tactics similar to what militias in the Niger Delta creeks did for years. By all accounts, however, as its campaign progressed, Boko Haram has far exceeded this modest outlook.

The first suicide bombings in 2011 were perhaps the initial sign that something had changed in the group's tactical doctrine. Four years later, at the height of its threat around January 2015, Boko Haram resembled a force numbering thousands of fighters, with military capabilities including light armoured vehicles, unarmoured technicals and protected mobility. With these capabilities came a subsequent pivot towards military fighting, and with that came a demonstrated ability to contest and hold territory across swathes of north-east Nigeria.

Ipso facto the insurgency in north-east Nigeria by Boko Haram has become the country's main internal threat, supplanting the Niger Delta insurgency as the Army's main domestic concern. By 2015 over 1.5 million people were reported displaced (The BBC 2015a) and several towns, within contested areas of north-east Nigeria, fell into Boko Haram's orbit (Blair 2015a). Boko Haram fighters, throughout the insurgency, numbered possibly over 10,000 (Freeman, Henderson and Oliver 2014). With a force of this size and attendant improvements in capabilities, territorial ambition followed, which was gradually realized between mid-2014 and early 2015. As one report from early 2015 put it, Boko Haram:

> Achieved mastery over 11 local government areas with a total population exceeding 1.7 million people [...] Once, the movement's fighters would launch hit-and-run attacks on defenceless villages. Now, Boko Haram's realm stretches from the Mandara Mountains on the eastern border with Cameroon to Lake Chad in the north and the Yedseram river in the west (Blair 2015a).

With such bold territorial claims, Boko Haram has indeed come a long way from its poorly timed and ill-fated confrontation of security forces in mid-2009. In the intervening period, so much changed in Boko Haram's tactics, its doctrine and its concept of operations that militarily the group came to be one of the most dangerous perpetrator groups in the world. From the preceding, two related questions emerge: first, what processes led Boko Haram to become such a formidable military threat? Second, why has the Nigerian military, with its superior capabilities, failed to stop this evolving threat? Parts II and III aim to answer the first of these questions; Part IV addresses the second.[10]

Beginning Part II's analysis of the factors that drive the insurgency, Chapter 4 discusses what the environmental drivers are that have sustained Boko Haram's military campaign and that have force-multiplied its threat. Before this shift away from an examination of Boko Haram and towards its environment, however, some developments into 2019 have informed an updated area of analysis, contained in Chapter 3. Infighting between Boko Haram factions, the influential central figures, ideological differences between the splinter groups, operational competition, and the implications for the Nigerian Army's campaign, into January 2019, are all considered next.

Boko Haram, Abu Mus'ab Al-Barnawi and ISWAP

Background: Organizational change as a sociological phenomenon

Most organizations are learning organizations, potentially, at least. Under the guidance of strong leadership, their constituent members can learn, imitate, adapt, evolve and sophisticate. Based on cues from the environment, as well as on perceived threats and opportunities, they may even transform over time (McChrystal et al. 2015). Nevertheless, even a so-called learning organization, due to institutional inertia, may remain seemingly change-averse and stagnated: failing to reconfigure itself, while the environment around it changes in ways that render existing doctrines and standard operating procedures less effective (and possibly even ineffective) compared to previous cycles. This effect is especially evident in larger and more bureaucratic institutions, whose older members may cite historical precedent and identify so strongly with a set of cultures, values, norms and practices, that even small changes to the familiar tend to be frowned upon or outrightly rejected by them (McChrystal et al. 2015).

A case in point is in established religious movements, wherein a departure from longstanding doctrines, or even criticisms of such doctrines via theological debate, may well be viewed as heretical. Such institutions, deeply traditional, frown upon even the idea of change and seldom embrace it with ease. Yet, somewhat ironically, because such institutional inertia may not sit well with certain actors within these organizations, internal schismatic tensions and infighting could mean that some radical factions push for a break with tradition and existing religious practices. Such schismatic tensions, driven by ideological cleavages, could change an organization's religious identity as rival factions jostle for power or try to break away to establish new doctrines or to employ new ways to promulgate old ones. In this regard, religiously motivated terrorist organizations such as Boko Haram are no different.

Splintering

Like any learning organization, terrorist perpetrator groups and insurgent movements are neither evolutionarily stagnant nor do they operate as a hive mind.

Although such entities, in general, are a like-minded collective, there nevertheless are individual views, strong personalities with leadership potential, shifting interests, and even different operational ideas around the prosecution of a group's conflictual strategies. Shifts in group identity could be due, perhaps, to longstanding group practices or ideologies that some members may not agree with (either because such thought processes or tactics are deemed too soft or hard). Such shifts invariably lead to growing concerns by more radical members around group purpose and cohesion. Such growing concerns, if they have a charismatic champion and reach a critical mass of support within the organization, could lead to the formation of ad hoc groups: splinter factions with ideas inconsistent with the parent group's conflictual strategies. Such splinter factions adopt new or considerably different identities, becoming so radical in the process that the parent group's core, by comparison, appears softened.

Within Boko Haram's case, there is a pattern of such organizational behaviour. As Chapter 1's analysis shows, moreover, Muhammad Yusuf, as Boko Haram's leader, himself created the movement as a faction that split ideologically away from a generation of new scholars looking to move beyond the softened core of Izala B teachings. Izala B itself was a departure from Izala, a Muslim group identity, which in turn was a departure from the teachings of the traditional Islamic establishment and, in particular, their rivals in the *Qadiriyya* and *Tijaniyya* (Sufi Brotherhoods). Indeed, such rivalries and ideological cleavages that led to splinter groups contributed to what Muhammad Sani Umar referred to as the 'crowded religious marketplace' of northern Nigeria (2012). So, here too is an observable pattern of organizational conduct, in the periodical emergence of offshoot movements, which challenge the status quo.

Do splinter factions, however, pose a threat to the parent organization? The answer, in short, is yes. The threat in question may be non-violent and ideological; it could be within the operational space without turning aggressive, or it could be conflictual. If this threat exists, then why? Splinter factions pose such a threat to the parent organization because the former could invigorate a stagnating movement by resonating with younger members who, having long hoped for change, could choose to align with this new organizational identity rather than keep faith with the old guard. In this way, new radical factions thus may prove increasingly popular within the movement. Also, in such cases, the group's right may well shift: becoming its centre over time. This shift invariably leads to a normalization of increasingly radical views, action and identity within the group context. Such an occurrence is significant as it may lead to even more profound changes as a radical internal faction gradually consolidates its base. Over time, as this happens, practices and ideologies that were once at the group margins become the status quo. Such changes may relate to identity, ideology, leadership, followership numbers and organizational tactics (if not to overarching strategic goals, *per se*).

Moreover, evolving group interests and idea systems could be so incompatible with the centre – either because they see it as too soft or too hard line – that a splinter cell, which fails to take over a group's leadership, could break away entirely to form its own organization. Sometimes, a splinter faction, perhaps for purposes of expedience, may continue to ally loosely with its parent organization, retaining an operational and tactical signature recognizable from its roots. Other times, however, not only is a new signature emergent upon splintering, there may even be ideological, operational and, in some cases, territorial competition between a new movement and the parent organization from which it split.

All of the considerations mentioned so far in this chapter are important to understanding the emergence of organizational 'splintering', as it relates to Boko Haram. Nevertheless, the rest of the chapter shifts from this theme of splintering within the organizational context and instead focuses on Boko Haram splinter factions until 2019 as well as some of the key personalities behind them. Influential personalities, after all, have been central to the emergence of these factions.

Emergent factions and personalities in Boko Haram

For some years now, there previously had been rumours of multiple factions within Boko Haram. Comolli points to no less than six groups that had splintered from, or existed as factions within, Boko Haram before 2014, with the existence of 'a number of smaller factions' additionally suggested (2015, 68–69). And circa 2012, no less than three Boko Haram factions were active, with the most popular of these factions being the splinter group Ansaru – notorious for its kidnappings and its trans-national links with AQIM (Zenn 2014, Comolli 2015). Comolli, for instance, writes, 'of all these [Boko Haram] factions Ansaru is no doubt the most threatening owing to the number of kidnappings of foreigners it has conducted, its closer cooperation with AQIM and other non-Nigerian Islamists, and its more international Agenda' (2015, 68–69). Over the past few years, however, a new actor has emerged as a significant Boko Haram rival, one that began as a splinter group but that has metastasized in ways that even now eclipse Boko Haram in Northern Borno.

In the first week of August 2016, there was considerable media chatter around a new figure, said to be Muhammad Yusuf's son (Nigerian Army 2011), becoming the head (*Walī*) of either Boko Haram or a splinter faction of the group. The appointment was made by Daesh (The BBC 2016d), which indicates that the individual in question, one Abu Mus'ab al-Barnawi, effectively becomes *Walī* of the so-called Islamic State's West Africa Province (ISWAP). ISWAP was the name used by Daesh to refer to Boko Haram after its erstwhile *Ameer*, Abu Shekau, swore allegiance to Abu Bakr al-Baghdadi, the 'Caliph' of the Islamic State (Daesh), in March 2015. As Aymenn Jawad Al-Tamimi points out, however:

> Shekau was eventually removed from his position by the Islamic State, and Abu Mus'ab al-Barnawi, who was announced to be the wali of West Africa Province in August 2016, has led the Islamic State affiliate ever since. Perceptions that Shekau's ideas are too extreme even for the Islamic State, his rejection of Islamic State leader Abu Bakr al-Baghdadi's authority as caliph, and Shekau's ruthless conduct against his internal critics, are the main reasons why Shekau was removed from his position as *Walī* of the West Africa province.

It has been claimed that Shekau's group and the Islamic State's West Africa Province represent two rival factions professing loyalty to Baghdadi and competing for recognition as the Islamic State's wing in West Africa. In fact, this claim is incorrect. Shekau clearly does not recognise the Islamic State as a legitimate authority whatsoever, and on multiple occasions, his group has actually fought the Islamic State's West Africa Province, which deems Shekau and his followers to be Khawarij [essentially rebellious to the authority of the Caliphate]. (Al-Tamimi 2018)

The designation of al-Barnawi as *Walī* is significant insofar as it carries with it a connotation of territorial responsibility (in this case, Daesh's territorial ambitions in West Africa). An *Ameer* (also 'Amir' or 'Emir'), on the other hand, denotes merely the leader of a group (whether small or large). Unlike the position of *Walī*, there could be, but need not be *per se*, territorial connotations attached to the position of *Amir*.

Nevertheless, with so little known about Abu Mus'ab al-Barnawi before his effective coronation as *Walī* of ISWAP, it is worth taking a closer look at this individual: to clarify some questions around his personage, but also to highlight some seeming discrepancies within the debate around his emergence. The section that follows raises several questions and evaluates them; it does not seek to authoritatively answer these questions which, all the same, are worth asking.

Who is Abu Mus'ab al-Barnawi?

A start point of this evaluation could be the name itself, in Abu Mus'ab al-Barnawi. Now, Muhammad Yusuf was from Yobe State. Therefore, any of his sons, by paternal lineage, should be from Yobe. This individual, however, in Abu Mus'ab al-Barnawi, appears not to be from Yobe; the suggestion, instead, is that he is from Borno. This is evidenced in the name 'al-Barnawi' as a suffix. Such suffixes are sometimes used to denote a person's home region often as part of a *nom de guerre* – a war name – adopted by, or perhaps given to, some jihadi fighters. In the specific example of 'al-Barnawi', it simply means 'from Borno'. Walker, writing for the BBC, correctly deduces that 'Barnawi is a pseudonym meaning "from Borno"' (2016b). A possible explanation, therefore, lies in the lineage of Abu Mus'ab al-Barnawi and in the names of his father, in Mohammed Yusuf. Yusuf, after all, also went by Abu Yusuf al-Barnawi, and so chose to identify with Borno (as a place of both tribal and ancestral connections) rather than with Yobe (as a place of birth as well as a maternal-side locality). More to this point, a new account of Abu Mus'ab al-Barnawi's origins comes from a publication supposedly by two of Muhammad Yusuf's sons, for ISWAP, in 2018. The text, published to, amongst other things, discredit Shekau, translates literally as 'Cutting out the tumour from the Khawarij of Shekau by the allegiance pledge of the people of nobility' (Al-Tamimi 2018). Here, the writers refer to Yusuf Muhammad (Abu Yusuf) as:

The father Imam sheikh, the reviver of jihad and tawheed, Abu Yusuf: Muhammad bin Yusuf bin Muhammad bin Ahmad al-Dagheri by origin, al-Maiduguri by residence, al-Jakusi by birth, and al-Barnawi by tribe and ancestry'. And as [to] the suffix al-Dagheri, it refers to Ghirghir, ' … a village in the locality of Geidam in the countryside of Yobe state in north-east Nigeria, and it is the locality of his mother in truth, but he did not claim affiliation with it out of fulfilment for it, and his birth was in Jakusko and it is the one embodied in al-Jakusi. (Al-Tamimi 2018)

The above excerpt helps clarify why the name Abu Mus'ab al-Barnawi may well be consistent with an heir of Abu Yusuf (Muhammad Yusuf). Moreover, the account of Yusuf's origins above is consistent with that of his widely studied background and origins, such as was discussed in chapter one of this volume. Nevertheless, what the above publication fails to do is discuss Abu Mus'ab al-Barnawi's origins; nor does it make, or substantiate, what should be a crucial bloodline linkage between Abu Yusuf al-Barnawi (Muhammad Yusuf) and Abu Mus'ab al-Barnawi. Shared lineage with Yusuf, we must remember, constitutes an undeniable claim: not just to legitimacy within Boko Haram circles but potentially even group leadership or, at the least, recognition within the group Shura (council). Such claims are common within other jihadist circles.

As examples, both Hamza bin Osama, Osama bin Laden's son, and Muhammad al-Masri, son of Abu Khabab al-Masri who was Al-Qaeda master bomb maker, were introduced based on their parentage first and foremost (Joscelyn 2015, Mekhennet and Miller 2016). Indeed, Daesh – already arguably the perpetrator group with the most demonstrable bomb-making experience in the world today (Doucet 2016) – nevertheless actively sought after Muhammad al-Masri. This courtship was not because the younger al-Masri had, himself, demonstrated any real bomb-making skill, but more likely because 'name recognition helped him [Muhammad al-Masri] build a following of several hundred fighters after he arrived in Syria in 2012' (Mekhennet and Miller 2016). It, therefore, is striking that in Daesh's introduction of Abu Mus'ab al-Barnawi as *Walī* of ISWAP, his supposed connection to Muhammad Yusuf was not made explicit or even mentioned at all (The BBC 2016e).

Another noteworthy point is that if al-Barnawi was a son of Yusuf that would make him fairly young, maybe in his early thirties and possibly even younger. This is because Ustaz Yusuf himself was not yet even forty when he died in 2009, a point suggested by journalist Ahmad Salkida in an earlier interview (Rice 2012). A report by Agence France Presse (AFP) from 2016, as an example, observes that 'Barnawi, aged in his early twenties, is none other than Habib Yusuf, the eldest son of group founder Yusuf. They said he was put under Shekau's care following the death of his father, but the pair fell out over ideological and operational differences' (2016). However, it remains unclear and has yet to be confirmed by either Boko Haram or Daesh, whether both individuals, in Abu Mus'ab al-Barnawi and Habib Yusuf, are one and the same.

This point on al-Barnawi's age is significant insofar as statements made by al-Barnawi in a second message from 5 August 2016 (Sahara Reporters 2016b), in response to an earlier audio message by Abu Shekau (Sahara Reporters 2016c) indicate three things. First, that Abu Mus'ab al-Barnawi had been active even before the events of July 2009. A second indication is that Abu Mus'ab al-Barnawi had a house where Shekau himself had resided. A third is that Abu Mus'ab al-Barnawi was part of the *Yusufiyya Shura* council that would 'would collectively go through and work on' Yusuf's Friday preaching (Sahara Reporters 2016b). Again, the idea that Yusuf would appoint his inexperienced son, who would still have been a teenager in the years leading to 2009, as a member of the *Shura* council of trusted Boko Haram leadership, is questionable. It also appears odd that any time before 2009, Shekau would have resided with Yusuf's teenage son, rather than with Yusuf himself, whose friends and confidants generally resided in his private lodgings (Abubakar 2012). As a final note on this point, it again seems somewhat unusual that a person so young at the time would have been so active, and privy to such internal matters, like those mentioned by Abu Mus'ab al-Barnawi regarding the period when Yusuf was still alive.

Then there is the issue of al-Barnawi's age and its relevance to his ability to have acquired the Islamic knowledge useful to leading a Salafi-Jihadist group without making fundamental theological errors in *Shura* council meetings, in publications, statements (and quite possibly fatwas, as such groups are wont to do) and so on. Even discounting the fact that Yusuf himself was accused of knowing little about the Islamic matters he preached about (Mohammed 2010, Umar 2012), and the fact that many jihadist groups make theological interpretations that are questionable, to begin with, Abu Mus'ab al-Barnawi's likely age and inexperience still makes questionable his knowledge of Islamic jurisprudence. Such likelihood of limited scholarly knowledge is more so the case because high-level involvement in Boko Haram's insurgency would have limited opportunities for any of its members to embark on rigorous Islamic study, local or abroad. Such studies, however, are crucial to developing the understanding required to avoid fundamental theological misjudgements. It, therefore, will be rare, although perhaps not without precedent, that someone so young would be an authority on Islamic law, while simultaneously being 'head of military operations', as Abu Mus'ab al-Barnawi was said to be for Boko Haram (Fick 2016). The absence of such Islamic authority may therefore further undermine the effectiveness of statements made, and of declarations made, by Abu Mus'ab al-Barnawi.

A final point is a question of how much military strategic and operational experience Abu Mus'ab al-Barnawi brings in, for one so young. This is not about infantry fighting or accrued hours in tactical warfare. It is about how to understand operations, and the ability to make sound decisions at all levels of war. Prosecuting a war, even an irregular war, requires tactical, operational and strategic understanding, in addition to consummate understanding of the environment and a good grasp of the enemy on top of that. The better this understanding, the higher the chances of campaign success. Such understanding, however, comes with command experience, with backroom staff duties – to better understand issues like logistics and planning – and with time. It is for these reasons that military decision-making at the operational and strategic level, requires a certain rank, and thus a certain age and level of experience, in professional militaries. It has been said that Abu Mus'ab al-Barnawi was head of Boko Haram's military operations (Fick 2016), since at least 2014. However, the responsibility required for such a position would have been considerable indeed. Giving that task to one young and inexperienced will be virtually unheard of within military insurgencies. The claim is even more incredible bearing in mind that some of Boko Haram's most significant military successes, such as the capture of Gwoza town, came since 2014. There is little evidence presented to suggest that Abu Mus'ab al-Barnawi has the relevant military experience to have masterminded Boko Haram's military successes in the period where the group took possibly the most territory in its history. Still, this is not to say that al-Barnawi has no operational experience at all.

In 2012, for instance, it was reported that one Habibu Yusuf alias 'Assalafi', at the time a deputy of another influential Boko Haram commander, Khalid al-Barnawi, was promoted by Shekau himself to plan and head operations in the Sokoto area; this was in 2012 (Africa Confidential 2012). How much operational experience this indeed gave Habib (especially since Boko Haram failed spectacularly at gaining a foothold in Sokoto), or whether Assalafi and Abu Mus'ab al-Barnawi are even the same person, is unclear, though this is quite likely.[1]

Such unanswered questions on Abu Mus'ab al-Barnawi's operational inexperience present food for thought. To this point, how much impact on Boko Haram's military ambition was the appointment of Abu Mus'ab al-Barnawi as *Walī* of ISWAP to have, *if* he was selected purely based on being Yusuf's son? Being Yusuf's son certainly lends him legitimacy but this does not make Mus'ab al-Barnawi an effective military leader. Nor does it make him the most strategic choice to deliver on Boko Haram's military ambition and the group's territorial hopes for a caliphate. For that, considerable operational experience is required. It is not clear that Mus'ab al-Barnawi – for all his claims to Yusuf's lineage – has that much experience, even though he likely possessed some experience.

There is, however, a possible explanation for such questions around al-Barnawi as the choice of *Walī* of ISWAP. Suppose al-Barnawi's legitimacy was the expedient here, rather than his operational pedigree or knowledge of Islamic law *per se*? So what that al-Barnawi was young and inexperienced? If his legitimacy as a son and heir of Abu Yusuf (Muhammad Yusuf) was what was primarily required, age and relative inexperience may have been seen as secondary to the legitimacy issue. Moreover, suppose Abu Mus'ab al-Barnawi's supposed legitimacy could pair with the unique leadership features, ideology, command experience and operational links of another influential individual within Boko Haram?

Such a scenario may well have been realized: with the role of Mamman Nur as the operational head and ideological leader of the ISWAP faction and with Abu Mus'ab al-Barnawi as de facto leader due to his connection to the Yusuf bloodline. The section that follows sheds light on the jihadist known as Mamman Nur, and his impact on Boko Haram's military success over the years.

The Mamman Nur factor

Abubakar Shekau, Mamman Nur and Khalid al-Barnawi at a time after Yusuf's death were, in that order, the three most influential leaders in Boko Haram's network. Research material obtained for this project from Nigeria's Office of the National Security Adviser (ONSA) states that 'the identified leadership of the group [Boko Haram] is Abubakar Shekau, [Khalid] Al Barnawi and Mamman Nur and it is strongly believed that there are some splinter groups with emerging leaderships as well' (ONSA 2012, 3). All three individuals share a long history, and enjoyed a friendship, within Boko Haram's earliest days, having:

Met as theology students in Borno. Yusuf admired the Taliban, Usama bin Ladin and al-Qaʿida (particularly AQIM), while Shekau preached takfiri (excommunication) ideology, but they both focused on their native Nigeria. Nur, who is Cameroonian, may have had an incentive to regionalise Boko Haram's ideology, and he was the mastermind of the bombing of the UN Headquarters in Abuja on August 26, 2011. (Zenn 2014, 23)

Born to Chadian parents in Maroua, the capital of Cameroon's extreme far north region (Région de l'Extrême-Nord) (International Crisis Group 2014, 19, Iaccino 2016), Nur is sometimes referred to as Cameroonian or sometimes as Chadian, due to his heritage and background of both countries. Being raised in Borno, however, Nur was effectively an indigene with fluency in the local Kanuri dialect. This helped the close relationship he shared with the group's senior leadership who also were either ethnic Kanuri (such as Shekau and Khalid al-Barnawi) or had strong ties to Borno (such as Yusuf).

Even from the group's early days, Mamman Nur was an influential member of Boko Haram, despite the group's mostly Hausa-Fulani and Kanuri ethnic make-up. In placing sanctions on Nur, for instance, the US Treasury notes that 'Nur was considered a most trusted lieutenant to US-designated Boko Haram leader Abubakar Muhammad Shekau and was one of approximately ninety extremists who had reportedly trained with US-designated SDGT al-Shabaab. Nur coordinated Boko Haram operations with SDGT Al-Qaeda in the Lands of the Islamic Maghreb' (US Department of the Treasury 2015). Nur's reputation as a high-profile commander of Boko Haram stretched even further back, however.

Nur, as an example, was one of Yusuf's main deputies, as of 2007, with the others being Muhammad Lawan from Potiskum (Yobe) and Shekau (International Crisis Group 2014, 19). Between 2007 and 2009, however, this order changed. In December 2007, Lawan left Boko Haram over ideological differences, increasingly divergent theological views, and disagreements of Qur'anic interpretation. Lawan, shortly after, 'issued an audio recording accusing Yusuf of insincerity and rejoined Izala. Boko Haram attacked his home in a failed attempt on his life during its 2009 uprising' (International Crisis Group 2014, 19). All of this meant that from December 2007 and perhaps even slightly earlier, Nur, Shekau and Khalid al-Barnawi (who as of the time of writing remains in the custody of the Department of State Agencies, Nigeria's intelligence agency) were de facto the most influential people in Boko Haram's leadership structure.

Mamman Nur was closer to Yusuf in the group's early years and is believed to have introduced Shekau to Yusuf (International Crisis Group 2014, 19). However, being Cameroonian, Nur would have been unable to obtain the local grassroots support with the Borno and Yobe areas, Borno in particular, which is dominated by the Kanuri – Shekau's ethnicity. This could explain why Habib Yusuf (Abu Musʻab al-Barnawi), due to his lineage and stronger ties to the area, may have been critical to any power coups against Shekau. Nur also has stronger regional connections compared to other influential leaders in Boko Haram's network. Boko Haram certainly has connections to AQIM, with later publications by ISWAP discussing these connections in considerable detail (Al-Tamimi 2018). However, these connections to Al-Qaeda affiliates in Africa are believed to be Nur's brainchild (Zenn 2014, 23, US Department of the Treasury 2015).

Nur had always retained a measure of operational control over some Boko Haram fighters, and, ideologically, he also had supporters within the group. With his links to both Chad and Cameroon in terms of heritage and birthplace, therefore, Nur commanded the respect of the non-Kanuri elements of the groups and likely was a key figure in attracting and recruiting from non-Kanuri and non-Nigerian demographics, especially those of Cameroonian heritage. Nur, as an example, was 'Boko Haram's coordinator for the group's training site in Cameroon' circa 2010. This was a chief reason for which the US Department of the Treasury placed sanctions on both Nur and Mustapha Chad, 'a Boko Haram Shura Council member and militant commander, [who] in 2013 directed activities in the Yobe State in northern Nigeria, one of five geographic areas in which Boko Haram operated' (US Department of the Treasury 2015). With his high-profile locally and his transnational links, as well as a less confrontational but effective approach to military campaigning, Nur appeared to have much of what was required to possible head Boko Haram's operations within Nigeria. Indeed, Nur was 'said to be more knowledgeable, mature and level-headed, was seen as Yusuf's deputy and eventual successor, but [despite these leadership traits displayed by Nur] Shekau was chosen after Yusuf's death because he was more radical and aggressive. [Although] Nur did lead in an acting capacity while Shekau recovered from a 2009 gunshot wound' (International Crisis Group 2014, 19).

Additionally, Nur's Al-Qaeda connections made him more technically proficient in operations than Abu Shekau. Moreover, 'Shekau's reported favouritism of ethnic Kanuris of Borno also may have driven Hausas, non-Nigerians and other non-Kanuris to ally with Nur, who was also non-Nigerian' (Zenn 2014, 23). Furthermore, Mamman Nur's ideology made a distinction between Muslims and Kafir (infidels or those who reject or disbelieve in Allah and the teachings of the Islamic prophet Muhammad). Such ideological differences left a noticeable footprint on operations. Nur's fighters were more respectful of Muslim traditions than Shekau's, with the former's faction attacking mainly military and Christian targets, rather than attacking Muslim civilian settlements, for which Shekau's faction became notorious.

Such operational manifestations of the differences between both men can be traced as far back as 2011 by which there already were local rumours of 'a power struggle between Nur and Shekau, with Nur and his faction of loyalists contending he was more competent to lead the sect given his exposure to Somali training and contacts' (Vanguard 2011b).

Moreover, this idea that Nur and his faction possessed some transnational terrorist links is consistent with reports like many Boko Haram fighters, including Nur himself, had recently returned from Somalia, having linked up with Al-Shabaab in that country for training and operational support, likely in the area of bomb-making and suicide bombing. Bomb-making operational expertise from jihadists in Somalia circa 2011 could, in turn, explain the fact that bombings and suicide bombings were only first employed by Boko Haram, later that year: in June, at the police headquarters; and in August at the UN building, both in Abuja. The UN building bombing left twenty-three people dead. Mamman Nur is believed to have masterminded both attacks (International Crisis Group 2014, 19).

Mamman Nur's operational pedigree that stretched back years, coupled with his documented ideological differences with Abu Shekau (Zenn 2014, Comolli 2015), likely contributed to a irreconcilable situation whereby Nur felt compelled – confident enough, at the least – to eventually splinter from Boko Haram, soliciting the support of Abu Mus'ab Al-Barnawi as the main figurehead of the new faction of ISWAP. One report, for instance, notes that Mamman Nur:

> Is the actual leader of the Boko Haram faction after they parted ways with Shekau. He (Nur) only put Habib (al-Barnawi) in the front as shadow leader because of his father (Muhammad Yusuf). The name Al-Barnawi is only being heard as symbolic leader; he was meant to lead so that followers would remain committed to the cause championed by his late father but he (Nur) is the major link of the faction with the Islamic State; the chief strategist around Lake Chad, including their cells in Nigeria, Niger and Chad. (Idris and Sawab 2018)

Nur's death

Mamman Nur's independence from Shekau and his influence within ISWAP proved relatively short-lived, however. Nur was reportedly murdered on 21 August 2018, by one of his closest lieutenants. The issue of contention, supposedly, was the ransom and release of a group of over a hundred girls kidnapped by the al-Barnawi faction on 19 February from Dapchi, a small town in Yobe. All but one of the girls were released around a month later, with the lone remaining abductee, Leah Sharibu, said to have been withheld because she refused to accept Islam and renounce Christianity (Maclean and Abrak 2018).

This kidnapping event, quite heavily publicized within Nigerian media, led the girls to be known as the 'Dapchi Girls' and provoked speculation over the payment of a heavy ransom for their release, though the ransom by itself may not have been the bone of contention. After all, little within the history of Boko Haram suggests that financial struggles have dominated the group's infighting calculus. Thus, although Nur 'was said to have been killed by his closest lieutenants on August 21, for releasing the Dapchi girls, without demanding ransom, among other reasons' (Sahara Reporters 2018), the ransom payment may have been less the issue than the fact that Nur's willingness to engage with Nigerian authorities constructively may have set him at odds with his top commanders. Such commanders, like Shekau and his faction of Boko Haram, may have been less minded to negotiate or otherwise come to terms with the Nigerian government outside of military fighting. Indeed, 'in this sense, Nur may have been seen as relatively moderate, or more willing to engage with the Nigerian government than others in his movement were comfortable with', which may have led to Nur's assassination (Mahmood 2018). As a local news source, the Cable, points out regarding Nur's murder:

The negotiation of the release of the girls did not go down well with some close associates of Mamman Nur who released the girls unconditionally, following a directive by Al-Baghdadi [Daesh's Caliph] […] Nothing was paid before the girls were released and besides, Mamman Nur's soft approach and close contact to governments and different levels angered his foot soldiers who rebelled against him and thereafter executed him. (Asadu 2018)

However, Nur's decision to return the girls gratis to the Nigerian government appears consistent with Al-Baghdadi and the Islamic State's views on the subject of which women captives it is permissible as a practice to enslave within jihad. As Aymen Jawad Al-Tamimi writes:

Though the Islamic State accepts that there has been disagreement on the matter [of whether women of Muslim background, or those who accept Islam, can be taken captive], Baghdadi has adopted the stance that it is not permissible. Instead, only the women of original disbelievers at war with the Islamic State (e.g. Yezidis, Christians etc.) can be taken captive. Since Baghdadi is deemed the caliph/imam, he is to be obeyed on this matter [by ISWAP] despite the disagreement. (Al-Tamimi 2018)

Such reasons contribute to the vagueness around whether Mamman Nur was assassinated on the orders of Abu Mus'ab al-Barnawi, or whether this was a rogue killing (by yet another splinter cell, this time within ISWAP). On the one hand, it is unlikely that such a senior figure as Nur within ISWAP could be murdered by anyone acting outside explicit orders from the movement's head, in Abu Mus'ab al-Barnawi. Yet, if this was an order from al-Barnawi, it raises questions. Abu Mus'ab al-Barnawi, after all, as *Wali* of ISWAP, is subordinate to, and was appointed by, al-Baghdadi. And Nur's actions, in freeing the captive Muslim girls, were consistent with the views of Al-Baghdadi on the subject of permissible (halal) and non-permissible (haram) female prisoners. Yet, the same actions may have led to Nur's murder within ISWAP. However, if the girls were to be free, they also had to be released into the care of an agent – in this case, the Nigerian government. In this sense, the decision to free the Dapchi girls was, by necessity, closely aligned to negotiations with the government; offence could not be taken against one view but not the other. Notwithstanding, it seems that offence to Nur's negotiations with government agents was a likely reason for his betrayal and assassination.

In any event, Nur's murder would suggest less ideological variance between the Shekau and al-Barnawi factions insofar as similar unit-level ideological and operational disagreements that had long existed between Shekau and Nur likely contributed to the latter's murder within ISWAP. Even so, it remains unlikely that both factions would merge or even cooperate closely in the future. Nevertheless, once things settle and ISWAP reconfigures over time – should slow progress within the Nigerian military COIN campaign allow it to – then Nur's death may well bring with it some potential for thawed relations between Boko Haram and ISWAP in the long term. Short term, however, Nur's death appears to have had a particularly destabilizing effect: causing a power vacuum within ISWAP that seems to have further exposed current security fragilities in north-east Nigeria and particularly in Borno State.

Impact of Mamman Nur's death on the conflict

In some cases, if it is targeted and planned, the death of a senior figure within an insurgency can sometimes have a stabilizing effect and work in favour of government forces (see Figure 7.1). Nur's death, however, reported by multiple news outlets, may have been problematic for the security situation in north-east Nigeria. This is insofar as the removal of this influential figure provoked more infighting amongst the insurgents, or what Nigerian security forces refer to collectively as 'BHTs': Boko Haram Terrorists. More to this point, since Nur's death, infighting in question has intensified both within the al-Barnawi faction and between the al-Barnawi and Shekau factions. Indeed, with this development, it would appear that al-Barnawi himself may have lost some operational control within ISWAP's ranks, with other senior commanders, loyal to Nur, likely to be disloyal to Abu Mus'ab al-Barnawi (even if he nevertheless continues as the assumptive leader due to his being part of the Yusuf bloodline). The Daily Trust newspaper for instance reports that, 'Al-Barnawi since Nur's death 'had also lost firm control of the group' and that, 'the man in charge of all the cells in the Lake Chad region is the former commander of the fighters who were directly under the control of late Mamman Nur' (Idris and Sawab 2018).

With Mamman Nur no longer a player in the jihadists' deadly game, organizational cleavages have become increasingly observable within ISWAP. Without Nur, and perhaps in part due to the nature of his death, Abu Mus'ab al-Barnawi's leadership now appears to be polarizing ISWAP in much the same way that Shekau's leadership also has for Boko Haram. Indeed, in a recurrent pattern of intra-group struggles seen many times before as Boko Haram evolved over the years, three factions are now observable within ISWAP. Each of these factions has differing loyalties. First, are those who see themselves as *Yusufiyya*: pledged to Abu Yusuf al-Barnawi and thus loyal to Abu Mus'ab al-Barnawi, his son. This faction appears to be losing control and most likely had a hand in Mamman Nur's elimination.

Next, are those ISWAP members who supported not just Mamman Nur's transnational goals but also his operational methods and his moderated views – including negotiations with the Federal Government of Nigeria, Nur's refusal to slaughter innocent Muslims, or to hold Muslim women captive and so on. This faction is likely to include Cameroonian and Chadian fighters, with whom Nur held kinship, and who may now feel more isolated without him. However, the fact that al-Barnawi seems to have retained this ideology of not killing Muslims (demonstrated in the months after Nur's death) may well see the more moderate elements, even non-Nigerian ones, pledge continued allegiance to Abu Mus'ab al-Barnawi.

The final faction of note after Nur's death includes rank and file fighters, and commanders minded to reunite with Abu Shekau's faction or at least to thaw relations with his group. Shekau, after all, retains broad respect across Boko Haram, being the person with the most prominent leadership and organizational role in the insurgency, since 2010. Indeed, so enduringly relevant is Shekau to the insurgency's narrative that the chapter's analysis shall once again turn to his role in proceedings especially with regard to ISWAP's emergence and the effect that has had on Shekau's influence. How has Shekau dealt with this blatant challenge to his hold on Boko Haram?

Shekau's response to ISWAP

Two chief reasons why ISWAP took issue with Shekau are (1) the extreme nature of 'Shekau's concepts of takfir (declaring someone to be a disbeliever/kafir)' and (2) Shekau's 'disobedience of Baghdadi's orders, such as on the controversy over whether it is allowed to take captive and enslave the women of those deemed 'apostates' (Al-Tamimi 2018).

Shekau, however, appears dismissive of such criticisms. Furthermore, Shekau remained defiant of Daesh's appointment of Abu Mus'ab al-Barnawi, claiming he, not al-Barnawi, is still in charge of Boko Haram. In an open response to Daesh's announcement, specifically, Shekau states that he was deceived and betrayed by members of his group. Shekau also alleges that his messages to Daesh and the statements of his ideologies (ostensibly to clarify Shekau's much-criticized use of takfir as well as the controversy of taking Muslim captives), which he sent to Daesh on request, were tampered with, en route (The BBC 2016d). Also, in what appears to be a veiled rebuttal of Daesh's rebranding of Boko Haram to be ISWAP, Shekau states (transcribed): 'please, understand that we still exist as a group and we shall not deviate from the Holy Qur'an and Sunnah. We still remain adherents of the Jama'atul Ahlus Sunnah Lidda'awati Wal Jihad. May Allah help us accomplish our mission' (Premium Times 2016b). ISWAP has since countered via its publications, in a clash of ideologies that eventually spilt over into the physical battlespace and beyond theological disagreements (Al-Tamimi 2018).

Still, Shekau's refusal to relinquish leadership of Boko Haram was, in many respects, a reasonable expectation. Pledging allegiance to Daesh appears to have yielded little if anything for Boko Haram since Shekau made that pledge in 2015. Consequently, it would be imprudent that Shekau, on Daesh's wishes, surrenders his leadership and hands over the keys of his kingdom to a person he has accused of betrayal, of 'trying to stage a coup against him' and of being 'polytheist' (The BBC 2016d). Abu Mus'ab al-Barnawi released a counter audio message to Shekau's accusations. Amongst other points raised, he counter-accuses Shekau of deviating from the tenets of Islam, of living in luxury, and of killing fellow Muslims and even fellow Boko Haram commanders. Abu Mus'ab al-Barnawi makes some threats against Shekau in his message, explicitly highlighting the fact that Shekau could have easily been killed if required (Sahara Reporters 2016b). Such mudslinging and threats helped make the break in rank a less than peaceful process.

English language transcripts from both Boko Haram leaders' statements, in Shekau and al-Barnawi, are available from Premium Times (2016b), although different Hausa and Arabic speakers may interpret the statements with slight differences – see, for instance, Sahara Reporters (2016b, 2016c). Nevertheless, what these transcripts indicate is that Abu Mus'ab al-Barnawi, even if he is not Yusuf's son, was very close to Abu Shekau, perhaps even one of the closest people, still alive, to Shekau. Furthermore, he was likely to have been part of, or privy to the decisions of, Boko Haram's *Wilaayah* (leadership) and *Shura* (council or parliament) for a while. Thus, Abu Mus'ab al-Barnawi's betrayal would have been all the more vexing to Abu Shekau.

Boko Haram and ISWAP: Conflicting ideologies, competing operations

Consequently, both Boko Haram and ISWAP have continued operations against Nigeria and its security forces but have done so in parallel rather than cooperatively. Both groups have clashed, and both have areas where each is stronger within the Borno axis. Within these areas, and especially by late 2018 when tensions between the factions escalated following the death of Nur, there is sometimes a change of territorial control: from the Nigerian Army to Boko Haram (Shekau faction) and then to ISWAP (al-Barnawi faction). As an example, by January 2019, locals in dozens of communities were said to now live under the control of the Abu Mus'ab's faction following the withdrawal of first the Nigerian Army forces protecting those areas and then Boko Haram (Shekau faction) fighters who went in to raid the towns after the military's withdrawal. Affected areas include communities in 'Gashigar, Zari, Granda, Gudumbari, Kukawa, Arge, Metele, Alagarnon Arewa, Kangarwa, Jilli, Birmari, Mairari, Mainari, Kuroskauwa, Mil 4, Mil 90'. As opposed to the indiscriminate killing by insurgents, as witnessed within these communities when under Boko Haram (Shekau faction) control, however, interviewees pointed out a difference when the same communities were taken over by ISWAP (al-Barnawi's faction): 'the (Abu Mus'ab's) Boko Haram fighters kill locals only when they show some form of resistance. They asked those who want to leave to leave but told those interested in staying behind not to worry' (Idris and Abubakar 2019). This practice would appear to be a continuance of fighter attitudes under Nur and is consistent with patterns of interaction between Boko Haram and northern Borno communities frequently at risk from attacks.

More to the above point, when the attackers on Nigerian villages have been from Shekau's faction, the killing of Muslims appears to be mostly indiscriminate – consistent with Shekau's controversial ideology on the subject (discussed towards the end of Chapter 2). Conversely, where insurgents under the ISWAP banner have raided Nigerian villages, they have been relatively lenient: generally leaving the largely Muslim villages intact but, nevertheless, imposing harsh levies on farmers, fishermen and local workers in return for 'protection' and the 'right' to continue their daily businesses without harassment (Idris and Abubakar 2019). However, as benign as it may sound compared to the prospect of death, the issue of taxes and imposed levies within Boko Haram-controlled communities around the Lake Chad axis and in the north of Borno has been a longstanding driver of the forced migration and humanitarian crisis experienced in the region. More details of this human security challenge are discussed in the Annexe to Chapter 9.

How Boko Haram and ISWAP regained tactical momentum: Mid-2017 to late 2018

Mamman Nur's death in August 2018 appears to have been a catalyst for ISWAP activity in Northern Borno between September of that year and January 2019. Likewise, the

Shekau faction has also been more active in the Southern and Central areas of the state. Indeed, since mid-2017, Boko Haram has made many probing attacks into territories meant to be firmly in Nigerian Army control. More to this point, in June 2017, Boko Haram released a video showing dozens of its fighters driving into the Maiduguri area. Abu Shekau, filmed brimming with confidence in that video, is seen to be taking responsibility (Salkida 2017). The June 2017 Maiduguri attack was one of the more brazen displays of overt military force by Boko Haram in a while. Moreover, in January 2018, another propaganda video was released showing Boko Haram using drones to spy on Nigerian Army locations, showing the wreck of a supposedly downed Nigerian Air Force (NAF) plane as well as captured ammunition, weapons and assets including an Unmanned Aerial Vehicle (drone) (Salkida 2018). The January 2018 propaganda video marked the first time that Boko Haram demonstrable some drone warfare and aerial surveillance capabilities – no matter how primitive.

More than at any other recent period in the north-east Nigeria conflict, therefore, the Nigerian military between 2017 and 2018 has been pegged back, with more territory changing hands, more tactical retreats by the Army taking place, more military casualties, more losses of equipment, hardware and matériel, and more military bases overrun or attacked than in the past few years. More to this point of military bases being attacked by insurgents, of the twenty military formations (at battalion or brigade level) in Northern and Central Borno, including Task Force Battalions, detachments and outfield units, fourteen were attacked to the point of tactical retreat or being overrun, within this period. In 2018, the security situation arguably worsened, moreover; in contrast to declarations by Nigerian Presidency as far back as 2015 that Boko Haram was already 'technically defeated' (The BBC 2015c).

What has enabled Boko Haram to resume such intense military activity, without drawing much attention to the group's unmistakable tactical and territorial momentum? Nur's elimination in 2018 and the resulting command vacuum indeed intensified infighting and territorial battles amongst Boko Haram factions. Nevertheless, some unrelated factors have contributed to this resurgence of insurgent activity.

To begin with, an active military campaign requires a war machine that is well-provisioned, well-funded and well-armed. For a greater chance of success, moreover, and especially for dealing with ambiguous situations or decision-making, warplanning also requires experienced leadership at the strategic level, commanders with an understanding of operational concepts, and fighters well-versed in tactical warfare. Where warfare is asymmetric, and the enemy is superior, then exploitation of the environment also is a vital component of success. Indeed, if the insurgent's odds against government forces are to be improved, then this rule practically has no reversal. Should all these requirements be met, however, then even a derailed military campaign may well regain tactical momentum. Parts II and III of this volume shall later focus on Boko Haram's exploitation of the environment and the nature of its tactics of operations before 2017. This section of Chapter 3, however, shall focus more on ISWAP: on how the group's leadership experience from the now-defunct Ansaru terrorist network, along with ISWAP's ability to generate funds and its success at recruiting, arming, paying and provisioning its forces, all translated to territorial gains and tactical momentum, by 2018 and into 2019.

Regarding ISWAP revenue between 2017 and 2018, part of this came via government and private ransoms paid to the group, which has a kidnapping pedigree directly linked to its leadership and worth discussing further. ISWAP's technical proficiency in kidnapping as both a terror tactic and funding source should come as no surprise insofar as Mamman Nur, as its ideological and operational head, was one of the former splinter group Ansaru's leaders along with Khalid al-Barnawi (Zenn 2014, Comolli 2015). Other sources indicate that at least one other individual and a former close Yusuf ally, Abubakar Adam Kambar, was just as influential in Ansaru's emergence (International Crisis Group 2014, 26). Nevertheless, this is where operational experience comes in. Ansaru, formally Jama'atu Ansarul Muslimina Fi Biladis Sudan (loosely translated as 'Vanguards for the Protection of Muslims in Black Africa') was a splinter faction that broke from Boko Haram in late January 2012. The group had at its core some Mamman Nur loyalists, 'sect members who, after the 2009 crackdown, fled to Somalia and Mali, where they joined and trained with Al-Shabaab and AQIM respectively' (International Crisis Group 2014, 26).

The now-defunct Ansaru's background of kidnapping, a years-old tactic now being exploited for financial gain by both Boko Haram's factions today, helps explain how ISWAP came by much of its funding circa 2018. Kidnapping was a tactic first introduced into the north-east Nigeria conflict, around 2012, on the strength of Ansaru's operational links with jihadists in Niger, Mali and the Maghreb. Indeed, in additional to Nur's previously discussed transnational jihadist links in Mali, Somalia and the Maghreb, Khalid al-Barnawi also had operational experience, specific to the tactics of kidnapping and smuggling, with notorious Algerian jihadist, Mokhtar Belmokhtar (Zenn 2014). Belmokhtar's group, circa 2012, was referred to as 'an offshoot of an offshoot of al-Qa'ida' (Armstrong 2014, 16). A seasoned jihadist, Belmokhtar was initially an influential figure within Al-Qaeda in the Islamic Maghreb (AQIM) and, and shortly after formed the jihadist group, Al-Mulathameen ('Masked') Brigade. Belmokhtar was an individual with operational and tactical pedigree within Algeria's jihadist circles. Therefore, Khalid al-Barnawi's relationship with both Belmokthar and Mamman Nur would no doubt have facilitated the expertize and hands-on experience required for Nur to integrate kidnapping tactics: first into Ansaru's terrorist activities and then, years later, into ISWAP's.

Aside from the tactical benefits of having ex-Ansaru fighters and the operational pedigree brought by senior figures like Nur, ISWAP, therefore benefited financially from the collapse of Ansaru's kidnapping network by gaining ransom revenue – generated as a direct result of this operational experience. ISWAP, however, also obtained funding for its military campaign in other ways. A primary means of this was ISWAP's control over fishing and transport routes along the Chad Basin, along with seasonal subsistence farmlands that served as the livelihood of entire communities. Such control means that substantial levies and taxes are placed on virtually the entire economic ecosystem of affected territory. Indeed, heavy taxation of administered areas historically has been a significant financial avenue for Boko Haram, for years. ISWAP, however, appears to have sophisticated this practice in controlling entire income ecosystems spread over tighter routes and economic corridors that are much further north away from strong Nigerian Army presences (as opposed to the Southern Borno areas contested by Shekau's faction, which have historically been harder to control and administer effectively). Thus, via kidnapping as well as the taxes and levies placed on entire economic ecosystems in Northern Borno and its frontier, ISWAP's military campaign revenue has increased between 2017 and late 2018.

Such a war chest indicates, amongst other things, that fighters can be better paid, regional allies can be co-opted within a training, logistical and operational capacity, and standing armies can be provisioned. A second noteworthy factor contributing to ISWAP's military campaign is the cache of arms that have been captured by ISWAP from Nigerian Army locations attacked. A key example is the loss of the Multinational Joint Task Force (MNJTF) base in Baga. That loss was said to have yielded, to ISWAP, military matériel, hardware and assets, including weapons and caches of ammunition, comparable in size and grade to the counterparts at HQ, 7 Div in Maiduguri (Salkida 2019b).

Moreover, the fact that ISWAP has accelerated its recruitment drive over this period, within the French-Speaking Cameroon, Chad and Niger, as well also in the North of Borno, is consistent with its narrative of establishing a cross-border caliphate across all four Chad Basin territories. ISWAP has demonstrated a willingness to conduct operations over a broad front across swathes of Northern Borno, yet also penetrates further south into Central and Southern Borno and further north too, beyond the Baga border areas and into Chad. The Nigerian military presence within the northern frontier areas, in particular, has therefore been targeted to preserve this so-called caliphate's integrity.

To summarize the escalation of territoriality and military fighting by ISWAP over this period, therefore, four factors are important to note. They are (1) kidnap-ransom funding, (2) captured hardware and matériel from the Nigerian Army, (3) a recruitment drive that transcends borders and (4) the weakness of Boko Haram (Shekau faction) in Northern Borno and around the Chad border areas, and, *c.* August 2018, the death of Mamman Nur. The remainder of this chapter shall discuss the extent of ISWAP's gains, the nature of its attacks, the role of the Nigerian Army in trying to recover lost ground, and the escalating territorial contests between ISWAP and the Abu Shekau faction of Boko Haram.

2018: The three-way contest involving the Nigerian Army, ISWAP and Shekau's Boko Haram faction

In attacking hardened Nigerian military targets, both Boko Haram factions generally aim to acquire military hardware, equipment and matériel and then beat a tactical retreat before Army reinforcements arrive. Such insurgent attacks, whether opportunistic by nature or merely probing, provide military replenishments for Boko Haram or otherwise test the water for more purposeful offensives. More to this point of more purposeful offensives, sometimes offensives on Nigerian military locations, especially larger ones, have seen Boko Haram employ a swarming tactic, as discussed in Chapter 7. Such large-scale 'swarming' offensives, where several hundred insurgent fighters along with motorized infantry and armour attack a single location, are rare compared to the main tactics of small teams attacking a Nigerian military location and then quickly dispersing. However, the gains for the insurgent, within such large-scale offensives, have been massive: not just in terms of equipment, hardware and matériel but also in terms of the destabilizing factor. A large Nigerian Army unit that is successfully dislodged or overrun may free up an entire town, or a swathe of territory, for enemy occupation.

In contrast to such attacks on hardened military locations, moreover, a parallel set of operations, conducted by both Boko Haram factions, is more directly territorial: aimed at gaining, defending and administering largely ungoverned communities and hamlets spread over large areas of rural Borno. People, after all, will only pay taxes to a regime that is present and in control of their livelihoods; for this, Boko Haram must control such territories and maintain a steady presence.

To contain this territorial push by the competing Boko Haram factions, the Nigerian Army has responded by accelerating its Mobile Strike Teams (MSTs) initiative, inaugurated in 2017. However, because Boko Haram, and Abu Mus'ab Albarnawi's ISWAP faction in particular, has also made substantial territorial gains, the Army may well need to mobilize on a massive scale to roll back those gains. MSTs by themselves may only be marginally useful within this task of reversing 2018-level territorial gains by both Boko Haram factions. Moreover, operations to push back or outright defeat Boko Haram on such a large scale, are not what the MSTs were purpose-built for (the Annexe to Chapter 9 discusses the Army's MST initiative in detail).

Between late December 2018 and early January 2019 for instance, 'the Abu Mus'ab Albarnawi-led group reportedly took control of Baga, Doron-Baga, Kross Kawwa, Bunduran, Kekeno and Kukawa, after expelling their military defenders' (Idris and Abubakar 2019). This resurgent territoriality of ISWAP, driven by ideological, schismatic and operational tensions between itself and Shekau's Boko Haram faction is consistent with reports that:

> The ISIS-backed Al-Barnawi [faction] had the upper hand in northern part of Borno State, Shekau remained dominant in the central and southern parts of the state, where the large swathe of the Sambisa forest is located. With the support of Mamman Nur, Albarnawi achieved a lot in consolidating his gains in northern Borno by trailing and killing "Shekau's boys" in places like Monguno, Kukawa, Damasak, Abadam, Marte and Kala-Balge. On the other hand, Shekau remained "strong" in villages in Gwoza, Damboa and Chibok, which are all not far from the Sambisa forest. (Idris and Abubakar 2019)

Shekau's faction, active around the Sambisa axis, has also exploited a peculiar seasonal rain effect that meant increased green and a thicker than usual forest canopy, by the last quarter of 2018. A more massive forest canopy around Sambisa has historically made it harder for NAF tactical air assets such as drones and fixed-wing reconnaissance platforms to conduct surveillance – especially under night cover, when the insurgent can, conversely, move easier without detection. Such exploitation of the terrestrial environment as a force multiplier has been a staple tactic of Boko Haram and shall be discussed further in Chapters 4 and 5. Nevertheless, it would appear that the al-Barnawi faction, stronger in the northern areas of Borno, as well as the border axis with Chad, may also have received an unwitting reprieve insofar as 'the "special arrangement" with Chadian authorities that allowed Chadian forces to pursue Boko Haram insurgents into Nigerian territory has virtually collapsed' (Idris and Mutum 2018). Towards the end of 2018, this meant that 'the Chadian forces are now limiting their activities to their border. This has emboldened the insurgents [the al-Barnawi faction in particular] to move nearly unhindered along the vast Nigerian borders with Chad, Niger and Cameroon, raiding military facilities and villages and carting away fighting equipment and foodstuff' (Idris and Mutum 2018). Such increased activity by Boko Haram around the frontier marks a turnaround from just a few years ago. As of mid-2015, for instance, Boko Haram had lost so much territory after massive Nigerian and Chadian military offensives, that the group appeared weaker than it had been for much of the conflict's preceding phases.

How the Nigerian Army has responded: Security implications of ISWAP's emergence by early 2019

ISWAP's activity around the border areas and its territorial gains within Northern and Central Borno, as of early 2019, make the Nigerian Army's outlook for an end to fighting as bleak as it has been for some time. By late 2018, Chadian state forces effectively ceased to play an assistive military role on the Nigerian side of the border. For the Nigerian Army's campaign, however, there has been even worse news on the external military assistance front.

US military counter-insurgency (COIN) tactical training of Nigerian Army troops, as of March 2019, is at an all-time low compared to 2014 when such activity peaked. Likewise, there has been an observable shift in expeditionary activity focus away from Nigeria within the British Army, not least because the British Army's 'Army 2020' restructuring project means it has problems of its own and cannot afford the budget, personnel or schedule commitments required for it to play a substantive military assistive role. In the past, the Nigerian COIN effort was propped up by private mercenary security contractors (PMSCs) who played active field roles training, embedding, mentoring and assisting Nigerian troops *in situ* against Boko Haram. However, these contractual arrangements have long since been completed (Omeni 2017). The Nigerian military, therefore, as it has been for much of the conflict, again finds itself virtually alone in the task of degrading and defeating Boko Haram within the country's borders. Moreover, this task now seems even more fraught with complications. If the war in north-east Nigeria was already problematic with just one enemy, then the emergence of ISWAP as a Boko Haram faction and legitimate insurgent threat may have made the task of security provision even more difficult in Northern and Central Borno.

Indeed, so far as this security task goes, the Nigerian Army, for almost a decade now, significantly expanded its COIN campaign. More units have been deployed (both incrementally, or as part of a troops surge as was seen in the second half of 2013). Additionally, more tasks – tactical and operational – have been added to the Army's COIN schedule. As a result, more strategic territory, to be protected, patrolled, policed and so on, has gradually been added to the Army's Area of Responsibility (AOR).

Here, however, both Boko Haram factions – al-Barnawi's fighters in the northern and frontier areas of Borno and Shekau's faction in Central and Southern Borno – exploit the Army's ever-expanding campaign responsibilities. This situation is worth explaining in detail.

Whereas the Nigerian Army's ORBAT is, on paper, stronger today than it has ever been in the institution's history, the Army's deployed Task Force Brigades, its Mobile Brigades, its outfield battalions and its frontier units have been spread thin within its campaign. Increasingly so since late-2016, this has meant that reinforcements and support capacity are often not viable *in situ*. Yes, the Nigerian Air Force has dramatically expanded the Army's air-land support options, but even here, the NAF has its own tactical and operational challenges (Omeni 2017). Consequently, relatively less capable insurgent forces have made the Nigerian Army ORBAT appear a lot poorer in practice than it comes across on paper. At times, moreover, the Nigerian Army has struggled against particular Boko Haram tactics, unable to stop the suicide bomber threat, as an example, and seemingly also failing in its task of ensuring that government writ runs the full span of Nigeria's borders. Simply put, for all the Army's talk of significant gains and improved capabilities, the territorial gains and the scale of attacks by both Boko Haram and ISWAP through much of 2018, as well as the Army's failure to often respond rapidly to these threats, have made the Nigerian military appear incompetent and hollowed out in practice.

Indeed, there are nuances to understanding this security situation, that should be considered (and which the rest of this volume shall aim to evaluate methodically). Yes also, in some ways, Nigerian government forces have already made progress here. The Annexe to Chapter 9, as an example, discusses how the Nigerian Army has attempted to redress this particular quick response challenge via its MSTs initiative. Indeed, this initiative, an attempt by the Army to innovate in war, has expanded sufficiently over the past two years to now have its own tactical doctrine. Likewise, there have been more training initiatives, such as Special Forces schooling and Counter-Terrorism and Counter-Insurgency (CT-COIN) training. There also have been crucial codified doctrine and training manual updates and promulgations.

Moreover, a range of new equipment and platforms has been inducted: from Mine Resistant Ambush Protected (MRAP) vehicles to Unmanned Aerial Vehicles (UAVs), rocket artillery battery sets, infantry fighting vehicles and so on. There even has been the induction of a motorcycle battalion, which has proved quite useful as a mobile and quick response asset. Nor is all this is meant merely as a morale boost. This capabilities build-up is very much meant to make the Nigerian Army a better fighting force: by improving its existing action set and lending it tactical momentum en route to building long-term security stability in north-east Nigeria.

Nevertheless, what the latter sections of this chapter indicate is that in this operational and territorial contest between ISWAP and Boko Haram, it would appear that the Nigerian Army, although better today than it was a few years ago in terms of military capabilities, is playing an unwitting role of spoiler within certain areas. NA 153 Battalion at New Marte is an example of this. This unit was created as a forward presence to build on the Army's stronger footprints at Monguno (where 8 TF Div is headquartered, with 333 Battalion, 195 Battalion and detachments from 7 Div and

5 Brigade all proximate units within the Monguno-Kukawa boundary). Warplanning around the positioning of 153 Battalion, however, was problematic. The unit effectively was deployed between Old Marte (up to the territories around the Lake Chad axis), where ISWAP has been dominant and New Marte, where Boko Haram has more control downwards towards Central and Southern Borno. Ordinarily, it would stand to reason that two proximate competing terrorist groups would have led to intense territorial struggles between both. ISWAP, for instance, has increasingly demonstrated a territorial doctrine. This competitive strategy may have forced Shekau's faction to begin again recapturing towns – out of fear of losing face, relevance and potential territory (along with the attendant taxation-based revenue from these areas) to its rival. Yet, what happened instead is that both sides, rather than circumvent the Army's presence to attack each other, besieged 153 Battalion and indeed Nigerian Army forces around the Marte axis. The enemy of your enemy, as they say, is your friend, at least until he becomes your enemy again.

By early January 2019, this latest territorial spin on the insurgency would be even more evident. Refocusing its efforts on the Nigerian Army's stretched forces once more, ISWAP captured multiple towns, some of which were highlighted in the previous section. Beyond this, however, Abu Mus'ab al-Barnawi's fighters began making territorial inroads within Central and even South Borno – that is, within Boko Haram (Shekau faction) traditional strongholds. Perhaps in response, Shekau's faction, in addition to contesting areas in South and Central lost to al-Barnawi's faction, also expanded its own territorial push northwards in Borno.

Faced with such territorial resurgence by both Boko Haram factions, the Nigerian Army, as of February 2019, was said to be planning a massive counteroffensive to push back the insurgent and recover some ground. Such an offensive, and possibly even a second significant troops surge, on a scale of that seen in 2013, may well be one of the better Nigerian Army options to stabilize an increasingly complex and fragile security situation. Some might wonder why the Army does not merely let Boko Haram's infighting destabilize the group from the inside out. Such ideas seem popular within informal military conversations as well as within the civilian space – on defence-related forums. This approach, however, would be a mistake. Even in a best-case scenario, whereby each Boko Haram faction expends its resources to defeat the other and gain territorial dominance, the fierce military fighting within these contests is likely to increase suffering for already strained and massively displaced Borno communities. Such chaos cannot be a win scenario for the Nigerian Army. Moreover, such infighting would not only harden fighters and provoke a new wave of recruitment for both factions, but also there is the risk: that either both sides would unify – putting up a stronger and more battle-hardened front, or that worse, yet more splinter factions may emerge, further destabilizing an already challenging security environment.

Conclusion

So far as insurgent tactics and operations go, Mamman Nur has to be in the conversation of Boko Haram's most experienced and influential personality. Such influence included the areas of planning and execution of suicide bombings, kidnappings, smuggling and transnational activity. This action set, moreover, made Boko Haram such a potent irregular threat that even transcends borders. With Nur now eliminated, the argument could, therefore, be made that the jihadists' overall threat is weakened. First, because the removal, by whatever means, of experienced terrorist leadership reduces the overall quality of opposition against state forces. Such quality is not readily replaceable. Although this is a general rule (Johnson and Sarbahi 2016), it also stands to reason that the same applies in the case of Nur's killing. Furthermore, because splintering, on paper at least, divides the enemy's forces and could make these forces easier to face off against. Whether these forces are fighting under Shekau's banner or Abu Mus'ab al-Barnawi's, logic dictates that they will be smaller divided than they would be together.

In practice, however, such upsides to Nur's death have yet to manifest for Nigeria. On the contrary, based on increased attacks on civilian settlements as part of an ensuing territorial contest, and in both factions' emboldened offensives on the Nigerian Army, such infighting within Boko Haram may well have made the security situation in the north-east more fragile, rather than less. Moreover, although ISWAP has been less violent than Boko Haram in its administration of Muslim communities in controlled territories, few would say that ISWAP's emergence has been an overall positive for the conflict.

The first part of this book, therefore, ends on a note that indicates Boko Haram's insurgency remains a significant security threat. The group is neither technically defeated nor has it even been forced to entirely relinquish its territorial ambition as seemed to be the case towards the end of 2015. Why, however, has Boko Haram's insurgency proved so enduringly resilient? Also, what factors must we consider within an examination of this entrenched security threat? The next part of the volume, in evaluating such questions, shifts away from unit level analysis and the role of influential individuals within the organizational context. Instead, domestic-level analysis, such as the role of the environment in the entrenchment of Boko Haram's threat, is the focus of the analysis that follows.

Part Two

The Environment

The Terrestrial Environment as a Force-Multiplier

Introduction

How is it that Boko Haram remains a legitimate security threat in 2019, despite a massively coordinated counter-insurgency (COIN) effort by Nigeria's military and security forces, and despite seemingly sufficient time – close to a decade – for these forces to defeat the enemy? Answers to this question, complicated as they might be, constitute the remainder of this volume's meditation. The previous chapter focused mainly on unit-level analysis: on Boko Haram's personalities and the impact of infighting in forming powerful factions with competing interests, operations and ideologies. From such infighting, ISWAP emerged as the most credible threat – both to Boko Haram as its parent organization and to the Nigerian government. Chapter 3 concluded that organizational splintering within Boko Haram, and ISWAP's consequent emergence, likely worsened the insurgency.

A more general lesson from Part I of this volume, I hope, is on the role of personalities: in agitating, mobilizing, and planning, for an armed insurgency as well as playing a role in leadership and command. Personalities, however, are not the only determinant of the causes, conduct and experience of insurgency as irregular warfare. Other factors, aside from human and organizational considerations, influence the direction of this conflict typology. A perpetrator's group ability to exploit the environment, as well as the capabilities required to prosecute and sustain military campaigning, could determine the likelihood of success, or failure, of an armed insurgency. Part II of this volume focuses on 'environment', whereas Part III focuses on Boko Haram's military campaigning.

Popular views on Boko Haram's 'environment'

The environment of north-east Nigeria has been said both to be conducive for Boko Haram's insurgency and to act as a conflict driver (Comolli 2015, Varin 2016, Walker 2016, Thurston 2018). However, the linkage – between such assertions and Boko Haram's success as a military actor – has not been well substantiated. Assertions that the environment of northern Nigeria was 'enabling' (Comolli 2015, 38), that a 'broader

Islamist environment' existed (Comolli 2015, vi) and that certain features of northern Nigeria made it an environment 'in which Boko Haram was able to prosper' (Varin 2016, 7) do little to substantively tell the reader how this linkage, between Boko Haram's military gains and the environment, is facilitated. Alex Thurston, as an example, writes that ' ... Nigeria's contentious politics, economic inequality, endemic corruption, and counterproductive conflict management strategies are part of the environment that contributed to Boko Haram's rise' (2018, 31).

Similarly, Freedom Onuoha writes that as '[religious] confrontations unfurl over an environment of economic marginality, political exclusion, and social destitution, a potentially fertile ground for radicalisation and recruitment [...] is being created for Salafi Jihadist groups such as Boko Haram' (2014, 185). Onuoha likewise talks about the 'distinctive local specificity and character shaped by the domestic environments in which they [Boko Haram and its jihadist affiliate groups] are operating' (2014, 181). However, exactly how has the domestic environment shaped Boko Haram's conflictual strategies? What even is this domestic environment? The answers to such questions tend to be taken as a given, or for granted, by the writers. Generalizations about what an enabling environment constitutes, as well as such claims as 'the larger environment also facilitated Boko Haram's resurgence' (Thurston 2018, 143), are problematic, without a substantive linkage created between 'environment' and Boko Haram's threat.

Aiming to fill this debate gap, Part II of this volume aims to show, in detail, how 'environment' acts as a potent force-multiplier for Boko Haram's military tactics and operations. Why, however, is it so important to view the environment as a force multiplier of Boko Haram's military campaign? Why, moreover, is it so important to dedicate so much analysis to Boko Haram as a military actor?

The 'Root Causes' thesis fails to emphasize Boko Haram's military threat

In examining an insurgency as complex as Boko Haram's, which may go several months without any actual military fighting to speak of, it becomes evident that much occurs away from the battlespace that warrants attention. Indeed, the debate's general lack of substantive analysis on Boko Haram's military function may be less indicative of an inability to conduct field-based research on this function and more representative of this idea that the 'root causes' of the insurgency, not the military conduct of the insurgent *per se* should inform the debate. This 'root causes' train of thought has gained much traction within the debate. Comolli, for instance, writes on how ' ... ideology feeds on socio-economic marginalisation, and what this means in terms of designing effective responses that produce lasting solutions' (2015, 6). Key to responding effectively to Boko Haram's threat, Comolli argues, 'is the need to look at the current problem comprehensively and within a very specific historical and societal context so that measures address both the insurgency and its root causes ... ' (2015, 6).

Within this narrative, however, there seems to be some failure to recognize the fact that in facing off against an internal perpetrator group with a standing army and territorial ambition, government forces must employ force (and sometimes a great deal of it). As the famous Ch'an Buddhist aphorism goes, 'when you meet a swordsman, draw your sword: do not recite poetry to one who is not a poet' (Greene 2000, 138). Indeed, it is not only natural that Boko Haram's military threat be met with a robust military response, it would also be problematic from a security perspective for this requirement to be neglected in favor of redressing the conflict's much-touted 'root causes'. Alex Thurston, for instance, alleges that 'resistance' of Nigerian authorities to 'examining the uprising's root causes, set the stage for more violence' (2018, 148). Johannes Harnischfeger similarly contends that '[the Nigerian] government, in order to stop the violence, has to address the root causes of the [Boko Haram] crisis (2014, 35).

Indeed, such perspectives have their merits. As Chapter 6 will later show, for instance, such factors as economic deprivation, ethnic identity, politics and society in northern Nigeria, and conflicting idea systems, all interact to influence Boko Haram's insurgency. Such influences, moreover, are consistent with the interdisciplinary nature of war and its study as themes that are not straightjacketed to the military function. Yet, within an analysis of military warfare, we must not relegate the business of warfighting itself, to the margins. Boko Haram's struggle, at its most primitive, is not merely ideological or social; it also exists in the conflictual battlespace. Armed men and boys fight this war. It is an insurgency complicated by the tactic of 'rigging' women and children as suicide bombers. Boko Haram's standing army employs refitted heavy guns, towed artillery, armoured vehicles and unarmoured technicals. Moreover, throughout its insurgency campaign, Boko Haram has fielded thousands of infantry. Such factors as these point to undeniable military elements within the insurgency, which the debate should feature. However, it is doubtful whether the existing narrative of Boko Haram's insurgency has considered the military warfare elements of the conflict in substantive depth.

The existing debate presents Boko Haram as a social actor, but Boko Haram is largely a military actor

Since 2011, an increasing number of publications[1] on Boko Haram's insurgency have become available to a broader audience. These texts tend to present Boko Haram as a social anomaly, focusing on the group's history, emergence and radicalization and impact on society. Implications of Boko Haram's threat for national and transnational security and the response challenge of a Nigerian government largely dismissed as corrupt constitute another part of the discussion, which today is also now paying more attention to the role of gender in the conflict.[2] Moreover, aiming to provide broader social context to conflict, much of this literature also devotes analysis to northern Nigeria: its religious history, its socio-economic challenges, the current role of Islam and politics, and governance failures as a contributing factor to much of the region's social caste system. For simplicity, let us refer to these sociological themes as the softer themes of insurgency, as opposed to military fighting as insurgency's hardest element.

Now, the value that such 'soft' analyses contribute to the dialogue on political conflict in northern Nigeria is evident. The academic discussion on Boko Haram has both broadened and drastically advanced, compared to just five years ago. Questions around the role of gender and vulnerable groups, for instance, must be addressed – and it is to the benefit of all stakeholders to understand this aspect of the conflict and seek solutions. Moreover, there are decidedly non-military elements to insurgency and to Boko Haram's insurgency. It, therefore, stands to reason that such social elements are adequately debated and understood.

However, much of this debate, in exploring the gamut of interdisciplinary themes of the conflict, strays far – sometimes too far – from the battlefield context of insurgency as a form of military warfare. Yes, this departure is typical: war is not just about warfighting, after all. What, nevertheless, is problematic here, is that having set aside the central theme of military warfare, the discourses seldom make a connection back to war as predominantly a military affair. Instead, the debate now leans towards such popular dominant narratives as, 'there is no military solution', or worse, that military intervention itself is the problem – one that the government must rectify by focusing on the political and socio-economic 'root causes' (Rice and Wallis 2012, Brett 2014, Whitehead 2015, The Will 2016). Along these lines, Onuoha argues, 'a more sustainable approach to addressing the challenge in Nigeria is to deal with the underlying ideology of the sect as well as the formative environment that enables such ideology to flourish' (2014, 186). The solution here, according to this train of thought is 'initiation of robust political, economic, and religious reforms' by the Nigerian government (Onuoha 2014, 186).

As common sense as such recommendations may sound, however, there is a fundamental problem here: Boko Haram is a formidable armed opponent actively waging an insurgency that stifles the pace and feasibility of reform in affected areas. Therefore, recommending that the debate shifts away from Boko Haram's military threat and focuses on governance issues, fails to consider that virtually no governance can take place if the insurgent is not denied activity in the relevant areas. Military force is the only means by which Boko Haram can be denied such access. Likewise saying that the compromised Nigerian military should more or less step aside as many have suggested,[3] because the Army is, according to this narrative, doing more harm than good (J. N. Hill 2012, 24, 26), is problematic. Boko Haram, without military obstacles, may well march all the way to Abuja to seize the seat of power.

So, as conveniently non-violent as much of the previously highlighted recommendations might be, the reality is that an extremely violent war is being fought. This war comes complete with battlefield elements and is waged by an enemy intent to kill and cause as many casualties as he can, in as little time as government inaction or incompetence allows. To understand such a war, as much as war in general, one cannot ignore its tactics, its features and the battlefield factors that lead to either victory or defeat (von Clausewitz 1976, 75–76). Skirting the issue of military warfare, therefore, as the final part of this volume will later show, does not help our understanding of Boko Haram as a military actor. It also does not make this enemy any less competitive within the military space.

Still, this is not to say that the non-military aspects of conflict, and in this case Boko Haram's conflict, only hold limited debate value. Insofar as insurgency constitutes a departure from the 'see-saw' model of war[4] – that is, Roman War as battlefield victory or defeat – military-centric analysis within Boko Haram's insurgency must likewise shift from war in its conventional sense. We must consider the battlefield impact of factors away from the battlespace and link this back to the insurgent's military operations. This in part is why the wider 'environment' is indeed important for assessing Boko Haram's military threat, just not necessarily in the way much of the literature appears to be interrogating it. To this point, I shall next provide a frame for the environment, beyond which I shall evaluate its implications for Boko Haram as a military actor waging an irregular war.

The context of 'environment'

An entire part of this volume is dedicated to the theme of environment because I discovered, in researching the discourses on Boko Haram, that this noun (or its adjectival form, 'environmental') was ubiquitous within the lexicon. Much of its use was mostly within a broader context, rather than focused on the term itself. Nevertheless, the extent of reference to this term was striking even though there has yet to be a single comprehensive analysis of the role of 'environment', in all its connotations, within the conflict. How has governance failure in Nigeria created an enabling environment for popular frustration and insurgency? What environmental features of north-east Nigeria has Boko Haram leveraged, as part of its conflictual strategies? How has the socio-economic environment influenced the rise of Boko Haram? What is the process by which Boko Haram emerged from the religious environment of northern Nigeria? What environmental vulnerabilities have Boko Haram exploited in its recruitment? In one form or another, such questions tend to punctuate the debate. I hope that by the end of Parts I and Part II of this volume combined, these questions would have been addressed.

In discussing the environment that has simultaneously enabled, and has been affected by, Boko Haram's insurgency, one thread will run through this chapter. Insurgencies tend to be localized phenomena. Understanding an insurgency's environment, and how the insurgent can manipulate its features, is not just relevant to understanding the conflict, it is critical. Consequently, this chapter discusses some physical factors, local to areas contested by Boko Haram and essential to the narrative of the insurgent's success in these areas. Some of these factors have no obvious battlefield link, yet, I shall show that Boko Haram may not even exist as a legitimate military threat without them. Some features of the geographic environment, however, have a more direct force-multiplier effect on Boko Haram's military campaign.

The geographic environment acts as a force-multiplier for Boko Haram's military threat

Of the features within north-east Nigeria, some of which are shared with Chad, Niger and Cameroon, the terrestrial environment is arguably the least studied within the debate on Boko Haram's insurgency. An insurgent's ability to swell his ranks, however, often is influenced by his immediate environment. Contemporary use of the word 'environment' within the context of the social sciences may, rightly so in most cases, connote the socio-economic and political. However, the terrestrial environment – physical terrain and the features of north-east Nigeria and its contested frontier – also lends Boko Haram a major tactical advantage in its military campaign. This geographic environment 'relates to where in the world (location) a character is' and factors in weather/climate, as well as landscape and topographical features (Patterson 2012). As will be shown in this chapter section, this category of environment lends Boko Haram an under-studied campaign advantage.

Reports on north-east Nigeria and the border regions suggest an open, arid nomadic geographic environment (Tuamanjong and Hinshaw 2016). For the most part, this is true; north-east Nigeria historically has always had vast stretches of Sudanian Savannah, with patches of Sahelian forest and an arid climate driven by high sunlight and low cloud cover (Nigerian Conservation Foundation 2001). Within the context of the tactical advantages this environment provides for Boko Haram, however, north-east Nigeria's geography, upon inspection, is far more nuanced. Over each calendar year, weather patterns change; humidity and rainfall levels considerably. These changes affected heavy vehicle mobility due to mud-clogged roads and highways and even worse off-road options, and such factors, in turn, impact war planning. Everything from logistics and the movement of troops and matériel, the timing of offensives, the element of surprise (or lack thereof) and even the viability of counter-ambush tactics, may depend on road and off-road conditions within a designated battlefield area. Indeed, failure to factor in such seasonal conditions, or even the possibility of them, within preliminary war planning and deployments, may well approximate military incompetence (Dixon 1979).

Short-term, 25-degree Celsius temperature swings between early morning hours and mid-afternoon occur in northern Nigeria. Such dramatic temperature shifts, unusual in southern Nigeria, are part of daily life beyond the country's middle belt, and are especially prominent in the extreme north-east. Climate swings of this nature, however, have consequences for mobile infantry. As an example, these mobile elements might be motorable in the early hours, yet crippled by heat by afternoon.

Climate and weather are not the only considerations relevant to this environment, moreover. Featurewise, local communities, dependent on where they reside, may have access to plateaus, mountainous regions, cave systems, wetlands, forest areas, and flatter arid stretches with little vegetation or cover. For the insurgent prosecuting an armed campaign, each of these is more than a mere afterthought. Such factors, after all, connive to influence the calculus of war, including the speed of deployment, the nature of forces deployed (such as foot soldiers, motorized light infantry and armoured platforms) and the scale of deployment. Even the timing of deployment may be affected by the environment. The presence of forest cover and mountainous terrain, for instance, could mean that, even during daytime, troops could be mobile and, simultaneously, fairly well concealed. Open areas such as plains and Sahelian savannah landscapes, on the other hand, might see night-time mobility as a more sensible option. What is more, although each of the points discussed next may not alone present a significant force-multiplier effect, collectively they make Boko Haram's military campaign considerably more resilient.

Mandara mountain range

Perhaps as good a physical feature as any to discuss, within the context of how the environment has force-multiplied Boko Haram's threat, is the Mandara Mountain Range in the north-east and frontier region of Nigeria. This volcanic range runs a border stretch about 200-km wide, shared by Adamawa and Borno states in Nigeria, with Cameroon's Extreme North region. The Mandara range has a network of partially unexplored caves, with populations that are non-Kanuri, non-Muslim and unlikely to be friendly to Boko Haram (Baca 2015, Schneider 2015a). Still, Mandara provides such a natural obstacle to heavy armour, in particular, that government forces would lose some tactical advantage if attempting to flush out Boko Haram from this hostile environment. Even its surrounding areas have relief features that make regular troop deployment more of a challenge. Part of this was evident in the engagement between the Nigerian Army and the Boko Haram presence in Michika, Adamawa State. Although Michika, in the north-east of Adamawa (see Figure 1.1), is not within the Mandara mountain range, it is close enough that heavy armour assets are logistically challenging to deploy eastwards beyond the town.

Mandara as a natural obstacle, therefore, creates two virtual certainties, both in favour of Boko Haram. First, due to geography, some aspects of the Nigerian Army's capabilities cannot be brought to bear. Second, Mandara begins in Nigeria and ends in Cameroon through a system of rocky terrain and complex caves. The Nigerian Army, therefore, must break off enemy contact beyond a certain point, so as not to carry out unsanctioned operations in a neighbouring country.

Such challenges however also affect Boko Haram's calculus of war. For instance, Boko Haram's few heavy armour vehicles it attempted deploying around Michika in 2015 – such as British Vickers MBT Mk IIIs captured from the Nigerian Army – were broken down or crippled in short order in the area. For an insurgent with only a handful of these Main Battle Tank (MBT) platforms, such losses inevitably prove costly. Heavy armour thus proves a double-edged source in these mountainous areas.

In theory, the presence of heavy armour acts as a force-multiplier for the Army's Infantry. In practice, however, due to the terrain, its absence may well quicken the Infantry, insofar as mobility (ingress and egress options and speed) improve. Removing heavy armour assets on the offence, however, may substantially lower the asymmetry of the engagement. As a second example, Gwoza, the capital of Boko Haram's so-called caliphate at a time when it controlled significant amounts of territory between 2014 and 2015, is situated at the Nigerian end of the Mandara range. Here, the natural barrier acts as a tactical defence to the town's eastern and southern flanks. Not surprisingly due to its tactical terrain advantages, Gwoza was one of the most difficult towns from which Boko Haram was dislodged. Indeed, Boko Haram's retreat from that axis came only on the strength of Intelligence, surveillance and reconnaissance (ISR) and air sorties[5] by the NAF in February 2015 to identify, track and bomb insurgent locations in the town. The NAF's sortie rate at Gwoza was force-multiplied by NAF 79 Composite Group's presence in Maiduguri, less than 150 kilometres away. Sequel to this combined effort from the NAF, a ground thrust by the Army in subsequent weeks was possible.

Moreover, although the Nigerian Army's armoured brigades, critical for motorized infantry support and cover, were deployed in towns much further northwards of Gwoza (Ngala, Dikwa, Bama), they could not be deployed in the mountainous terrain around Gwoza itself. Consequently, Boko Haram's standing army was able to hold Gwoza for almost a year. Even then, faced with a major offensive by the Nigerian Army by March 2015, the insurgent slipped away into the mountain range, which runs across the border into Cameroon.

Adaptations for Mandara, by Nigerian forces

Understanding the above tactical advantages provided by Mandara, as well as the military reorganization required to counter its use as a natural tactical barrier, is essential to recognize the geographic environment's relevance in war. The environment is of particular tactical significance in insurgency, as rebels must exploit even the most seemingly trivial terrestrial features in a bid to bridge the asymmetry against far superior government forces. As a reversal to this argument, however, the same environment could just as well provide opportunities for battlefield innovation by counter-insurgent forces. There is a ring of truth to this in the Nigeria case.

A terrain-specific battlefield innovation on the part of the Nigerian Army in 2016 was the induction of a motorcycle battalion into HQ, 25 Task Force Brigade (25 TF) at Damboa, the town immediately west of Gwoza and in proximity to the Mandara area.[6] A significant but slightly unorthodox battlefield introduction, the induction of a dirt bike 'combat' battalion in 25 TF makes it the Army's first-ever motorcycle unit, at formation level. 25 TF shares some area responsibility with HQ, 26 TF, Gwoza. At the tactical level, the motorcycle battalion's induction into 25 TF appears a sound decision for forward recce (reconnaissance), mobile raids and counter-ambush tactics. The mobility of the motorbike battalion also means its elements have been widely deployable across Damboa, one of Borno's largest local government areas. Specifically, to the east of Damboa, the battalion supports 254 Task Force Battalion (254) in patrol-and-escort duty within the Army's assistive capacity to the National Union of Road Transport Workers (NURTW) in the area (Nigerian Army 2016). Boko Haram had abused the Biu–Maiduguri–Damboa road since 2013, making it impossible for private and government transport to function normally in the area. To the west of Damboa also, and into Gwoza, the motorbike battalion assists HQ, 26 TF in securing the axis up until Mandara. As a motorized formation with light assault, but largely recce duties,[7] the motorbike battalion will likely consist of a supporting light armour car company, two specially trained motorcycle infantry companies as the formation's nucleus and at least one engineering regiment. Moreover, from what has been discussed here so far, motorcycles could force-multiply the Army's mobility capabilities, not just in areas such as Mandara (including Pulka and Gwoza), but also across much of the terrain in north-east Nigeria which seems tailor-made for dirt bikes. Indeed, *Okada* (motorcycles) have long featured as a fast mode of transport for Boko Haram within both its overt and covert fronts, but never by the Army at formation level.

Although the environment around Mandara provides a unique tactical benefit for Boko Haram, that location, however, poses its own set of challenges. Boko Haram's fighters aiming to seek refuge in the Mandara axis have to confront not just Nigerian military forces, but also the Cameroonian Army special forces (BIR). Likewise, elements of the Cameroonian regular army (*Armée de Terre*) and gendarmerie supporting units that form part of Operation Alpha, the Cameroonian COIN against Boko Haram around the country's borders, are also active in the axis. Mandara falls under these border areas of Cameroon's North and Extreme North regions. For Boko Haram, therefore, Mandara also brings this added disadvantage, which may affect its calculations around Mandara as a viable base.

Biu plateau

Should Boko Haram wish to entirely remove Cameroonian military pressure from its war calculus but retain some of the tactical barrier features seen within Mandara, it could move much deeper inland into Nigeria, to Borno's Biu Plateau to the south of Biu local government area, Borno. Like Mandara, aspects the plateau's relief features make it a natural obstacle against mobile units, especially those with heavier technicals and platforms. Moreover, unlike Mandara, with the local ethnicity being Kanuri, Boko Haram should find a less hostile and more ethnically familiar people.

Hadeja-Nguru wetlands

As another option to lend it a tactical advantage within the north-east environment, Boko Haram could relocate its forces deeper still west, into the iconic Hadeja-Nguru Wetlands of Yobe State (Baca 2015). This axis falls within the area of responsibility of the Nigerian Army's 3 Division[8] and lies outside of the major axis where 7 Division, tasked with the Nigerian Army's COIN since 2013, is widely deployed. The Hadeja-Nguru Wetlands also possess a sufficient population of Kanuri and Fulani in addition to Bede ethnic groups (Olalekan et al. 2014) and Boko Haram is likely to find less hostility within this ethnic population comparative to the dominant Mofu ethnicity in Mandara.

Sambisa forest

The vast forest range of Sambisa is another feature of the geographic environment exploited to Boko Haram's advantage. Marked as a game reserve by British colonialists likely due to its vibrant fauna and megafauna earlier in the past century, Sambisa forest today has formed a base of operations for Boko Haram with the group's kidnap victims also said to be stashed away there (Kayode 2014).

Recognizing the strategic nature of Sambisa to the war outcome, the Nigerian Army in 2016 had elements of no less than four brigades in the towns and areas surrounding

Sambisa (see Figure 9.1): 21 Armoured Brigade deployed at Bama and Mafa (north-eastern and northern flanks of Sambisa, respectively); 25 Task Force Brigade (25 TF) deployed at Damboa (western and southwestern flanks); 26 Task Force Brigade (26 TF) stationed at Gwoza (southern flank); and elements of 7 Garrison (7 Gar, detached from the garrison at Maiduguri) deployed at Konduga East (north-western flank). One of the Army's newly formed Task Force Brigades, 29 TF, also was initially instructed to capture Sambisa; this was early in 2016. The task, however, was likely underestimated and was never fulfilled. Indeed, despite substantial troops deployment in the axis, the Army as of September 2019 has been unable to dislodge Boko Haram from the forest entirely.

Notwithstanding a slower timetable to the Army's Sambisa operation, unchallenged egress opportunities for Boko Haram from the axis, have reduced. Several Nigerian Army formations, within a coordinated troops deployment strategy by HQ, 7 Div, now surround the location.[9] These are not merely patrols, moreover; the presence of these Army units is permanent for the duration of ongoing operations. The Army's engineers are also deployed there to create roads and assist with mobile unit's access deep within the forest axis. However, the challenge ahead, in the complete dislodgement of Boko Haram from the forest, is nonetheless considerable.

To understand the Nigerian Army's challenge of taking jungle terrain as vast as Sambisa, it is important to recognize the area's tactical advantages for Boko Haram. The forest's foliage is punctuated with non-uniform woodland, dense shrubs and trees in clusters up to two meters high but with an average height of less than a meter. Two features are standard across Sambisa's woodland. First, the species of vegetation present for the most part low visibility from above; second, it is physically challenging to penetrate from the ground (Nigerian Conservation Foundation 2001, Google Maps 2017). A top-down view of the vegetation, for instance, highlights only a relatively small incidence of *Adansonia digitate L* (Baobab) and other megaflora vegetation (Bamalli et al. 2014, Nigerian Conservation Foundation 2001). Despite such low occurrence of larger plant life, the forest canopy, somewhat surprisingly, remains thick, or very thick in many places (Google Maps 2017). The forest's areas of dense foliage negate some tactical advantages of airpower by the Air Force. The dominance of clustered Sudan-Guinea and Sahelian features (Nigerian Conservation Foundation 2001) also contributes to the denial of access from the ground and reduced visibility from above. This combination of features lends Sambisa its unique geography:

> It is not the typical forest one sees along some southern states [of Nigeria] which could be as high as 100m, creating a primary, secondary and tertiary scenario. It is a single dimensional forest which is visible driving on the main road that connects Maiduguri, Konduga and Barma [sic]. It also graduates from trees as low as half a metre to the extremely dense areas where human skins cannot penetrate without being hurt by thorns if you do not have a cutlass or something to ward them off. That is the nature of the forest which is being manipulated and controlled by Boko Haram who have become masters of the Savannah. (Kayode 2014)

There are multiple implications of this feature set, for tactical warfare. First, Sambisa's features serve as natural camouflage for defensive positions under the forest canopy.

The nature of woodland and shrubs within the forest also removes the force-multiplier effects of Nigerian Army heavy armour and motorized infantry. Artillery likewise is out of the question; even inordinate amounts of blind shelling might level entire sections of the forest and change the landscape without hitting a single enemy position. Furthermore, ISR that typically would employ unmanned aerial vehicle (UAV) platforms, as well as crewed recce flights for low-level reconnaissance, becomes ineffective, especially in areas with taller woodland, shrubs and tree vegetation. Indeed, this final point may well be the main advantage of camping in Sambisa. The NAF, within its combined role in COIN operations against Boko Haram, cannot deploy its platforms the way it would over flatter terrain. Under cover of night, at which time Boko Haram's tactical movements would more than likely peak, this makes ISR even more problematic. Such factors limit the Air Force's contribution, again lending Boko Haram another critical tactical advantage, in the preservation of its 'super bunkers underneath the Sahel [vegetation]' (Kayode 2014).

Sambisa's terrain lends the insurgent another tactical advantage, one that is more primitive. The nature of jungle warfare is such that combat requires a specially trained type of infantryman and local knowledge of the forest terrain itself (Bull and Noon 2007, Cross 2008). In this form of warfare, the other combat functions such as the Armour (whether light, motorized or heavy) and the Artillery become clumsy integrations amongst the arms, and in some cases, may not even be viable as land assets. Moreover, jungle warfare and its requirements, have changed little since the days of warfighting in the Pacific theatre of the Second World War (Bull and Noon 2007, Cross 2008, Perrett and Walker 2015). Indeed, despite technological advancements, 'without the man on the ground to dominate an area, nothing else can secure it – and that is as true for jungle warfare as ever it was' (Cross 2008, 3).

All of this points to the eventuality that operations to recapture Sambisa must be infantry centric and, beyond that, must limit or may entirely preclude the use of airpower, motorized infantry or heavy armour within the engagement. The insurgent, in a sense, has forced the Army's infantry to engage him under what classic jungle warfare theorists refer to as a 'canopy of war' (Perrett and Walker 1990). Under these conditions and due to Boko Haram's terrain familiarity, its tactical advantage is force-multiplied by choice of battleground. The Nigerian Army and especially the combat arm of the Infantry, therefore, must take the time to adapt specifically to jungle warfare or press ahead into the forest and encounter heavy losses (many of which are unlikely to be documented for the public). The stalemated nature of military activity *in situ* around Sambisa circa mid-2016, the adaptations the Army is making elsewhere in northern Nigeria in preparation for a full-blooded thrust into the forest (more on this shortly), and indeed, the theory of jungle warfare, all support this thesis. As Stephen Bull comments, ' ... Only one arm of service [is] truly suited to jungle warfare. As the US manual *Jungle Warfare* tersely explained: Jungle fighting is performed largely by infantry. Close fighting usually characterises combat. Support of infantry by other arms will frequently be impractical or impossible' (2007, 7).

However, even with a highly infantry-centric Nigerian Army thrust to recapture Sambisa, supported by artillery barrages and air sorties, Boko Haram's advantage in Sambisa still will be hard to take away. Boko Haram has had years to understand, map out and fortify that terrain. Early attempts by the Army to penetrate the forest, for instance, saw it heavily mined. Moreover, although the Army recently acquired, in 2016, BOZENA+ Mine Sweepers, these platforms are not suitable, nor were they built, for forest terrain. Instead, the sort of flatter terrain in Alagarno (where the platform deployed successfully) is where the BOZENO+ remote vehicles excel. It thus is unlikely that these platforms will find much utility in a jungle offensive against Sambisa forest defences where Boko Haram employs anti-personnel and anti-armour improvised devices and mines. Rocket artillery units may have more success, once the Nigerian Army can map the interior of the forest. Despite the potentiality of such combined arms approaches, however, the Nigerian Army has been largely untested in jungle warfare combat on the scale required for infantrymen to occupy, and entirely dislodge Boko Haram from, Sambisa. Effectively, the Army will need to learn and adapt *in situ*. On this point, since April 2016, the Nigerian Army began jungle simulation training and live fire exercises at Alkaleri Forest in Bauchi State. Such training is to better simulate warfighting conditions within a jungle-oriented campaign in Sambisa, Borno State.

Size matters

A final feature of Sambisa that makes it a problematic battleground from which to dislodge Boko Haram is its size. The Nigerian military has focused on the forest expanse to the Central-East of Borno (see Figure 4.1). For operational purposes, this area, to the Army, is designated Sambisa. However, there seems to be some confusion around the sheer scale of the forested areas in question. Rear Admiral John Kirby, the former Pentagon Press Secretary, referring to Sambisa, commented that 'we are talking about an area roughly the size of West Virginia and its dense forest jungle' (Londoño 2014). Now, West Virginia, in the United States, has an area of 62,755 km²; Borno State, by comparison, has an area of 70,898 km². Kirby's assertion, therefore, suggests that a contiguous and densely forested area covers roughly 90 per cent (88.5 per cent) of Borno's land mass. Such a claim is fanciful because the associated natural obstacle associated with a jungle is absent through most of Borno. Much of Borno State (and indeed most of north-east Nigeria), in contrast to this assertion, is highly arid.

The expanse of Sambisa identified by the Army as a critical area of interest is roughly about 686 square kilometres (686 km²). Sambisa Forest – to use the analogy of Lt. General T.Y. Buratai, the Army's chief of staff – 'is as big as Enugu State' (Igata 2016). General Buratai may have meant to make the comparison to Enugu City (556 km²), which is the capital of Enugu State and which is closer to the land area highlighted in the map above. In any event, Sambisa, even just the area highlighted in Figure 4.1, is large enough that it requires a major military effort to secure. On this point, there appears to be agreement. As Rear Admiral Kirby comments regarding the US search task around the Sambisa area, 'It is very difficult in terms of the geography, the actual size, just square miles, of what we are trying to search' (Londoño 2014).

Figure 4.1 Cross-section of Borno Highlighting Sambisa Forest (Relative to Army Positions).

By 2014, Borno's flat, arid, topography helped a highly mobile Boko Haram trade space for time

Although forest terrain impedes state forces' movement, provides cover, and creates a natural obstacle in favour of the insurgent – with Sambisa's attributes as a case in point – the presence of vast stretches of arid, flat, terrain provides a different set of advantages. Boko Haram's ability to swiftly conduct large-scale offensives and make quick getaways exploited these vast open spaces to great effect. Indeed, in 2014, Boko Haram's mobile warfare doctrine and the hybrid form of desert warfare it employed would scarcely have been possible on any other terrain (Omeni 2017). Although this category of terrain – the 'flatter' topographical option – lends itself to highly mobile desert warfare by the insurgent, the heat and the excessive dust also tends to degrade Government forces' heavy armour. Even under the best form, heavy armour platforms of mobile units run a risk of breakdown, if movement pace is indeliberate.

To effectively 'police' contested spaces, Army patrols need to cover a wider area. Due to the extreme heat and dust conditions more typical later in the north-east

Nigerian day, however, heavy platforms that were motorable in the early morning may well struggle and may even require maintenance *in situ*, when temperatures peak mid-afternoon and convoys are still on the move. With the Nigerian Army having to cover large spaces, mobility inevitably takes time, and yet, time spent in the harsh arid terrain has a degrading effect on man and equipment.

If from the preceding, we conclude that the Nigerian Army's COIN campaign has assumed a slower pace within these flatter and arid areas, Boko Haram, on the other hand, adopted the opposite approach for phases of its campaign. Borno's open arid spaces and the sheer size of its plains have meant that Boko Haram's smaller, leaner, forces often demonstrated superior mobility in pre-dawn motorized infantry offensives against Nigerian Army locations. These offensives often employed a 'swarming' tactic, which emphasized movement, numbers and speed, both in the ingress and in the egress.[10] So, in employing such tactics – opting for war avoidance and then suddenly launching massive probing counter-offensives between entire periods of the 2013 and 2014 calendar years – Boko Haram evolved its campaign. This insurgent, in conceding territory to expanding Nigerian military (land and air-land) operations, embraced a doctrine of mobile warfare. In so doing, Boko Haram opted to trade space (territory) for time. There are three ways to view this time trade.

First, the ability to move quickly across the plains made Boko Haram a hard target to plan against and hit decisively, in a way that a territorial doctrine (and hence Boko Haram's occupation of territory) would not have permitted. That is, this speed factor gave the insurgent added defensibility in the offence. Second, speed, as the essence of momentum, is distance covered relative to the time taken to cover that distance. Being able to cover more considerable distances in less time, by having a leaner and more mobile structure, gave Boko Haram significant momentum in its military campaign. The flat, arid plains force-multiplied this momentum as the tactical mobility lent by this topography meant that Boko Haram could hit military formations and cart away weapons and ammunition or attack civilian communities to kidnap and loot, and then beat rapid tactical retreats. The brief time spent by the enemy on such offensives limited contact with Nigerian forces as well as enemy losses. Third, by temporarily giving up territorial ambitions and shifting to small-scale guerrilla operations, Boko Haram gained time to recalibrate its overt front,[11] even as the Nigerian Army gradually began reorganizing around the same period, *c*. late 2013.

Hundreds of kilometres of border areas lend Boko Haram a tactical advantage

Another related feature of the terrestrial environment worth considering, are the stretches of borders in play – several hundred kilometres of them – shared by north-east Nigeria with three different countries in Chad, Niger and Cameroon. Policing these borders presents as much a challenge for Nigeria as for the countries involved. It is, for this reason, the boundaries between Nigeria and its neighbours are described as 'porous'. This porosity has been much discussed within the literature, as has been Boko Haram's exploitation of the insecure borders.[12] Less discussed, however, and the domain of much equivocating, are the particular cross-border features of Cameroon, Chad and Niger, that make insecure national boundaries problematic for these countries and Nigeria, yet advantageous for Boko Haram. Indeed, words like 'exploitation' and 'exploit' are used often but largely unclarified, within the discourses on Boko Haram's movement across national boundaries. Whereas this chapter focused on the terrestrial environment within north-east Nigeria, Chapter 6 examines the insecurity around north-east Nigeria's borders, as it affects and relates to the three neighbouring countries of Cameroon, Chad and Niger.

To begin with, each of these neighbouring countries has unique geographical and political features that make them attractive to Boko Haram's cross-border and transnational ambitions. Thus, 'exploit' used within the context of this section's analysis, refers to how Boko Haram takes advantage of the specific features within each country's border areas, for its activities. The activities in question are conducted on both sides of the borders and include kidnappings, small town raids, government forces ambushes, movement of troops and *matériel*, recruitment activity, and onward transit for training further along the Sahel (such as has occurred in Mali and Mauritania (Udounwa 2013)). Such exploitation is not one-way. There is evidence indicative of egress of small arms and light weapons (SALWs), as well as ordnance: from post-Gadhafi Libya southwards through the Sahel, to north-east Nigeria (Omeni 2017).

Conclusion

Having established what border 'exploitation' means within the context of Boko Haram's cross-border activity and available tactical options, let us now return to the question of why (and how) each of Nigeria's north-east neighbours is of import to the insurgency's debate as it relates to 'environment'. The answers range from the tactical to the strategic, from the geographic to the ethnic.

As a caveat to the analysis that follows, some of the geographical features observable in the border areas shared by Chad, Niger and Cameroon with Nigeria are, invariably, applicable to Nigeria as well. Therefore, rather than duplicating the nature of these physical features, Chapter 6 shall aim to discuss implications of these shared features – geographic, ethnic, cultural and socio-political –for the conflict environment. Also, how these countries have responded to Boko Haram's threat in the border areas, what the main military challenges are in responding to this threat, why these challenges exist and their inferred consequences for Boko Haram's cross-border activity shall also be considered.

The North-East Nigeria Border Environment: Cameroon, Chad and Niger

Cameroon's military response around the Mandara axis

With the Mandara range also a key geographical feature shared with Cameroon's Extreme North region, its tactical barrier features are likewise exploited by Boko Haram on the Cameroonian side. Consequently, the Nigerian Army is not the only force protecting state territoriality against the jihadists around the Mandara axis. Boko Haram's egress across the border to the Cameroonian side of Mandara in 2014 triggered increased activity by Cameroon's 3rd *Bataillon d'intervention Rapide* in the area, as part of Operation Alpha (OP Alpha). OP Alpha is the designation of the Cameroonian military counter-insurgency (COIN) effort against Boko Haram, active since August 2014 when the insurgents first seized Gwoza town and thus gained access to the Mandara axis.

Cameroon's army has identified the tactical advantages brought by Mandara to Boko Haram; several of the insurgent fighters hide and operate from makeshift bases there. Consequently, Mandara and the surrounding terrain has become a key battleground for elements of Cameroon's special forces. In August 2014, the same month as Boko Haram captured Gwoza, Cameroon's forces began OP Alpha. It is unclear whether OP Alpha's activation was coincidental, or whether it was an expedited operational timetable, on the part of Cameroonian military planning, in response to Boko Haram's increased threat at the frontier with Nigeria.

Cameroon's Special Forces Rapid Response Brigade (BIR, by the French acronym) spearheads its COIN effort. BIR is composed of three rapid response battalions each of which, due to their size, has no General Staff and is headed by a colonel. These battalions, stationed at Douala (Littoral Region), Tiko (South-West Region) and Koutaba (North-West Region), respectively, are Special Amphibious Battalion (*Bataillon Spécial Amphibie*; BSA), *Bataillon des Troupes Aéroportées* (BTAP) and Armored Reconnaissance Battalion (*Bataillon Blindé de Reconnaissance*; BBR). BIR's battalions, as part of the Cameroonian army's order of battle, are designated 1st *Bataillon d'intervention Rapide*, 2nd *Bataillon d'intervention Rapide* and 3rd *Bataillon d'intervention Rapide*.

BIR has a total strength of 2,000 special forces upon formation, although initially, only the BTAP was operational. BIR, within OP Alpha, has extra support from around a thousand regular troops, in addition to between 600 and 700 police and gendarmerie, deployed to, or based in, Cameroon's Far North Region. This combined force patrols and protects 'the 400km border with Nigeria, disrupting Boko Haram supply chains and targeting the group's in-country leadership' (Schneider 2015a).

3rd *Bataillon d'intervention Rapide*

The battalion headquarters of each of BIR's battalions are stationed virtually on the other side of Cameroon around its coastal south and quite some distance from the extreme north region where Boko Haram poses a threat. Consequently, elements of 3rd Battalion, supported by redeployments from the other two battalions, have been redeployed to Maroua, the capital of the Far North Region. Here, an officer at the rank of army colonel is in command. The Maroua base, which coordinates BIR activity around the Mandara axis, is subordinate to operational orders from the BIR brigade HQ, itself designated as a tactical battle unit under the army's headquarters.

One of 3rd Battalion's main strengths is that its forward reconnaissance elements stationed at Maroua have benefited from an eight-week sniper course. Such tactical expertise has direct battlefield implications, insofar as Boko Haram commanders and its most experienced fighters, in combat situations, were conspicuous: these individuals often held walkie-talkies and coordinated the young and inexperienced fighters (Schneider 2015a). The ability of BIR's forward sniper teams to identify and remove these experienced commanders *in situ* has made otherwise difficult engagements easier for BIR's combat effort.

It is worth pointing out, on a final note here, that BIR is, for all intents and purposes, the tip of the spear of Cameroon's response to Boko Haram. Moreover, the combat formation has been active in this task for some time (and even before OP Alpha commenced in 2014). Coordination and liaison with other Cameroonian Army units, especially the motorized elements, are critical to BIR's task due to the stretches of arid desert and border areas it is tasked with protecting/patrolling/policing. For instance:

> During the May 2013 Nigerian offensive, Cameroon deployed around 1,500 troops of its Rapid Battalion Intervention (BIR), Infantry and Motorised Brigade (BIMA) and gendarmerie to the northern border. The BIR has an agreement with the Nigerian JTF that allows each to pursue bandits and criminals across the border for up to 8km. (International Crisis Group 2014, 26)

Cameroon–Nigeria borders

Cameroon–Nigeria border areas around the latter's north-east axis have, since the beginning, been central to the two-way movement of man and *matériel* within Boko

Haram's insurgency. Regarding the physical advantages of these borders, the Mandara mountain range provides tactical barrier features that force-multiply Boko Haram's defensive capabilities. Five north-east Nigerian local government areas (LGAs) are the most affected here, within the context of Mandara as a natural barrier beginning in Nigeria and ending in Cameroon. The LGAs are Gwoza (Borno), Madagali (Adamawa), Michika (Adamawa), Mubi North (Adamawa) and Mubi South (Adamawa).

The Mandara mountain range, however, is not the only reason Cameroon attracts cross-border movement by Boko Haram. Also relevant is shared ethnic identity, in particular between the above LGAs in Adamawa on the Nigerian side and Cameroon's North, Extreme North and Adamaoua regions. These LGAs have overwhelmingly been the targets of Boko Haram's insurgency within the Adamawa axis, leading to a higher than usual Nigerian Army presence there, in the deployment of some existing formations as well as new task force battalions, since 2016. Some examples of this mobilization by the Army include 117 Task Force Battalion (117 TF Bn) deployed at Mubi North and Mubi South as part of the Area of Responsibility of 28 Task Force Brigade (shared with 3 Div Tactical). 28 TF has an Area of Responsibility around the shared border regions with Cameroon and Madagali. At Gwoza, close to the Cameroon border and not far from Borno's shared boundary with Adamawa (separated by Michika, Madagali and Mubi, respectively), the Nigerian Army also deployed infantry units including elements of 26 TF, 82 Bn, 121 TF Bn and 122 TF Bn.

More so than most other troubled areas, therefore, why is Boko Haram's presence such a threat around this Borno–Adamawa–Cameroon axis, enough to necessitate more-than-usual deployments of Nigerian Army forces as a deterrent?

Nigeria and Cameroon have enduring historical ties

Arguably more than any of Nigeria's other north-east neighbours, Cameroon has been affected by the regional fractures brought about by Boko Haram's threat. One explanation is that shared ethnic identity between Adamawa region in Nigeria and the nearby Adamaoua region in Cameroon disregards national boundaries and increases the ease of cross-border activity. Both features are self-reinforcing: weak borders expand interactions, movement, trade and other business between both sides of the frontier. Such activity, however – mostly existing unregulated within the informal market and predicated mainly on the permanence of cross-border ethnocultural ties – itself leads to the further diminishment of the practical relevance of political boundaries. Shared ethnic identity and its marriage to cross-border activity is, after all, a natural part of life in these areas. Both features of this part of Nigeria, moreover, have existed for centuries,[1] with the historical Adamawa Emirate spanning Nigeria and Cameroon. Locals are well aware of the historical cross-border ethnic identity shared with their Cameroonian kin. Indeed, many locals view the boundary between Adamawa area of north-east Nigeria and Cameroon as artificial and divisive. Famously, in 2014, during a rowdy session of the National Conference in Abuja, the Lamido Adamawa (the region's traditional ruler) made a controversial point:

My people and the people of Adamawa [state in Nigeria] have got somewhere to go. I am the Lamido Adamawa, and my kingdom extends to Cameroun. The larger part of my kingdom is in Cameroun. Part of that kingdom is today called Adamawa State [Adamaoua region] in Cameroun. You see, if I run to that place, I will easily assimilate [...] My Kingdom has been in existence hundreds of years before the so-called entity called Nigeria and the so-called civilised people from the West who are the people who came and divided us. The larger part of my kingdom is now in Cameroon, and a part of it is named a state that is Adamawa State in Cameroon. If you go to Cameroon, you verify that. (Umoru, Erunke and Nwabughiogu 2014)

There virtually is no disputing Lamido Adamawa's comments. Powerful and long-standing identity linkages have transcended political cleavages, and they still exist: between Cameroon's far north and Adamaoua regions, and north-east Nigeria – specifically the Adamawa area. Mokolo for instance, whereas a Far North Cameroon region[2] today was, a hundred years ago, in 1916, still subordinate to Madagali in north-east Nigeria and was administered from there. Adamawa, today, constitutes a region split across Nigeria and Cameroon, with both a north-eastern Nigerian state (Adamawa) and the third largest Cameroonian region (Région de l'Adamaoua), bearing effectively the same name and retaining similar ethnic Fulani constitution (Njeuma 2012). Indeed, Adamawa's history is vital to the present-day instance of Boko Haram's seamless movement between Nigeria and Cameroon and integration of fighters from both the Cameroonian and Nigerian sides of the border, into its ranks.

The impact of colonial legacy on Nigeria–Cameroon territory and ethnic identity

Two centuries ago, before the German and British colonial Balkanization of West Africa, these regions were part of a single empire ruled by Modibo Adama. The Adamawa Emirate constituted a subordinate region to the vast Sokoto Caliphate, which encompassed parts of northern Nigeria, Cameroon, Niger and even modern-day Burkina Faso (Falola and Genova 2009). Amongst much else Balkanized by colonialists in the region in the nineteenth and early twentieth centuries, the Adamawa Emirate was split between the English and Germans, after the latter Annexed Modibo Adama's empire (named Adamawa after him) in 1884 (Neba 1987, Ngoh 1996). This dismantlement of the Adamawa territories had come decades before an additional political wedge was driven into this region. On 10 July 1919, the Franco-British treaty defined the boundaries between Nigeria and Cameroon under the British-French colonial government, 'presided over by Sir Viscount Milner, the British Secretary of State for the colonies and Henry Simon, the French minister for the colonies' (Enaikele, Olutayo and Aluko 2009, 232).

As part of the so-called Scramble for Africa, such arbitrary boundary definitions are now widely recognized as problematic. After all, European powers partitioning new territories were doing so without fully understanding the long-term social, ethnocultural and political implications of their actions. As former British Prime Minister, Lord Salisbury, remarked, 'we have engaged in drawing lines upon maps where no white man's foot ever trod, we have given away mountains, rivers and lakes to each other, only hindered by the small impediment that we never knew exactly where the mountains, rivers and lakes were' (Enaikele, Olutayo and Aluko 2009, 229–230).

Part of the political consequences was that autonomies and long-existent empires, in the years and decades following the Berlin Conference of 1884–1885 would be split apart (Ajala 1983). In north-east Nigeria, which now shares borders with three other countries, this would have a particularly profound effect compared to the rest of the country. In these areas, cross-border ethnic identity would stubbornly endure for centuries, despite the difficulties of keeping close cross-border ties (Ajala 1983). To the ethnic Hausa, Fulani, Fulɓe (as the Fulani are called in Cameroon), Mafa, Kanuri, Beri Beri and various other cross-border identities, these rapidly implemented political boundaries were confusing. People who one day belonged to the same community woke up the next to find:

> That they could no longer move freely across areas which they and their ancestors had for centuries regarded as their virtual backyard. If they wanted to get across, they were required to cross at specified frontier posts which were usually great distances apart. They also soon realised that they were subject to different sets of rules as their brethren on the other side of the new 'barrier'. (1983, 181)

With the British likewise absorbing the section of Adama's empire within its Nigerian territories (Neba 1987, Ngoh 1996), the Europeans effectively killed off the idea that Adamawa was a single kingdom. Close and long-standing ethnicities, practically overnight, and without any form of social contract to participate in the decision-making process, were given new and artificial identities.

For these ethnic groups and indeed the subregion, however, more change was yet forthcoming. With Germany's loss in the Great War, France would assume Germany's African territories, effectively putting Cameroon under French rule. Colonies of Chad, Niger, Cameroon and Nigeria in this way were shared amongst France and Britain. Consequently, the Hausa, Fulani, Kanuri, Mafa and other ethnicities, who used to be part of a single vast empire of indigenous peoples less than a century earlier, were divided by political lines (Neba 1987, Ngoh 1996, Njeuma 2012).

Some of these ethnic identities, however, disregarded the British colonial boundaries: across Borno and Adamawa states in Nigeria, the North, Extreme North and Adamawa (Adamaoua) regions in Cameroon and south-west of Chad. As an example, a community from northern Borno, in practice, is closer in almost every way imaginable to another across the lake in Chadian territory, than it is to a riverine community in the Niger Delta in the south-south of Nigeria, even though the latter is likewise a Nigerian community. Such shared ethnic identity from the ancient and pre-colonial 'Hausa States' (Lange 2010), along with the 'permanence' of Borno's boundaries (Hiribarren 2016), has been exploited by kings and powerful rulers for centuries (Lange 2010, Hiribarren

2016). Today, they likewise have been exploited by Boko Haram in swelling its rank and file. Combined with the power of radical Islamist demagoguery – which, as one police officer in Maiduguri puts it, 'helps individuals see themselves as dispensable alone but part of a greater religious calling together' – shared regional identity has enabled Boko Haram to integrate its fighters (Adeoye 2012). Political boundaries, to such individuals, matter little as a result. Whether in Cameroon, in Chad or back in north-east Nigeria, Boko Haram's fighters appear well integrated.

Seini Boukar Lamine, the Lamido (local ruler) of Kolofata, a town in the Far North region of Cameroon pointed out that within Boko Haram units in Cameroon, the Kanuri constitute the largest ethnic group, followed by the Hausa, Fulani and other ethnicities (Schneider 2015b). What is striking from Lamido Lamine's account is that nationalities were entirely subordinate to language, shared ethnic identity and religious identities of Boko Haram fighters. This issue of shared ethnic identity, therefore, remains a single thread that connects all the areas that Boko Haram has contested in north-east Nigeria and its three Chad Basin neighbours. However, it is particularly relevant to the cross-border threat in Cameroon.

Chad

In the case of Chad, weak borders also mean that Boko Haram's transnational ambitions to hit a major city have become operationally feasible. Chad has its capital city of N'Djamena a little more than 300 km from Nigeria. This proximity greatly expands Boko Haram's operational ambitions as a transnational threat, although, in practice, the insurgent's penetration into N'Djamena has been limited (Ngarmbassa 2015). Even so, N'Djamena is the only other country capital to be hit by Boko Haram, besides Nigeria's capital of Abuja. The capitals of the other two north-east neighbours in Yaoundé (Cameroon) and Niamey (Niger) are much too far away to be viable targets; comparatively, N'Djamena is next door.

Chad is relevant to Boko Haram at all three levels of war, therefore. At the tactical level, Chadian fighters feature within Boko Haram's ranks. Indeed, as pointed out by police personnel in Maiduguri, the Chadian contingent within Boko Haram is substantive enough that earlier speculation about Boko Haram not being entirely Nigerian is credible and supported by evidence (Adeoye 2012). At the operational level, shared ethnic links, combined with Chad's proximity to Nigeria, enable Boko Haram's cross-border activity. Such activity includes cross-border covert operations, relocation of kidnap victims, and the transit of mujahideen and matériel. Chad's proximity provided Boko Haram 'succour' (Ahmed 2012), such as during periods when intensified military COIN operations on the Nigerian side of the border forced Boko Haram to lay low. There also were rumours that Shekau, injured at a time, spent months recuperating in Chad. Such rumours are difficult to verify. However, the technicalities of such a scenario – Chad's proximity, Boko Haram's record of activity around the Chadian frontier, and the high incidence of Chadian fighters within Boko Haram – make it eminently feasible that Boko Haram and Shekau have a Chadian base of operations, near enough to Nigeria.

At the strategic level, Boko Haram's ability to strike a country's capital, in N'Djamena, make it significantly more legitimate, both as a standalone terrorist threat and as the Islamic State's West Africa Province (ISWAP). However, there is another and often overlooked geographic advantage lent to Boko Haram by the Nigeria–Chad border area; this comes by way of the boundary itself, in Lake Chad.

Over the last half-century, Lake Chad has eroded to a tiny fraction of its former self. In the 1960s, the lake's surface area was about 25,000 km^2, making it 'one of the largest water bodies in the world' (Vanguard 2016d). Today, however, the situation is much different. Lake Chad 'has lost 90 per cent of its water and shrunk to about 1,350 square kilometres' (Vanguard 2016d). Indeed, Lake Chad's enduring lake status is questionable insofar its features now resemble those of a wetland (Braun 2010). With less than half the original lake bed flooded with water over each year and with rich yet traversable vegetation, there is a stronger argument that what remains is a wetland, not a lake. Indeed, depending on the seasonal flooding of wetland areas, some areas of the former lake bed may be dry enough for the crossings of large groups of people (though certainly not motorized convoys). Here again, there are tactical implications for Boko Haram's threat.

Water level's erosion, combined with changes to the lake topography over time, has opened up footpaths and points of crossing on *terra firma* – solid earth – which neither the Nigerian nor the Chadian military forces can fully exploit. As Figure 5.1 indicates, there is no substantive land border between both countries: Lake Chad, degraded as it is, remains the most significant shared demarcation. Moreover, tactically speaking, wetland crossings for motorized convoys would be problematic or impossible.[3]

Neither the political nor tactical technicalities that hold back Nigerian and Chadian forces are necessarily relevant to many locals on either side of the lake, however. Having access to solid earth crossings, shallow pools of water and a wetland to traverse (dependent on season), these locals can now move between national boundaries without the need for boats. A few decades ago, this would have been impossible, with areas such as Baga, on the Nigerian side of the border, surrounded by water. Today, however, whereas locals can exploit the emergence of an environmental anomaly, so too can Boko Haram. Especially at night, when covert crossings are more likely, the current form of Lake Chad could provide a tactical military advantage for even a few Boko Haram fighters.

Niger

Nigeria's shared border, with just Niger, at around 1,500 km (900 miles), is the longest border stretch shared by Nigeria, without the presence of any significant natural barriers (such as Mandara, shared with the Cameroonian side). Nigerian, Nigérien and multinational joint task forces share policing and security duties. Since 2012 for instance, small amounts of Nigérien special forces have been deployed along the border to check Boko Haram's cross-border threat in the area. Moreover, for years, the Zinder region in Niger, across the border from Nigeria, has been a point of ingress and egress for the insurgents (Massalaki and Valdmanis 2012). Like some cross-border

Figure 5.1 Lake Chad as the Most Substantive Crossing Between Chad and Nigeria.
Source: United Nations Cartographic Section

areas of Cameroon and Chad, Zinder shares a collective ethnic identity with north-east Nigerians across the border. Indeed, the city of Zinder itself was initially a small Hausa settlement within the Kanem-Bornu empire and, for centuries, was a major trade hub for onward traffic from the Sahel, southwards into Nigeria (Geels 2006). Some Tuareg settled across the border in Nigeria and integrated, after escaping French Colonialist occupation and losing the 'Hausa Revolts' of the late nineteenth and early twentieth centuries (Geels 2006). So, there is evidence of historical, two-way, cross-border movement and settlement between both sides of the boundary.

Going back earlier in Niger's history and pushing even deeper into Niger beyond Zinder, both 'Hausaland and Kanuriland' were at the nucleus of the pre-colonial region (Fuglestad 1983). Indeed, as Finn Fuglestad comments in his historical study of Niger, the Hausa, one of Nigeria's three dominant ethnicities today, have historically dominated Niger's population since pre-colonial times. By Niger's independence in 1960, when an official census was conducted, 'between 45 and 48 per cent of the total population' identified as Hausa (Fuglestad 1983, 1). This percentage was more than the Tuareg or any other ethnic group in the country at the time and remains the case today (Central Intelligence Agency 2015). Populating entire towns such as Birno in the old area of Zinder, some of the Hausa-dominated locations even today are virtually identical to communities to Borno, across the Nigerian border (Geels 2006). Hausa communities across the demarcation share culture, architecture, language and ethnicity. This shared cultural identity also extends beyond Niger's Hausa ethnicity; two other ethnicities, in particular, are noteworthy.

The Kanuri (or Beri-Beri as they are referred to in South-Eastern Niger) have historically been present in substantial numbers; with the 1960 census putting Niger's Kanuri at 'between 6 and 8 per cent' of the population (Fuglestad 1983, 1). This population has been mostly sedentary in South-Eastern Niger, in areas across the border from north-east Nigeria (around the Borno frontier, in particular). The Kanuri, as discussed earlier in the chapter, have a long history with their kith and kin in Borno State, Nigeria, where they also dominate that population.

Case Study: The Fulani and cross-border migratory tendencies of nomadic groups in West Africa and the Sahel

The Fulani, finally, as another primary Nigérien ethnicity with strong cross-border ties with their Nigerian kin (who also are called Fulani), made up between '11 to 13 per cent' of the post-colonial Nigérien population (Fuglestad 1983, 4). Even today, the community remains significant in Niger, estimated at over 1.5 million (Central Intelligence Agency 2015). Unlike the Fulani settlements who also are present in Chad, Mali, Guinea and Sudan, the Nigérien Fulani ethnicity remains culturally close to their Nigerian kin. The closeness of ethnic and familial ties correlates to Niger–Nigeria border proximity. Furthermore, there is a considerable amount of cross-border movement and interaction between both groups. More so than virtually any ethnicity in the proximate LCBC subregion, the Fulani disregard political borders and have a robust migratory culture.

Indeed, unlike the mostly sedentary Kanuri, the Fulani are more migratory and a highly dispersed ethnic group across West Africa and the Sahel. The Nigérien Fulani ethnicity was not, for instance, always indigenous to the south of Niger. Instead, the Fulani, as 'newcomers to the area', migrated from across the Nigérien border, from the north and north-western parts of Nigeria in pre-colonial times (Fuglestad 1983, 4). This strong migratory nature of the Fulani ethnicity is related to the fact that some Islamist militant groups have Fulani fighters active within a subregional, transnational map that includes West Africa and the Sahel (Weiss 2016). Moreover, 'the Fula is one of the largest ethnic groups in West Africa, which could help in the transnational recruitment of Fulani fighters' (Weiss 2016). This migratory feature of Fulani moving in clusters as primitively armed marauder bands continues to endure till date. In Niger, Chad and northern Cameroon, they remain a feature of the landscape. In the north of Nigeria, these clusters are a security threat in their own right, aside from Boko Haram.

Even further down to the south of Nigeria, the phenomenon is identifiable as the so-called 'Fulani Cattle-rustlers' in the Middle-Belt South-West and the South-East states of Nigeria. This armed migratory tendency and the non-recognition of political boundaries is likewise identifiable in the movement patterns of Boko Haram whose ranks feature Fulani fighters.

To better comprehend this migratory nature of Boko Haram's cross-border activity, therefore, it is useful to situate it within the broader phenomenon as it manifests in the activities of nomadic groups that have roamed and raided this region of West Africa and the Sahel for centuries. As such groups expand in size, they assimilate more significant numbers of nomadic cross-border fighters of similar ethnic identity. Increasingly, the idea of 'the State' becomes less preponderant to decisions around where these groups go to raid or to the consequences of their actions. Such groups, moreover, do not have what many might see as a normalized view of what it means to be a marauder, a cattle-rustler or a human-raider. They do not respect political boundaries, and this reflects in the cross-border nature of their activities. This region of West Africa and the Sahel, moreover, has a rich migratory history that goes back five centuries and more. To such marauder groups, cross-border kidnapping today was slave-raiding then; it was a practice that came with killing, loot and plunder, and torching of houses: effectively what Boko Haram does when it attacks small communities. Such raids were, of course, an unpopular practice centuries ago in the areas now contested by Boko Haram.

Moreover, like kidnapping, cattle rustling, or village raids today, these practices remain unacceptable within the existing legal frameworks. To many locals within this subregion, nevertheless, such acts of violence and lawlessness are not new and unrecognizable, regardless of their current form. 'Boko Haram's actions are thus to a great extent understood in terms of slave-raids and borderlands. Those actions are not some mysterious, unprecedented eruption of violence and savagery: they can be understood within local contexts of politics and history' (MacEachern 2018). On this note, it probably should be added that Boko Haram's cross-border activity should also be situated within the framework of the weak borders of the countries it targets. In Niger, Boko Haram has found a prime candidate for a state with weak, vast borders, both at the boundary with Nigeria and even further north-west through Niger, right into Northern Mali.

Niger's border problem

Beyond its longstanding ties with the Fulani, Hausa and Kanuri ethnicities across the border in Nigeria, Niger presents a second advantage for Boko Haram's insurgency. This is insofar as Niger itself has a border policing problem with its other four large neighbours: Mali, Libya, Algeria and Chad. This border issue is exacerbated by Niger's sparse frontier areas exploited by Boko Haram in its use of 'several crossing points to transit towards Mali and Mauritania' (Udounwa 2013, 14–15). Indeed, on the Nigérien border axis with Nigeria, Nigerian task force operatives fighting Boko Haram were categorical: the vast stretch of border shared with Niger across the north of Nigeria was being exploited both ways by the group (Adeoye 2012). The police knew it; the Army knew it. However, workforce issues meant it was not practicable to patrol and protect the entire border (Omeni 2017). Furthermore, this exploitation of border insecurity in Niger went beyond the shared boundary with north-east Nigeria.

To better understand why Nigérien territorial access remains advantageous to Boko Haram beyond the Niger–Nigeria boundary, two comparative statistics of Niger are worth bearing in mind. First, its size. Niger is one of the biggest countries in West Africa with a land mass of 1.267 million km^2. To put this size into context, Niger is larger than the UK, France and Germany combined; and about a third bigger than Nigeria (923,768 km^2). Despite being a third larger than Nigeria in land mass, however, Niger has about a ninth of Nigeria's population and about a twelfth of its army. Simply put, the Nigérien terrestrial environment is, relative speaking, sparsely populated. Moreover, Niger's security forces, comparative to its land mass – Niger is landlocked and with no operational need for littoral activity has no navy – are understaffed and poorly equipped.

For instance, the Nigérien regular army had about 5,300 active personnel as of 2015 (IISS 2015). Of this, light infantry constitutes just seven infantry companies, with four armoured recce squadrons and two airborne companies as the remainder of the army's entire combat arms. Even counting additional Nigérien paramilitary forces with Gendarmerie (1,400), Republican Guard (2,500[4]) and National Police (1,500), the Nigérien forces are still at a fraction of the workforce required for its vast borders. Especially with Boko Haram now an added threat to the existing jihadist insurgents from Mali to the west, border insecurity is a manifestation of Niger's military challenge.

Nigeria's border challenge certainly puts the Nigériens in context. In contrast to Niger's military forces, for instance, the Nigerian Army at the start of its COIN in 2011 had over 62,000 army personnel. As of 2017, this number has almost tripled due to the war effort. Six Nigerian Army manoeuvre divisions and a task force division now exist, with the Army's Chief of Staff hoping for a 240,000-man Army restructuring in the future (Buratai 2016, 24). Even with the Nigerian Army's forces considerably larger than Niger's, however, this border issue itself remains a significant challenge for Nigeria, and thus has been much more so the case for Niger.

The above analysis highlights the regional challenge of Boko Haram's movement across borders, and it is a problem which, in affecting Niger, also affects Nigeria. For instance, Boko Haram fighters who 'try to cross the [Niger-Nigerian] border nearly daily […] likely transit … towards rebel-occupied northern Mali instead of setting up camps in Niger' (Massalaki and Valdmanis 2012). In particular, the Zinder region around Niger's southern border with Nigeria 'was seen as a natural conduit for militants moving between northern Mali and northern Nigeria' (Comolli 2015, 90). Indeed, this idea that Boko Haram exploited weak Nigérien borders and vast unpatrolled physical spaces within the country, mostly as a transit route to Mali (often to the Gao and Timbuktu regions) and, sometimes, to Mauritania, has enjoyed some popularity within the literature and media.[5]

The Non-Physical Environment to Boko Haram's Insurgency

Introduction

As the previous chapter's analysis has shown, certain features of the border areas shared by Chad, Niger and Cameroon with Nigeria help to extend Boko Haram's transnational threat by lending it tactical advantages. However, the chapter's analysis also indicates that, within this conversation on 'environment', physical features and topography were not the only drivers of Boko Haram's military resilience: in north-east Nigeria but also in the spaces shared by Chad, Niger and Cameroon with Nigeria. This chapter builds upon this idea that the broader environment, the context of which now goes beyond the features of a given locality, plays a vital role in insurgency.

The environment and the population as variables

It is often said that insurgency is people-centred conflict, and that the winning of hearts and minds of the local populace should at least feature in the conversation of how to defeat an insurgency. This is the so-called 'battle for hearts and minds' (Rid 2010). As Part Four of this volume will show, it is today a dominant narrative within modern counter-insurgency doctrine. This, however, does not mean that perpetrator groups directly exploit the populace.

Instead, where the assertion is made that an insurgency is a battle between government forces on one side, insurgent sources on the other, and the people in the middle (Mackinlay 2012), the suggestion here is more that perpetrator groups exploit specific features of the environment in order to benefit from the support of the people who depend on that environment. 'Support' for the insurgency may be voluntary, or it may be coerced. In this sense, a spectrum of participation exists (more on this later). Furthermore, 'dependence' on the environment, in this context, could be for community; it could be socio-economic; it could be for religious conviction; and it could be for ethnocultural or political identity. Such things matter to people; indeed, they influence peoples' cost-benefit calculus in everyday decision-making.

If therefore, the government can positively change that environment or otherwise prevent the insurgent from controlling it, victory is more likely for state forces, because people are more influenced to support the government (or at least not take up arms against it). If, on the other hand, the insurgent can get a foothold in this environment and exploit it in a range of ways this chapter shall explore, then he gains popular support or at least some semblance of it, and the government has a real counter-insurgency challenge on its hands.

Simply put, positively influence the environment as the government and the people's mindedness for insurgency changes. Fail to do so, then you may fail to have the people on your side and might already have lost the war, no matter how many battles your war planners win. The key here, however, is not the people, *per se*; it is the environment that accommodates them.

To this point, the chapter's analysis shall focus on how inequalities within the social, political, ethnocultural and religious contexts, which coincide to magnify existing feelings of disenfranchisement and grievances against authorities, hold explanatory power for Boko Haram's ability to exploit the environment that engenders these differences within vulnerable population groups. The chapter shall show, very specifically, the features of this environment that makes it exploitable by Boko Haram. Indeed, as a different form of the environment – the presence and interaction of social and economic factors and their influence on individuals or groups – this environment was one of Boko Haram's first battlegrounds, exploited even as the group started making religious inroads in north-east Nigeria. Rather than geographic features such as wetlands, or political demarcations that denote national boundaries, it is the population that is the main feature of this environment.

In this sense, the population is the dependent variable within this chapter's analysis: the variable that reacts in different ways, depending on changes to the independent variable (environment). Conversely, the environment is the independent variable: the variable to which changes made cause a noticeable impact on the dependent variable (population). Figures 6.1 to 6.3 later in the chapter build on this concept to illustrate, within a hypothetical marketplace model, the impact of ideology on a population audience already rendered pliant by the environment in which they find themselves. This variable relationship and dependency were absent in Chapters 4 and 5's analyses insofar as 'environment', as previously interrogated, refers to the physical connotation of the term, not to its wider connotation, which is this chapter's emphasis.

This chapter's analysis also shows a spectrum of participation (illustrated in Figure 6.4)[1] that involves persuasion and socio-economic incentives at one end, and coercion and outright abduction at the other. The spectrum corresponds to the fact that many locals caught in conflict spaces, within this socio-economic environment, face a difficult choice and have few good options. The rest of the chapter shall work its way towards an evaluation of this spectrum of participation in insurgency.

The socio-economic environment in insurgency: Role of the disenfranchised, the poor and the delinquent

Long before there was a war to fight, or an insurgent to fight against, there was governance neglect and socio-economic failure in the north-east of Nigeria that made the most vulnerable within these societies susceptible to insurgent influence (Falola 2001). This environment, with large numbers of the disenfranchised and the 'downtrodden', has been exploited for political and religious violence in the past (Isichei 1987). In this regard, Boko Haram is the latest in a line of groups, movements and individuals who tap into society's vulnerable youth groups, employing this groups to drive conflictual strategies against the government and religious establishment (Danjibo 2010, Adesoji 2011). This narrative on insurgency and society in northern Nigeria has gained virtually popular dominant status. And according to this debate, entire demographics of disenfranchised youth – the poor and the 'disinherited', as Elizabeth Isichei calls them (1987) – have populated that environment for decades, seemingly waiting to be recruited in 'revolt' against governance failures and indeed the state that had seemingly disowned them (Isichei 1987, Falola 2001). Whereas this thesis was proposed long before Boko Haram, the group's emergence seemingly validated this dominant popular narrative that the indignance of the government and the Yan Boko (the political elite) towards broad swathes of the poor and vulnerable in northern Nigeria has created a socio-economic environment ripe for insurgency.

Caroline Varin, for instance, suggests that the human development indices of poverty, unemployment, illiteracy are amongst the ' … greatest factors for Boko Haram's successful recruitment strategy' (2016, 4). Walker meanwhile is of the view that 'the general poverty and the poor state of northern Nigeria' are issues that 'feed' Boko Haram (2012, 13). Indeed, 'it is anger at these issues', Walker argues, 'that sustains the group and gives it recruits to continue its work' (2012, 13).

Adesoji likewise alludes to a '… scholarly agreement on the centrality of economic factors' within the emergence of insurgency in northern Nigeria (2011, 101). Other writers on Boko Haram's insurgency are even more adamant regarding the explanatory power of the socio-economic environment. David et al. present a 'central argument [...] that the high level of socio-economic inequality in Nigeria can meaningfully explain the emergence and persistence of the Boko Haram terrorism … ' (2015, 6). Even Nigeria's former National Security Adviser, Sambo Dasuki, in a 2015 paper delivered at Chatham House, London, seemed fixated on local corruption, socio-economic discontents and lack of opportunity as drivers of Boko Haram's insurgency. Quoting Col Dasuki:

> For Nigeria to address the underlying conditions conducive to the spread of violent extremism leading to insurgency, the cancerous menace of corruption must be fought with all elements of its national power. [We must] build badly needed infrastructure, put our children in schools, ignite economic activities and accelerate upward mobility for a majority of our people. (2015, 4)

Within this dominant popular narrative in Nigeria – that poor governance, socio-economic decline, failed educational systems, and vulnerable youth groups all drive insurgency – some areas have been the debate foci. A case in point, so far as the narrative in the country's north is concerned, is the *almajiri* phenomenon, the related madrassa system of Qur'anic learning in northern Nigeria and the also related challenge of regulatory mechanisms around open-air teaching/preaching in the region.

So important are the above aspects of this insurgency debate that an analysis of political conflict's supposed drivers in north-east Nigeria will be incomplete without a closer examination of what these issues are. Specifically, what is the almajiri phenomenon; why is it often linked to the debate on Boko Haram's rank and file? In the following case study, I examine key aspects of this established popular narrative on insurgency's drivers in northern Nigeria.

Case study: Are the 'almajiri' bred, and is their madrassa system of Qur'anic learning a breeding ground, for political violence?

A longstanding narrative has existed in Nigeria, that, for decades, the *'almajiri'*, an entire social caste of some of the poorest and most vulnerable youth in the country's northern areas, have swelled the memberships of recalcitrant preachers, insurgent actors and political rabble-rousers. To many observers, especially those who fail to grasp what exactly *'almajiri'* means, the system as well as the related madrassa scheme – an unregulated, uncensored, non-Western and often 'forced' educational approach – from whence *almajirai*[2] come, are a monument of governance failure in Nigeria's north. Boko Haram, this narrative goes, like the 'Yan Tatsine and Yan Kala Kato from previous decades, are merely the latest in a line of rogue societal elements to not only exploit the pliant *almajirai* and vulnerable madrassas but also to capitalize on a lack of regulation and censorship of open-air preaching, for political violence. The solution, according to this train of thought? Drastically reform or remove the almajiri system. As for the madrassas, replace them with Western educational alternatives or, at worst, regulate whatever teaching goes on there as part of a larger push around Islamic teaching/open-air preaching censorship in northern Nigerian.

Over the course of this subsection, I shall explore the views of many prominent critics of the almajiri system. I also shall examine three counter-narratives. First, on the *almajiri* youth as social victims as opposed to being delinquent, violent and potentially terrorist. Second, I take a closer look at this idea that the Islamiyyah system (Qur'anic schooling) and madrassas are 'imposed' on the 'ignorant' in northern society in place of their Western counterparts *karatun boko* (Western schooling). Third I shall discuss why it may be problematic to indeliberately censor open-air teaching and preaching in northern Nigeria and what steps at the state level have, nevertheless, been taken in recent years to redress this problem. Before all of this, however, let us discuss what exactly the almajiri phenomenon of northern Nigeria is.

An *almajiri* is a young boy sent off by his parents or guardians to an older, and often, a respected, Islamic scholar, as part of a years-long process of Qur'anic education. Girls cannot become *almajirai* as the system is masculine and forbids female participation. Once enrolled, the expectation is that the young boy, just one of several under an *alim*, or a *malam* (a Qur'anic teacher) will (1) study the Qur'an, (2) will contribute to his teacher's welfare and upkeep via social activities that we shortly shall discuss and (3) will conduct a range of duties attendant to his status as a young student. These processes generally would continue uninterrupted until graduation, although students are sometimes allowed to go back home to visit parents or guardians in-between. Graduation (*Sauka*) occurs typically by the boy's early twenties.

This practice is shared across northern Nigeria, with an official census from 2010 putting the total number of *almajirai* close to ten million (Höchner 2014). Often found begging for arms and money and in wretched physical states, *almajirai* exist within the lower strata of society. Within the literature and media, this demographic of boys and young men has a blanket portrayal as the primary source of foot soldiers for insurgents in northern Nigeria (Höchner 2015). Thus,

> Rightly or wrongly, *almajirai* have over the years have thus been generalised as fanatics conditioned within the *almajiri* system for the violence they would perpetrate eventually against society. In reality however, there is more to understanding '*almajiri*' that suggests a simplistic causal linkage between them, and social violence, may be problematic. (Omeni 2015)

'*Almajiri*', the dominant argument goes, are uneducated, impoverished and 'disinherited'. They, therefore, must be delinquent, violent and easily inclined to participate in armed insurgency. Indeed, according to this line of reasoning, many of the males that make up Boko Haram's foot soldiers in north-east Nigeria are likely *almajirai*. Such thinking is pervasive within the discourses on drivers of Boko Haram's insurgency. Both Danjibo (2010) and Adesoji (2011) for instance attempt to link '*almajiri*' to Boko Haram's insurgency. Some writers, however, take this socio-economic thesis further. Iro Aghedo, as an example, posits that 'a large chunk' of Boko Haram's membership are ' … Almajirai, who are not only easy to brainwash but [are] also ready to do anything, including peak battles for a little amount of money' (2015, 516). Similarly, Ngbea and Achunike are scathingly critical of the *almajiri*, situating the phenomenon as a driver of terrorism and insurgency. The writers argue that the *almajiri* system has 'outlived its purpose and has become a breeding ground for child begging and potential terrorist's [sic] camps in Nigeria' and that 'the Almajiri system typifies child abuse, social exclusion and chronic poverty in all ramifications' (2014, 269). Within this established popular narrative, the *almajirai* are not the only ones singled out for criticism, however. Even their places of traditional Qur'anic learning, in the madrassas, have also been criticized as breeding grounds for Boko Haram terrorists.

Whereas such writers as Nobel laureate, Wole Soyinka have 'repeatedly declared that Boko Haram's recruits were "bred in madrassas" where they have presumably been "rendered pliant, obedient to only one line of command, ready to be unleashed at the rest of society"' (Höchner 2014), such generalizations are problematic. Such views, rather than helping, may limit broader public understanding of both the nature of Qur'anic learning for these youngsters as well as its roots in northern Nigeria's traditional Muslim society. Moreover, such accusatory rhetoric, observes Hannah Höchner, 'rests on a weak empirical footing' (2014). Along the same lines as Höchner (2014) and Omeni (2015), Tahir Mehmood Butt cautions that political constructions of madrassas as problematic learning centres due to the '"socio-economic system of Islam", "historical rivalry of Jews and Christians against Muslims" and "conservative ideology of madrassa", undermine the important cultural, religious and learning roles of madrassas as traditional learning institutions (2012, 402). Within northern Nigeria moreover, such roles apply to *Islamiyyah* more broadly. Moreover, such reasons are part of why the suggestion that Western education is a local strong preference being 'denied' local youth (Griswold 2014), or that *makarantun boko* will (or even should) replace *tsangayu* (Qur'anic school for youth), reflects a poor understanding of the role and importance of Qur'anic teaching in northern Nigeria.

As an example, acclaimed journalist and writer, Eliza Griswold, expresses an opinion on the role of *almajirai* in Boko Haram's insurgency that exemplifies the extent to which the phenomenon has been misrepresented. For Griswold,

> Boko Haram's swelling ranks are filled with boys and young men who attended almajiri schools, West African madrassas [...] in the slums, many of these boys sleep with their begging bowls under their heads for safekeeping. To make money, corrupt teachers rent out their students to commit acts of violence. In this way, many have become foot soldiers for Boko Haram. (2014)

Griswold further suggests that many of these *almajirai* did not have the chance to attend Western schools. This assertion is dubious because it assumes Western education is the preference for many in north-east Nigeria. Whether this indeed is the case, however, is questionable, perhaps even improbable (Crisis Group 2010). Moreover, many *almajirai* are sent to Qur'anic boarding schools by fathers who themselves experienced, or are well versed with, the system. The idea therefore that *almajiranchi* (the process of begging for food and money as part of being an *almajiri*) is somehow misunderstood by those who send their boys to become *almajirai*, underestimates social understanding and acceptance of the practice. This, however, is what Ngbea and Achunike appear to do where they contend that parents who send their boys off to board as *almajirai* are 'ignorant' and that 'northerners and the parents of the street children have abdicated their obligations of properly caring for and educating their children' (2014, 269). This is not necessarily the case, though. Many parents might prefer *Islamiyyah* (Qur'anic schooling) over *karatun boko* (Western education) because of the traditional and Islamic virtues the former instils in young males, and because it is a centuries-old local practice (Omeni 2015).

Furthermore, to those familiar with the *almajiri* system, the criticized boarding practices, the begging for arms, and the austere lifestyle as a whole, are known to be historically integral to the experience of *almajirai* (Abubakar 2012). Indeed, such practices, known collectively as *almajiranchi*, a subsystem within *almajirci*, are 'ostensibly designed to prepare them [*almajirai*] for some of the hardships they may encounter later in life' (2010).

Another misunderstanding within this established popular narrative is that many youth categories that are not *almajirai* ironically are also often accused of being delinquent and prone to criminality because they lack the very discipline imbibed by *almajirci* and the *almajirai*'s strict Qur'anic learning regimen. Some examples of these categories include *yan ci rani* (seasonal immigrants), *yan tauri*, *yan daba* (street corner boys), *yan banga* and *yan dauka amarya*. Often, moreover, no distinction is made between *almajirai* and such other youth categories, even though it is essential to make these distinctions within the discourses on northern youth participation within insurgency (Omeni 2015).

Now, the argument here is not that *almajirai* are not potentially exploitable by Boko Haram. Nor is it even that some Boko Haram members may well have emerged from the *almajiri* system or may have failed to complete their studies before joining the insurgency. As Höchner writes, '*Almajirai* may well be, and probably are, amongst the followers of Boko Haram. But there is no systematic evidence to support such assertions' (2014). Still, to highlight the socio-economic fragilities of northern Nigeria, link those fragilities to the *almajirai* identity and then link the latter to insurgency, is to simplify what is anything but a simple set of insurgency drivers. Such an approach moreover 'implies that Qur'anic school enrolment can somehow explain why some young people decide to join Boko Haram. It suggests easy answers where they do not exist' (Höchner 2014). Military-aged males (MAMs) *do* play an important role within Boko Haram's military strategy; much of this chapter's discussion is centred on this argument.[3] Nevertheless, whereas most *almajiri* fall into the category of MAMs, this does not make the reverse true; most MAMs are not necessarily *almajirai*. Too many other male youth demographics exist in northern society for accurate blanket assertions. The '*almajiri*' therefore, as Höchner observes in interview, have far too conveniently, albeit falsely, been blamed for extremist and political violence in northern Nigeria (2013).

So, to summarize, are the deprived and disenfranchised *almajirai* truly the rank and file of Boko Haram's army? It is likely – even inevitable perhaps – that many *almajirai* may find themselves, for reasons discussed throughout this chapter, within Boko Haram's ranks. Still, to single out the *almajirai* as the insurgency's chief culprits is disappointingly reductive, not least because this demographic is one of many young demographics within northern Nigerian society, neglected enough to be pushed to delinquency's fringes.

Structure vs agency: Are young Boko Haram members' victims, extremists or both?

Indeed, so far as vulnerability to radical views goes, it may be problematic to make blanket assumptions that children so young as *almajirai* enter Boko Haram's ranks already radicalized. Suppose, however, this is not the case? Suppose these children, too young to even understand the extremist views to which they are exposed, were integrated into the Boko Haram group setting and then were radicalized, over time, *in situ*? Surely, this makes them victims? Moreover, if the argument is that even though they are children, they nevertheless joined Boko Haram wilfully and so are every bit as radical as the average members, then this is a complicated train of thought to substantiate. These are just children, after all, without the agency, or 'the capacity to act', often associated with adult decision-making (Barker and Jane 2016, 16). Research also suggests that the youngest and most vulnerable youth groups that join Boko Haram may not entirely, or even in part, recognize what they are getting into (Mercy Corps 2016). So then, how exactly does one end up within a group setting they do not understand nor necessarily support?

The answer is that social structure might influence the decision-making for joining the insurgency. In sociology, 'structure' includes such considerations as norms, social caste, economic conditions, religion, sense of belonging, gender, ethnicity, culture and identity (Barker and Jane 2016). These constructs influence decision-making within a social context. In assessing Boko Haram's broad membership, therefore, structure, rather than agency (or its lack thereof) *per se*, may also hold explanatory power.

The decision to join an insurgency, as an example, especially where young and vulnerable groups are concerned, may be strongly influenced by structure. Structure, in this context, involves the patterned arrangements, underpinned by culture and social life, which effectively limit choice and influence the decision-making of individuals and groups. These 'predictable regularities lie outside of any given person', yet affect that person's choices, behaviours and decisions; they are driven by 'the constraining patterns of culture and social life' (Barker and Jane 2016, 18).

Again, however, we must acknowledge a nuance here. Yes, some Boko Haram members are indeed influenced by structure – wilfully integrated into the insurgent's group setting for other reasons to do with ethnicity, culture and social options – without first being radicalized. Nor does it even have to be entirely voluntary for structure to be still playing a role here. Suppose acquiescence to coercion coincides with structure? Later parts of this chapter, as an example, shall examine how some Boko Haram members get coerced into the group setting. With few, if any good social alternatives to choose from, with a culture that neglects their class, with an ethnicity shared with the insurgency, with no true sense of political identity, or real commitment to a failed social contract with the Nigerian government, these vulnerable youths may have little choice but to eventually acquiesce and join the insurgency. In assessing Boko Haram's broad membership, therefore, structure, rather than agency (or its lack thereof) *per se*, may also hold explanatory power.

Radicalization, viewed from this lens, certainly is not the only factor at play here. However, just because some members did not wilfully join Boko Haram as radicals, does not mean there are no members who do so. Boko Haram also depends on ideology as a soft form of influence on audiences that make informed decisions, employing agency. Moreover, especially where agency is present, persuasion and its influence become all the more critical to emotive decision-making of individuals and groups (Barker and Jane 2016, 480).

The persuasive power of extremist ideology

An insurgent's persuasive power employs ideology in wresting popular support away from the authorities. Ideology by itself, however, is unlike to force people with agency to make a simple cost-benefit calculation and then choose conflict over 'normalcy'. What, however, counts for 'normalcy' for disadvantaged social groups? If normal life for them means poor socio-economic conditions, high marginalization and low social mobility, would this still be seen as acceptably normal if an alternative comes knocking? It is, therefore, such conditions and conditionalities that ideology aims to exploit. However, no matter how appealing an insurgent's ideology and political manifesto might be, or how charismatic its wielders are as orators, the environment must play a role.

Where there is weak governance, social inequalities, and a sense of disenfranchisement and marginalization within lower classes, then discrediting authorities via an alternate narrative – extremist or otherwise – becomes more manageable for the insurgent. The aim here is not simply to make a case that the government has failed, or that lower classes deserve better. Instead, the insurgent also aims to insinuate his agenda – presenting himself and his ideologies as viable alternatives. This is where extremist ideology can be an effective influence; it persuasively presents violence as the only viable contestation mechanism and so lends the insurgent a form of soft power which, employed effectively, could transform into sufficient hard power in his quarrel against the government.

Soft power, on its part, is 'the ability to influence the behaviour of others to get the outcomes one wants' (Nye 2004, 2). As an example, in all those years of preaching as the head of Boko Haram, Yusuf's primary goal was to persuade: that he was right, that the government was wrong, that he should be obeyed, that his views were supported by the Qur'an (and so endorsed by God). Yusuf, in his way, was influencing the behaviour of his followers. This method is consistent with the wider thinking around the idea of soft power as persuasive power:

> There are several ways to affect the behaviour of others. You can coerce them with threats; you can induce them with payments; or you can attract and co-opt them to do what you want [...]. Some radical Muslim fundamentalists may be attracted to support Osama bin Laden's actions, not because of payments or threats, but because they believe in the legitimacy of his objectives. (Nye 2004, 2)

Ideology, therefore, like coercion, can also be its form of power. During its formative years, Boko Haram attracted a handful of middle-class and even some upper-class followers. The overwhelming majority of its target audience, however, was lower class: *the talakawa*, or common folk. It was this lower social class that would fight and die in the hundreds, during 2009's rampage. In amassing this sizeable followership, Boko Haram's influence was not military, even though its influence was nonetheless considerable. Boko Haram's power, instead, was soft power – a scaled-down version of soft power at the state level, to be sure, but soft power nonetheless. Now, since Boko Haram's primary power resource in its formative years was, at its core, soft, why then is the Nigerian government's response a 'hard' response – that is, use of military force? The answer is because soft power can, over time and with careful calculations, translate to credible hard power. Indeed, insurgents from Mao Tse-tung to Che Guevara have depended on this ability of soft power to, eventually, transform into politico-military power (Guevara 1968, Greene 2007, Tse-tung 2007). Here, timing is key.

If at the point where wielded power is soft, then a military (hard) response against the wielder is heavy-handed at worst and disproportionate even with the best of outcomes. Indeed, such a response could expedite the timetable of insurgency by turning more people against the state, or by making the section of the population who already are anti-establishment and indignant, to become violent. Conversely, where soft power has transformed to hard power and the insurgent has begun an armed campaign, a military response becomes necessary. Attempting to persuade an enemy's armed battalions, without the metaphorical stick to assist such persuasions, may prove idealistic at best and catastrophic at worst.

Transformation of soft power to hard, however, takes time. This rule has no reversal. Just because people agree with an insurgency's idea system does not mean they are strong enough to violently contest state power (or that they will even do so, putting their lives at risk, when it comes down to it). Now, the insurgent might be tempted to subvert the lengthy transformation process and prematurely leverage soft power. In so doing, however, he faces the risk of finding out the hard way that whereas soft power may eventually give way to hard power, soft power is *not*, in itself, hard power. In the case of Boko Haram, Yusuf paid the ultimate price for this cardinal error in his group's premature rampage of 2009. Such misjudgement is typical of insurgent groups who grow too powerful too quickly, within permissive environments. Such groups, often inexperienced despite their momentum, fail to realize that 'converting resources into realised power in the sense of obtaining desired outcomes requires well-designed strategies and skilful leadership. Yet strategies are often inadequate, and leaders frequently misjudge' (Nye 2004, 3).

Moreover, ideology alone is not soft power. Indeed, to persuade poor populations, ideas by themselves are unlikely to hold sway that translates into action. Where the insurgent plays the role of seducer, there often has to be some tangible incentive, such as financial rewards, food, shelter and so on. If segments of the population are to arm and put themselves at risk for a cause, their simple cost-benefit calculations may need to be influenced beyond rhetoric. For instance, not only did Yusuf preach, but he also employed economic incentives to influence his followers' decision-making. Thus, we see that whereas the population plays a central role in insurgency as military warfare, the mechanism by which the insurgent engages it differs from the way that states historically have tried to leverage the same human resource in time of war.

The role of the population

French diplomat and political scientist, Alexis de Tocqueville once famously wrote,

> Remove the secondary causes that have produced the great convulsions of the world and you will almost always find the principle of inequality at the bottom. Either the poor have attempted to plunder the rich, or the rich to enslave the poor. If, then, a society can ever be founded in which everyman shall have something to keep and little to take from others, much will have been done for peace. (de Tocqueville 1840, 268)

This idea that inequality and social challenges coincide with political violence is a useful proxy for this chapter's analysis of the population's role in insurgency. It is an analysis that sees the population as playing a different role in what is a different, and in many ways a unique, war form.

In the past, the local population was seen as 'strength for war' (Nye 2004, 3–4). Governments could use the population not just for large-scale recruitment for the Infantry, but also as a tax base. In this way, the population was critical to a state's war machine. Indeed, Major War and 'the primacy of land power', through much of the nineteenth century to the mid-twentieth century was influenced by states' leverage of massive populations in recruitment, conscription and taxation for military campaigns (Mearsheimer 2001, 83–137).

Now, the insurgent also requires access to the population to campaign successfully. Insurgency, however, is not Major War; the twenty-first century is not the nineteenth, and the insurgent is not a legitimate government. So, his reasons for getting funding, tax and recruitment from the local populace need to be driven by something other than nationalism or compulsory civic duty that forms part of the terms of some states' social contract with citizens. Moreover, entire populations can no longer be regimented and deployed as in the past. As is shown later in the chapter, the ways by which locals participate in insurgency occupies an entire spectrum and is a great deal more nuanced than might have been associated with Major War of the past. Ideology as a key instrument of soft power, therefore, is of particular importance.

'Hearts and minds'

Ideology effectively becomes the insurgent's vehicle to winning over and employing the population in similar ways as the government itself might have done in the past. Depending on who ends up winning locals' hearts and minds, the population could swing matters decisively one way for another. On the one hand, if perceived inequalities within the population's environment – whether acting as a proxy for greed or grievance – encourage the population towards insurgency, then the government may have a long and challenging internal security situation on its hands. Indeed, in a worst-case scenario, the conflict might even escalate into civil war.

If on the other hand the insurgent can be ideologically and physically isolated from the population's environment, then support for the insurgency dries up, and the insurgent is left to fight with fewer and fewer resources over time. Conflict, in this scenario, devolves into very low-intensity skirmishes. Guerrilla warfare with limited aims could be the best that the insurgent might eventually hope for.

In both scenarios above, the population's support is now at risk. Therefore, the incumbent must now fight the insurgent, in untraditional battlegrounds, to retain it. As the Counter-Terrorism (CT) Section of the Office of Nigeria's National Security Adviser (ONSA) observes, 'we must build resilience among the populace […] We must counter Boko Haram's ideologies, indoctrination and propaganda. We must gain the upper hand in the war of ideas; to win the hearts and minds of those whom BH [Boko Haram] claim to speak and fight for' (ONSA 2012, 6). Along these lines, the government and its agents, by influencing the environment of the populace, could make it less permissible for extremist movements like Boko Haram to be accepted, thus undermining the insurgent's 'war of ideas'.

Mostly, therefore, authorities are in a scramble to fix issues that might cause people to view insurgency as a viable social option. The insurgent's job is to argue otherwise: get the population to support his campaign wilfully. This is not a traditional battlefield contest, however. Nor is it even a battle that directly occurs between insurgent and counter-insurgent *per se*. Instead, this is a proxy battle: the population is 'prize', their environment is the battleground (Rid 2010).

Demand curve of ideology

From the preceding, if we think of insurgent ideology as a good (fundamentally, an idea) sold in a marketplace (a socio-economic and political environment) to an audience. We can relate this to the view that certain goods require a particular type of marketplace if they are to attract an intended audience. In return for finding the right marketplace and reaching his target audience, the goods merchant (in our example, a radical movement/an insurgent) gains a valuable resource as 'payment'. That resource is soft power. Ideology is not soft power. Rather, ideology, for our marketplace model, can be seen as a good, the return for which is soft power: the power over people to make them do things they would not have done, were they not in the ideologue's orbit of influence.

In our marketplace model, illustrated within Figures 6.1 to 6.3, the demand curve is the relationship between radical ideology and number of the population who are open to such ideologies. The Y-axis shows the 'price' of ideology – what those who 'buy into' the insurgent's idea system, have to give to the cause. The X-axis shows the number of people willing to take up the ideology, on the strength of the corresponding payment; generally, the higher the sacrifice demanded by the insurgent, the fewer people will willingly pay that price. Although, as is argued later in this chapter, not all active participants in insurgency are willing actors.

Also, within our marketplace model, two features are noteworthy. First, the demand side of ideology is similar to the concept of demand in conventional market economics. Where the 'price' of ideology – what adherents commit to doing in return for accepting the ideology – is high, the 'demand' for the ideology is low (that is, fewer people have the stomach for the ideology). In Boko Haram's case, the group's non-violent ideology attracted many thousands by 2009, yet only a fraction of these so-called adherents would take up arms at the time violence ensued that July. Moreover, in the six years since 2010 with Boko Haram now proscribed as a terrorist organization, its ideologies now have a much higher price for which fewer people can afford to subscribe openly.

Consequently, ideology is all the more unlikely to have remained the primary driver of Boko Haram's rank and file, as the insurgency matured. Whereas Boko Haram may indeed still have recruits that join it purely on the strength of ideology, 'demand' (that is, local appetite) for the movement's ideology has plummeted since its formative years. There are caveats to this particular thesis within our marketplace model.

First, where the socio-economic environment permits, the insurgent's ideology may appeal to a larger-than-expected audience insofar as extreme violence, as an operational outcome of the idea system, is embraced by troublingly more significant numbers. Within the marketplace model, these shifts in the environment will reflect the position of the demand curve. Socio-economic improvements that disadvantage the insurgent and benefit the local populace may cause the curve to shift to the left (inward) and reduce the numbers willing to buy into the insurgent's ideology. On the other hand, socio-economic insecurities that benefit the insurgent and disadvantage the local populace may cause the demand curve to shift to the right (outward). Such a change will increase the numbers ready to accept even the most violent operational outcomes of embracing the insurgent's ideology. Figures 6.2 and 6.3 highlight the effect of socio-economic changes within the environment, on the demand curve. In all three figures, the population is the dependent variable: the variable that reacts in different ways, depending on changes to the independent variable (ideology). Whereas ideology is the independent variable: the variable to which changes made influence the dependent variable (population).

In Figure 6.1, the demand curve indicates that, under normal circumstances, very few people agree that the high price of volunteering for a suicide mission, in the insurgency, is acceptable. Those who do pay such a high price voluntarily, without being coerced, drugged or heavily explicitly indoctrinated for the task, may do so due to a personal vendetta against the military or police, extreme socio-economic hopelessness, a genuine conviction in the ideology or a combination of such factors. That is, ideology may play a role here but it unlikely that it dominates the cost-benefit calculus of the typical suicide bomber in non-Western settings such as in north-east Nigeria.

At lower levels of commitment (actions that exclude voluntary suicide missions), voluntary support scales dramatically, particularly when the insurgent maintains his end of the informal social contract with fighters and provides them with food, shelter and, where applicable, payments and financial incentives. At this level, there is some base level of ideological commitment within the fighters' group setting; however, as later sections of this chapter will show, there again are a range of competing factors.

At the lowest levels of membership, where radicalization may not necessarily require action and where there is a limited penalty for supporting the insurgent (nothing like the death guarantee of a suicide mission), 'support' is likely to be highest. Indeed, at such relatively low levels of commitment, ideology and its influence, even if only at a subliminal level, now play a more significant role. Even those without any need for the economic or social alternatives offered by the insurgency may support its fight against the government, in principle, without voicing their thoughts or ever acting on them.

Vulnerable younger people especially may more wilfully buy into violent radical ideologies if the price of participation is low or very low. This tendency towards radical ideology might be influenced by 'a very wide range of experiences and social factors; a lack of resilience in some places and communities; and grievances, some real and some imagined, which were frequently exploited by apologists for violence and made a reason for engaging in it' (Home Office 2011, 17–18). Scaling down this general assertion to the Nigeria case, we see some consistency with views of scholars like Jon Hill, who asserts that 'The Federal Government's failure to take adequate care of its citizens is driving some to support one or other of the insurgent or separatist groups operating in the country [Nigeria] today' (2012, 1).

In order words, governance failures reduce the reward for compliance with the state and increase the incentives for vulnerable and frustrated citizens, especially the socio-economically hopeless, to buy into insurgent ideologies. Indeed, where governance failures are so disruptive that insurgent ideologies become a more viable alternative to the state offering, more people are likely to view joining insurgencies as the least bad option. The motivations here could be 'greed', such as in socially vulnerable groups' search for better economic options (Collier and Hoeffler 2001). However, motivations for joining insurgencies could also be 'grievance': against authorities that have ignored these vulnerable social groups and thus driven them to support insurgent ideologies (Stewart 2008, 2009, 1, Keen 2012). In some cases, such as Nigeria, the motivations may well be both but with grievance nevertheless remaining a major underlier of such tensions.

Frances Stewart, as an example, contends that 'horizontal inequalities', which, essentially, are 'inequalities in economic, social or political dimensions or cultural status between culturally defined groups' hold explanatory power as to why people join insurgencies against governments (2008, 3). Stewart's theory rests 'on the notion that when cultural differences coincide with economic and political differences between groups, this can cause deep resentment that may lead to violent struggles' (2009, 1). Within the Nigeria context, such views are consistent with those of scholars like Hill (2012). In such scenarios, government and governance, rather than military action of any kind, has a central role to play in influencing the demand curve within our theoretical marketplace model.

Suppose, therefore, favourable government policies and reforms were introduced, which influence a shift of the demand curve to the left. What happens then? Figure 6.2 shows the relationship between the price of ideology and the number of adherents when the previous demand curve shifts inward. On the new demand curve, *no one* views suicide bombing as an acceptable price for the ideology.

Moreover, far fewer people are even willing to commit to more extreme forms of actions consistent with the ideology. Put another way, extremist ideology is now losing its value for the insurgent. Real government policies and reforms have either improved the socio-economic environment or have directly incentivized locals not to rebel.

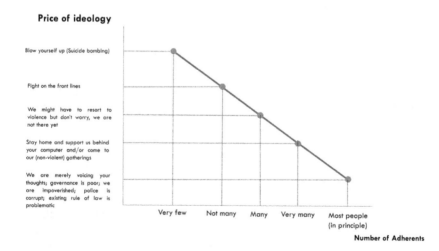

Figure 6.1 Demand Curve in a Hypothetical Marketplace, Relating Ideology and Its Reception by an Audience.

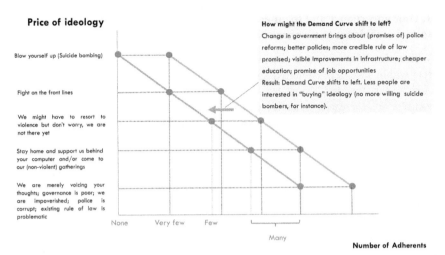

Figure 6.2 Adjusted Demand Curve. Shift to the Left Means the Insurgent's Ideology Is of Less Value.

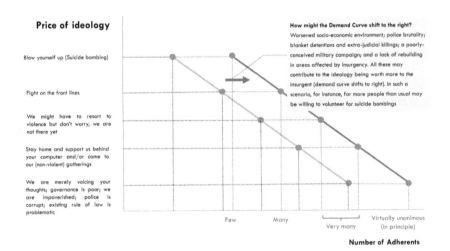

Figure 6.3 Adjusted Demand Curve. Shift to the Right Means the Insurgent's Ideology Is of More Value.

Consequently, the insurgent's soft power cannot be transformed into hard power as readily as before: that is, the insurgent's soft power, even where initially substantive, becomes less fungible with longer-term hard power as the government makes social reforms. People might feel, at this point, that the opportunity cost of joining the insurgency is higher (or much higher) than that of buying into government reform. Government policies and a parallel set of non-military calculations aimed at long-term stability of pacified areas, therefore, are critical to whether or not a conducive environment exists for insurgent ideologies to take root.

1. Poor governance and socio-economic insecurity have historically driven sectarian violence in northern Nigeria

Within the debate on insurgency's drivers, this theme of poor governance and its role within insurgent-contested spaces is identifiable. Governments in Iraq, Syria, Afghanistan, Iraq and Nigeria have been said to at times resemble 'glorified criminal gangs' with little regard for suffering masses (Chayes 2015). In such countries, 'acutely corrupt governance does not just aid terrorist organizations by driving indignant citizens into their arms; it provides haven and logistical support for those very same groups, as officials avert their eyes in exchange for a bribe' (Chayes 2015, 184). Moreover, even where governance failures may not drive insurgency as directly as Chayes suggests, at the very least it creates an opportunity for insurgent movements to integrate the failures of the government and pro-establishment *status quo*, into their written or implied political manifestos.

In Nigeria, as an example, anti-government exhortations, government blame for poor socio-economic conditions and politically charged, highly divisive anti-establishment rhetoric have been central to insurgent narratives for years, in both the Niger Delta and the north-east.[4] This theme, moreover, is also evident within the discourses on why insurgencies exist in Nigeria. 'That Nigeria is a failed state is now beyond doubt – present tense not future' (J. N. Hill 2012, 1); these were amongst the opening remarks by Jon Hill who goes on to severally argue that government failure has been a driver: for insurgency in Nigeria and Boko Haram's insurgency in the north-east specifically.

Furthermore, this issue of poor governance is itself closely linked to the idea that a poor socio-economic environment drives insurgency. As an example, the human development indices of poverty, unemployment and illiteracy have been presented as amongst the 'greatest factors for Boko Haram's successful recruitment strategy' (Varin 2016, 4). Poverty in northern Nigeria has likewise been said to 'feed' Boko Haram, sustaining the group and providing it with 'recruits to continue its work' (Walker 2012, 13). Other writers allude to a ' ... Scholarly agreement on the centrality of economic factors' within the emergence of insurgency in northern Nigeria, as evidenced in the cases of Maitatsine and Boko Haram (Adesoji 2011, 101). Some commentary on Boko Haram's insurgency is particularly adamant about this role of the socio-economic environment. David et al., as an example, present a 'central argument [...] that the high level of socio-economic inequality in Nigeria can meaningfully explain the emergence and persistence of the Boko Haram terrorism ... ' (David, Asuelime and Onapajo 2015, 6).

Faith, politics and society in northern Nigeria

Within the Nigeria case, an intersection of the effects of weak governance, socio-economic inequalities and ethnocultural differences feature prominently within the insurgency debate. As an example, Hill asserts that the 'failure of the Nigerian state' as a whole, is 'inextricable from the country's insurgencies' and 'helps explain the origins of the anger and desperation fuelling the insurgencies in the Niger Delta and North-east' (J. N. Hill 2012, 3).

Indeed, such views form part of the dominant popular narrative which holds that 'failing governance' is, in effect, a 'catalyst' for insurgency in Nigeria (Comolli 2015, 60). Incumbent government indifference to poor local conditions and a culture of impunity has long featured within the system of government in Nigeria. Along these lines, Boko Haram, initially at least, was not just kicking against *karatun boko* (Western education), it also was kicking against government corruption and 'the mechanics of colonial rule' (Chayes 2015, 130). This is insofar as Western education was framed as contributing to the former and as being a by-product of the latter. Western education, in this sense, 'was seen as a tool for corruption, for oppression' (Chayes 2015, 130).

There also is a religious angle within this debate, and it is a theme that coincides with that of politics and social problems. Boko Haram has pushed strongly for Sharia. However, Sharia adoption, for the jihadists, was but a step towards a puritanical shift in northern Nigeria society. Aside from the theological debate, Boko Haram pushed for a moral system whereby the government and exploitative *Yan Boko* – the educated political elite – no longer would be the oppressors of the commoners (Mohammed 2010). As Kano bar association chairman, Ibrahim Aliyu Nasarawa, puts it, 'when they [Boko Haram] say Sharia, they are not just talking about legal technicalities, they mean politics, economics, social justice' (Chayes 2015, 130). Indeed, Boko Haram's formative years saw the sect frame itself not just as an increasingly militant religious outfit but also as a counter to political and governance failures. Along these lines,

> Boko Haram exposed the misbehaviour of politicians who did not hesitate to manipulate Islam and hire private militia to kill their opponents. The sect certainly benefited from the lack of legitimacy of fraudulently elected leaders. Conversely, it contributed to delegitimise a mafia-like parliamentary regime that did not follow Islamic principles of government. More than poverty, bad governance in Borno helped Muhammad Yusuf to become popular and politicise his struggle. (Montclos 2014, 149)

In this way, locals who were sympathetic to Boko Haram's idea system viewed the entire issue not just within a religious frame but also within a socio-economic and political one. Boko Haram became the focal point, the 'focus', for those within the population, who wanted a platform to voice their indignance but did not have one. However, this climate may not have boiled over without an environment where government and the established religious order stood seemingly idly by as matters worsened, people got angrier, and opportunities for anti-establishment ideologues and ideologies emerged.

Anti-establishment Islamic movements in northern Nigeria

Boko Haram, violently championing the darkest elements of this anti-establishment argument, displaced even the most radical deviant movements in the north of Nigeria. In this way, the group positioned itself as the anti-establishment bogeyman. Moreover, within the nonviolent religious debate amongst the more traditional rival Islamic groups, the potentiality for overspill into the arena of political violence has long existed in northern Nigeria (Loimeier 1997, J. N. Hill 2010). Faith and politics, after all, are inextricable from the local Islamic debate. Ideological disagreements within the Islamic establishment, but also popular indignance against the government, over the decades, contributed to the creation of several anti-establishment movements (J. N. Paden 2008). These emergent 'Muslim identities' face off against other groups all of which vary in doctrine, methods and alignment (within or against the establishment). Amongst these groups are the old and powerful Sufi Brotherhoods, the 'Traditional Ethno-Religious Affiliates', the 'Anti-Innovation Legalists', the 'Intellectual Reformers', the 'Antiestablishment Syncretists', the 'Antiestablishment "Muslim Brothers"' and the 'Unemployed Youth and Qur'anic School Movements' (J. Paden 2002, 2–5).

Now, for the most part, scholarly religious debate amongst these groups, even where it has led to tensions, remains civil. The existence of large and influential anti-establishment groups does not mean such groups are violent. Whether by self-moderation and the preference of religious and scholarly debate or by establishment pressure and government-enforced regulation, even the more substantial and influential anti-establishment embodiments of such 'Muslim identities' persisted with a non-violent approach.

On the other hand, however, some of these ideologies and their parent movements over time have also been significantly more confrontational. Moreover, in some cases, unchecked by the government and Islamic establishment, such ideologies have found an audience and exploited the environment to tap into local frustrations. The result has been that the potentiality of a military threat, by such renegade movements, increased in a relatively short space of time; Boko Haram falls into in this category. The difference between Boko Haram and most of the anti-establishment movements, however, is that the former's leaders failed to moderate both its idea system and the operational implications of its ideology. Quite the contrary, as Boko Haram's ideologies matured the group shifted these anti-government and anti-establishment agitations to an extreme conclusion. It is a conclusion that goes much further than any of its anti-establishment predecessors: a literal war against the state.

Moreover, Boko Haram, in waging its insurgency, has not employed its mobilized numbers for political currency or the spread of spiritual influence within the competitive religious setting of northern Nigeria. Instead, the group over the years has reorganized its numbers into covert and overt operatives, with a destructive and militaristic agenda. Consequently, 'mobilization', for Boko Haram, connotes the co-option of recruits, willing and unwilling, across an entire spectrum of participation. The final part of the chapter brings us to this spectrum.

1 The broad spectrum of participation in insurgency drives protraction and evolution of conflict

Earlier in the chapter, the emphasis was on persuasive power and its effectiveness in mobilizing elements of the population, for insurgency. Persuasion, however, falls into a broader spectrum of participation in insurgency; it is but one way the insurgent recruits for his rank and file. Indeed, the notion that all or even most of the insurgent's rank and file are persuaded to fight is dubious, at least within Boko Haram's case.

Figure 6.4 shows the spectrum of participation in Boko Haram's insurgency. Now, recruitment methods that lean towards persuasion indeed feature prominently within this spectrum; indeed, for reasons already explored in this chapter, some of the local populace willingly and without any initial coercion fight for Boko Haram. As this chapter's final section argues, however, coercion likewise plays a vital role within this spectrum of participation.

'Ungoverned spaces' where government writ is nominal and insecurity is high typically make it easier for the insurgent to encroach upon civilian daily life (Solomon 2015, 1–2). Kidnappings and violent attacks, as disruptors of such permissive environments, tend to dominate the news and security debate. For the insurgent, however, such tactics are borne out of a lack of control of such areas – they are an indication that the military's counter-threat is relatively strong which has led to tactics of last resort by rebels. Where the insurgent's standing army is strong enough to control such spaces, on the other hand, 'soft' actions become viable, and these are even more powerful as a power projector than guerrilla attacks. Such activities include propaganda, preaching and control of places of worship, taxation, financially based persuasion and even primitive forms of administration within insurgent-controlled territories. Effectively, the insurgent fills the vacuum left by the lack of strong governance. The same argument is viable for the north-east Nigeria case.

As the Nigerian military COIN reorganized, a commanding Nigerian Army presence in built-up areas such as Maiduguri and Bama made penetration of the urban space problematic for Boko Haram. The expanding Nigerian military orbit lowered insecurity within larger and more strategic towns and forced Boko Haram not only to recede territorially but also to rethink its concept of operations in the urban space (Omeni 2017). Retreating to more rural areas, however, where police authority was virtually non-existent, and the Army's presence was nominal, Boko Haram found

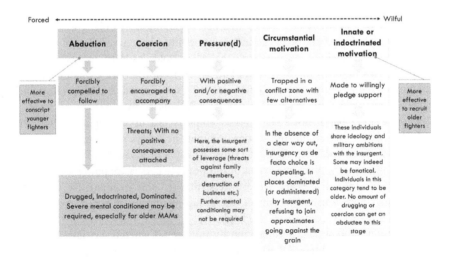

Figure 6.4 Boko Haram Participation Spectrum. Credits: Olonisakin (2004), Mercy Corps (2016, 12).

more success. A chief example of one such location was Gwoza, which Boko Haram captured, defended and administered – even passing laws and enforcing them within the town. However, even within such strongholds and in the urban spaces that Boko Haram tended to contest more heavily, resilience building through task force battalions deployed by the Nigerian Army since 2015[5] forced Boko Haram to abandon these softer forms of influence that territorial control allowed it to exercise. Overreliance on persuasion, especially as the environment shifts from permissive to non-permissive due to COIN operations, may spell doom for the insurgent's recruitment drive. Ergo, other tools also had to be employed for Boko Haram to swell its ranks initially, and to replenish them as they depleted during hostilities.

Mixed motivations for Boko Haram fighters

Boko Haram recruits, on average, might well fit the profile of socio-economically hopeless and angry individuals, mostly male and frustrated enough to consider unlawful alternatives to their current state. Insurgency is an outlet for these frustrations, and there might even be some personal gain in it. One theory, for instance, holds that 'recruits must be paid, and their cost may be related to the income forgone by enlisting as a rebel. Rebellions may occur when foregone income is unusually low' (Collier and Hoeffler 2001, 4). In other words, recruits effectively make an informal cost-benefit calculation of joining the rebellion and, if the 'benefit' of joining is greater than the 'cost' of leaving their present economic circumstance, they are more likely to enlist. There is a ring of truth to this popularized greed-grievance model when applied within Boko Haram's insurgency.

Boko Haram fighters have indeed been known to enjoy certain 'comforts' within their camp settings. Access to laptop computers, generators for electricity, meals – no matter how modest, places to sleep, hard drugs (more on this soon) and camaraderie are all available in their camps (Schneider 2015b, Hinshaw and Parkinson 2016). Some of these are non-operational 'luxuries' that fighters are unlikely to have access to for 'free', without being part of Boko Haram's group setting. There have been, for instance, reports of Apple MacBook Air notebooks, as well as stolen 'gadgetry', provided within Boko Haram camps. In this way, 'boys kidnapped from mud-brick homes came to live amid satellite internet terminals, flat-screen TVs, walkie-talkies, refrigerators and kitchens run by diesel generators' (Hinshaw and Parkinson 2016).

On the other hand, Boko Haram also employs fear as a weapon of coercion and control; 'for even minor infractions, militants beat boys nearly unconscious or denied them food and sleep for days' (Hinshaw and Parkinson 2016). Boko Haram may no longer possess the same extent of soft power – persuasive power – employed in the group's formative years. Nevertheless, through this manipulative approach that employs both fear and incentives, the group retains a viable pathway towards maintaining scores of 'committed' child fighters.

Over time, moreover, it becomes mostly immaterial whether (1) false financial incentives seduced fighters, (2) they were abducted or (3) they bought into Boko Haram's ideology and wilfully joined the insurgency. All three sets of individuals ultimately get conditioned for violence and violent conduct. All three may feel increasingly trapped as they realize the true nature of the group, and all three may find it just as tricky, once locked in, to escape Boko Haram's clutches.

Still, let us not be so focused on this idea that every Boko Haram fighter is a trapped young boy who just wants to go home. Some fighters may well relish the prospects of going out to raid to earn additional economic benefits, through loot for instance (Schneider 2015b). Indeed, the common criminal idiom, which holds that 'crime pays', influences the behaviour of Boko Haram raid participants. One Boko Haram fighter, for instance, claimed that 'he was paid just 30,000 naira ($150) for the attack [on Kolofata]' (Schneider 2015b). Payments of that nature may act as a real incentive for many fighters to willingly stay. Some fighters may no longer have homes to go back to, after all, either because Boko Haram destroyed their homes or because such individuals may be identified as militants and set upon by vigilantes. In such instances, the results of fighters' informal cost-benefit calculations are likely to favour staying with the insurgency rather than returning home.

Despite such factors as considered above, economic incentives or selection of the least bad option are not the only reasons why Boko Haram fighters stay and fight or even to enlist in the first place. Rather than just 'greed' or 'grievance', therefore, a third explanation – coercion – further explains why Boko Haram, as the insurgency matured, retained significant numbers of its fighters and indeed added more recruits to its ranks.

Other reasons for participation

Since coerced individuals tend to fit the same profile as those who wilfully join insurgency, this makes it all the harder to separate the 'accidental guerrilla', who is a circumstantial insurgent, from the voluntary recruit with a calculated interest in participation (Kilcullen 2009). This spectrum of participation, therefore, should be interpreted with some caution insofar fighter motivations are not necessarily discrete. Coerced Boko Haram militants, for instance, may nonetheless have some intrinsic motivation to either join the insurgency or to remain with the collective once enlisted. Group setting and familial bonds (including marriages), as an example, may form. Unforeseen socio-economic opportunities could also emerge *in situ*, which for recruits would cease to be an option if they leave from the Boko Haram group setting and attempt a return to former lives (Mercy Corps 2016).

Moreover, even those who joined Boko Haram voluntarily, being initially persuaded by its anti-*boko* idea system, may over time – through being drugged and mentally conditioned – lack the psychological strength to quit and return to normal life even if they wanted to. In other words, whereas the extreme ends of the spectrum have 'abduction' and 'intrinsic motivation' as discrete pathways to participation on paper, in practice, these pathways may interact with one another in shaping the calculations of Boko Haram youth recruits. As Mercy Corps writes regarding this spectrum of participation, 'the paths that youth take to joining Boko Haram defy neat categories of "voluntary" and "forced"' (2016, 11).

As Boko Haram's insurgency matured and it became impractical for persuasion to dominate recruitment-based participation, kidnapping of both male and female minors became more frequent, although each plays different roles. An exception lies in Boko Haram's use of both sexes in suicide bombings (more of this in Chapter 8). Even so, kidnapped females typically are not deployed in frontline roles for Boko Haram, although in rare instances women featured in raids and 'were sometimes tasked with burning homes during attacks' (Mercy Corps 2016, 15). By and large, and notwithstanding these exceptions during raids, kidnapped women and minors were, initially at least, a lot more likely to be married or sold off. It is unlikely that Boko Haram forcibly recruits women, so they become fighters-in-waiting. Rather, away from frontline roles like their male counterparts, women 'were most often confined to cleaning and cooking in the context of forced marriage' (Mercy Corps 2016, 15).

Female minors and younger women were less likely than men to join the insurgency voluntarily, even though such individuals sometimes stayed on wilfully, even where presented with the opportunity to leave (Matfess 2017a). Male juveniles, young men and even fathers could leave their parents, extended families and wives to voluntarily recruit for Boko Haram. Wives and daughters, on the other hand, were unlikely to leave either their parents and husbands and sign up with Boko Haram. With a lot more males wilfully participating or forced to fight, it follows, therefore, that male youths remain more likely to be used for active duty, in overt or covert roles (Hinshaw and Parkinson 2016, Mercy Corps 2016).

Overall, as an aggregate of both male and female members within the mature insurgency, 'about half of the youth were coerced or pressured to join, or perceived joining Boko Haram as the least bad option to address a challenge given their circumstances' (Mercy Corps 2016, 12). The situation earlier in Boko Haram's life cycle, by contrast, saw youth more likely to join because Boko Haram's ideology had a lower price and individuals were more likely to be persuaded under such circumstances. As Boko Haram got desperate in its interactions with the population, coercion went beyond just social pressure, threats and strong-arming to include more extreme tactics.

Boko Haram's coercion mechanisms: Kidnapping

Mass kidnappings by Boko Haram became a dominant coercion mechanism around 2014 (J. Hill 2014). Before then there had been kidnappings, both in north-east Nigeria and around its border areas, but in addition to being much smaller in scale – foreign individuals or small groups of people tended to be victims – there was little indication that these incidents were anything but a cash grab: an attempt to monetize insecurity. Moreover, kidnappings in the broader subregion around and beyond the north-east frontier hitherto appeared more connected to the short-lived offshoot movement, Ansaru, rather than to Boko Haram *per se* (Comolli 2015).

It was the Chibok mass Kidnappings of April 2014 that generated considerably more local and international threat awareness of this evolving tactic (The BBC 2014b), although other less-publicized mass kidnappings have occurred since. In the town of Damask, for instance, captured by Boko Haram in 2014, over 300 students were separated from their parents and sequestrated for months in classrooms, under the supervision of older Boko Haram members who attacked the town. Almost all the victims were boys, and minors aged no more than seven, with the oldest no more than seventeen. This incident appeared to be a pre-planned attempt to hastily recruit a large number of new members, *in situ*. The boys were eventually taken away, unceremoniously, by Boko Haram (Hinshaw and Parkinson 2016).

Such incidents are not out of place, according to other child soldiers who left Boko Haram (Hinshaw and Parkinson 2016). They just have not gathered as much attention as the Chibok Kidnapping. Male minors kidnapped in this way, some no more than their early teens, eventually are likely to play active roles, in combat or combat support areas, for Boko Haram. Chapters 7 and 8 discuss such themes.

As a final point, this phenomenon of child combatants within Boko Haram's rank and file army is one that has spread beyond north-east Nigeria. In Cameroon, for instance, 'children have now become something to fear' within local communities terrorized by Boko Haram (Hinshaw and Parkinson 2016).

Drug abuse and addiction as coercion, manipulation (control) and inhibition removal mechanisms

It is, however, crucial to note that – by ex-Boko Haram combatant accounts and indeed by the account of military personnel who interact with these individuals – minors who play frontline roles within the conflict tend to be drugged, indoctrinated over time and not necessarily in control of their actions. Colonel Dier Badjeck of the Cameroonian Army cites an example where hundreds of boys, conscripted by Boko Haram, once ran screaming at an army position. 'Many of them barefoot and unarmed and most were swiftly gunned down [...] Soldiers found in many of their pockets packaging from the opiate tramadol' (Hinshaw and Parkinson 2016). This idea of Boko Haram members in drug-induced states and possibly even 'high' on narcotics is scarcely a new phenomenon. Military and police task force personnel in Maiduguri as far back as 2012 noted that Boko Haram camps often had syringes, leftover hard drugs including opiates and sex-enhancing drugs such as Viagra.

Indeed, the Nigerian military and security forces in Maiduguri[6] painted Boko Haram in less than flattering light. To them, Boko Haram was not some model religious sect with a strict and exemplary moral compass; that was the movement's created myth. For the military and security personnel who came to know and understand this enemy, the reality of Boko Haram was that the so-called jihadists were depraved, drug-addicted sociopaths who did not conform to the high moral standards their false religious doctrines suggested.

The point of drug use, in particular, primarily overlooked within the debate on the internal workings of Boko Haram, requires further examination. Substance abuse within Boko Haram's ranks was not just the antithesis to Boko Haram's supposed morality. Instead, Boko Haram's use of narcotics also highlighted a tactical use in the insurgency. Substance abuse appeared systematic and employed to enhance some abnormal battlefield behaviours exhibited by Boko Haram fighters, specifically a lack of inhibition to violence. On a similar note, the Civilian Joint Task Force (CJTF), a paramilitarized collective of local amateur vigilante groups that has metastasized within the military effort against Boko Haram (Omeni 2017), has likewise been accused of drug abuse. CJTF members have admitted to misuse of the opiate-like drug,

Tramadol (NSRP 2017). Substance abuse could explain the extreme and uninhibited violence that the CJTF has sometimes displayed against suspected Boko Haram members. There is no conclusive evidence linking substance abuse and uninhibited violence by CJTF, but there have been uninhibited displays of violence on a scale that suggests drug-abused fighters. On 1 November 2014, as an example, CJTF vigilantes beheaded forty-one Boko Haram suspected members and subsequently mounted their heads on pikes (Marama 2014). Such behaviour is as abnormal as Boko Haram's own extreme displays of violence. Now, some of those who conducted these beheadings and similar acts of extreme violence in the north-east conflict may well have been violent sociopaths expressing themselves by being militants. However, uninhibited behaviour as a direct consequence of drug abuse also cannot be ruled out.

Substance abuse: OxyContin, cannabis and other substances

Nigerian Army reports have listed the narcotic analgesic, OxyContin (Oxycodone), as a substance recovered from Boko Haram (Odunsi 2016). OxyContin is not illegal in Nigeria. However, it requires a prescription as it is a common abuse substance. As a class of drug within the opioid analgesic family, OxyContin changes the way the brain and nervous system respond to pain. Simply put, the drug significantly reduces sensitivity to pain thus lowering the pain threshold. It also inhibits anxiety and provides a narcotic 'high', effectively feelings of euphoria (although its effects vary across individuals). For these reasons, OxyContin is highly addictive amongst substance abusers.

3 Division, Nigerian Army also confiscated large quantities of more widely available abuse substances in the Geidam area of Yobe State. This incident occurred in September 2015. 'Cannabis (Indian Hemp), Chlorofone substance (AKA Madaran suck and die) and Tramol [Tramadol]' were amongst the seized substances, according to the Army's statement (Mutum 2015).

Drug abuse: Tramadol

Tramadol in particular, 'a synthetic opioid-like drug used as a painkiller', is already illegally abused by jihadist combatants in Libya. Moreover, in Syria, 'it is widely seen as fuelling the conflict [...] as the drug has generated millions of dollars in revenue and has been used by combatants' (The BBC 2017).

Referred to as 'jihad pills', Tramadol is used 'by jihadist fighters as a stimulant and to heighten resistance to physical stress'. Specific to Boko Haram's case, a March 2017 report by British Council Nigeria and the Nigeria Stability and Reconciliation Programme (NSRP) found evidence of Tramadol abuse within Boko Haram's ranks. Specifically, the report notes that JAS [*Jama'atul ahl alsunnah li da'awati wal jihad*, or Boko Haram], 'had targeted drug users for recruitment during its early days. Use of tramadol, an over-the-counter painkiller that is related to morphine and other opiates, was said to be rampant in JAS ranks and was perceived by many interviewees to have played a role in enabling atrocities ... ' (NSRP 2017). Boko Haram's child soldiers have also been reported to frequently abuse both Tramadol and marijuana (Schneider

2015b). By targeting vulnerable existing drug users to join its rank and file and, also, by using hard drugs and opiates to condition the minds of rank and file, Boko Haram fighters are made obedient to the point of death and numb to horrific acts of violence. This approach is part of a system of psychological indoctrination that normalizes the extreme violence perpetrated by Boko Haram's fighters. Over time, as substance addiction is normalized, these fighters look forward to drug sessions with peers in camps where such abuse is widespread (NSRP 2017).

Use of drugged minors in battle situations is also a tactical weakness for Boko Haram

Now, on the one hand, use of drugged up minors as fighters has helped Boko Haram maintain a semblance of an army of irregulars, even after years of being degraded by Nigerian military COIN operations. On the other, the use of minors for combat purposes also reveals tactical weaknesses that can be exploited by opposing forces.

Take the case of Cameroon's military response to Boko Haram's threat around the Mandara axis, where Boko Haram came to hold territory. In Chapter 5, reference was made to BIR's eight-week sniper course and its relevance in helping forward sniper teams destabilize Boko Haram's battlefield coordination. Where older and experienced walkie-talkie bearing commanders can be identified and neutralized, the remaining inexperienced minors have little chance of fighting skilled Cameroonian forces. These exposed minors, typically in drug-induced states, could either stand and attempt to fight or flee the battlefield (Schneider 2015a). In such situations, it becomes clear that use of coerced and drugged up minors, or even minors who are highly motivated by other economic incentives, may yield a poor return on Boko Haram's human investment.

Boko Haram's coercion mechanisms: Psychological conditioning

Faced with a string of empty promises made by Boko Haram, youth in its ranks have often been 'left disillusioned, whether because the violent tactics were too extreme or because their expectations were not met' (Mercy Corps 2016, 15). To control the disillusioned within its rank and file, Boko Haram has, therefore, employed substance abuse, illegal highs and hard drugs. However, these are not the only control mechanisms in play. Recruits are kept in check through a methodical process of indoctrination by psychological conditioning. The aim is likely to entirely desensitize fighters, even very young ones, to the horrors of war. Especially combined with drug abuse, such psychological conditioning is a potent control tool – one that makes young fighters more malleable, less sensitive to battlefield chaos and killing. Furthermore, conditioned fighters become less inhibited in displaying violence.

There are some ways by which young fighters over time become psychologically conditioned. For instance, 'Boko Haram tries to collect the bodies of their militants slain in action … [and] use children around the age of 11 on the frontline to collect these corpses' (Schneider 2015b). This intentional exposure of children to mutilated human corpses is likely to have a major psychological impact on how such individuals conduct themselves when tasked with violence. To further accelerate the transition from innocent child recruit to cold-blooded murderers, children in Boko Haram camps are also said to be 'brutalised from an early age' and encouraged to mete out similar violence to others. Indeed, in one instance, the grotesque account was given 'of a 9-year-old who had beheaded a victim' (Schneider 2015b). Stories have likewise been told, by escaped Boko Haram child members, that 'dozens' of boy fighters are made to watch public beheadings within the camps and told not to 'have feelings about it' (Hinshaw and Parkinson 2016).

The actions above are consistent with studies by on the exploitation of child soldiers by armed groups (Olonisakin 2004). Not only do rebels wilfully expose minors to the horrors of war from a very early age, but child soldiers are also exposed to violence in popular culture, such as movies, so they can aspire to enact such 'heroic' behaviour (Olonisakin 2004, 247). Testing this theory in the case of Boko Haram, we see that militants 'encouraged boys to watch American war movies: 'They cheer for the U.S. soldiers, actually [...] They say these are the kinds of things they want to replicate' (Hinshaw and Parkinson 2016).

Summary

From the preceding, it could be surmised that especially where younger fighters are concerned, there are complex social and psychological factors that influence recruits' calculations around participation in insurgency. Whereas for child recruits brought into a perpetrator group, there is likely to be some enduring excitement attached with 'empowerment' around the use of a weapon, this attraction is less relevant to the adult fighter. Indeed, the price on average for supporting Boko Haram has come to be so high, that fewer adults than ever are likely to pay it willingly. The population, however, remains the lifeblood of insurgency. If the insurgent cannot persuade or otherwise exploit locals in his campaign, he cannot hope to achieve his strategic goals, and he is doomed to eventual failure. So, if adults refuse to join his campaign wilfully, the insurgent must find ways to redress this issue or face even worse odds against government forces.

If the insurgent cannot persuade the crowds through ideology like he used to, and if unable to entice common folk through economic incentives, then he may decide to drastically lower the age of participation and abduct, coerce, drug and psychologically condition a new generation of young and under-aged irregulars. Indeed, this is a potent strategy that insurgents in sub-Saharan Africa have used effectively for decades (Olonisakin 2004). Boko Haram is just one in a long line of rebel groups in the region who have exploited the child soldier. Moreover, there are operational benefits, for the insurgent who looks to the child fighter as a staple of his rank and file.

Compared to adults, child recruits and young minors are more likely to be exploited with flimsier promises and comforts and are easier to control and keep 'trapped' within the group setting, once enlisted (Olonisakin 2004). Over time, with constant drug abuse, psychological conditioning and punitive measures for those who attempt to escape, such dysfunctional group settings become normalized. An audience this young, we should remember, is significantly more malleable. Recruits' initial despair turns to resignation, resignation to acceptance. The social, economic and political environment where these recruits come from is also important to this transitioning. If the socio-economic environment is poor, if good governance is virtually non-existent, and if hopelessness is all such recruits have known, then the insurgency option may dominate recruits' informal cost-benefit calculations.

Stockholm syndrome

Additionally, for some abductees, after several months or even years of being subjected to extreme psychological conditioning and with little or no prospects of returning to home, Stockholm syndrome – the emotional dependence and bonding between captive and captor, often due to abuse and intimidation – becomes a real possibility. Abductees stop seeing senior Boko Haram members as captors but rather as benefactors with whom to be sympathized and cooperated. Consequently, the notion that former captives-turned-fighters would easily give up their Boko Haram captors should the opportunity present itself may not be entirely accurate.

This decision to support the insurgency, despite being its victims, applies to male abductees who eventually become fighters. Just as much, however, the same could be said of female abductees who wilfully stayed with Boko Haram, even when given the option to leave (Nwaubani 2017). For instance, some females captured by Boko Haram, even when rescued by the Nigerian military, preferred to rejoin the insurgency and the insurgents. Moreover, as has been pointed out, 'there certainly are women who deploy as suicide bombers, who have agreed to do so' (Matfess 2017a). For Boko Haram, this idea that captives could voluntarily invest in the group setting, if not in its ideology *per se*, creates an unintended opportunity whereby coercion mechanisms could potentially be relaxed or made entirely redundant, whereas control of some recruits stays uncompromised. For state forces countering insurgency, and indeed for the government, it is a horrifying prospect that even when given the option to leave the insurgency, some recruits voluntarily stay on and support it.

Final notes

It would appear as though the chapter's analysis stacks the odds in the insurgent's favour and there is indeed much that tends to favour the insurgent who goes irregular. Such an insurgent avoids pitched battle. He frustrates the government's conventional forces, and circumvents rather than engages, except perhaps in highly favourable contact scenarios such as ambush and counter-ambush settings. This insurgent's likelihood of battlefield defeat reduces because, to begin with, he tends not to engage and is flexible. Where he loses adult fighters, he recruits children. If his armour and artillery units are destroyed, he shifts to martyrdom operations. If dislodged from the urban space, he fights a bush war. If his orbit is perceived to be waning, he conducts a bombing in a far out area to remind of his strategic threat. Such an insurgent, therefore, is better situated to protract his military campaign, compared to if he fought a conventional war. A protracted war, moreover, is not in the incumbent's favour. Indeed, it runs counter to the counsel of Chinese General and military strategist, Sun Tzu, where he cautions that it is hard to see 'any skill in lengthy campaigns. No country has ever profited from protracted warfare' (2003, 21).

Consequently (as Chapter 9 of this volume later discusses), there is a real counter-insurgency challenge here. Militaries, especially those of developing countries, must come to accept that, faced with the complexities of irregular warfare, they will likely struggle against insurgency. The state military's capabilities, even where superior, will not matter as much here; most of its equipment and matériel cannot be employed in the determination. The shrewd insurgent, moreover, despite sophisticating as the conflict matures, will avoid battle and exploit features of the environment to lower asymmetry and protract war. Unless it suits him, and even then, rarely, he will not engage at scale. This is the insurgent's way. Boko Haram's military campaign in the Nigeria case is no different. Part Three of the book, which follows, discusses this campaign. This next section of the volume shows that Boko Haram's military ambitions led it over the years to prosecute a campaign on two fronts. The first of these is a covert front with a strong emphasis on tactical goals and immediate terror. The second is an overt front with a strong emphasis on long-term strategic goals and territoriality.

Part Three

Boko Haram's Military Campaign

A Resilient Threat: Boko Haram's Military and Organizational Sophistication

Introduction

Part Three of this volume conducts a military-focused analysis of Boko Haram's insurgency. This threat has sometimes been covert: small enough and clandestine enough to altogether avoid the Nigerian Army, thereby frustrating the latter's traditional military advantages. However, Boko Haram's threat, for entire phases of the insurgency, has also been overt: large enough to employ 'swarming' tactics that have overwhelmed even hardened Nigerian Army formations – forcing them into a tactical retreat. Within Chapter 7's meditation, this insurgent-side analysis of the north-east Nigeria conflict is combined with counter-insurgent-side reflections on how the Nigerian military has tried, failing sometimes and succeeding at others, to counter Boko Haram's increasingly sophisticated tactics.

Analysis within this chapter[1] builds on previously discussed broad themes from Parts One and Two of the volume. Part One of this volume emphasized the role of leaders and influential individuals within Boko Haram's organizational structure. The start of this chapter takes a look at that structure from an operational lens. The evaluation then shifts to how the Nigerian military's 'decapitation'-focused approach at one time aimed to dismantle and degrade Boko Haram's organizational structure by placing operational emphasis on the killing or capture of Boko Haram senior leaders, influential figures and high-value targets (HVTs). The limited success of this top-down decapitation strategy circa 2012, however, necessitated a bottom-up approach that was task force and intelligence based. This approach has since been replaced by a land warfare model that emphasizes the deployment of Task Force Brigades (Omeni 2017) and Mobile Strike Teams[2] to deter and repel Boko Haram's territorial ambitions, respectively.

Likewise, Part Two of this book focused on 'environment' and analysed how different connotations of it had certain force-multiplier effects for Boko Haram's insurgency. Building on this theme, Chapters 7 and 8 discuss how specific tactics, within specific phases of the insurgency, have exploited various aspects of the physical environment to create a more favourable operational environment.

The chapter also evaluates Boko Haram's military capabilities and details the process of how its standing army, driven by these capabilities, came to pose a phased threat between 2013 and 2015 in particular. This was a period when Boko Haram's offensives employed a larger-than-usual number of fighters within its standing army, and thus coincided with a period when military fighting dominated the insurgency in north-east Nigeria. Whereas literature is abundant on Boko Haram's histories and the impact of its insurgency on north-east Nigeria, analysis of Boko Haram's military campaigning is still deficient. Attempting to fill this gap, Chapter 7 of this volume uses field findings and battlefield case studies from north-east Nigeria to highlight how Boko Haram's overt front – its standing army – came to supplant its guerrilla operations as the main security threat to the frontier area.

This pivot towards military fighting, for a group initially composed of a few ragtag combatants, on the surface might seem surprising. Yet, whereas Boko Haram may lack the popular support required for 'people's war', classic insurgency theories nevertheless hold some explanatory power for this deliberate shift: away from guerrilla warfare as the expedient of the weaker side, and towards the use of a large standing army of locals to swarm, and sometimes successfully overrun, government forces.

Background to military fighting in north-east Nigeria

Boko Haram's insurgency, which began in north-east Nigeria but also came to affect the neighbouring countries of Chad, Niger and Cameroon, remains one of the deadliest conflicts in the Chad Basin subregion of West Africa. Over the years, the nature of Boko Haram's threat as shifted – away from motorized infantry forces as the backbone of a territory-seeking armed force, and towards suicide bombings and a covert threat more consistent with guerrilla warfare.

At the heart of Boko Haram's threat, therefore, lies its ability to operate on two fronts. Boko Haram's overt front, effectively its standing army of irregulars, has been instrumental to its territory-seeking strategy, a strategy that greatly expanded between the later months of 2014 and early 2015. Here, bandolier and assault rifle-wielding fighters, and light motorized infantry columns facilitated a demonstrable pivot towards military fighting. Where this standing army has been strong, Boko Haram has demonstrated a credible territorial ambition. A covert front, on the other hand, drives Boko Haram guerrilla terrorist threat, while prosecuting a doctrine of war avoidance. This front does not seek to hold territory or gain strategic ground. Instead, it is for the most part employed as a psychological weapon, a reminder not only that Boko Haram has given war avoidance a new meaning in Nigerian conflict but also that it can still project its threat further than its typical strongholds. Moreover, guerrilla tactics as part of insurgency generally are the expedient of the weaker side, and so, Boko Haram has reverted to such covert tactics at times when it has gotten the worst of military fighting (such as after significant territorial losses).

Boko Haram's covert operations have emphasized *istishhad* (martyrdom operations) mostly, since 2011. However, by 2014, the tactic had matured. Improvised explosive devices (IEDs) now caused more casualties, and as for the question of detection, young boys and increasingly girls, booby-trapped as suicide bombers, posed a threat to any location that was not heavily barricaded and/or operated by tactical assets aimed explicitly at recognizing the suicide bomber. In 2017, this threat further evolved to include individuals who masqueraded as pregnant or nursing mothers.

The actual number of operatives across both fronts is tricky to ascertain. The broad demographic of fighters may be easier to identify, however. For instance, Boko Haram's rank and file within its overt front is dominated by military-aged males (MAMs). Combat roles for female operatives are atypical; however, studies by Warner and Matfess indicate that Boko Haram female operatives who do feature in covert roles tend to be of a lower average age than their male counterparts (Warner and Matfess 2017).

That Boko Haram operates on two fronts, switching between both or using them simultaneously, has complicated the Nigerian Army's counter-insurgency (COIN) campaign. Boko Haram's covert front emphasizes guerrilla warfare and terrorist tactics such as bombings, kidnappings and early-dawn raids. Conversely, Boko Haram's overt front – its standing army – emphasizes strategic objectives including territoriality and counter-denial of the Nigerian Army's localized presence. When capabilities and conditions on the ground favoured a territory-seeking strategy, the overt front has played the lead role. Examples here are the periods around late 2013, and then between late 2014 and January 2015. The formation of several new task force battalions, deployed in forward areas, has been an effective hard counter to this threat, by mid-2015.

However, during the periods Boko Haram's overt front has been degraded, or where the Nigerian military has too strong of a presence, Boko Haram has dispersed its overt front and has dramatically lowered conflict intensity (think: ambushes on small convoys, rather than frontal assaults on brigade HQs). Or, in such scenarios, it has avoided the engagement altogether, focusing instead on martyrdom operations. At such times, between 2010 and 2013 for instance, and again since mid-2015, Boko Haram's covert front became the tactical fulcrum of its operations.

Since 2015 precisely, when the holding of territory has become problematic, a spate of suicide bombings and mining of areas with IEDs has impeded the ground troops' COIN progress. This was an indication that Boko Haram was, once again, reverting to guerrilla warfare as its main plank of operations, marking a pivot away from military fighting and territory-seeking activity. To combat this shift to guerrilla tactics (such as in Boko Haram's observed rigging of highways with IEDs), expensive minesweeping equipment, such as autonomous vehicles, has sometimes required induction in the theatre. The progress recorded by government forces in some areas, such as in the heavily mined areas of Alargano, is one example (Omeni 2017, 211, 218).

For war planners, however, having to frequently adapt to Boko Haram's evolving insurgency – by inducting new equipment, deploying more troops to more outfield locations, setting up new campaign tasks, conducting new forms of training, and near-constantly adjusting the scope and ambition of projects taken on within the COIN – is both exhausting and resource-intensive. Boko Haram, on the other hand, has proved a lot more adept at shape-shifting its tactics over the years. This relational dynamic invariably favours Boko Haram and puts the Nigerian Army under operational strain: forcing troops to dabble in untraditional roles they typically would not (and at which they might not be excellent, to begin with). Government forces, as a result, have explored other campaign methods to degrade Boko Haram that can accelerate campaign pace. One such approach relates to COIN operations aimed specifically at degrading Boko Haram's organizational structure. Even here, however, there are problems for Nigeria's military and security forces. To better appreciate this operational challenge of weakening Boko Haram's organizational structure, we should, to begin with, take a closer look at Boko Haram's organization.

Understanding Boko Haram's organizational network and command structure

Boko Haram's ability to switch between different forms of doctrine, from territory seeking to war avoidance and vice versa, has confounded the Nigerian Army. To counter this shape-shifting threat, the Army has been forced to allocate inordinate amounts as it attempts to pre-empt the possibility of various forms of attacks – by either front or a combination of both, across hundreds of kilometres of urban and rural space. Within both fronts, however, fighters do not retain individual agency. Contrary to what some might assume, Boko Haram fighters are not a bunch of uncontrolled 'riffraff' running unorganized in the countryside. Rather, both Boko Haram fronts exist within a loosely defined but identifiable organizational and command structure (Ahmed 2012).

Boko Haram's fighters function in a hierarchy and command structure which, although organized, may not have strict command and control. This lack of tight control as the organization flattened out over the years could help explain the number of splinter factions emergent throughout the group's history. Nevertheless, fighters within factions follow decision-making from the top, which is passed down from a council via commanders in a hierarchical process discussed below.

There is less bureaucracy than expected in a group of this size, and decision-making is generally streamlined; this is mostly down to the authoritarian style of Abu Shekau and contrasts what was described as a group with 'diffuse organisation and leadership', under Yusuf (International Crisis Group 2014, 18–19). A top-down view of Boko Haram, for instance, indicates that:

> It is formally led by an amir ul-aam (commander in chief) with a Shura (council) of trusted kwamandoji (commanders in Hausa) that is its highest decision-making body. The amir ul-aam cannot speak for the group without Shura approval. In major cities and towns where the group has a presence, a local amir is in charge, beside a commander who oversees and coordinates armed operations. Depending on his influence, the commander may be a Shura member. He is assisted by a nabin, (deputy), who is in turn aided by a mu'askar, who passes orders from the commander and the deputy to foot soldiers. Cities and large towns are divided into lajna (sectors) supervised by sub-amirs for operational and administrative purposes. (International Crisis Group 2014, 18–19)

Decapitation: Target-based weakening of Boko Haram's command structure in Nigeria

The emphasis on town and city-specific networks is critical to understanding how the above structure works, insofar as Boko Haram operates a cell-based network within municipalities. This contrasts the group's presence in rural areas where large camps with fighters who live, eat, train and conduct operations together exist – or at least existed in the past. Within larger towns and cities such as Maiduguri, a local amir would likely know some details of individual cells as well as the larger cell-based objectives of the Boko Haram presence in his area. Consequently, the killing or capture of such individuals designated as extremely HVTs, at a time at the task force level, was amongst the highest operational priority for Army intelligence and for the Department of State Services – Nigeria's domestic intelligence agency. HVT targeting is otherwise known as 'decapitation': the tactic of targeting leaders and HVTs within perpetrator groups to deny, deter, degrade and dismantle the organization. Successful mapping and persistent surveillance of a town-based terrorist network could lead to the identification of a local amir, influential militant figure or similar HVT within a Boko Haram cell. This, in turn, could lead to the killing or capture of such individuals, an event that Nigeria's military and security forces would present as a huge blow to Boko Haram's military campaign.

The theory to support this idea that decapitation works, appears compelling (Johnson and Sarbahi 2016). Figure 7.1, as an example, highlights research findings indicative of targeted killings' utility. There are, however, counter-arguments suggesting that even where successful, decapitation remains problematic. A range of issues underpins this target-based approach to degrading a terrorist organization. These include poor intelligence, which might lead to civilian collateral, political and humanitarian risks and blowback within Muslim communities particularly where such strikes, even where successful, lead to the deaths of civilians and non-combatants, too (D. Byman 2009, Zenko 2012).

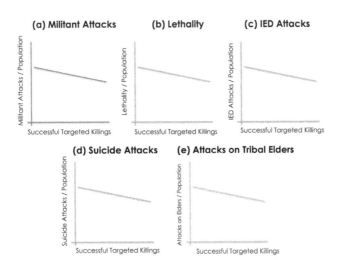

Figure 7.1 Substantive Effect of Successful Targeted Killings. Adapted from: Johnson and Sarbahi (2016, 203–219, 214)

Has Decapitation Degraded Boko Haram's Terrorist Network?

Nevertheless, within the Nigerian military's COIN campaign over the years, there is evidence to suggest this target-based approach to degrading Boko Haram has been met with some success: that is, amirs, commanders and a range of HVTs have indeed been killed or captured within the insurgency. Trickier to substantiate within the Nigeria case, however, is the impact of successful decapitation on reductions in insurgency-related violence. There is no clear correlation between any reduction in casualties and the successful targeting of Boko Haram's most senior commanders and influential figures around the same periods. This, however, is not to say that successful decapitation does not ever impact Boko Haram's ability to conduct violent attacks.

In 2012, as an example, interview data for this book, from the Office of the National Security Advisor (ONSA) indicated that targeting of HVTs has yielded a trove of information for the COIN effort, particular in the first two years of the government's inaugural COIN effort (Bello 2012). Such actionable intelligence led to COIN gains and, by inference, losses by Boko Haram. In other instances, the elimination of an HVT directly contributed to a de-escalation of violence. One example would be the killing of Boko Haram's bombmaker in Maiduguri in 2012, which led to a lengthy period with little or no bombings in the city including an unusually quiet period of no bombings at all, throughout the December holidays (Omeni 2017). In other cases, such as in the capture on 3 April 2016 of Khalid al-Barnawi, the amir ul-aam of Ansaru, such target-based efforts have even led to the dismantlement of network-wide operations and strategic removal of particular threats.

Notwithstanding such apparent success stories, however, claims that decapitation has a measurable impact on the reduction of insurgency-related violence in Nigeria should be made cautiously. Indeed, insofar as sometimes it appears to exist, and yet, other times fails to, a substantive correlation remains tricky to determine. If, however, decapitation does not seem to be degrading Boko Haram's organizational structure (to the point where there is a demonstrable impact on its operations), there is an explanation.

Over the years, Boko Haram has become a flatter organization. This flattening out has led to more cells, more fighter units and, correspondingly, more commanders. As of mid-2017, as an example, whereas Shekau remained atop the organizational chart wire diagrams designed by the Nigerian Army, the Army was already on its third edition of 'Images of Most Wanted BHTs' [Boko Haram Terrorists], the published image charts of all the most wanted Boko Haram figures. With serial numbers on this third edition chat numbering over 240 for senior Boko Haram commanders alone, it was evident by 2017 that despite how many Boko Haram members had been killed or captured over the years, their ranks remained swollen. Now, it probably can be safely inferred, by the law of numbers, that such a large number of amirs and senior commanders within Boko Haram's organizational structure should mean that decapitation strategies as a whole are likely to yield more casualties or captures of senior commanders. On the other hand, overall quality (value) of HVTs killed or captured is also likely to reduce. This, in turn, would lead to less actionable information. As a result, the impact on Boko Haram's conflictual strategies might be even less substantive. Indeed, even when key figures are killed or captured at reasonably high rates within a short period, this has not appeared to have had a substantive impact on Boko Haram.

As some examples, on 11 June 2017, Abu Nazir, Boko Haram's appointed amir for Jrawa village, was killed. The Nigerian Army, in a press release, celebrated this as a significant win (Attahiru 2017), whereas Boko Haram did not even acknowledge Nazir's death. This event was similar to what occurred just months before, on 27 April 2017, when Abu Fatimah, one of Boko Haram's senior leaders on the Army's wire diagram and the group's most senior commander in the Buk – Talala – Ajigin axis, was targeted and killed by a Nigerian Army operation. Abu Fatimah's death was publicized by the Nigerian Army, which was quick to point out that, before his elimination, the terrorist was one of Abu Mus'ab al-Barnawi's three most trusted commanders (Attahiru 2017). Abu Fatimah was, therefore, part of the Shura council of the al-Barnawi faction of Boko Haram. Here again, however, Abu Fatimah's elimination, whereas celebrated by the Nigerian Army, was not even accorded a mention by either Boko Haram faction.

Similarly, when Mustapha Salihu, another high-profile Boko Haram target was arrested in March 2017, despite being a long-term suspect and featuring on the Army's wire chart, no real changes were seen after his capture, and neither faction recognized his arrests. Arrests of other high-profile Boko Haram members have also gone seemingly unnoticed by the group. Examples are the arrests of Kolo Adam, a Cameroonian as well as that of Matta Francois, a Chadian, both in April 2017 (Attahiru 2017).

That decapitation seems to be having such limited operational impact within the insurgency may well be an indication of the nature of Boko Haram's organizational structure today. In the past, when Boko Haram was younger, had a less flat structure and was less bureaucratized, such arrests and killings would likely have degraded the group's organizational structure at least to the point where some operational impact would be observable. Today, however? Probably less so. This situation, to some degree, is consistent with research by Jenna Jordan (2014) on the subject of why terrorist groups survive decapitation. For Jordan, bureaucratization (lateral freedom to act and operationalize, within perpetrator groups), as well as some local support, could make a group remain active even if it has been 'degraded' by the killing or capture of senior leaders, commanders and influential figures within the movement (2014). Older, larger and religious groups, moreover, are more likely to have these traits (bureaucratization and local popular support) than smaller or younger groups (Jordan 2014). Thus, an older and religiously based terrorist movement is more likely to be resilient: that is, more likely to resist 'decapitation'. This especially would be the case for a perpetrator group that has been active, and that so would have accrued operational experience and co-opted a range of irregular and conventional warfighting tactics within its operations. Such experience in older groups would not be centred on just one individual or a group of individuals. Over time, experiences are shared amongst several members in much the same way as the knowledge and adeptness at certain tactics is gradually disseminated across the group structure. Under such circumstances, successful decapitation, in most cases, may not substantively impact operations by the perpetrator group.

More to this point, Figure 7.2 shows that despite many senior Boko Haram figures being killed or captured over the years, there is no clear pattern in the casualty figures throughout the conflict. Decapitation's precise impact on this enemy's overall resilience remains unclear. This lack of correlation becomes all the more apparent when plotting the chart and viewing the monthly data,[3] too. Figure 7.3 does show a slightly more discernible pattern, whereby as of March 2019, casualties seem to be at an all-time low. Also, overall, there have been fewer casualties in 2019 (as of March), but even also in 2018, compared to 2017. Nevertheless, by the end of 2019, this trend may yet have been upset, and even if it is not, how much of this apparent reduction of Boko Haram's violence, if any part at all, should be credited to the Nigerian Army's decapitation strategy?

This is difficult to say, but it is unlikely that successful decapitation is playing much of a role here if any. Indeed, it may be difficult to say with certainty which particular COIN tactics have the greatest degradative effect on Boko Haram. For instance, it may be tempting to assume that the Army's expanded Mobile Strike Teams initiative had the most significant impact on the reduction of casualties since mid-2017 when the MSTs became operational. The timing certainly appears to fit. Nevertheless, a more realistic view is that any number of COIN-related efforts could have acted synergistically to reduce the impact of Boko Haram's violence over the same period.

Moreover, any observed reduction in violence could also be because the insurgent factions are either regrouping or simply planning offensives for later in the year. Lower incident numbers, such as indicated towards the ends of both Figure 7.2 and Figure 7.3, could also be because the insurgency has already displaced so many people in north-east Nigeria that Boko Haram, by this fact, may be running out of fully populated communities and areas to terrorize.

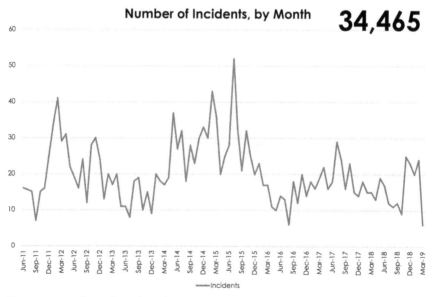

Figure 7.2 Total Number of Deaths, Monthly, in Boko Haram's Insurgency. Data Source: Nigeria Security Tracker[4]

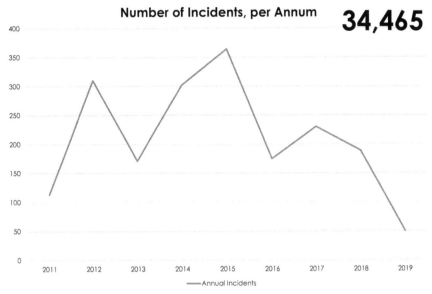

Figure 7.3 Total Number of Deaths, Annually, in Boko Haram's Insurgency. Data Source: Nigeria Security Tracker[5]

Also, even if successful decapitation can take credit for some of the reduction of violence, it is worth observing that, relative to the number of senior figures and commanders in Boko Haram,[6] the incidence of HVT captures or killings has been extremely low in Nigeria. Moreover, most of the killings or arrests outlined above came during a particular period when Operations DEEP PUNCH and RAWAN KADA by the Nigerian Army and with the assistance of the Multinational Joint Task Force (MNJTF) troops, were active.[7] Indeed, aside from such heavily manned operations tasked specifically with targeting and eliminating Boko Haram's senior leadership and fighters, HVTs, more often than not, are both difficult to locate and difficult to kill or capture. All this points to a likelihood that Boko Haram could stay resilient for the foreseeable future. After all this is a group that significantly escalated its military ambitions, just little past a year since its ranks were first decimated and its spiritual leader killed, in July 2009.

Dismantling Boko Haram's network via grassroots intelligence and Civil-Military Cooperation (CIMIC)

With the chances of constantly stumbling upon HVTs low, and the potential of actionable intelligence on such individuals not high enough, Boko Haram's command and organizational structure, as a result, appears unlikely to collapse on the strength of decapitation strategies alone. Notwithstanding if these strategies have been moderately successful. At a time, therefore, Boko Haram's terror network had to be pieced together differently and then dismantled bottom-up so to speak, using untraditional activities not typically associated with the Nigerian Army. It is worth looking at that time, at the methodology employed by the Nigerian military and security apparatus, and at the success of this methodology. This approach, after all, remains operational within the government's COIN effort.

Critical to this bottom-up approach, circa 2012 when the military first began putting together Boko Haram's organizational wire diagram was a military-led schema of a five-process plan, signed off by Defence Headquarters (DHQ) and supported by the Office of the National Security Adviser (ONSA). The schema is broken down as follows.

(1) Trust-building within vulnerable communities, as a prerequisite for actionable intelligence. Trust-building occurred via a range of processes. These included 'use of traditional leaders, community and religious leaders as well as patriotic legislators from Borno State to denounce Boko Haram in rallies and make regular broadcasts in local languages [including Kanuri, Hausa and, in some cases, Arabic]' (JTFC 2012). (2) A form of influence operations aimed at changing perceptions: negatively against Boko Haram and positively towards the Army and security services. Townhall meetings, outreaches and medical projects were the first steps. Then, over time, infrastructural initiatives became another plank of the civil-military cooperation (CIMIC) task here. One example was in the 'execution of quick impact projects by the relevant FG agencies to include medical facilities, boreholes, renovation of schools and construction of roads' (JTFC 2012). (3) A bounty-based incentives programme aimed at 'championing the use of bounty from the State Government to kill or arrest key Sect members'. Table 7.1 reproduces this bounty schema. (4) Network building involving a broad range of stakeholders: from clerics, influential community heads, state ministry parastatals (such as in the area of civil engineering and infrastructure works) the police, the Department of State Services (DSS) and military intelligence personnel *in situ*. (5) Intelligence Operations within the grassroots. This also involved, to various degrees of action, support or assistance, inter-agency government cooperation. This inter-agency effort included the Nigerian military and the Defence Intelligence Agency (military intelligence) at its nucleus, the DSS (domestic intelligence) and the ONSA. Insofar as I have previously researched with military intelligence personnel tasked with the COIN effort in 2012, I have extracted lengthy excerpts from fieldwork findings at the time. In particular, it is worth highlighting:

> [The] planning methodology known internally as the joint intelligence preparation of the operational environment (JIPOE). Initiated but also mostly managed within Battalion HQ, JIPOE involves contributions and close working between the staff branches of G2 (Intelligence) and G3 (Operations). The JIPOE includes collection, study, analysis and implementation of intelligence as part of a battle plan, such as a joint campaign plan (JCP). The JIPOE effectively allows the JTFC [Joint Task Force Commander] and his staff to penetrate and disrupt the enemy's decision-making cycle. In this context, threats and weaknesses, as well as available course of actions (CoAs), for both the enemy force and the JTFC's force, are used to facilitate a more robust planning and contingency process in the operating environment. Intelligence, surveillance and recce by the various military and non-military components, are critical to the JIPOE. (Omeni 2017, 152)

Take the case of the Boko Haram network in Maiduguri circa 2012, as an example. 2012 is an important year because it was the period within which the first wire diagram of Boko Haram's network was drawn up by the Nigerian military and security apparatus. 2012 also was the year when that wire diagram, and thus the Army's overall understanding of Boko Haram's network and command structure was greatly expanded (Omeni 2017, 152–153). Previous chapters within this volume also have discussed why Maiduguri remains the most important city within any narrative on Boko Haram. Whereas the city was at a low risk of a full-blooded thrust by Boko Haram circa 2012, due to the extent of military assets and combat-ready units within the municipality, there was always the risk of internal sabotage by Boko Haram cells already resident in the city. Maiduguri, therefore, had to be cleansed inside-out of the terrorist cells as well, if casualties in the city were to be kept to a minimum. This required an understanding by the Nigerian Army and its taskforce units: first, of what the city-specific Boko Haram network looked like was and second, of what individuals in particular needed to be removed to weaken or dismantle the network. Information from arrests and lucky breaks such as raids that yielded unexpected Boko Haram network details were certainly not off the table for the Army and security agencies. More than anything else, however, a grassroots intelligence initiative, driven by task-based multi-agency methodology, was the priority. To this end:

> Throughout 2012, civ–mil interactions which drove the [Army's Joint Intelligence Preparation of the Operational Environment] JIPOE[8] would gradually increase after failed Boko Haram attacks in Maiduguri earlier that year. These civ–mil interactions would bring together DSS, police and military intelligence personnel from HQ, JTF ORO [Joint Task Force Operation Restore Order].[9] With the help of local civilians, tactical intelligence teams would eventually construct a wire diagram detailing Borno State's 20-man insurgent network. This wire diagram will later increase to 100 men, and would be retranslated into various local sub-dialects. Intelligence for this exercise was entirely sourced from local civilians, having built on trust relations with military and security agency intelligence personnel. JTF ORO's tactical intelligence team, its Joint Intelligence Committee, in the latter half of 2012, would build a comprehensive understanding of the history of network members: names and familial connections; who had worked together; social relationships of network participants, and their roles in Boko Haram's cross-state networks in north-east Nigeria. Mapping of this nature, similar to the way the task force came to understand Boko Haram's Shura (its governing council) and the individuals on it, came about not by kinetics but by months of civ–mil interactions and painstaking intelligence activity by the tactical intelligence team (interviews in 2012 with Danmadami and JTF Intelligence Office, Suleiman). Precision targeting of individuals on that list, at company level, could then take effect because the targets were clearer and had been confirmed by local human intelligence sources. An example is the killing of Boko Haram's IED maker in 2012 and the detainment of many Boko Haram suspects by JTF ORO's [intelligence] component in the same period. (Omeni 2017, 152–153)

This bottom-up approach to unravelling Boko Haram's command structure also paid further dividends later that year (2012). In particular, the use of the JIPOE methodology by the Army-led joint task force in Borno, led to the elimination of a top-level commander in September 2012, and to the elimination of the group's bomb maker later that year. Local intelligence was also responsible for one of the Army's closest attempts at eliminating Shekau. Around 24 September 2012, Joint Task Force Operation Restore Order (JTF ORO) forces stormed a Boko Haram camp in Damaturu, and simultaneously, the military forces tried capturing Shekau at his home; also based on local intelligence. The was one of the closest the military has ever come to capturing Shekau, who:

> Had sneaked in the day before for the naming ceremony of his six-day-old baby. Fighting was fierce: 35 militants were killed and two soldiers injured. Shekau escaped, with a thigh wound; his wife and three children were taken into military custody. Three SUVs, seven laptops and a large arms cache reportedly were recovered from the house. Shekau was said to have been spirited to Gao, in northern Mali, when Islamist armed groups held it. This is one reason Nigerian troops were deployed to Mali in January 2013 to support the French Operation Serval that expelled Ansar Dine and the Movement for Oneness and Jihad in West Africa (MUJAO) from that country's northern cities. (International Crisis Group 2014, 19–20)

Table 7.1 Incentive-Based Approach to Influence Operations: Boko Haram Bounty Schema for the Nigerian Army (*c*. 2012)

RANK	NAME	REWARD	TARGET VALUE
1	Abubakar Shekau	N50,000,000 ($138,888.88)	Head/Shura
2	Habibu Yusuf (AKA Asalafi)	N25,000,000 ($69,444.44)	Operations/Shura
3	Khalid al-Barnawi	N25,000,000 ($69,444.44)	Shura
4	Momodu Bama	N25,000,000 ($69,444.44)	Shura
5	Mohammed Zangina	N25,000,000 ($69,444.44)	Shura
6	Abu Saad	N10,000,000 ($41,666.67)	Commander
7	Abba Kaka	N10,000,000 ($41,666.67)	Commander
8	Abdulmalik Bama	N10,000,000 ($41,666.67)	Commander
9	Umar Fulata	N10,000,000 ($41,666.67)	Commander
10	Alhaji Mustapha (Massa) Ibrahim	N10,000,000 ($41,666.67)	Commander

RANK	NAME	REWARD	TARGET VALUE
11	Abubakar Suleiman-Habu(AKA Khalid)	N10,000,000 ($41,666.67)	Commander
12	Hassan Jazair	N10,000,000 ($41,666.67)	Commander
13	Ali Jalingo	N10,000,000 ($41,666.67)	Commander
14	Alhaji Musa Modu	N10,000,000 ($41,666.67)	Commander
15	Bashir Aketa	N10,000,000 ($41,666.67)	Commander
16	Abba Goroma	N10,000,000 ($41,666.67)	Commander
17	Ibrahim Bashir	N10,000,000 ($41,666.67)	Commander
18	Abubakar Zakariya	N10,000,000 ($41,666.67)	Commander
19	Turkur Ahmed Mohammed	N10,000,000 ($41,666.67)	Commander

Anybody with relevant information should call the following GSM numbers: 080–64174066; 07085464012; 080154429346. Note: Informants' Identities Will Be Protected.

Military capabilities of Boko Haram's overt front

Within this chapter's analysis of Boko Haram's evolving military threat, however, it will be problematic to focus mainly on its leaders and commanders and the impact that their killing or capture will have within the Nigerian military's COIN effort. Low-level fighters and foot soldiers are, we must remember, the backbone of any land army. This is no different in the case of Boko Haram. So, have exactly have Boko Haram's rank and file featured in its military campaign? Moreover, how, along with other military capabilities, has this contributed to Boko Haram's overall threat sophistication? The answers to these questions should begin with a closer look at the capabilities of Boko Haram's rank and file, as the most fundamental representation of the insurgent's overt threat.

Fighters deployed in Boko Haram's overt front – its rank and file – are generally non-disabled[10] MAMs. Boko Haram's fighters are trained in the rudiments of soldiering and basic infantry tactics. This aspect of training is universal across the group's MAMs. Video evidence recovered by Nigerian security forces shows that even Abu Shekau himself, Boko Haram's leader since 2010, is not exempt from such tactical training lessons, or at least had them in the past (Bello 2012).

Training initially came from external terrorist groups, primarily in Somalia and Mali, but over time has localized. Research material obtained from the ONSA in 2012 for this project observes that Boko Haram 'has a strong affiliation to Islamic terror groups operating in N. Mali (Mujai, Ansar Deen and AQIM) for training, mentoring and financing' (ONSA 2012, 2). Further, 'elements of the Sect [Boko Haram] are well trained by AQIM and Al Shabaab in weapon handling, IED making, operational planning and execution, and media management' (ONSA 2012, 2).

Within this training exists some opportunity for specialization (such as the use of PSG-1 sniper rifles, recovered from the insurgents). Also, as with insurgencies elsewhere, such as Daesh's campaign in Iraq and Syria, pre-existing occupational skills are carried over. Mechanics, artificers, healers, cooks, carpenters, and huntsmen/trackers all feature in Boko Haram's ranks. Such duties are likely perfunctory to the males' primary function of foot soldiering, however.

These foot soldiers are the light infantry fighters of Boko Haram's backbone military. Typically, each carries a Kalashnikov (AK-47) assault rifle, and some carry bandoliers also. A few carry machetes or even simple sticks when part of large-scale offensives. This suggests a greater personnel-to-weapon ratio, although there might be other reasons (such as these individuals being part of the offensives simply to video proceedings, to ride *Okada*[11] with gun-wielding fighters on the passenger seats, to drive unarmoured technicals). Weapons are mostly seized from Nigerian and Cameroonian forces – Boko Haram videos show large caches of these weapons. However, the heavier guns do not always originate from local military and security forces. Fieldwork with military, police, and security forces in north-east Nigeria, strongly indicate a large amount of Boko Haram's heavier weapons and ordnance come all the way from post-Qaddafi Libya (Omeni 2017, 216).

There is also evidence from the ONSA detailing a broader cross-section of Boko Haram weapons at the unit level. These:

> Include AK 47 Assault Rifles, General Purpose Machine Guns, Rocket-propelled Grenades, Pistols, Light Machine Guns, telescopic Sight Sniper Rifles, Katyusha Rockets, Biological and Chemical capability (different types of poisons including cyanide), IED capability. The fall out of the Libyan crisis and the readily available Gaddafi's stockpiles has further boosted the group's arsenal. (ONSA 2012, 2)

At the section level, Boko Haram squads are a mix of machine gunners, rocket artillerymen (typically using the ubiquitous RPG-7 Rocket Launcher) and at the platoon level these are supported by motorized infantry (essentially gun-mounted Toyota Hilux vehicles, unarmoured technical and light armoured infantry fighting vehicles). Guns are vehicle-mounted using improvised mounts and could either be anti-air, general-purpose machine guns or even 23-mm twin-canons, with mount grips. Individual fighters are universally unkempt; most are poorly fed and do not carry the appearance of professionalized forces. Similarly, foot soldiers, for the most part, are without uniforms, regardless of the propaganda videos filmed by Boko Haram to suggest otherwise. It is likely such videos are engineered to over-embellish the professionalization and capabilities at unit and formation levels.

To this point, Boko Haram's light motorized infantry, when on the move, is not structured like the typical columned and highly regimented impedimenta of modern warfare. The lead vehicles, to begin with, have been captured old Soviet T-55 tanks and rinky-dink armoured personnel carriers (APCs), with other unarmoured technical punctuating these lines. Look closely, moreover, and the mobile warfare capabilities on display are even more modest. Boko Haram's convoys more closely resemble a bizarre assortment of private vehicles, Okada, 'mammy' wagons, cattle trucks. Fighters, within these ranks, are almost entirely clothed in civilian garments. Indeed, those with uniforms tend to be the exception as these are not issued within the ranks. Instead, killed Nigerian military personnel are stripped of their uniforms and arms. If you were Boko Haram soldier and you came across a dead Nigerian Army soldier wearing a helmet, that helmet became yours. This is in addition to the uniforms, equipment, platforms and hardware obtained via looting Nigerian Army locations during successful Boko Haram offensives. Despite these apparent shortcomings and limited overall capabilities, however, Boko Haram's light motorized infantry has been deceptively effective. These forces are the backbone, of Boko Haram's overt front, in the offence.

Armoured Fighting Vehicles (AFVs) and Main Battle Tanks (MBTs) complement motorized infantry elements where available. However, Boko Haram possesses very few of the former and even fewer of the latter, both of which often originate from Nigerian Army units, before capture by the insurgents. The low count of heavy armour means Boko Haram fighters need to be heavily supported by lighter armour and motorized infantry. Put another way, heavy armour does not support motorized infantry for Boko Haram because the group's modest armour and towed artillery capabilities mean that, within battlefield scenarios, it has to be the other way around. Support elements of Boko Haram's motorized infantry have as a backbone, unarmoured 'technicals'. These are technical pick-up trucks, improvised fighting vehicles, 6 × 6 transports, and smaller 4 × 4s with improvised/bolted-on heavy weapons mounts. Such 'technicals', including flatbed trucks, have increasingly been employed by armed groups, in Libya and Syria for instance, to tow heavier (and large amounts of) ordnance, as well as in the mounting of artillery guns, most typically the Soviet-era ZU-23–2. I examine elsewhere how Boko Haram came to possess some of its 'technicals' capabilities, and how it has improvised, and even innovated, in this area (Omeni 2017).

Boko Haram's light infantry – large numbers of fighters on foot, typically supported by nominal light motorized elements – have raided villages and towns, ambushed military patrols, and attacked small military outposts. However, the real test for Boko Haram's overt front came since 2014, in its willingness to initiate the engagement against more massive Nigerian Army formations at company (COY), Battalion (Bn) and Brigade (Bde) levels, respectively. For such larger offensives, the insurgent's motorized infantry described a little earlier takes the lead, with the light infantry acting as support elements.

Since 2011, Boko Haram's overt front capabilities have also been improved by small arms and light weapons (SALWs) obtained from Libya in 2011 after the fall of the dictator, Qaddafi. Boko Haram's irregulars also benefitted from foreign training in the past, likely from Al-Qaeda affiliates in the West and Horn regions of SSA (Omeni 2017). A train-the-trainer indirect approach that culminates in in-country training, rather than out-of-country training options, which are mostly infeasible for large numbers of fighters, would be more likely. Trained irregulars also need to be armed.

Here, confiscated and looted SALWs and ammunition from Nigerian security forces, as well as other tactical assets, have helped upgrade and upscale the group's motorized infantry, on which it is highly dependent for more massive offensives. One such offensive, which deserves some discussion, is Boko Haram's massive assault on HQ, 21 Brigade of the Nigerian Army in March 2014, located at Giwa Barracks, Maiduguri.

Case study: Boko Haram's jailbreak offensive at Giwa Barracks

Giwa Barracks is the headquarters of 21 Armoured Brigade (21 Bde) of the Nigerian Army – a unit at the heart of the Army's COIN since its earliest days. Indeed, due to its location (the barracks have been situated in Maiduguri for decades as the nucleus of the Nigerian Army's north-eastern divisions), the brigade garrison has been the tip of the spear against Boko Haram in the city. Such reasons are in part why Boko Haram's ability to overwhelm 21 Bde was a declaration of intent and a demonstration of the insurgent's standing army strength.

In the morning of 14 March 2014, Boko Haram, using hundreds of foot soldiers supported by motorized infantry and light armoured fighting vehicles, penetrated Maiduguri's defences and took control of HQ, 21 Brigade for several hours. Several hundreds of suspected Boko Haram members, detained by the Nigerian Army in that facility, were freed. Nigerian Army forces at the location beat a retreat, overwhelmed by Boko Haram's swarming tactics (see later in this chapter). Few casualties resulted for the Nigerian Army during this offensive, but for Boko Haram, and the hundreds of captive suspects it freed from detention, the successful offensive on 21 Brigade nonetheless was a great moral victory and, beyond that, a demonstration of Boko Haram's strength in a scaled offensive.

Boko Haram's vehicles as a roadmap of its capabilities

Boko Haram's motorized infantry was central to its mobility and speed, and thus the tactical momentum, generated in its success against 21 Brigade. Ground assets deployed by Boko Haram — many of which originate from Nigerian Army and police units – include tactical vehicles such as Armoured Personnel Carriers (APCs), infantry fighting vehicles (IFVs), 4 × 4 pick-up trucks (Toyota Hilux vehicles appear commonly used), transport trucks, and other forms of ground mobility assets. Included here is towed artillery, such as a captured Nigerian Army ZSU-23 quad-barrel anti-aircraft tank, known locally as *Shilka* tank. In 2015, one *Shilka* was recaptured from Boko Haram, by Chadian military forces at Gambaru, Ngala, a significant supply route via Fotokol, less than half a kilometre away in Cameroon's Extreme North region. Whereas the *Shilka* is a light tank, Boko Haram has also fielded heavy tanks.

With the Nigerian Army's Armour acquisitions sharply pivoted towards the T-55 and Vickers Mk. 3 Eagle MBTs, it also comes as no surprise that both these tanks, as an example, have ended up in Boko Haram's possession. At Mubi, in December 2014, a Nigerian T-72 AV tank destroyed a T-55 tank captured by Boko Haram from the Army. This might have been the first time both these armour platforms were deployed in proximity by opposing sides in Nigeria. A Vickers Mk. 3 Eagle, also a main battle tank (MBT) was also recaptured by the Nigerian Army, from Boko Haram, late January 2015 (Dempsey 2015). In May 2015, another Vickers Mk.3 Eagle tank was seized by Nigerian troops from Boko Haram, at Bazza. And in March the same year, a T-55 tank in use by Boko Haram was destroyed and captured by Nigeria Army forces at Uba (Askira).

Notwithstanding incidents such as these, the overall numbers of armoured assets, especially heavy armour, fielded by Boko Haram are modest. Here again, the extent to which Boko Haram has innovated to make up for its critical lack of armour and artillery platforms, should not be underestimated. As an example, whereas the Nigerian Army does not operate track or truck-mounted 105-mm artillery guns, one such gun – an improvised self-propelled 105-mm truck-mounted gun – was captured from Boko Haram at Gwoza, early April 2015. It is unclear how Boko Haram acquired the technical expertise required to improvise and refit equipment as heavy as the 105mm, either for track or truck-mounted use. For the Nigerian Army, this demonstrated capability of Boko Haram, to modify lighter field guns for track or truck-mounted use as of 2015, is worrisome. Such instances of significant modifications to existing artillery appear to be rare, nonetheless. Boko Haram's artillery guns, towed or otherwise, have typically been captured and after that used with minor modifications if any. An example would be the 90-mm-gun-armed Panhard Sagaie AFV, captured and deployed by Boko Haram, and eventually destroyed by Nigerian Army T72 tanks, in 2014.

Despite the above portrayed picture, Boko Haram's capabilities, including its entire haul of tanks, light armour, towed artillery, unarmoured technicals and artillery guns (considerable amounts of which were deployed by the insurgent at Monguno, in 2015, discussed in the case study that follows shortly) barely matches a traditional armoured or mechanized brigade of the Nigerian Army. Such has been the typical insurgent's challenge against traditional government forces: comparative to the latter, the former tends to be inferior. Moreover, in many cases, the asymmetry in question is in orders of magnitude of troops, equipment and *matériel*. Such considerations complicate the Boko Haram's ability to close the already wide military fighting gap between its overt front and Nigerian military forces.

Boko Haram's concept of operations

On occasions where Boko Haram has favoured the engagement as an escalation of its military ambition, sheer numbers of motorized infantry, within these offensives, have been used for overwhelming effect. It has been typical, for instance, that Boko Haram forces deploy *en masse* – in numbers least one unit-level above Army and security forces being attacked. Thus, platoon-sized insurgent forces have been pitched against Nigerian Army and police joint fire teams or sections, battalion-strength units face off against Nigerian Army companies, and regiment-strength forces are used either to ambush outfield Army battlegroups (battalions) or to assault brigade garrisons or HQs. For Boko Haram, this is a way to mitigate traditional military advantages possessed by the Nigerian Army's outfield battalions (such as better weapons, availability of the

Armour and the fact these formations were in the defence). Indeed, this is a classic 'swarming tactic' in military warfare.[12] Employed in the offence, such tactics have become a staple of Boko Haram's general concept of operations against deployed Nigerian forces.

This approach is consistent with Sun Tzu's maxim: 'in general, the strategy for employing the military is this: If your strength is ten times theirs, surround them; if five, then attack them; if double, then divide your forces. If you are equal in strength to the enemy, you can engage him. If fewer, you can circumvent him. If outmatched, you can avoid him' (Tzu 2003, 28–29). Boko Haram, consistent with this maxim, has generally circumvented the Nigerian Army's larger forces and largely stuck with guerrilla warfare's classic hit-and-run principles. Yet at the same time, the group nevertheless has, in employing classic swarming tactics, has overwhelmed Nigerian Army outfield formations with sheer numbers on a number of occasions. Perhaps the most pertinent case of Boko Haram's swarming tactics was demonstrated in Boko Haram's capture of Monguno, in January 2015.

Case study: Battle of Monguno

On 25 January 2015, Boko Haram attacked and overran HQ, 5 Brigade of the Nigerian Army, stationed at Monguno (see Figure 9.1). As some background, 5 Brigade forms the nucleus of Nigeria's contribution to the cross-border security outfit, the Multi-National Joint Task Force (MNJTF). MNJTF itself is a buffer security force around the border areas of north-east Nigeria. The task force has army units 'from Chad, Niger, Cameroon, Nigeria; collectively known as the Troop Contributing Countries (TCCs)'. The main task of this force is to secure the border areas straddling the TCCs, which have been targeted by Boko Haram over the years of its insurgency. Indeed, with its main garrison in Monguno town, HQ 5 Brigade could, therefore, be considered one of the stronger ground forces in that area of Borno, in charge of a vital Area of Responsibility (AOR) within the Nigerian Army's COIN campaign.

To overrun HQ 5 Brigade, Monguno Barracks, therefore, thousands of fighters were employed by Boko Haram. This was more than what had previously been deployed by the group in a single assault, at least since the hundreds of fighters previously seen in combat, during Boko Haram's Harmattan Offensive at Konduga, in September 2014.[13]

The Monguno offensive came as part of the insurgent's increasingly credible-looking strategy to control northern Borno and its frontier, beginning within a series of Harmattan offensives between October 2014 and March 2015. Within this offensive, some features are noteworthy. First, 'large numbers of combatants, several times more than the Army had deployed at Monguno at the time, were fielded by Boko Haram. Second, armour pieces, equipment, supplies and SALWs were all captured, with dozens of military personnel killed or unaccounted for, after the attack' (Omeni 2017, 239). Also, so far as swarming tactics are concerned, the Battle of Monguno was not just about enemy numbers *per se*. Indeed, in addition to the thousands of light infantry deployed by Boko Haram, it also, 'employed a surprising amount of firepower in capturing HQ, 5 Bde; recoilless rifles, anti-aircraft guns, 60-mm and 81-mm mortar pieces, APCs and gun-mounted Toyota Hilux 4 × 4 vehicles were deployed with over a thousand fighters in that offensive'. Moreover, Boko Haram, in that engagement, also deployed more RPGs than usual (Omeni 2017, 239). To everything discussed above, add in the element of surprise. Add in the fact that a Nigerian Army battalion is seldom a full-complement battalion. Then consider that Boko Haram has demonstrated tactical warfare proficiency and that it exploits the terrain as a force-multiplier. Suddenly the outcome of such engagements, especially where smarming tactics are employed, pivots away from a supposed easy military decision for Nigeria's forces.

Boko Haram's military fighting tactics

Boko Haram's increased dependence on its overt front, demonstrated at the Battle of Monguno, brought about changes to the way it operates in the offence. Adjustments include the rapid movement of its motorized infantry; its use of the terrain, weather patterns and darkness for its offensives; and use of *istishhad*, martyrdom operations, to strike terror just before some offensives. Other tactics employed by Boko Haram on the offence includes the use of reconnaissance detachments and even children as innocuous scouts, to gain as much advantage as possible, prior to an offensive. Also, use of theatricality *in situ* – microphones duct-taped onto Kalashnikovs for exaggerated sound effects; megaphones attached atop unarmoured technicals, blaring the words of the *Takbīr* ('Allāhu akbar') as swarms of fighters congregate on overwhelmed Nigerian Army units – likewise help exaggerate Boko Haram's battlefield threat. Each of the above is a tactical adaptation by which Boko Haram has come to make an otherwise unremarkable infantry fighting force punch far above its weight on the battlefield. Such tactics, within the battlespace, have signalled a change in the insurgent's concept of operations over the years.

Still, even where the engagement has favoured Boko Haram, and whereas this enemy has indeed demonstrated a surprising extent of technical proficiency at military fighting, it should not be assumed that Boko Haram is militarily superior to the Nigerian Army. Paul Lubeck for instance comments, 'these guys [Boko Haram] are better organised, more highly motivated and have better arms than the Nigerian military'. 'The Nigerian military', Lubeck declares, 'is decayed' (Londoño 2014). Lubeck does not localize this dominance of Boko Haram, suggesting that, against the Nigerian military, it is strategic rather than tactical and highly situational. This assertion is dubious.

Localized battlefield successes, attributable to Boko Haram in between late 2013 and early 2015 (Omeni 2017, 233–241), do not, *per se*, equate to strategic superiority over the Nigerian military. Localized success, or even dominance, does not mean theatre-level superiority; it just means that at a certain level of conflict intensity, at a particular location and time, the insurgent gained the upper hand against government troops. This distinction might confuse writers like Lubeck to assume that Boko Haram is the superior military outfit. However, tactical edge (which Boko Haram often possesses in terms of speed, mobility, methods, the element of surprise etc.), need not be confused with strategic advantage (which the Nigerian Army possesses in terms of overall military capabilities including airpower, available ordnance, force size, manoeuvre assets and so on). Strategically, therefore, it is a different matter, as the Nigerian military is the far superior fighting force. To what extent, however, has this mattered in practice? In evaluating this question, the likes of Paul Lubeck now have a point.

Boko Haram, after all, is aware that it is the weaker side and thus, that guerrilla warfare, not the engagement at scale, is the expedient of the weaker side. Indeed, it is for this reason – the existential capabilities deficit faced since day one – that Boko Haram has fought a highly irregular, network-centric, low-intensity war that exploited both the environment and the local populace. Boko Haram has not dominated the Nigerian military at scale; but then again, it does not need to. In sometimes employing guerrilla tactics, Boko Haram demonstrated different set of strengths, which neither required it to engage the Nigerian Army at scale nor required a territorial map that could be hammered by Nigerian Air Force (NAF) air strikes.

Against such a threat during phases of the insurgent, do the Nigerian Army's traditional military advantages count for as much – compared to say against a much larger state force that decides to engage directly on the battlefield and employ similar doctrine and operational concepts as those used by Nigeria's forces? The short answer is no. The idea of an armed force's order of battle (ORBAT),[14] after all, does not necessarily account for an unconventional enemy without a traditional structure. Nor does ORBAT necessarily account for irregular war, where most of the ORBAT may not deployable. Indeed, in practice, the nature of insurgent warfare renders key traditional advantages of government forces, within an ORBAT, ineffectual. Military operations to counter insurgency, therefore, tend to be frustrating, because untraditional roles need to be adopted and decades of culture and doctrine may require changes in a relatively short space of time. Chapter 9 shall explore this idea in more depth.

Nevertheless, what all this information suggests is that Boko Haram's battlefield successes have not occurred despite this capabilities asymmetry; they have occurred, in part at least, because of it, and because of the nature of insurgency. Boko Haram's inherent limitations to its ability to escalate open confrontation – its battlefield inferiority, if we can call it that – have led this enemy to wage a form of warfare, in insurgency, where military superiority is of less import to the determination: the achievement of war objectives. In this way, Boko Haram's concept of operations accommodates for, and in some cases even exploits, the permanence of battlefield asymmetry, because guerrilla warfare suits its war object.

Despite the previous emphasis on the conflict's asymmetry and irregular elements, it would be misleading to assert that Boko Haram is unable to function within the conventional military space. Indeed, even in aspects of warfighting where Nigeria's forces, on paper, should dominate, the reality on the ground turns out somewhat differently to what many, including war planners, might have assumed a foregone conclusion before this conflict. The section below highlights airpower as one such area and attempts to explain why, even here, Nigeria's forces have failed to force a capitulation of Boko Haram's forces.

Some notes on airpower and air-land operations

Whereas much of the debate on military operations against Boko Haram has focused on warfare on *terra firma*, solid earth, Boko Haram has also faced a significant threat from the air. Since 2013, the NAF has conducted thousands of sorties against Boko Haram positions and has reorganized its forward presence in the north-east of Nigeria on an unprecedented scale, as part of its contribution to COIN joint effort. However, despite considerably escalated NAF operations, conducted in coordination with the Army's land activity and integrated amongst the arms, Boko Haram's forces have remained resilient. Why has the NAF's airborne threat, much like that of the Army on solid earth, failed to put an end to Boko Haram's military ambitions? The answer to this question is linked to the nature and robustness of surface-to-air defences as a historical counter to airpower.

Whereas armour (the battle tank) was introduced during the Great War as a hard counter to the static and cumbersome nature of heavy artillery (Guderian 1999), by the Second World War, armour would itself face a new threat: airpower. The impact of this threat to entire columns of heavy tanks was near-immediate. Military thinkers such as Heinz Guderian and Erich von Manstein, who watched this threat emerge, were concerned about the implications for land warfare (Guderian 1999, Lemay 2010). After all, over a century earlier, Carl von Clausewitz in his seminal work, *On War*, argued for the pre-eminence of the Infantry, relative to the other combat arms (von Clausewitz 1976, 667–668). However, with Armour's emergence as a combat arm, and with airpower as an evolved threat to the Armour, the great tank and air warfare battles of the Second World War suggested a pivot away from Clausewitzian thinking around the pre-eminence of the Infantry, within the engagement (Trigg 2016).

War planners who utilized long logistics chains by land would be particularly vulnerable to the air threat. Moreover, in the field, land assets without air defences could be swiftly wiped out by even a single combat aircraft. This susceptibility would endure even much later in the twentieth century, and held even within less evolved forms of air-land engagements within the developing world context. As an example, during the Civil War of Nigeria (1967–1970), air sorties by federal forces laid waste the entire motorized columns of rebel land forces; in some cases, setting back rebel war planning by weeks or even months via mere minutes of successful air-land operations (Alabi-Isama 2013).

Rebuttal: The surface-to-air counter

Let us pause here, so as not to run away with the idea that land defences are rendered obsolete against the air threat. There is, after all, a reversal to this thesis. The surface-to-air aspect of warfare, as a counter to some forms of airpower, is formidable, and is one of the most rapidly advanced aspects of tactical warfare. Such has been the pace of innovation in this area of modern warfare[15] that by the 1990s the Bosnian

Serbs could at times defend entire airspace against even advanced NATO aircraft (Byman and Waxman 2000). In September 2016, Air Commodore Martin Sampson, Air Officer Commanding No 83 Expeditionary Air Group and United Kingdom Air Component Commander,[16] Al Udeid, Qatar, observed that militant jihadist insurgent group, Daesh,[17] 'in theory', could shoot down some of the UK's most advanced operational fighter platforms, its Tornado GR4 jets and Typhoon fighter aircraft (Brown 2016). Now, Daesh has persuasive, but certainly not exceptional, surface-to-air capabilities (Brown 2016). Both Tornado GR4 jets and Typhoons, on the other hand, are incredibly advanced fighter platforms. The issue is that fixed-wing fighter platforms have been relatively slower to advance than surface-to-air warfare, over the decades. Good surface-to-air capabilities, therefore – the sophistication of which can scale dramatically to include radar-guided and battery missile systems if conventional surface-to-air capabilities owned by states are taken into account – remain a hard counter to the threat of airpower in general.

Thus, upon introduction to the battlefield, whereas airpower indeed changed the calculus of war, it did not render the threat of the Infantry and other combat arms obsolete. Even so, the Vietnam War, the Gulf War and NATO's bombing campaign in Kosovo, respectively, sparked a classic debate around the preponderance of airpower at the lower rungs of the conflict escalation ladder, and its effects on the decision-making of commanders on the ground.[18]

Airpower and Boko Haram's resilience

Such deliberations on airpower and its land-based counter are not abstract to war, or to the calculus of war, of both insurgent and counter-insurgent, in Nigeria. Still, it would appear that airpower and Boko Haram's response is possibly the least-discussed military theme within the north-east Nigeria conflict. Either due to a lack of information on its role or to a lack of understanding around its role, the NAF has been primarily sidelined within the academic debate on COIN warfare in north-east Nigeria. Only recently has there been some shift towards the airman's role within military operations against Boko Haram.[19] Indeed, within the discourses, it is common for 'military' to be used in reference to the Nigerian Army, altogether ignoring the NAF's operational role. Such conflation of the service arms' roles, however, fails to adequately account for the air threat posed by the NAF, and Boko Haram's calculations around the nature of this threat against its overt front.

For an irregular standing army like Boko Haram's, with limited armour and inevitable maintenance issues around motorized infantry assets, air strikes can be crippling to field operations. Indeed, Boko Haram since 2012 has learned hard lessons regarding the threat posed by the NAF's sorties. However, because Boko Haram has no air assets of its own, there is no possibility of an air-based counter-deterrent to the NAF's threat.

Boko Haram consequently has had to leverage advances in surface-to-air warfare to defend its overt front and its motorized infantry in particular. As an example, by way of captured hardware from the Nigerian Army and with evidence also suggesting capabilities acquired sequel to the Civil War in Libya, Boko Haram has come to possess limited amounts of protected mobility and anti-aircraft capabilities, including SA-7 'Grail' and SA-24 'Grinch' man-portable, shoulder-fired, low-altitude surface-to-air missile systems (MANPADs).[20] Boko Haram's protected mobility and surface-to-air capabilities give it some air defence options against the NAF's air threat, especially against the Air Force's rotary platforms, and its older fixed-wing platforms such as the Alpha Jet E variant.

This situation, whereby otherwise poorly equipped insurgents challenge air dominance is not isolated to the conflict in north-east Nigeria. As Loren Thompson points out, 'places, where enemies have no air forces and no air defences […], are fast disappearing, because cheap surface-to-air missiles are ubiquitous in global military trade' (L. B. Thompson 2016). Simply put, insurgent-controlled spaces can, with relatively affordable surface-to-air capabilities, can go from being 'permissive' to 'non-permissive' environments for rampant air sorties.

Even with Boko Haram's modest surface-to-air capabilities, however, this aspect of the conflict leans heavily in favour of the NAF. In June 2016, as an example, airpower interdiction destroyed a convoy of congregated Boko Haram unarmoured technicals (Roblin 2016). And between 2013 and 2015, thousands of ISR sorties were flown by the NAF in north-east Nigeria (Today 2015). In coordination with the Army, these air missions were instrumental to dislodging Boko Haram from the considerable territories it was contesting or occupying, at the start of 2015. Moreover, the more Boko Haram insists on using its army of irregulars to, in particular, defend territory, the more of a target it makes itself to such air-land operations.

As a final point on this discussion of airpower's threat to Boko Haram's overt forces, whereas the NAF has conducted the vast majority of air sorties against Boko Haram, a small number of sorties have also been conducted by the Chadian Air Force component of its army (*Force Aérienne Tchadienne*) (Massalaki 2015, Al Jazeera 2015b). However, despite now fielding depleted forces, and having to contend with more than a single cross-border COIN actor, Boko Haram has not entirely lost the ability to launch surprise attacks on Nigerian Army formations in frontier areas. Indeed, years after an enduring campaign of airstrikes became operational against it, Boko Haram retains the ability to field not just motorized infantry but also large numbers of highly mobile ground troops (Vanguard 2017).

Phases of Boko Haram's military threat

The analysis so far in this chapter suggests that Boko Haram has come a long way since its clumsy opening gambit against Nigerian authorities in 2009. No longer is Boko Haram an 'unsophisticated', amateurish, military outfit. Sophistication, after all, is relative. And relative to the armed forces of Nigeria and the troop-contributing countries (TCC)[21] conducting COIN operations against Boko Haram, the capabilities asymmetry between both sides – in terms of numbers, equipment and combat capacity, and campaign sustainability – has reduced over the years. However, Boko Haram's sophistication has been so phased and gradual, it has appeared virtually organic to the conflict. Let us consider these phases.

From September 2010 when it executed a jailbreak at Bauchi Prison, Boko Haram conducted a string of covert attacks and bombings, for the next three years in the north, the north-east, the Middle Belt of Nigeria and the Federal Capital Territory (FCT), Abuja. However, the use of IEDs, and shortly after, vehicle-borne improvised explosive devices (VBIEDs) would not become prevalent until mid-2011. Beyond this point, until Christmas Day of 2011, there was a spate of bombings in what was a highly guerrilla affair.

Now, Boko Haram's use of bombings as a critical plank of its threat is not unprecedented in Nigeria; militias in the Niger Delta had been conducting attacks and blowing up pipelines and infrastructure using IEDs, for years hitherto. What sophisticated Boko Haram apart from these other insurgent groups in Nigeria was, in particular, its use of *istishhad* – martyrdom operations – as the central tactic of its covert front. The tactic of the use of the suicide bomber, never before used in Nigeria, gave war avoidance a new meaning in the north-east conflict.

Such emphasis on highly irregular military tactics dominated Boko Haram's calculus of war between 2010 and 2013, beyond which guerrilla warfare was complemented with mobile warfare doctrine, as Boko Haram's motorized infantry exploited vast areas of arid terrain to rapidly strike and disperse before Nigerian Army reinforcements arrive. Since 2013, Boko Haram began fielding its unarmoured technicals, heavier guns, towed artillery, light infantry fighting vehicles, MANPADs and other forms of protected mobility. However, this doctrine of mobile warfare, unlike Boko Haram's guerrilla threat, would be highly limited in operational reach, identifiable primarily within the north-east and extreme north-east of Nigeria until late 2013.

By early 2014, escalated territorial contests between large numbers of Boko Haram's irregulars and the Nigerian Army and security forces were the dominant form of the engagement. By this period, Boko Haram could field several hundred fighters in the offence; its unarmoured technicals now had higher-calibre guns and twin-cannons refitted, not just general-purpose machine guns from the preceding eighteen months. Boko Haram now had more heavy armour platforms supported by its motorized infantry. It was also increasingly proficient in both ambush and counter-ambush against Nigerian Army outfield battalions. Moreover, Boko Haram could now defend and administer captured territory for several months – indeed, over a year, in the case of the extreme north-east town of Gwoza, the capital of Boko Haram's so-called caliphate. These territorial contests, limited in area to the north-east (mostly in Borno, but also some parts of Yobe and Adamawa states) continued until 2015 when a degraded Boko Haram would gradually revert to first principles: guerrilla warfare, across a broader geographical area.

From the preceding, it can be surmised that in a half decade, Boko Haram became a credible military threat. Table 7.2 highlights three critical phases of Boko Haram's insurgency, between 2010 and 2015. Since then, Boko Haram's tactics have primarily reverted to an approximate of its phase one activities, highlighted in the table.

Table 7.2 Boko Haram's Transitioning from Local Nuisance to Regional Military Threat

Boko Haram Before Battle of Maiduguri, 2009	Boko Haram (2010–2011) PHASE 1	Boko Haram (2012–2013) PHASE 2	Boko Haram (2014–2015) PHASE 3
• Ultra-Salafist Islamist group. Non-violent at this phase.	• Having attempted to tackle Nigerian police and security forces head-on, Boko Haram failed and disappeared.	• People know more about them • Technically proficient at this stage: attacks more frequent, more spectacular	• Military capabilities have increased sufficiently to realize territorial ambition.
		• Numbers of combatant fighters increase, compared to phase one	• By this phase, the group, • Can now successfully challenge state writ and realize territorial ambitions as seen in capture (or heavy contestation) of areas such as Konduga, Delwa, Gwoza, Bama and Monguno.
• Were active in spreading ideology more openly; in the group's *masjid* (mosque), though leafleting, tapes and across other states in north beyond Borno.	• Guerrilla warfare on re-emergence	• Active recruitment within this phase.	
	• *Istishhad*, martyrdom operations, give war avoidance a new meaning	• Expect stalemate(s) here	
	• No real territorial ambition.	• The insurgent is counting on an over-reactive state target response: do not take bait ('courageous restraint').	• Has sufficient military clout to negotiate from position of power. This is a bad time for government to seek terms.

Boko Haram Before Battle of Maiduguri, 2009	Boko Haram (2010–2011) PHASE 1	Boko Haram (2012–2013) PHASE 2	Boko Haram (2014–2015) PHASE 3
• Minor skirmishes with police but little more than a local nuisance.	• Targeted killings of senior leadership (such as IED experts, tacticians and overall head) more likely to degrade group at this stage	• Police role crucial – Strong military presence amongst civilians may be mistaken as 'occupation'. • Counter-insurgent should go non-kinetic: *Durbars*, town hall meetings, community initiatives, Civil-Military Operations (CMOs) as 'carrot'.	• Can demand inclusion in political process, if so inclined Furthermore, • As military offensive against the insurgent increase, expect counter-coercion by punishment here. Attacks on schools, marketplaces and Mosques.
	• Deterrence by denial as main COIN concept of operations (CONOPS). Hard targets should be harder; soft targets, hardened.	• Attacks on military assets by insurgent more rampant here. This is to bait an over-reactive target response • Classic example of phase 2 attack: Attack on 21 Bde, Maiduguri	• Expect a smoother pathway to political legitimacy, if group is successful here
	• You do not need troop surge here • Intelligence plays key role		
• However, message resonated with locals; so, followership was large and increasing			
• No notable military capabilities at this phase	• Classic examples of phase 1 attacks: Edet House, UN building suicide bombings (2011); Bauchi prison break (2010)		

Maoism, post-Maoism and Boko Haram's military evolution

In the few years where it fielded its battlefield forces, Boko Haram amassed the numbers, but also demonstrated an understanding of the logistics and cross-border supply chain requirements, to successfully field a highly mobile army of irregulars. This helped to scale its territorial threat considerably and made Boko Haram, in localized instances, a bona fide conventional threat. Consequently, compared to historical threats of *Maitatsine* and *Yan Kala Kato* in northern Nigeria, where machetes, fetish charms, Dane guns and modest fighter numbers were the height of resistance to the Nigerian Army, and where rebellion was fleeting and unsustainable, Boko Haram is in an entirely separate military space of its own.

As unthinkable as this may have sounded back in 2009, Boko Haram gradually evolved its threat to a position whereby military fighting against Nigerian forces and those of the TCCs, became feasible within its concept of operations. This is not to say that guerrilla tactics were abandoned as a result of the emergence of this standing army. However, it does mean that Boko Haram, through phases, manoeuvred itself into a position of such conventional military strength, that guerrilla warfare no longer was its only recourse to action.

There is precedence to this gradual evolution of revolutionary and insurgent groups, and there are similarities here with classic insurgent warfare theory and the third phase of classical Maoist insurgency. Maoism ideology emphasizes the importance of the peasantry and common folk in revolution (Tse-tung 2007). For Mao Tse-tung, 'people's war' was the insurgent's ability to mobilize the 'proletariat' against the 'exploiting classes' and the state (Tse-Tung 1967b, 292). The process is lengthy, taking years or even over a decade, across three broad phases.

Mao's three phases of 'People's War'

In the first phase, the insurgent begins by mobilizing the disadvantaged majority against the state but also must plan for a guerrilla war, which aims to undermine governance while simultaneously providing military experience and successes (which could be used to highlight government weakness further). In mobilizing this class of society (phase two), particular emphasis is to be within fringe areas – 'the countryside', as Mao calls it – with an abundance of poorer folk and limited government presence. Gradual envelopment of more built-up areas with a stronger government presence comes only after the insurgent has a stronger base. The aim is for this base to be eventually militarized and of sufficient numbers, to shift away from guerrilla tactics, and challenge the state in open warfare even in areas where the government presence is strong. Due to relative inexperience, a large number of 'revolutionaries' inevitably end up being casualties of war; this is warfighting at its ugliest. Yet, the insurgent must press on towards this final phase (three), if territory and writ are to be wrested away from the state, via open military confrontation.

Underpinning the thought process of phase 3 is the Marxist theory of the state, whereby 'the army is the chief component of state power [and] whoever wants to seize and retain state power must have a strong army' (Tse-tung 1967, 225). Here, however, the 'people's army' is made up not of the political elite, or even the middle class, but of lumpen proletariat and common folk at the bottom of the social ladder. Mao is at pains to point out the role of the socio-economically hopeless, in this war form:

> Without the poor peasants (the 'riffraff' as the gentry call them) it would never have been possible to bring about in the countryside the present state of revolution [...] Without the poor peasants there can be no revolution. To reject them is to reject the revolution. To attack them is to attack the revolution. Their general direction of the revolution has never been wrong. (Tse-tung 1927)

Insofar as Mao emphasizes this role of the lower class within insurgency, and whereas this social class indeed dominates Boko Haram's rank and file, it nonetheless is worth pointing out that Boko Haram's insurgency is not, strictly speaking, a Maoist insurgency. Boko Haram's ranks are indeed dominated by local combatants who number in the thousands. Moreover, Boko Haram's demographic constitution, from interviews conducted for this project, was severally referred to as a 'Kanuri problem', a reference to the Kanuri ethnic group of Borno State, which dominates the ranks of Boko Haram fighters (Omeni 2017, 141). This should not come as a surprise, *per se*. Insurgencies are, after all, people-centred conflicts.

Moreover, the people in question invariably tend to come from the region affected by conflict. The Nigeria case is no different. Even so, such mobilization is not enough to classify the insurgency as the Maoist archetype. Large numbers of locals as participants in an insurgency does not necessarily mean the insurgency is popular. Nor does it necessarily mean that a 'people's war' is being waged by the insurgent. Nevertheless, whereas it thus is important not to overcook the people's war thesis here, it may be worth investigating the link between theory and practice within the Boko Haram insurgency case.

Similarities between Boko Haram and the Maoist insurgent archetype

Certainly, Boko Haram, especially in its formative years, displayed the potential of a movement very much looking to leverage popular support, and that of the lower social classes especially. Boko Haram's onetime leader, Muhammad Yusuf, for instance, exploited large numbers of 'illiterates, indolent, the unemployed' to swell the ranks of his following (Mohammed 2010, 42). Such an approach is a classic feature of the Maoist insurgency. Other features of Boko Haram's insurgency are likewise observable within Maoist-style insurgencies.

Boko Haram's insurgency, also similar to the classic Maoist archetype, is 'the expedient of the weaker side' (Mackinlay 2012, 20). Yusuf and his anti-*boko* followers did not initially set out to become armed revolutionaries, of the calibre that Boko Haram later evolved to be. In the beginning, these were but a small group of radicals, enthusiastic young men, some of whom were University of Maiduguri graduates bitter against corrupt government practices and hoping for a puritanical society (Abubakar 2012). These radicals, initially at least, had little more than rhetoric to assist their ambitions. This, however, may have been enough to attract the numbers. After all, some of the espoused ideological tenets resonated with locals, especially the poor and disenfranchised, whether Western educated or not. Indeed, as Sarah Chayes points out in *Thieves of State*, ' ... Boko Haram's vilification of "Western education" should be understood – at least in the early years [...] the system of going to school and getting a job in the civil service and skimming off contracts – that's what they are angry at [...] If they had taken a secular approach, all Nigeria would be with them' (2015, 129). As it stood, Boko Haram's radical views *did* attract large numbers as the group first formed, and then matured as a movement, between 2003 and 2009 (Mohammed 2010). However, whereas Yusuf and his followers for years preached and complained against the *status quo*, and attracted the crowds in Maiduguri, Boko Haram remained little more than a local nuisance, even at the times when the police got involved with its activities (Adeoye 2012).

Consequently, as the years passed, it became clear to Boko Haram's leadership that preaching alone or local skirmishes with the authorities, would not suffice to realize Yusuf's absurd views regarding the expungement of Westernization and its influence from society. Now, Boko Haram had no political legitimacy, and could not force the issue through political discourse or Islamic debate – the powerful Islamic establishment in northern Nigeria had, at several points, dismissed Boko Haram's ideology as deceitful and un-Islamic (Mohammed 2010). Yusuf's power base, considering its extremist and unnegotiable objectives, therefore had military contestation as its only recourse to relevance as an anti-state and anti-establishment actor. The dilemma for Boko Haram was that, notwithstanding its political objectives, it was, at the time, poorly positioned to force the issue militarily. Compared to Nigeria's forces, it posed no substantive threat. Still, resurfacing late 2010 and this time sticking to guerrilla warfare principles, this weakness did not mean insurgency was impossible. This shift, towards an asymmetric force posture due to relative political and military weakness, is yet another classic feature of the Maoist insurgency model.

Boko Haram and the Maoist insurgency archetype share yet another trait, in the centrality of ideology to the movement's early appeal. Many Boko Haram adherents may not have fought and died solely on the strength of ideology, but ideology did play a role in amassing the extent of followership, local support and broader recognition of Boko Haram.

Another similarity between Boko Haram and the Maoist insurgency archetype is the former's exploitation of the environment, both physical and socio-economic. Exploitation of the physical environment, in particular, has proved unusually prevalent, relative to recent insurgencies elsewhere; this perhaps was born of the relatively diverse terrain options available to Boko Haram, in the subregion contested. These terrain options have greatly facilitated the movement and security of Boko Haram's army of irregulars. They include some relief features of north-east Nigeria and its bordering areas, discussed in Chapters 4 and 5.

A final resemblance between Boko Haram's insurgency and the Maoist model lies in the nature of Boko Haram's irregular war. Virtually from day one, much of Boko Haram's campaign has been orchestrated to prompt an over-reactive 'target response' (Neumann and Smith 2005). Such a response effectively provokes the government to institute increasingly disproportionate military measures against the slippery yet lethal insurgent. Such state measures, in turn, may increasingly disrupt life for the local population, and better still for the insurgent if government decisions come across as draconian – they then serve to alienate the population from the government's response further. This, in itself, is a win for the insurgency.

In the case of Boko Haram, the north-east of Nigeria came to experience a military campaign unprecedented in scale.[22] The Nigerian military, within this campaign, has been accused of heavy-handedness towards some locals (Amnesty International 2012, Amnesty International 2015, HRW 2012). At least two states of emergency were declared as a result of Boko Haram's threat in the north-east, disrupting civilian freedoms. Furthermore, not one, but now two Nigerian Army divisions have been created to combat the insurgency – HQ, 7 Division, with 7 Div Garrison in Maiduguri, and HQ, 8 Task Force (TF) Division at Monguno. Both divisions are situated in Borno State, further saturating an axis, which already is war-weary, with more troop numbers. Indeed, the entire subregion of north-east Nigeria and the border areas of the neighbouring Chad Basin countries have become heavily militarized, leading some senior local politicians to compare the Army presence there to an 'occupation force' (Scan News 2014). All of this approximates a government target response, a feature characteristic of Maoist insurgencies.

Similarities between Boko Haram and the post-Maoist insurgent archetype

If despite these similarities, Boko Haram's campaign is not a Maoist insurgency, what then is it? A post-Maoist insurgency? Boko Haram also does not necessarily fit classification as a post-Maoist insurgency type form for several reasons. First, Boko Haram does not depend on social movements or popular mobilization in the same way that scholars like Mackinlay picture post-Maoist insurgencies (Mackinlay 2012, 143–170). Nor can it be said that Boko Haram emerged from a global movement. Yusuf indeed had expressed admiration for Bin Laden and Al-Qaeda. However, Boko Haram's ambitions and its vision for jihad are embryonic, compared to the global view of Al-Qaeda's idea system.

Additionally, unlike Mackinlay's post-Maoist insurgent (Mackinlay 2012, 143–170), Boko Haram has (or at least had between 2014 and 2015), a concept of operations that was very much territory seeking, rather than one that was strictly guerrilla and always clandestine. Notwithstanding dissimilarities with the post-Maoist model, Boko Haram does share an important feature, in the Propaganda of the Deed (POTD). This operational technique essentially means that Boko Haram's tactics are intended to be as bold as possible because the bolder the action, the more intense the media reporting around it. As Mackinlay comments:

> POTD is defined by its violent deeds, not by the promulgation of explanatory texts. As long as the deed is dramatic, after the dust of the explosion has settled and the bodies removed, the insurgents' job is done for them by the media. It is the photographers and their editors who select the most powerful images and propagate them onwards to the intended targets. It is their presentation techniques – not the

insurgent's – and the brand aura of their newspapers and satellite TV channels that gives the deed its necessary reach and authority. (Mackinlay 2012, 150–151)

Shades of the above are identifiable within the insurgency in north-east Nigeria. Boko Haram, as the police in Maiduguri pointed out to me, 'do not do anything to make a statement' (Adeoye 2012). Each attack, each activity, had a specific purpose for the insurgent; they were not just meant to be spectacular and done for notoriety's sake. Moreover, on the strength of the POTD argument, Boko Haram's actions were the statement, quite aside from whatever tactical or operational objectives the actions themselves were meeting. The dramatic fashion in which news sources report Boko Haram's actions – the pictures, the description, the depiction of dread – already make a strong statement of its actions. POTD, therefore, means Boko Haram's duplication of effort is redundant. Simply put, Boko Haram takes action, and the news media does the rest: by delivering its message and thus expanding the reach of its propaganda effort, including to jihadist affiliates elsewhere that may be keen to offer assistance. This feature is standard to post-Maoist insurgencies, including other radical Islamist insurgencies elsewhere (Mackinlay 2012).

Boko Haram's threat spectrum

As argued above, whereas Boko Haram is neither Maoist nor post-Maoist, it nevertheless shares features of both insurgency archetypes.[23] Indeed, the range of Boko Haram's tactics, its use of new media and social media and its exploitation of the physical and social environment in a range of ways, make Boko Haram a threat form that transcends the conventional battlespace. Moreover, Boko Haram's insurgency, in part due to 'the interconnected nature of modern society' (Deep 2015, 1), has evolved into a threat that Nigeria's military forces have struggled to contain. Somewhat like the elephant to the many blind men in the famous allegory, therefore, Boko Haram's threat has come to mean different things to the different military, security and non-security stakeholders in Nigeria. In part due to the group's broad spectrum of activity, some writers have even referred to Boko Haram's insurgency as 'a hybrid security challenge' (Comolli 2015, 153–154).

It is, nevertheless, problematic to conflate an insurgent group that employs a range of tactics with a so-called hybrid threat. Such categorizations, moreover, may prove in practice to be little more than a label of convenience: as much for policymakers in Abuja as for military commanders in the theatre. Additionally, radical Islamist movements like the Shabaab over the last decade in Somalia, as well as Daesh in Iraq and Syria, share features of both Maoist and post-Maoist models. In this sense, Boko Haram's spectrum of activity is hardly unique.

Still, the mostly undefined and shifting nature of Boko Haram's threat – like those of Daesh and al Shabaab – makes it a more difficult COIN challenge, both in the overt and in the covert battlespace. Thus, whereas I am averse to situating Boko Haram's archetype of political violence within the conflicted debate on hybrid warfare, it nonetheless is worth highlighting how the group's spectrum of activity makes it a more potent, and certainly more unconventional, threat.

To begin with, Boko Haram's ability to deploy over its overt and covert front contributes to its threat on and off the battlefield. On the one hand, Boko Haram's standing army elevates it above criminal outfits which do not possess its military capabilities. However, the nature of Boko Haram's covert operations, on the other hand, make the group far more dangerous than regular armies which, as an example, cannot (or refuse to) employ suicide bombings. This mix of the conventional and the asymmetric has helped protract Boko Haram's threat against a Nigerian Army that was formed not to combat irregular warfare but to counter-balance the local threat of conventional land forces: from Francophone West Africa, and from the most extensive regional military force and Nigeria's great rival, in South Africa (Omeni 2017, 24–25).

Boko Haram's blending into the civilian population, moreover, means that government forces set up an ever-increasing number of urban checkpoints, with an ever-increasing number of troops to operate them. Boko Haram's formlessness also means that even innocent civilians, within these heavily policed areas, may constitute potential suspects. This is a classic insurgent warfare tactic: the insurgent gets the government to flood the theatre with troops. Once this happens, it is these forces as well, not just the insurgents, that make the news for disrupting civilian life. Boko Haram also operates as a networked enemy: using a spider web of spies, lookouts and informants, including young children, to quickly exhaust the intensity of intelligence operations against it. Such behaviour, again, is archetypal of weaker guerrilla forces waging an insurgency. So too is criminality, such as in the robbing of banks and village raids. Such forces, after all, require financing from a range of illicit sources. Kidnapping also features within this archetype: with women used as rewards for fighters. Abductees of both sexes are also held for ransom or could be strapped to Person-Borne Improvised Explosive Devices (PBIEDs) and sent on suicide missions. Male abductees are more likely to be used as reluctant foot soldiers by Boko Haram.

Another classic insurgent warfare feature identifiable within Boko Haram's campaign is the spectrum of minor actions removed from the battlespace (such as psychological warfare waged via the power of film: the beheadings, canings and demonstrated authority with Boko Haram-controlled hamlets). A final feature in this non-exhaustive list is the role of the technological environment in shaping external perceptions of the battlespace. Boko Haram's embrace of social media and new media is both hypocritical to its worldview of Westernization and essential to its threat projection. Features such as these are essential to situating Boko Haram's military threat within the broader debate on newer threat forms posed by post-Maoist insurgent groups (Mackinlay 2012).

Frank Hoffman defines this new threat form as one that, typically, 'incorporates' in parallel or at different points of its campaign, 'conventional capabilities, irregular tactics and formations, and terrorist acts including indiscriminate violence, coercion, and criminal activity' (Hoffman 2008). As this chapter has shown, such a spectrum of activity indeed coincides with Boko Haram's tactics. This shifting nature of Boko Haram's threat, whatever its label, connives to make it a more difficult COIN challenge, in both the overt and the covert battlespace and even beyond. It is a threat that has come a long way, from when a ragtag group of riotous individuals first took up arms in the name of Boko Haram, in July of 2009. From the warfighting tactics such as that demonstrated within the Battle of Monguno, to the use of information warfare and unconventional methods such as suicide bombings, there is little doubt, as this chapter has shown, that Boko Haram's military threat has indeed sophisticated beyond the conventional and perhaps even hybridized to a degree.

Conclusion

Historically, covert activity and guerrilla warfare have been the mainstay of insurgencies. As conflict matures, however, territorial ambition may become increasingly feasible for rebel groups. In such a scenario, insurgents may well begin to assemble and field an irregular army, in order to realize that ambition. This is consistent with phase three of the Maoist insurgency archetype. Moreover, unless carefully managed, insurgencies that mature to this extent – whereby heavy military fighting comes to dominate the calculus of war – have a good chance of further escalating to full-blown civil war. Such a state is the revolutionary's ultimate objective.

Boko Haram's insurgency, while not entirely conforming to the classic Maoist model, demonstrates some of its archetypal features. For instance, in eventually being able to field a standing army, and in using that army to capture and hold territory between 2014 and 2015, Boko Haram's insurgency has certainly matured within the military space. By 2014, motorized infantry offensives, and capabilities that include unarmoured technicals, light and heavy armour, and artillery, came to underpin the escalation of Boko Haram's military fighting ambition. This improvement in Boko Haram's military capabilities caused the engagement to move up higher up the conflict escalation ladder. To this point, conflict character assumed a higher intensity as Boko Haram deployed its manoeuvre elements, such as those listed above, against Nigerian Army formations.

In amassing a standing army and in seeking territory, however, Boko Haram had opened itself to the possibility of counter-offensives and tactical air strikes, by the Nigerian Army and Air Force. The Air Force, in particular, was instrumental to the degradation of Boko Haram's overt front. Since 2013 the NAF escalated its sorties and played a central role in COIN joint effort (JE). This enduring role by the NAF posed a considerable threat to the movement of forces and *matériel*, by Boko Haram's overt front and to its territorial ambition (Omeni 2017, 190–199). Territorial control, after all, meant Boko Haram could not refuse the engagement when NAF fighter jets came by. The insurgent had to stay and fight *in situ*. In such territorial battles against Nigeria's land forces, Boko Haram's rank and file, its standing army, had a fighting chance. However, against fighter jets and without anti-aircraft defences? These insurgent land forces stood virtually no chance.

As a counter-adaptation, Boko Haram began demonstrating the use of anti-aircraft guns that have afforded it a measure of protected mobility against the air threat. Airpower by and large still comes out on top within these confrontations. However, the nature of surface-to-air technological advances drastically increased the odds of Boko Haram's survivability. Boko Haram's surface-to-air capabilities, demonstrably modest as they have proven, nevertheless elevate insurgent-controlled spaces from 'permissive' to 'non-permissive' environments for rampant air sorties.

For Boko Haram, the sum of the above considerations means that threats of establishing an Islamic Caliphate within Nigeria, which rang hollow early in the life cycle of the insurgency, became a real possibility by late 2014. Indeed, so relatively sophisticated did Boko Haram's overt front become by late 2014, that police units long since stopped being the group's primary opponent. Even toughened and foreign-trained Nigerian military garrisons, and outfield battalions, deployed to the north-east, became battlefield targets.

Considering that security forces initially viewed Boko Haram as little more than a nuisance made up of riffraff, this military evolution of the movement, in about a half-decade of operations, is difficult to ignore within the conversation of Boko Haram as a threat form. Individually, Boko Haram fighters may be a mix of coerced and poorly motivated volunteers, an unkempt, unprofessional, motley bunch of *talakawa* – common folk and country bumpkins. Together, however, and with training and arms, this army of irregulars has proved a tough opponent for Nigerian army units up to formation level.

This chapter's study of the Boko Haram case, moreover, suggests that, for the insurgent, the *nature* of tactical deployment of ground forces, and the timing of this deployment, could be just as crucial as troop numbers or aggregate capabilities. Irregulars may have the numbers, training and equipment, but the asymmetric nature of insurgency means that government forces tend to have more – sometimes orders of magnitude more – of everything the insurgent can field. Moreover, there is a considerable threat of airpower, which few insurgents across the world have managed to demonstrate.[24] Due to such asymmetry, the insurgent must adopt untraditional approaches, and deploy his forces in ways that frustrate government forces' traditional manoeuvre advantages.

Firm grasp of infantry tactics, speed and highly mobile motorized infantry, dispersion of forces, the element of surprise, knowledge and exploitation of terrain; these are all ways by which Boko Haram has come to make the most of an otherwise motley army of irregulars against a Nigerian Army that manoeuvres poorly at scale. Training and affiliations with other terror groups likewise also helped the maturation of Boko Haram in military fighting (Udounwa 2013). All of this indicates that by early 2015, using its standing army, Boko Haram had demonstrated enough territorial ambition to startle even the most sceptical observers of its military sophistication.

Despite this, and unless the odds of a battlefield decision are stacked heavily in his favour, the typical insurgent cannot rely on military fighting, and his standing army, as his sole plank of operations. No matter how active military fighting is for the insurgent, his most potent threat typically remains in the area of covert operations. For Boko Haram, this has proved correct. For all the display of belligerence by its overt front between mid-2014 and 2015, overall gains in this area were wiped away in a matter of weeks by the superior Nigerian land and air units (Omeni 2017). This decimation of its standing army forced Boko Haram's gradual reversion to guerrilla tactics – suicide bombings in particular, but also gun attacks – between 2015 and 2019.

Chapter 8 shall next discuss the technicalities of these tactics and how they have sustained Boko Haram throughout its campaign. Especially during periods of the conflict when war fighting, or indeed any significant activity by the insurgent's standing army, has proved an unrealistic operational objective.

8

Suicide Bombing and Guerrilla Warfare: Boko Haram's Covert Front

'I suppose it is tempting, if the only tool you have is a hammer, to treat everything as if it were a nail.'

– Abraham Maslow (1966, 15)

Introduction

In contrast to Chapter 7, which discussed the technicalities of Boko Haram's overt front, Chapter 8, continuing this volume's meditation on war and insurgency in Nigeria as it relates to Boko Haram, shall discuss the group's covert threat.[1] Guerrilla warfare, Boko Haram's approach to it, and why it has been so successful within this plank of operations – specifically in the area of suicide bombings – are the main areas to be examined in this chapter. Within this examination, the theory around suicide bombing shall be used to explain the practice as it occurs within Boko Haram's case.

From Chapter 7's analysis, it becomes apparent that the insurgent has much to consider if he is to field, and is to be successful at fielding, an overt front. Mobilizing, equipping, training and deploying a standing army for a long-term campaign is, typically, an enterprise for a qualified General Staff and several supporting military and non-military structures such as an Office of Training and Operations, an Office of Policy and Plans, multiple civilian contractors, foreign partners, and so on. The process of preparing such an army, moreover, itself takes time. Thus, an army that is operational today may have had months, even years, of planning, forming and preparations.

Even where the insurgent can field a well-trained and well-equipped army, however, he still faces an uphill task if open confrontation of government forces is the object of war. Traditional government forces, after all, tend to have the doctrine, capabilities and, often, the experience, for pitched battle and the heavy mechanized engagement. Government armies were historically formed up and armed for this purpose. Herein lies the problem for the government's army in counter-insurgency, however.

Maslow's hammer

With state forces historically attuned to employing traditional military advantages, they swear by those advantages – even when faced with insurgents who opt for guerrilla warfare and choose not to engage government forces using the doctrine and concepts with which the former is familiar. However, as one British Army colonel interviewed for this study intimated to me, counter-insurgency is not warfighting, and to even consider framing a COIN campaign along conventional lines, as though facing a similar-sized traditional military adversary, is problematic (Hall 2012). Still, it takes a while for this reality to sink in for government forces, and the insurgency may well have matured by then.

This attitude is what psychologists refer to as 'Maslow's hammer', a cognitive bias that makes an actor too reliant on an instrument which they have always wielded, and with which they have become too familiar. The phrase is coined from Maslow's statement in his classic text, *The Psychology of Science*, where he observes, 'I suppose it is tempting, if the only tool you have is a hammer, to treat everything as if it were a nail' (Maslow 1966, 15).

With the Nigerian Army so used to employing its traditional advantage (its 'hammer'), even non-traditional threats like Boko Haram, for such an institution like the Army, still approximate a 'nail': that is, an adversary that can be defeated by a familiar tool. Now, this might apply, to some degree, to Boko Haram's overt front. Where the insurgent wises up and shifts to guerrilla warfare and covert operations, however, these traditional advantages do not count for much. Indeed, they may become counter-productive in some scenarios. Using Maslow's analogy, a hammer ceases to be the right tool, and attempting to force the issue with that tool may only lead to problems. How so?

Well, over time, the guerrilla gets better at his tactics. Bombs lead to more casualties. Gun attacks become bolder and more effective. Ambushes get more spectacular; sabotage, more disruptive for the government and people. This saps the military's restraint on the one hand, and even relatively small acts of terrorism add up to discrediting governance and the rule of law, on the other. At this point, moreover, the incumbent might interpret the insurgent's low-intensity activity to mean that his threat is weakened and that a massive military operation – a final full-blooded thrust, so to speak – is what is required to overwhelm the seemingly diminished enemy. However, such misreading of insurgency's battlespace could lead to what Neumann refers to as an over-reactive target response (2005): the detention of people, the kicking down of doors, indiscriminate use of force and similar acts of coercion. Essentially, the employment of a hammer where there are no nails in sight, so to speak. The insurgent feeds off the blowback from this sort of target response; he is invisible and difficult to strike; and, as frustrated government forces lash out, they further alienate the population.

Boko Haram and guerrilla warfare

Guerrilla warfare has historically been appealing to the insurgent because 'it is cheap and easy; waging guerrilla warfare does not require procuring expensive weapons systems or building an elaborate bureaucracy. And it works. At least sometimes' (Boot 2013, xx). Boko Haram has exploited such advantages of guerrilla warfare, as its tactical fulcrum throughout its campaign. Certainly, as Boko Haram's standing army sophisticated, there was some reduction in covert activity and a spike in military fighting. This was discussed in the preceding chapter. Even with that trend towards military fighting, however, the guerrilla threat did not go away. Indeed, with its overt front losing 90 per cent of territory and being considerably degraded by March and April of 2015, Boko Haram reverted to its first principle of guerrilla tactics. This reversion is not surprising insofar as Boko Haram had always run an efficient guerrilla campaign.

At a time, for instance, Boko Haram was causing so many civilian casualties, with so few attacks, that no other perpetrator group in the world – not even Daesh – had its casualties-per-attack ratio. Figure 8.2 highlights relative casualties-per-attack ratios of Boko Haram and Daesh, between 2013 and 2014.

A second argument for the operational efficiency of Boko Haram's war is that its financial and military cost of war – comparative to the millions displaced, the thousands killed, the military mobilization to counter its threat and indeed the scale of the conflict it has generated in north-east Nigeria – is negligible. Insurgency, as has been pointed out, is 'cheap' (Boot 2013, xx).

In addition to being efficient, Boko Haram also has been an effective guerrilla. A strategic level argument to support this assertion is that Boko Haram, through the violence of its campaign, has come closer to achieving its goals of destabilizing north-east Nigeria than could ever have been imagined in the group's formative years. At the tactical level, Boko Haram's attacks have been able to penetrate even hardened Nigerian Army, security and government locations. Moreover, at the operational level, the extent to which Boko Haram has been able to project its threat is evidence of its effectiveness and an indication of just how dangerous this threat is. In 2011, even before Boko Haram became prolific at martyrdom operations (*al-amaliyyat al-istishhadiyya* or *istishhad* for short), the group bombed the United Nations building and the Nigeria Police Force (NPF) headquarters (The BBC 2011b, The BBC 2011c). Both locations were in Abuja, the Federal Capital Territory, far away from Boko Haram's contested areas in north-east Nigeria.[2] The police HQ bombing at Louise Edet House, Abuja, was Nigeria's and Boko Haram's first ever suicide bombing.

Since then, Boko Haram has further demonstrated its technical proficiency at IED making. Loss of its bomb makers in 2009, and 2012 slowed the pace of bombings but did not stop them as the driver of its covert threat; bombings still occurred frequently and still did so increasingly further away from the insurgency's heartland of Maiduguri. Indeed, between 2013 and 2014, Boko Haram was so effective as a guerrilla that it became one of the most lethal perpetrator groups in the world. In 2014, Boko Haram's share of global deaths caused by terrorism increased by 300 per cent over 2013 (Varin 2016, 3). Figure 8.1 shows the relative threat of Boko Haram within the period between 2013 and 2014.

As seen in Figure 8.2, moreover, between 2013 and 2014, Boko Haram arguably came to surpass even Daesh in terms of violence resulting in civilian deaths. It is striking, moreover, that even with almost 2.5 times the number of attacks conducted by Boko

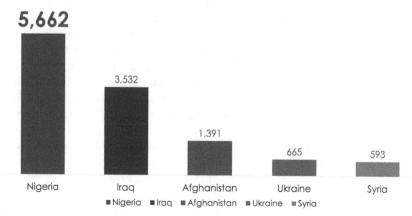

LARGEST INCREASES IN DEATHS: 2013 TO 2014

Figure 8.1 Largest Increases in Terrorism-Related Deaths, Globally (2013–2014)[3]

Haram, Daesh caused considerably fewer casualties – specifically, deaths – over the same period. Also, in relative terms, Boko Haram was responsible for almost a quarter of worldwide terrorism-related deaths at the time. For instance, 'on a global scale, out of 32,658 people killed by terrorism in 2014, Boko Haram was responsible for 7,512 deaths, equivalent to 23 per cent of all terrorism-related deaths worldwide' (Varin 2016, 3). Boko Haram's rise to infamy, as the deadliest perpetrator group in the world, did not stop there, however. The next year, in 2015, Boko Haram 'became the deadliest terrorist group in the world, outstripping the Islamic State, al-Qa`ida, al-Shabaab, and the FARC in terms of the total number of people killed within the calendar year' (Warner and Matfess 2017, 1). The distinction here is that, between October 2014 and April 2015, Boko Haram escalated its threat through military fighting. Whereas, before that insurgency phase (and, for the most part, since), guerrilla warfare outstripped the group's territoriality and military fighting ambitions.

Figure 8.3 also indicates that whereas Boko Haram has been a deadly insurgent throughout its campaign, the phases of military fighting and the deployment of its overt front, in particular, saw an overall increase in casualties. Compared to deaths caused during periods of heavy military fighting, for instance, suicide attacks tend to bring about fewer casualties – typically under half a dozen and very often even less (Warner and Matfess 2017). Sometimes, no casualties may be recorded if the suicide vest fails. This all pales in comparison to the potentiality and actual incidence of overt attacks by Boko Haram. Where the group has deployed an entire battalion or more of fighters, the damage that 800 odd fighters can do in a single instance of contact with civilians or military forces, is considerable. Consequently, it is not unusual for dozens of casualties – military, civilian or a mix of both – to be recorded in a single Boko Haram attack that involved heavy military fighting (Omeni 2017). So why, therefore, has Boko Haram not just stuck to guerrilla warfare as the weaker side's expedient?

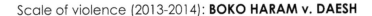

Scale of violence (2013-2014): **BOKO HARAM v. DAESH**

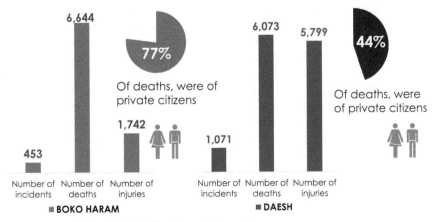

Figure 8.2 Relative Scale of Boko Haram Violence.[4]

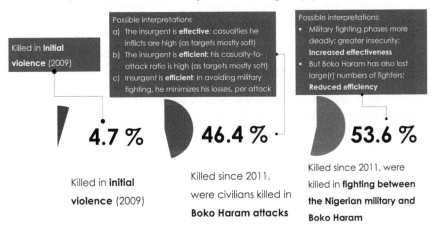

Figure 8.3 Casualties as a Consequence of Boko Haram's Insurgency, as of 2015.

I shall revisit this question in a bit more detail, shortly. For now, however, it is suffice to say that military fighting has been a double-edged sword for Boko Haram. On the one hand, it facilitated the group's pivot away from war avoidance towards territorial battles fought by its standing army. On the other hand, military fighting has brought about heavy losses for Boko Haram. By deviating from a war avoidance doctrine and engaging the Nigerian military up to formation level, Boko Haram has lost large numbers of fighters, platforms and equipment. Some of these platforms (heavy armour in particular), initially confiscated from the Army, would be difficult or impossible to replace. Such losses, consequently, have forced a shift in Boko Haram's calculus of war back towards a guerrilla action set. Central to this action set, for Boko Haram, has been the tactic of suicide bombing.

Suicide bombings as the tactical fulcrum of Boko Haram's guerrilla war

More so than any other capabilities demonstrated by Boko Haram in its rebellion, the tactic of suicide bombing has complicated Nigerian Army operations to stabilize the country's north-east. No military today has a failsafe doctrine against the suicide bomber, particularly when seemingly arbitrary civilian targets, rather than likely military formations, are the primary targets of the bombers. Suicide bombings are particularly damaging to the government's narrative of progress against the insurgent. More so than other forms of attacks, suicide bombings instil terror and deepen the sense of insecurity within targeted areas. Furthermore, martyrdom operations give the lie to the notion that government forces can dominate the insurgent at every rung of the conflict escalation ladder.

On the contrary, what conventional wisdom suggests, and as is observable in the Boko Haram insurgency case, is that government forces often struggle to contain, much less dominate, seemingly inferior insurgents: so long as these rebels stick mainly to guerrilla tactics. Indeed, at the lowest levels of combat intensity – such as in suicide attacks where the engagement is altogether avoided, and yet casualties still occur – it is the weaker insurgent, not the strategically superior counter-insurgent, who dominates. Thus, in avoiding the engagement yet dominating the battlespace and forcing government forces to expend inordinate amounts of resources in the defence, suicide bombings give war avoidance a new meaning.

There is some theory to explain this observation wherein government forces fighting weaker insurgents underperform and seemingly experience a plateau of operational progress as the conflict protracts. In conflicts where one side is much more powerful than the other, and where the stronger side has weapons it cannot deploy due to the nature of the conflict, then the restraint shown by the stronger side means that it is, effectively, handicapped to a degree against the weaker. With this apparent handicap in place, the engagement devolves to the low-intensity space where the weaker, not the stronger, may have an edge. In the words of Martin Van Creveld:

> Given time, the fighting itself will cause the two sides to become more like each other, even to the point where opposites converge, merge, and change places [...] a strong force fighting a weak one for any length of time is almost certain to suffer from a drop in morale .... (Van Creveld 1991, 174)

With over eight years of operations as of the time of writing, such a drop in government forces' morale is observable within the Nigerian Army's COIN.

The cost of military fighting for Boko Haram

If suicide bombings as a subset of guerrilla warfare activity, in particular, seem to lower the cost of insurgency relative to warfighting, when then did Boko Haram seem to prefer, for extended periods, a territory-seeking and engagement strategy over a doctrine of war avoidance and suicide bombing?

Part of the explanation here may be that the cost to Boko Haram, of a territory-seeking strategy underpinned by military fighting, was not immediately apparent. Rapid gains between late 2014 and early 2015 may have misled the group into believing that an enduring doctrine of military fighting will serve it as well as one of war avoidance. After all, towns and communities had fallen before Boko Haram; Nigerian Army units were overrun; and, in taking Gwoza as the capital of its so-called caliphate, the Mobile Police (MOPOL) School there also was overrun. Indeed, by January 2015, it seemed like neither the police nor MOPOL and not even the Army were a match for Boko Haram. Confidence in the territorial gains made by its overt front, for instance, led Boko Haram to quickly declare its captured territories as the Islamic State in West Africa Province (ISWAP) (Comolli and Robertson 2015b).

Along these lines, and brimming with confidence in September 2014, after a particularly lethal year of campaigning, Abu Shekau, Boko Haram's leader, would say that 'Allah used us to captured Gwoza [so-called capital]; Allah is going to use Islam to rule Gwoza, Nigeria and the whole world' (Windrem 2014). Shekau's comments came in the months preceding the start of Boko Haram's Harmattan Offensive, a period that led to dramatic territorial gains by the end of Harmattan season, in February/March 2015. Shekau's remarks, however, ultimately proved illusory. Over the next six months, the Nigerian Army defeated Boko Haram's forces at Gwoza and recaptured the strategic town. As Boko Haram's overt front tried to assert itself in defence of other captured territories, losses within the enemy's standing army began to mount. The inefficiency of military fighting compared to guerrilla warfare became, increasingly, stark. It was a bitter experience, one the group is yet to recover from as of September 2019, where Boko Haram continues to fight, for the most part, a guerrilla war.

With military fighting unrealistic and territoriality increasingly abandoned, guerrilla warfare may well be the one approach that can protract Boko Haram's campaign and simultaneously make the regional counter-insurgency effort look poor. Moreover, Boko Haram as a guerrilla outfit at this stage of the conflict may well be at its most dangerous. There now is less need to calculate for the long term, less incentive to be methodical and more benefit in being spontaneous and highly unpredictable.

Cumulative campaign losses also mean that, for Boko Haram, objectives must now be smaller and limited. This insurgent must now think tactically, rather than strategically. In this tactical recalibration, few tactics are more lethal, controversial, or generate as much academic and media debate, than suicide bombing. Indeed, so instrumental has this tactic been to Boko Haram's enduring threat that it is worth a more detailed investigation.

The (suicide) bomber might not always get through, but istishhad (martyrdom operations) still gives war avoidance a new meaning

Increasingly since 2011, Boko Haram's suicide bombings or martyrdom operations (referred to as *istishhad* for short) have, overall, been central to its calculus of war. Why, however, is this tactic favoured by guerrillas? 'What does it [self-sacrifice] offer that could not be gained from the skilful use of an ordinary weapon?' (Géré 2007, 392)

There are some responses to this question. One is that, with *istishhad*, Boko Haram has the means to redress the asymmetry between its forces and those of Nigeria. Chapter 6 discussed the concept of the ORBAT and its role in COIN. Despite having irregular elements of the Infantry, Artillery and Armour as the three combat arms of its standing army, Boko Haram remains vastly inferior to the Nigerian military in conventional terms, except in highly localized instances of the engagement. As an aggregated series of confrontations, therefore, that is, at the theatre level, Boko Haram cannot hope to dominate in any of these three combat arms.

Moreover, Boko Haram also cannot rely on airpower as an additional arm – a potentially crippling handicap for the insurgent. Finally, at least one of Boko Haram's other three combat arms, in armour, is highly underdeveloped with only a few motorable pieces. All of this makes the task of military fighting, as a sustainable objective, daunting for Boko Haram. A battlefield decision against the Nigerian Army consequently is improbable, to say the least, due to such asymmetry. In *istishhad*, however, Boko Haram has introduced a highly unconventional tactic, by which it can redress this asymmetry. Suicide bombers can penetrate hard targets; they can project the enemy's threat much further than his standing army; and, unlike, traditional land-based capabilities, the suicide bomber is not seen or heard until it is too late. Furthermore, in *istishhad*, Boko Haram has a tactic the counter-insurgent cannot ever use, no matter the desperation of proceedings.

A second possible response to the question around the appeal of suicide bombing to guerrillas has to do with the nature of suicide bombing itself. No government can claim to be entirely defensible against suicide tactics. To borrow a statement by Stanley Baldwin (Middlemas and Barnes 1969, 722), reinterpreted for the contemporary popular discourses on martyrdom operations, 'the [suicide] bomber will always get through' (The Economist 2005, Bishop 2004). Now, as has been pointed out, suicide bombers do not always get through (The Economist 2004, Corte and Giménez-Salinas 2009). Countermeasures can indeed reduce the probability of a successful suicide attack (Dzikansky, Kleiman and Slater 2012). However, surprise and subterfuge drastically improve the chances of the bomber reaching the target. At that point, it is left to the skill of the bomb maker, to the bomber's discretion, and to the availability of nearby soft targets, to determine casualty numbers.

With so much in consideration for detonation at the pre-planned location to be successful, it is inevitable that quite a few bombings fail. This certainly has been the case in Boko Haram's experience (Warner and Matfess 2017). Moreover, some Boko Haram PBIEDs, who are involuntarily selected for *Istishhad* but are aware they have a suicide vest, have surrendered to security forces, or cried out for help. Such individuals, at the last minute, changed their minds about the mission (Matfess 2017). Still, the broader point of the 'suicide bomber always getting through' argument is that, on the balance of probability, if the insurgent keeps refining his plans, reselecting targets and sending more bombers, the chances of one eventually getting through, are high (Dzikansky, Kleiman and Slater 2012).

More than just an ability to penetrate defences, however, the tactic of suicide bombing also gives war avoidance a new meaning insofar as the insurgent can project power 'cheaply', with a low relative cost to overall campaign resources (Dzikansky, Kleiman and Slater 2012). Moreover, the larger the capabilities gap between insurgent and counter-insurgent, the greater the impact of each successful bombing, as a show of strength aimed at bridging that asymmetry. This is consistent with the fact that 'the suicide volunteer is the response of last resort in a strategic situation marked by [a] fundamental asymmetry between the adversaries' (Géré 2007, 392). Perpetrator groups tend to adopt guerrilla warfare because they are weak and have few options (Boot 2013, 43). Take the case of Boko Haram, for example. Around the period when it was able to reduce asymmetry by other means – such as by fielding an overt front, training it and acquiring platforms and equipment – Boko Haram's tactical dependence on *istishhad* also reduced. By contrast, Boko Haram's defeats within the Nigerian military's late-Harmattan offensives between February and April 2015 forced a swift reversion to guerrilla attacks. Suicide bombings, in particular, have increased since 2015 even as heavy military fighting as reduced.

Hard versus soft targets

Boko Haram has conducted numerous suicide attacks on public venues and institutions linked to the Nigerian government, since 2014. Noteworthy here is that such attacks have been on civilian institutions, rather than on military formations. Targets of this nature, where casualties are more likely to be civilians going about their day-to-day, are generally known as soft targets. This is because such targets are more accessible for a suicide bomber to penetrate, often demonstrate crowd disorganization, and thus, in many instances, lead to significantly higher deaths and injuries than bombings at hard targets. Hard targets, by contrasts, tend to be military locations or heavily reinforced police and civilian locations. In the case of ad-hoc events and venues fortified by troops and a police presence specifically deployed as a preventative measure against the threat of suicide bombings, such locations may also be said to be temporarily 'hardened'. In this sense, they differ from military installations and bases which, especially in areas at risk of insurgent attack and influence, generally operate in a perpetually hard state.

Hard targets, generally speaking, have not yielded as much success for Boko Haram (in terms of casualties, media coverage and overall utility) in its suicide bombing attempts. This in part is because suicide bombings on military formations (not checkpoints) are problematic for Boko Haram for a range of reasons. To begin with, over the years since the first bombings in 2011, Nigerian military and security units deployed in the north-east have become increasingly familiar with the tactic. Multiple barricades, antipersonnel obstacles, specialist police bomb squads and bomb detection units, and road checks are amongst the range of preventative measures now employed *in situ*.

Moreover, unknown individuals walking up to a hard target, such as a military formation, without clearance, identification and possibly a military escort, could be shot dead – with little notice unless they heed early warnings. By contrast, the same person walking into a marketplace, religious institution or public space may not be searched on many occasions; they certainly are less likely to be shot dead.

For Boko Haram, therefore, an informal cost-benefit analysis of where to send its suicide bombers and PBIEDs, with the highest chances of success, leaves a stark choice, a choice that puts the civilian population at a substantial disadvantage, yet that also complicates the Army's security task.

Thus, as reprehensible as martyrdom operations against soft targets are, such targets and the attendant suicide bombings aimed at them are deemed acceptable as a wartime mechanism. This holds not just for Boko Haram, but also for some violent jihadist perpetrator groups and radical Islamist movements around the globe. The section that follows aims to shed some light on the controversy around such use of the suicide bomber, as an asymmetric warfare instrument, by such groups.

Controversy around use of suicide bombing

For perpetrator groups and rebel movements that adopt the tactic, suicide bombing constitutes a legitimate tactic given that such groups are fighting government forces that they cannot otherwise openly confront. The insurgent, we must remember, has no Cruise Missiles or precision ordnance; he possesses no airpower (or at least he rarely does). Indeed, perpetrator groups possess no credible means to project power within the most hardened locations in contested areas, except using the suicide bomber. After all, how can government forces claim to be prepared against a suicide bomber, which is just a face, similar to everyone else around? Still, this idea that martyrdom operations are acceptable in irregular warfare, even where the insurgent is being hammered and faces imminent defeat, is mired in controversy.

The term 'martyr' today connotes a willingness to sacrifice one's self for a religious cause. Some suicide bombers – 'martyrs' – may indeed, willingly and conscientiously, sacrifice themselves, embracing the illusion of some paradisal reward awaiting them in the afterlife, after detonation. The dark reality of the suicide bomber, however, is that many individuals – men, women and children of both genders – are forced, drugged, coerced and even tricked, into self-sacrifice. Moreover, in virtually every setting the tactic is used; it is deeply controversial, even when adopted by the most violent perpetrator groups.

As much today as historically, the debate on whether or not *istishhad* is permissible, as a military option in violent (lesser) jihad, is conflicted. Shi'a Islamist militant group, Ḥizbu'llāh, who at a time was prolific in the use of *istishhad*, said in 1999 that 'if we [Ḥizbu'llāh] had possessed conventional weapons with which to fight the Israeli invader, martyrdom would have been an illegitimate means. It was necessity that permitted recourse to martyrdom operations' (Géré 2007, 392). Some adopt the opposite view, that use of *istishhad*, by Islamist militant groups, is an ideological fundamental for such groups; the tactic is not merely an expedient employed based on necessity and/or the threat of imminent defeat. *Istishhad* in this context is not some a last resort but is always a viable tactic said to be, 'in a deeply malicious corrupting of the religion's true tenets' by Salafi-Jihadist networks like Al-Qaeda, 'a sixth pillar of Islam' (Schweitzer and London 2009, 321). Suicide bombing along these lines 'has become the archetype of Muslim violence …' (Feldman 2006). There are, however, a series of critical rebuttals of this thesis.

It is, for instance, a commonly held view that 'there is no link whatsoever' between terrorism tactics and religion (Schmid 2011, 23). Other counter-arguments present variations of this broad position. Shaykh Afifi al-Akiti, in his fatwā (response by a qualified Muslim scholar) against the killing of civilians in the name of Islam, notes that suicide bombing is an innovated practice that has no basis in Islamic law (Sharia). Indeed, Shaykh al-Akiti disputes the notion that suicide bombing is ever a form of martyrdom, writing that 'murderous suicide is never martyrdom but rather perversion' (al-Akiti 2005, 8). This view is consistent with other refutations of the permissibility of martyrdom operations in Islam: 'the technique of suicide bombing is anathema, antithetical and abhorrent to Sunni Islam. It is considered legally forbidden, constituting a reprehensible innovation[5] in the Islamic tradition' (Ihsanic intelligence n.d.). An important fatwā in this area is also that issued by Ayatollah al-Udhma Yousof al-Sanei, important as Ayatollah al-Sanei is one of the highest ranking Marja clerics within Shia Islam.[6] Ayatollah al-Sanei dispelled the notion that *amaliyat istishhadiya* (martyrdom operations) are permissible in Islam, decreeing a fatwā against suicide bombing, which he declared to be a terrorist act.

Despite this demonstrable degree of consensus within both Sunni and Shia Islamic jurisprudence on the illegitimacy of martyrdom operations in jihad, some schools of thought, and of course the perpetrator groups that employ *istishhad*, do not view the practice as innovation. Many of these groups even justify its operational use; specific examples are Al-Qaeda, Ḥizbu'llāh, Fatah al-Majles al-Thawry (Abu Nidal), Haqqani network, Boko Haram and Al-Shabaab. The notion, moreover, that these groups do not understand the Qur'an or that they are 'misguided' may not be entirely true. Such groups simply may have chosen to interpret it differently. Groups using terrorism in the name of Islam do not necessarily represent 'deviant sects', but are often guided by a radical interpretation of the religion (Schmid 2011, 25).

The debate of whether it is permissible under any circumstances aside, the fact remains that, on the strategic, operational and tactical levels, *istishhad* is a viable tool for the insurgent. Strategically, it 'at least partially redresses imbalances [in military capability]. On the logistical level, it is a useful, effective, inexpensive, easily renewable weapon. And on the tactical level, it is effective because it relies on human intelligence' (Géré 2007, 392).

The tactic of istishhad in Boko Haram's insurgency

Within the tactics employed by Boko Haram's covert front, *istishhad* in particular has been an area the Nigerian Army has failed to grasp, much less implement a fail-safe counter against. Boko Haram's mastery of *istishhad* is consistent with the experience of other terrorist organizations. This area of guerrilla warfare is one where other perpetrator groups, globally, tend to get proficient fairly rapidly (Moghadam 2011). After all, the logistics themselves are relatively unsophisticated: a belt, explosives, sometimes a vehicle and either a willing or a coerced suicide bomber (Géré 2007, 391–392). Still, so much could go wrong between bombmaking and eventual detonation that many suicide attacks also end up being unsuccessful. Suicide bombings seldom yield a hundred per cent success rate. 'Success' is dependent on factors outside the bomber's control. For instance, even a last-minute change of venue, or additional unscheduled security measures on site, could mean that even if everything else goes to plan, the bomber has much fewer victims, or limited access, upon arrival. For such reasons, whereas the tactic of suicide bombing has a relatively low entry barrier, the casualties-to-suicide attack ratio has in many cases been typically low (Moghadam 2011), especially considering the bomber is usually counted as a fatality in each successful detonation.

Consistent with the preceding argument, use of *istishhad* so relatively early in its life cycle, and the frequency of employment of such attacks, indicated that Boko Haram quickly became technically proficient at the tactic of suicide bombings. Moreover, as this particular guerrilla tactic had never featured in Nigeria, the shock and awe effect of the earlier attacks was magnified. Indeed, scepticism greeted the first few suicide bombings. Some Nigerians who heard of the new tactic dismissed it as a one-off or said it simply confirmed suspicions that Boko Haram fighters were not Nigerian. Nigerians, according to this popular view, were too in love with life to blow themselves up. The rampancy of suicide bombings since 2011 when the first bombers struck, however, shattered that myth. Suicide bombing was not a one-off tactic by Boko Haram; it was now a Nigerian problem to be redressed.

The female suicide bomber presents a unique challenge

Use of female suicide bombers since 2014 further evolved Boko Haram's covert threat and cast an even darker shadow over the practice in north-east Nigeria. Whereas the employment of women in martyrdom operations indeed presents a unique security challenge, it is, however, not a uniquely Nigerian phenomenon. Indeed, an examination of terrorist operations, in general, suggests that 'Islamist groups are by no means averse to recruiting women. Even nowadays women arouse somewhat less suspicion, and they are as highly motivated as men' (Géré 2007, 389).

Nonetheless, in Nigeria and even by the standards of Boko Haram, the use of female suicide bombers introduced a disturbing element to political conflict. There already had been stories of Boko Haram paying young boys in Borno paltry sums, or otherwise coercing them, to act as IED couriers. Such individuals are referred to as 'mules': they act without knowing the package contents, or that their packages might even be set off remotely. Indeed, 'in especially blunt terms, some have referred to children's roles as undetectable bomb-carriers as "little carts," for "their ability to sneak hidden weapons through military checkpoints without arousing suspicion"' (Warner and Matfess 2017, 34). However, in the introduction of women and young girls as suicide bombers, Boko Haram has been further exploited, to the fullest extent, every possible advantage within its bombing campaign.

Increasingly since 2014, a tactic has been adopted by Boko Haram whereby an IED is strapped to females and concealed using some form of the veil covering – the hijab, niqab or burka. Now, only females use these coverings as part of their attire in northern Nigerian public spaces. Such coverings, moreover, are mandatory in many of the Sharia adopting states of northern Nigeria. This category of the suicide bomber is one where a woman or girl, using the secrecy afforded by the veil covering, effectively becomes a human vehicle for the eventual detonation of an improvised explosive device (IED). Especially when the individuals are ignorant of the situation they are in, they sometimes are referred to as Person-Borne Improvised Explosive Device (PBIEDs). Regardless of whether the PBIED tactic utilizes willing or coerced females, from the perspective of Nigerian military forces prosecuting COIN operations, it is harder to guard against, when a female PBIED is employed.

To begin with, males are typically forbidden to interact inappropriately with females publicly, in many parts of northern Nigeria that have adopted Islamic law. The north-east of Nigeria, and more specifically Borno, Yobe and Adamawa states, have amongst the strictest Sharia laws. There are punitive consequences, typically canings, for civilian men who run afoul of this custom. In the case of soldiers deployed in these states, such interactions could provoke outrage in situations where they have to pat down (search) local females. In an area like Borno for instance, with stringent Sharia laws, females to be patted down would typically, for reasons of modesty, be wearing the veil covering in any of its forms (ḥijāb). Unless related by blood or marriage, however, certain interactions, especially potentially intimate ones between males and females, are forbidden in public. That the men in questions are soldiers prosecuting COIN and that the women to be patted down could be Boko Haram operatives does not create a waiver for such local customs and religiously influenced traditions.

The above situation is not just a Nigerian situation, moreover; it is a broader form of the counter-insurgent's dilemma in dealing with local customs and religious requirements in traditionally Muslim areas. Where counter-insurgencies are prosecuted in such strict Muslim cultures, male soldiers who pat down female civilians in public view might be breaking the taboo between the sexes, a situation that could aggravate the local climate. On the other hand, military forces could choose to be more sensitive to the customs and daily life of locals and relax the rules around such pat-downs. However, this might increase the risk that female suicide bombers, with the ḥijāb, are viewed as less of a security risk than protocol would usually demand. Boko Haram, as an example, has become all too aware that hijabi female suicide bombers create a unique problem for a male-dominated military force, in an environment where women live under a set of laws and customs.

Let us also remember, moreover, that the mere prolongment of a military presence takes a toll on everyday civilian life. Civilians, universally, are nervous if heavily armed soldiers suddenly show up everywhere and refuse to leave. In north-eastern Nigeria, some prominent voices such as the governor of Adamawa State, Vice Admiral Murtala H. Nyako (retd), have already likened the Army presence there to an occupation force (Scan News 2014). Similarly, critical views have been echoed for some time now in that part of Nigeria (Daily Trust 2012). Such outspoken views tend to be the minority, but this is very much an unspoken local concern. However, when soldiers begin to pat down women wearing the veil covering, whether in intentional or inadvertent disregard of local customs, they may be perceived as having gone too far. Such forces may well have crossed religious and cultural lines in a situation where the hearts and minds of a deeply traditional and religious local population is a vital battleground to be won. This has been the case elsewhere, moreover; the Nigerian Army is not alone in this dilemma.

Boko Haram's female bomber threat in context

In Iraq, a serving US officer points to a similar problem: 'you really have to have female counter-insurgents if you are expecting to have a successful counterinsurgency strategy [...]. If you cannot access or even deliver a message to half of the population just because of this taboo between the sexes, you're at an enormous disadvantage in trying to persuade people that you're there for reasons that are in their interests' (C. Thompson 2011). Trying to solve the problem during counter-insurgency operations in Iraq, the United States deployed 'lioness' teams of female Marines to 'conduct searches of local women' (C. Thompson 2011). A similar approach has been trialled in the Nigeria case as far back as 2012. Joint Task Force Operation Restore Order (JTF ORO) was the first phase of military operations against Boko Haram between 2011 and 2013. The Army's Operations Officer in 2012, Colonel Musa Danmadami, pointed out in an interview for this book project that the task force employed female personnel, typically from the Nigeria Security and Civil Defence Corps (NSCDC), for this task (Danmadami 2012). Female NSCDC personnel were trained and assigned to pat down and search local females at checkpoints and duty posts, but also in public gatherings and mosques in Borno (Danmadami 2012).

However, this role of non-military female personnel within Nigeria's COIN effort should not be overembellished. Female military and security personnel in Nigeria play a role that, at best, is at the margins of what is a predominantly male operation. Consequently, female-specific searches typically are infrequent, relative to male-to-male pat downs. This, in turn, may have influenced an important statistic worth highlighting within this analysis.

Statistics of Boko Haram's female suicide bombings

For Boko Haram, the lower incidence of female searches, relative to males, meant that hijabi suicide bombers typically had easier access through checkpoints and military roadblocks. In some cases, mainly before Army and security personnel identified the security risk, female suicide bombers quietly walked up to their targets, without being 'harassed' (that is, patted down). When it first emerged, moreover, there was no doctrine for dealing with this threat category. Perhaps government forces had not thought that Boko Haram would go that far with its bombing campaign. So it is explainable then why, since 2014 when the first female suicide bombing was recorded, the spike in this bombing category has been dramatic.

Between 2014 and 2017 alone, there have been 244 female suicide bombings attributed to Boko Haram, 80 of which occurred between January and August of 2017 alone (Warner and Matfess 2017, 31). To put that number into context, the next highest perpetrator group to use female bombers, the Tamil Tigers in Sri Lanka, conducted a total of forty-four female suicide bombings throughout its entire insurgency (Matfess 2017, Warner and Matfess 2017, 30).

What is even more indicative of Boko Haram's dependence on this tactic is that, before 2014, the group had only used males in its bombing campaign. Moreover, compared to Boko Haram's use of the male suicide bomber between 2014 and 2017, the incidence of female bombers is much higher. Figure 8.4 illustrates the female-male ratio within Boko Haram suicide bombings in the period between 2014 when the first female suicide bombing was registered and 2017.

As Figure 8.4 shows, around seventy-six bombings were conducted by males (compared to 244 attributed to female bombers) within the same period (Warner and

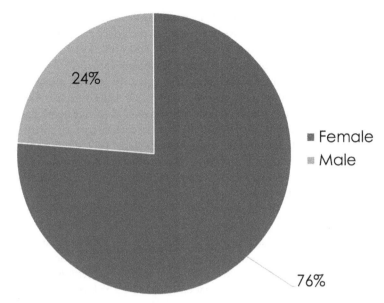

Figure 8.4 Female-Male Ratio of Boko Haram Suicide Bombings (2014 to 2017).

Matfess 2017, 31). Within the same period, therefore, Boko Haram conducted about three times more suicide attacks using females than males. How can this spike in the use of the female suicide bomber be explained?

Mandatory use of some form of covering, typically the niqāb in areas affected by the insurgency, appears to have provided a tactical opening for Boko Haram. The group's perversion of everything from Islamic practices to local customs and traditions has now been put to use in war, and precisely the tactic of suicide bombings. Whereas the veil covering in all its forms has typically been a mark of respect for the privacy of the Muslim female in northern Nigeria, Boko Haram' abuse of this local custom has contorted its perception. The veil covering may now be viewed as an insurgent tactic and thus could provoke suspicion, and possibly even stigma, in ways previously unthinkable. Not even women, girls, pregnant mothers or mothers nursing infants, are safe any longer from the suspicion of being a Boko Haram member.

Female suicide bombers in north-east Nigeria are less effective than males, but more frequently employed

The spike in Boko Haram's use of female suicide bombers in 2017, however, should not be confused with the success of the tactic. First, because, into 2019, female suicide bombers have not emerged as the credible tactical alternative to other forms of Boko Haram's terrorist campaign, that their first use might have suggested. But also, because the use of female suicide bombers raises 'a really interesting question', insofar as female bombers typically register fewer casualties compared to use of male bombers (Matfess

2017) Why then is Boko Haram so dependent on female bombers, 'when they are not as lethal or as necessarily destructive or effective, as their male counterparts' (Matfess 2017)? The answer to this question lies in the insurgent's need to stay active, that is, to be seen as continually staking his claim against the incumbent.

If a single attack with massive casualties or frequent attacks with minor casualties per incident were offered to most insurgent groups, the latter option is likely to be preferable. Why so? This in part is because the frequency of suicide bombings creates a perception of an enduring threat and indicates sustained terrorist activity. A high incidence of several attacks, however small each one might be, has more potential to tie down government resources over the long term. Several dispersed attacks (both timewise and spacewise), moreover, are also more likely to encourage overall security vigilance over sustained periods.

An example could be in the renewals of a State of Emergency, in the creation of more military units, in the deployment of more troops, in the territorial extension of a strategic security perimeter, and so on. A bombing spate also ensures enduring infamy for the perpetrator group. Let us remember that groups of people, whether in the media, in policy circles, within the security environment or in academic settings, will continue to actively debate a group's security threat only for as long as it remains a legitimate concern – a situation best demonstrated by constant activity or at least enduring signs of activity in the long term. If a perpetrator group stops being active, general interest reduces. The group, therefore, becomes increasingly less-debated within the political, military, media and political conversation. However, if a perpetrator group can conduct different terror attacks, even if these attacks are relatively infrequent, it may generate more chatter, and strategic interest, than otherwise.

Thus, whereas female suicide bombers may not be as lethal, they generate more media interest and thus more public debate, per attack, than male bombers – *ceteris paribus*. Use of the female suicide bomber, we must remember, in addition to being even more taboo (relative to other terrorism tactics), is also far less common amongst perpetrator groups than the use of male bombers. Furthermore, the hijabi suicide bomber in north-east Nigeria, again, *ceteris paribus*, is slightly more likely to evade detection than her male counterpart. Moreover, if the female bomber is very young, is either pregnant or is masqueraded as being pregnant, this may yet increase her chances of success even more.

Istishhad as an incredibly asymmetric weapon

Along with the above operational features, which have made the use of female suicide bombers attractive to Boko Haram, we should add the fact that the female suicide bomber is an incredibly asymmetric weapon with great tactical value to the insurgent. Especially when government forces have developed resilience against male suicide bombers by implementing the necessary counterbalances *in situ*, the sudden introduction of the female suicide bomber into the theatre could prove to be a tactical game changer. The tactical advantages provided by female bombers include 'stealthier attack, [an] element of surprise, hesitancy to search women, female stereotype (e.g., nonviolent); increased number of combatants; increased publicity (greater publicity = larger number of recruits); [and] psychological effect' (Zedalis 2004, 7). For a guerrilla that has more or less exhausted his tactical options and thus spent his element of surprise, introducing female and child suicide bombers reignites that element and could present the illusion that a degraded and weakened insurgent is still potent and able to strike at will. Such is the power of *istishhad*, particularly when women and children become operatives of the tactic. Indeed, in the guerrilla's world where asymmetric tactics already dominate, the female suicide bomber '... is the ultimate asymmetric weapon' (Don Van Natta 2003).

Conclusion

Chapter 8 of this volume has focused on the asymmetric nature of Boko Haram's threat. Moreover, in evaluating Boko Haram's covert front of operations, it is crucial, in particular, to emphasize the threat of *Istishhad*. The tactic, after all, is both terrifying and hard to defend against. In Nigeria, suicide bombings have been Boko Haram's most consistent threat projector. The suicide bombings in 2011 at the police headquarters in Abuja, as an example, would have been considerably more difficult for Boko Haram, if conventional foot soldiering was employed. Boko Haram's mastery of martyrdom operations, moreover, extends its threat beyond Nigeria's borders. The twin bombings conducted in the Chadian capital of N'Djamena in 2015, are an indication of the broad operational orbit lent Boko Haram, by *Istishhad*. By comparison, virtually all of Boko Haram's defensible territory, throughout its lifetime, has been in Borno State in north-east Nigeria, and just parts of the state at that – not even most of it.[7]

Beyond the threat that it poses in the Nigeria case, moreover, suicide bombing is so controversial that perpetrator groups employing it anywhere in the world attain new heights of infamy and thus attract more interest from academic, political and practitioner circles. Suicide bombings carry with them a shock and awe effect that gives the tactic staying power within the academic debate space (Warner and Matfess 2017, 2). Boko Haram's instance is no different.

It is nonetheless worth remembering in debating suicide bombing that Boko Haram's guerrilla tactics occupy a broader threat spectrum. Kidnapping, ambush tactics, roadside IED explosions, early-dawn raids, gun attacks on civilian targets, and probing offensives on military and police outposts, are other manifestations of this threat. Nor is the threat in question just a covert one. Chapter 7's analysis shows that Boko Haram's overt front – its standing army – also posed a territorial threat over phases of the insurgency. Moreover, in 2019, with ISWAP and Boko Haram now contesting territory and returning to a military fighting plank in north-east Nigeria, the covert threat may well have become subordinated yet again, within the insurgent's operational schema. How do such conclusions, along with everything else discussed in this chapter, tie into this volume's overall narrative?

More to the preceding question, Part III's combined summary suggests that in addition to its overt territorial threat, Boko Haram generates such a broad range of asymmetric attacks at such a high rate that an analysis of the group's campaign risks focusing on the tactical side of things. There consequently is the risk of losing sight of more significant questions around insurgency and intra-state political conflict as a broad interdisciplinary area of war theory and strategic studies. Such questions, moreover, whether for the conflict scholar, government lawmaker or military commander, are seldom isolated. The lessons from one aspect, or one phase of an insurgency, can be linked, using the right analytical tools, to other phases and other aspects of the same conflict.

In understanding the full-spectrum 'environment' of an insurgency, for instance, it becomes clearer why certain tactics – whether overt or covert – are adopted by the insurgent at certain times and why one tactic instead of another may be problematic if opted for at a given time. On this point, as an example, Part Two's analysis of 'environment' helps explain, amongst other things, why even with its diminished ideological appeal, Boko Haram could still find ways to field sufficient fighters in a standing army. Without this standing army, Boko Haram had to be reliant on guerrilla tactics and relinquish territorial claims. With this standing army, however, Boko Haram has gone on to demonstrate territorial ambition in north-east Nigeria: leading to a shift in insurgent tactics from suicide bombing as the weaker side's expedient, to military fighting.

Furthermore, as both this chapter and Chapter 7 together show, such shifts within the insurgent's calculus of war indicate phases of insurgency and help explain why particular state responses that work at one time might be problematic at another. An insurgent who pivots towards military fighting may struggle against superior fire and the combat arms: the Infantry, Artillery, Armour, airpower and so on. This, moreover, may encourage government forces to invest in those areas of conventional capabilities – leading to an arms race of sort as both sides focus on arms, ammunition and mobile platforms to give them an edge. A situation similar to this could be observed in the escalating arms build-up between Nigeria's Federal Forces and Biafra rebels' conventional army, during the Civil War of Nigeria (Curtis 2004, 174–181, Venter 2015, 91).

Suppose, however, unlike the Biafra rebels who chose to go conventional for particular reasons,[8] the adversary declaring war chooses to go unconventional against government forces? To this point, suppose the enemy switches tactics, relocates its threat from the countryside to municipalities, hides within the population, and employs suicide bombers, what happens then? This approach, precisely, is what Boko Haram has adopted. In response, state forces must recalibrate to confront this threat in a different and more population-friendly way. Outfield battalions may need to change their concept of operations (CONOPS); the military institution at large may need to change its doctrine to be less firepower-oriented; airpower may need to take a diminished operational role as the threat shifts from rural areas and ungoverned spaces to municipalities; and so on.

In the case of the Nigerian military in counter-insurgency operations, whether the institution has indeed recalibrated itself and its CONOPS against an evolved Boko Haram threat is a more complicated affair (Omeni 2017). This is a question that requires an examination of the Nigerian military, its doctrine, and its organizational and cultural challenges. The issue here, moreover, is not purely one of Boko Haram and its tactical and operational strengths. Indeed, in some ways, it is a topic of discussion for an entirely different project.

Nevertheless, in the final part of this volume, I shall attempt to present an abridged version: of why this failure to recalibrate has occurred, and of why the Nigerian military has, consequently, struggled in its operations to counter Boko Haram's insurgency. Before the Nigeria-specific discussion, however, and sometimes stitched into it, there will be some interrogation of COIN theory and case studies to help situate Nigeria's counter-insurgency challenge within the context of the broader debate. Furthermore, Part Four, in the Annexe to Chapter 9, shall also feature an updated evaluation of what theatre-level steps have nevertheless been taken by the Nigerian Army to address Boko Haram's sophistication between 2017 and 2019.

Part Four

The Counter-Insurgency Challenge

War and the COIN Challenge

[Theory] is an analytical investigation leading to a close acquaintance with the subject; applied to experience – in our case, to military history – it leads to a thorough familiarity with it. Theory will have fulfilled its main task when it is used to analyse the constituent elements of war, to distinguish precisely what at first sight seems fused, to explain in full the properties of the means employed and to show their probable effects, to define clearly the nature of the ends in view, and to illuminate all phases of warfare through a critical inquiry. Theory then becomes a guide to anyone who wants to learn about war from books [...] it is meant to educate the mind of the future commander [...] not to accompany him to the battlefield.
– Carl von Clausewitz, *On War* (1976, 141)

Introduction

As Prussian general and military theorist Carl von Clausewitz observes, war theory is essential to the study of war itself (1976, 141). Centuries of the scholarship of war, even of irregular war, hold some explanatory power for observable patterns within modern-day insurgency and counter-insurgency (COIN) (Boot 2013). At the least, we should not entirely discard those past lessons. After all, 'much can be learned for today's population-centric operations by looking more closely at nineteenth-century colonial campaigns' (Rid 2010, 728).

Thomas Rid, along these lines, cautions, regarding the doctrinal lessons from COIN theory, that we are better served by not taking ' ... theoretical lessons for granted that had been distilled from more than a century of practice' (2010, 751). Indeed, insofar as 'staff colleges and military academies debated and captured lessons' from militaries countering insurgencies in the mid-twentieth century, it can be inferred that this war form, in COIN, lends itself to study and to lessons (2010, 751).

Certainly, a grounded understanding of each insurgency's uniqueness is vital to campaign success (Sepp 2005, Ucko 2012). At any rate, such a focused study, in the Nigeria case, has been the object of much of this book. However, useful dots can also be connected by taking a step back and looking at the Nigeria case – at any modern COIN case, most likely – within the broader context of the academic scholarship on insurgency and COIN. This chapter aims to make such connections between theory and practice within what is effectively an abridged summary of Nigeria's COIN challenge.[1]

Conducting a limited critique of the COIN debate while also employing contemporary case studies aimed at testing the theory against the actual practice of COIN by state armies, I shall weigh the pros and cons of this debate and, at each stage of analysis, interpret the implications for the Nigerian military in COIN.

Furthermore, the chapter's examination of COIN concepts aims to balance previous analysis, on the resilience of Boko Haram's military threat, conducted earlier in the volume. In a sense then, Chapter 9 of this book is a coda to Chapter 7. And as for lingering questions around the phases of the insurgency discussed from Chapter 8, hopefully, this chapter's analysis shall help address those too.

Countering insurgent warfare

Insofar as COIN shall be this chapter's focus, it is worth briefly touching upon its definition. COIN entails a legitimate government-mandated military contribution to counterbalance the armed threat posed by perpetrator groups waging an insurgency. Necessarily, if there is a consensus that a particular typology of conflict can be classed as insurgency, then, ostensibly, the government's politico-military architecture aimed at ending that conflict is a COIN.

Part of the issue with the dominant narratives on COIN today, however, is precisely this fact: there is too much a government might be doing which, by definition of the concept, falls under COIN. Indeed, critics argue that that the concept of countering insurgency now encompasses such a broad range of military and non-military activity that it sometimes is difficult to clarify what exactly is *not* COIN. Others say that militaries have no business doing the things they are asked to do in COIN and that, consequently, the core military tasks of soldiering and warfighting within the institution may suffer (Gentile 2008, 2009, Manea 2010). And then there is the terminology and phrasing of objectives, which can be problematic.

Hyphenated compounds like 'nation-building', 'population-centred' and 'enemy-centred' are routinely used to define the concept of operations (CONOPS) in COIN. Such explanations, however, are both 'awkward and unsatisfying'; indeed, 'the vagueness inherent in these statements is a testament to the lack of specificity in the discussion as a whole' (Ucko 2012, 68). This has led some theorists to declare that COIN is 'something impossible to define' (Ucko 2012, 69).

Whereas COIN may be a tricky concept to define, an insurgency is arguably more straightforward to characterize. Going with the Nigerian Army's definition from its capstone COIN operations manual, an insurgency is:

> The actions of a minority group to force political change using a mixture of subversion, propaganda and military pressure; aiming to intimidate the broad mass of people (normally within a state) to accept such a change. It is an organised armed political struggle, the goals of which may be many and diverse. (2011, 4)

Conflicts categorized as insurgencies typically share some features. First, an insurgent, by definition, opposes the State; his quarrel, therefore, is primarily within the borders of the State – the authority of which is contested. The parameters of the contest, however, change throughout the conflict. As Chapter 3 shows, for instance, cross-border considerations may drag neighbouring states into the conflict as politico-military stakeholders. However, a group that violently contests the power of a foreign state is not, strictly speaking, waging an insurgency, because insurgency is a people-centred conflict that requires a *local* group, as the primary actor, for *foco*. Boko Haram, by this definition, is waging an insurgency in northeast Nigeria but is conducting terrorist attacks in Chad, Niger and Cameroon. Boko Haram might have territorial ambitions in these countries; its main quarrel, however, is with the Nigerian authorities and Islamic establishment.

The second feature of insurgency is that the insurgent tends to have a political angle to his quarrel. Rebels might want to change (overthrow) the government leadership or they might demand a change in a particular aspect of the governance system. Armed groups might be contesting territory with the government, or they could be fighting for reparations – such as for some perceived past ill against the population they ostensibly represent. Again, in the case of Boko Haram, its original political manifesto was clear: the establishment of Sharī'ah law is an objective, with the ' ... the [overall] aim to Islamise Nigeria and ensure the rule of the majority Muslims in the country ... ' (Vanguard 2009). Certainly, there is a religious undertone here. In this case, however, the religious and political objectives are inextricable.

A third feature most commonly linked with insurgency is that it is perpetrated with the assistance – coerced, willing or circumstantial – of a section of the local populace. With little relative popular support, armed groups are more likely to be branded terrorists. If so, the government might respond within a counter-terrorism legislative and security frame. Here, the local police, security agencies or limited 'police action' by military forces in a worst-case scenario is likely to be the government's response. Unanimous popular support, on the other hand, might mean the State has a 'people's war' with which to contend. Such a scenario might require the mobilization of the military, with a mandate to defeat rebels by force. The greater the popular support, however, the less likely it is that the army will operate without divisions as it might be perceived as supporting a few individuals in power rather than the wide masses of the population. Indeed, perhaps more than any other feature, this concept of popular support is central to insurgency. As General Alberto Bayo remarks in his classic text, *150 Questions for a Guerrilla*, 'it is necessary to be on the side of the oppressed masses in their struggle against foreign invasion, the imposition of a vile dictatorship, etc. If this prerequisite is not met, the guerrilla will always be defeated. Whosoever starts an uprising against the will of the masses or against a popular regime will fail' (1963, 19). In Boko Haram's early years, Nigerian security and intelligence forces maintained that the insurgency had some local support and, more to this point, a strong Kanuri character to it. For this book project, specifically, there were accounts provided in interview by the Borno State DSS Director highlighting the fact that the Army and intelligence services were battling Boko Haram in areas where locals would not give up the group; that is, where the group retained local support (Ahmed 2012).

A fourth feature, linked to the third, is that the insurgent, especially initially, tends to be a great deal weaker than the State forces he opposes. This in part is why he needs the voluntary or coerced support of the populace to surmount this wartime asymmetry in typically untraditional ways. External actors could and indeed often do, play a role in helping the insurgent surmount this asymmetry: either by giving him the skills and training to become an irregular threat or by giving him the capabilities to pose a battlefield threat. However, this role is perfunctory to local support. If external actors drive conflict from day one, without popular support in the country targeted, the population may view the insurgency as a foreign threat, making it more likely to fail. In Boko Haram's case, it has, *ab initio*, struggled against the asymmetric nature of the conflict. Nigeria's forces are superior in virtually every respect. Not even transnational support from jihadist affiliates, as well as the endorsement of Daesh, has helped Boko Haram bridge this considerable capabilities gap. It is no wonder, therefore, that Boko Haram, early in the conflict, turned to terrorism as the weaker side's expedient.

All of the above features do not, one way or another, make insurgency harder for government forces to counter. They merely are identifiable attributes within this war form as a whole. There exists, however, a set of features peculiar to insurgency, which indeed make the COIN task difficult – primarily because they require government forces to recalibrate from a warfighting action set to a more population-friendly action set. Within the theory, this attitudinal and operation switch is posited as critical for effective COIN (Kilcullen 2010a). In practice, however, such recalibration is neither easy nor guaranteed to yield results. This is part of the counter-insurgent's dilemma: does he stick with what he knows – that is, to tradition – only to find himself using the wrong toolkit (in kinetics) to pry out the insurgent from the population? Alternatively, does he risk recalibrating *in situ*, only to find out that the process of innovating in the crucible of war is neither natural nor a guarantee of better results against a shape-shifting enemy? In evaluating such nuances of the debate, the rest of the chapter presents three reasons why this COIN challenge exists.

1. *Insurgencies frustrate traditional military advantages: Unlike in conventional warfare, a body count may be a perverse success measure. COIN maths runs counter to the Roman model of war*

In conventional warfare, a military's most powerful unit – its most capable armoured corps, for instance – has historically been its centre of gravity, or at least important to its *points d'appui* (tactical fulcrum). Cripple such units, conventional wisdom goes, and you gain a significant battlefield advantage that could provide a manoeuvre advantage over the enemy (Martin 2010, 1). This ability to effectively manoeuvre in proximity to the enemy has been central to land warfare doctrine and concepts for centuries. Suppose, however, the enemy's centre of gravity is not some powerful conventional unit but something else altogether? Suppose the enemy can also frustrate traditional military advantages of state forces by failing to employ external or internal lines, bases and territorial maps?

Much to the disadvantage of conventional state forces, both of the above scenarios manifest when facing off against insurgents, insofar as this threat archetype tends to exploit the population and the environment more than it depends on superior firepower and traditional warfare elements (Van Creveld 1994). Indeed, even where irregulars have some conventional capabilities, destroying an insurgent's most powerful field units is unlikely to provide the pathway to victory that commanders are taught at staff colleges.[2] Such battlefield victories may not even serve to shorten conflict at all. This all suggests that reliance on traditional manoeuvre advantages, which served conventional state armies so well in the past, against today's insurgent might lead to victories that are hollow at best and pyrrhic at worst – if we take into account the cost of war and the toll that protracted insurgency takes on the government and its forces.

To counter insurgency, therefore, militaries directly cannot employ their most powerful conventional armoured and artillery units as though the threat in question was symmetrical: that is, an army of similar size, fighting with a similar land warfare doctrine and concepts and possessing roughly equivalent military capabilities. The sobering reality is that, in this war form, the longstanding stereotype of war as the clash of heavy mechanized brigades fielded by opposing sides – whereby each aims to attrit the other and leave with the fewest casualties – is illusory. The nature of combat here, if indeed the insurgent decides to engage, tends to be low-intensity, and often brief skirmishes: fought on rooftops, in streets, in alleys and hallways, in forests and on dirt roads, and sometimes requiring the most basic infantry tactics on both sides. Further, in COIN, by contrast to the Roman model of war, a body count may well be a perverse measure of success (Farrell 2010). More civilians killed by government forces does not necessarily mean the war is being won (Kolenda 2013). Each insurgent killed might have family members and sympathizers, and each offensive by state forces could lead to casualties that have a 'rally-around-the-flag' effect, whereby the local population is no more keen to support the government (and might even look to joining the insurgency as the least bad option). Let us explore this notion further, using Boko Haram's military emergence, within the Battle of Maiduguri, as a case in point.

Case study 1: Military-aged males (MAMs) and the battle of Maiduguri

The summary execution of Boko Haram's leader in 2009, Abu Yusuf al-Barnawi (Mohammed Yusuf), by Nigerian authorities, the related killings of hundreds of suspected Boko Haram members who went on the July rampage that year, and the subsequent police and security forces crackdown from August 2009 after the Battle of Maiduguri, have been discussed in Chapter 2 of this volume. Building on that incident, I argue here that the nature of military and security forces' response to Boko Haram's riots in that event set in motion a role – one that endures to date – for local military-aged males (MAMs) within the insurgency. I have defined a MAM as a male between the ages of 10 and 54: essentially males within the age brackets of those active within Boko Haram's campaign. This differs from the National Bureau of Statistics definition of a Nigerian 'youth' male as being between the ages of 18 and 35 (2012).

It may seem a little odd that I have listed boys as young as ten, as being military aged. Within the context of Boko Haram's military activity, this age bracket, however, is not at all unusual. Boko Haram has a documented history of deploying child soldiers as young as ten in combat (Hinshaw and Parkinson 2016). To understand the child's role in the conflict, it must be understood that not all MAMs carry guns and charge into battle as fighters in Boko Haram's standing army. As Part Three of this book showed, numerous combat and non-combat opportunities exist for MAMs who are used (kidnapped, trained and conscripted; or willingly recruited), covertly, by Boko Haram.

Picture a scenario whereby a Nigerian Army convoy passes an inconspicuous ten-year-old, walking along a dusty road in rural Borno. The boy is armed, not with a gun, but with a cell phone. A few minutes later, the same convoy is ambushed, based on actionable intelligence provided: by that boy to his Boko Haram handlers. This is just an example of how Boko Haram has exploited young, and sometimes very young, foot soldiers. Thus, whereas MAMs have been defined elsewhere as males between the ages of 16 and 60 (Ricks 2009, 107–108), Boko Haram tends to prefer younger fighters and uses relatively fewer older men. It would, therefore, be inaccurate to define a MAM, within the context of Boko Haram's insurgency, as a male aged from sixteen and above (as this would neglect the much younger fighters preferred by the group).

Boko Haram's preference of males within the youth end of the MAM spectrum should not come as a surprise. As at the time of census data around the Battle of Maiduguri (2009), most Borno males were aged between 10 and 34 (National Population Commission 2010, 71). Further, younger males were, in general, far more numerous than older ones. Moreover, the youngest males had the highest population (National Population Commission 2010, 71). It seems only reasonable, therefore, that Boko Haram's fighters, regardless of how they ended up in the group setting, fall within this very young age group.

More to this point, Borno's sizeable MAM demographic, over 1.2 million as at 2006, made the July 2009 killing and detention of hundreds of insurgents and civilians combined, a short-sighted approach that failed to see the impact it could have on sections of the population. As Table 9.1 shows, that military strategy was flawed, regardless of the tactical and operational success it brought at the time. Coupled with an already unfavourable local view of the police in particular – a sentiment that Mohammed Yusuf had been loudly vocal about for years (Mohammed 2010) – this approach had a negative impact on the availability of MAMs for insurgency. Sections of this demographic likely became sympathetic to Boko Haram, even as the sect got better at persuading and coercing MAMs into its ranks. Moreover, some of these MAMs may just have wanted retribution; Boko Haram's ideology or its caliphate ambitions may have been perfunctory, or entirely irrelevant, to the vengeful state of such individuals. Comolli, making a comparison, for instance, challenges the notion that every Afghan who joins the Taleban 'fully embrace[s] their ideology' (2015, 78). US Army Colonel Kolenda (retd) similarly suggests that, for many MAM insurgents, reprisal against counter-insurgent forces, rather than support for the insurgent's cause *per se*, may be the reason for joining, to begin with (2013, 19–21). Such considerations are pertinent to the role that MAMs came to play within Boko Haram's insurgency, and it was the Nigerian military and security forces' opening gambit, within the Battle of Maiduguri, that first served to exacerbate such factors through the use of kinetics, as an operational expedient, against civilians.

Now, at the tactical level of war, this opening gambit, and this use of kinetics as an expedient, was a success. After all, Boko Haram's ability to wage war was taken away, in the space of a few days. The importance of an outcome like this, from a military planner's perspective, cannot be overemphasized: for commanders leading a campaign, shorter tends to be better. At the operational level of war, the Battle of Maiduguri also was a success; 21 Armoured Brigade fulfilled its military assistance to the civil authority (MACA) task, in record time. Further, there was a clear and documented handover process back to the police, and no additional unplanned assets – airpower, as an example – needed to be deployed as a contingency.

At the strategic level, however, the security forces' intervention was a failure because local support for Boko Haram amongst the Borno MAM demographic was suppressed, not removed. This strategic failure was influenced by the nature of the initial military response. The conduct of the force operations to end Boko Haram's riotous behaviour in July 2009 – including the raiding of the sect's mosque, the streets littered with corpses, the summary execution of Mohammed Yusuf – violated human rights with impunity. This is problematic for a MAM demographic watching events with consternation. People are not won over by seeing a 'hammer' employed that way. On the contrary, depending on how such events affect them, they might even be driven towards the insurgency.

Table 9.1 Tactical, Operational, Strategical Outcomes of the Battle of Maiduguri

Battle of Maiduguri, July 2009. Belligerents: Boko Haram (*Yusufiyya*); Nigerian security forces from Armed Forces of Nigeria (AFN), with 21 Armoured Brigade (21 Bde) as Nucleus.		
TACTICAL OUTCOME: *Victory*	**OPERATIONAL OUTCOME:** *Victory*	**STRATEGIC OUTCOME:** *Loss*
Few losses recorded on the part of AFN	21 Bde was tasked by the GOC 3 Div, to mobilize for MACA.	Support for the *Yusufiyya* was not removed, merely suppressed (for a period).
Unrest quelled, Boko Haram activity put to a stop, attacks on police structures halted	Task came within stipulation of paragraph 8 of the National Defence Policy document.	Overall support for the *Yusufiyya* increased, upon its re-emergence.
Artificial security returned to Maiduguri, with police resuming enforcement of law and order, shortly after Army handover	Task fulfilled without the need to deploy any additional unplanned assets. Indeed, not all assets within the operation's ORBAT had to be strained to achieve its victory.	Yusuf's death – the way he was killed, extra judicially by the police – complicated things. The movement was effectively handed over 'from a demagogue [Yusuf] to a madman [Shekau]'.
Enemy leadership decapitated (as was discussed in Chapter 7, whether decapitation works, in the long term, is a different matter)	Military operation, with Army spearhead, was successful in just three days. No lengthy military campaign needed.	The number of people killed or taken into custody – seemingly at random in some cases – provided a base of MAMs. Extent of problem would only begin to manifest circa 2011, during JTF ORO.

Battle of Maiduguri, July 2009. Belligerents: Boko Haram (*Yusufiyya*); Nigerian security forces from Armed Forces of Nigeria (AFN), with 21 Armoured Brigade (21 Bde) as Nucleus.		
Group's HQ was destroyed. This removed the possibility for the structure (near the Railway Terminus) to remain a congregation point. However, the HQ in question, *Ibn Taymiyyah Masjid*, was a mosque. So its destruction must have aggravated locals.	Clear and documented handover from Army back to police, for stability operations (SO).	Boko Haram, as a long-term security threat, did not go away. Ethnic identities that link the insurgent to his population base transcend religion, and cannot be severed by military operations.
	No NAF Close Air Support (CAS) required from 79 Composite Group, Maiduguri (this could have been a worst-case scenario).	Security in Maiduguri remains artificial. The outcome of Battle of Maiduguri effectively failed to translate the artificial security at the time, to long-term stable piece (which can only be provided by the government, not the Army).

Table 9.1 denotes the outcomes of the Nigerian security forces' opening gambit against Boko Haram, in July 2009. Despite the decapitation of Boko Haram, via the elimination of its leader, and despite the killing and capture of hundreds of suspected insurgents within this opening gambit, thousands of more males would emerge to battle the Nigerian military and security forces in the years to come as the insurgency matured. How is this possible? In classical warfare, after all, the more enemy combatants are killed, the fewer, by definition, should be left to pose a threat. However, the reverse of this paradigm is what COIN theories refer to as a form of cause and effect, specific to insurgencies, that 'turns "attritional math on its head"' (NATO-ISAF 2009, 2). Why is this so? NATO COIN doctrine offers some explanation,

> From a conventional standpoint, the killing of two insurgents in a group of ten leaves eight remaining: 10–2 = 8. From the insurgent standpoint, those two killed were likely related to many others who will want vengeance. If civilian casualties occurred, that number will be much higher. Therefore, the death of two creates more willing recruits: 10 minus 2 equals 20 (or more) rather than 8. (NATO-ISAF 2009, 2)

Kolenda refers to the above dynamic as 'COIN math – counterinsurgency math' (2013, 19–21). Kolenda is asked what most MAMs would do if family members were killed or wounded by military forces deployed to defeat an insurgency? If there was a possibility of revenge (by joining the insurgency), Kolenda suggests that even he in that position, 'would probably fight' (2013, 20). Relating this to the emergence of Boko Haram's overt front, whereas the events of July 2009 did not create that front *per se*, it facilitated an environment whereby 'COIN math' came into effect, leading to a considerably more viable recruitment environment for the insurgency. Moreover, more significant MAM numbers in a locality might lead to the higher the risk that the insurgent targets such areas to recruit and coerce into joining (Kolenda 2013, 19–21). And with such a large MAM demographic to tap into, Boko Haram would eventually form a standing army that it could persuade or otherwise coerce into fighting for it.

Therefore, as a result of the strategic failure of the Nigerian military and security forces' approach, an entire population category, MAMs, went from being passives – historically disaffected passives with a bunch of social inequalities to contend with, but passives nonetheless – to actively participating in the insurgency by 2013 (Bello 2012). These MAMs would over time be armed and extensively trained in basic infantry tactics, sometimes by jihadists groups outside the country as Boko Haram first began to leverage its transnational terrorist links for operational use (Bello 2012). It is this standing army that helped transform Boko Haram's calculus of war: encouraging a pivot away from limited guerrilla tactics, towards a larger territory-seeking strategy driven by a more significant number of available fighters.

Linking back to the COIN theories discussed earlier in this section, what the above Battle of Maiduguri case indicates is that a government, therefore, cannot deploy its military forces to attack the populations that harbour insurgents, as though it is attacking a foreign invader. Whereas the insurgent, in a matter of speaking, 'invades' the state and aims to take control of the hearts and minds of the people, and whereas there inevitably will be some grassroots support and local sympathy for the insurgency, the humanitarian and political cost of such a kinetic counter-revolutionary strategy by the state, is, strategically, simply too high. Achievement of short-term objectives is often confused for sensible strategy, but it should not be.

Moreover, there is COIN math to contend with, whereby the use of kinetics to bring about what seemed to be a tactical win at the time could create near-irreversible strategic setbacks. This blowback effect is arguably what the Nigerian government still faces today. Such measures as curfews and states of emergency, which flood communities with troops and limit everyday life, also make locals uncomfortable and increasingly resentful of the 'occupying force'. One mistake by these troops, such as a public show of force by a restless private that leads to local civilians being killed or unfairly detained, could create a blowback effect of heightened anger towards the Nigerian government and sympathy towards the insurgency. This ties back to this section's central theme: despite strategic superiority, government forces are at a relative disadvantage in a people-centred war form that generally discourages force.

Reversal: Whereby the soldier changes action-set and becomes more civilian-friendly

If, however, coercive force operations, which potentially could backfire, are a poor option in COIN, what others are there? Another approach by some contemporary militaries is the deployment of forces into affected areas, but with a de-emphasis on kinetic force operations and an emphasis on a more civilian-friendly action set. The aim here is to build local networks and to conduct influence operations. Such operations, quite aside from the task of preserving peace and protecting strategic territory, have three key objectives. First, they aim to gain the trust of local communities and to build networks within these communities. Second, in helping troops gain the trust of the host communities, influence operations try to dissuade locals from supporting the insurgency, by leveraging local trust and already-built networks. Such networks may include civilians, influential leaders, clerics, pro-government militias (where available), and local law enforcement such as the police, intelligence services and state paramilitary outfits. Third, having built robust community-level networks, influence operations aim to persuade moderate or passive grassroots supporters of the insurgency to switch allegiance to the COIN effort.

In focusing on civil-military cooperation (CIMIC) as a way station along the typically tricky route to winning locals' 'hearts and minds', military planners hope eventually to isolate the insurgent. This population-centred approach, conducted largely by military forces advised by a few civilian experts embedded within the operation, is less about kinetic operations to dislodge the insurgent and more about friendly actions and civil gestures that send positive signals, win over locals and limit the insurgent's ideological and social influence within vulnerable communities.

A risk here, however, is that the level of protection that government forces typically enjoy, within barracks, for instance, is compromised. By interacting with locals – even attempting to integrate troops within communities – the counter-insurgent makes himself vulnerable. The insurgent, over time, could continually attack, and bleed out government forces. The aim? Frustrate troops' attempt at reinventing their identities to match the tea-sipping, group selfie-taking, community-friendly soldier archetype.

This strategy to gaining influence in the civilian space, therefore, appears counter-intuitive notwithstanding its potentiality for long-term stabilization. The notion that troops should coexist with locals and 'assume greater risk in order to gather much-needed intelligence and, in the end, achieve greater safety' runs counter to the military's historical instinct. This, however, is the paradox of expected conduct in modern COIN. As former United States Ambassador to the United Nations, Samantha Power puts it in her review of US COIN doctrine Field Manual 3–24, 'sometimes, the more you protect your force, the less secure you may be.' 'Sometimes, the more force is used, the less effective it is.' 'Sometimes doing nothing is the best reaction' (2007).

2. Smaller armies, Nigeria's included, struggle to shift from the Roman model of war and embrace COIN's doctrine and concepts. Yet, larger armies, including those that formulated such concepts and that influence contemporary COIN theory, have also underperformed in its operations. A critique of the COIN literature, therefore, indicates that the theory is at odds with practice.

As relevant as Ambassador Power's words might be to COIN theorists, however, they are an unnatural maxim to military traditionalists. The traditional approach to military warfare, after all, often connotes an ideology of the offensive (Snyder 1984). War, in this frame, is a soldier's occupation, one that historically has involved violence and the employment of superior firepower to inflict injury and death on enemies. The more conventional capabilities an army possesses compared to its battlefield opponent, the stronger the urge to go on the offensive and remove the threat by force. Losses on the part of the superior army may only serve to infuriate its General Staff and deepen its resolve to inflict battlefield defeat on a weaker enemy, especially where the capabilities asymmetry is particularly pronounced. 'If stronger foes than you could not withstand our offensive power', such generals might be thinking, 'how then could you?' Over time, this attitude self-reinforces, becoming culturally entrenched within the institution. The more victorious an army is by employing the offence, the more reliant it tends to be on the offence, the more institutionalized the offence becomes, and more the offence comes to dominate its calculus of war, over all else, in plans and operations (Snyder 1984).

In the case of Nigeria, an institutionalized predilection towards firepower and strategies that favour the offensive are what Nowa Omoigui refers to as the military's 'ammunition mentality' (2015). During the Civil War of Nigeria (1967–1970), against rebels employing similar doctrine and operational concepts to the Army, but who, capabilities-wise, were vastly inferior, warfighting and the cult of the offensive drove the Army's strategy successfully. This success, partly what Brigadier General Alabi-Isama refers to as 'the tragedy of victory' for the Nigerian Army, stifled reform and served to reinforce the institution's reliance on strategic dominance and superior firepower (Alabi-Isama 2013). Against Yan' Kala Kato and 'Yan Tatsine rebellions in northern Nigeria in the 1980s, again this ideology of the offensive worked (Isichei 1987, Falola 2001). And, again, it served to entrench negative pathologies within the Army's institution. Against rebels in Liberia, and in Sierra Leone during the Army's 1990s' peacekeeping adventures in West Africa, the same outcome: success, and yet more confidence in superior fire and traditional military advantages. Against Niger Delta militias, force worked – to a degree; rebels were more minded to accept the 2010 Presidential Amnesty Programme incentives (Bello 2012), because they were not confused: the government, via the military as its most coercive tool of statecraft, was prepared to wield a heavy stick indefinitely. So, here we effectively see over three decades of kinetic force yielding utility for the Nigerian Army. Could this institution be, perhaps, forgiven for assuming that force is the preponderant requirement for 'battlefield' successful against any threat?

Against people-centred insurgency and a formless enemy, however, this kinetic mindset, on the one hand, is damaging to the civil-military interface, and on the other, it has caused the Nigerian military to have a problematically narrow view of COIN and network-centric warfare. Consequently, the military's recalibration for a COIN culture, all the more urgent due to Boko Haram's Proteus approach to war today, has been slow and fraught with problems (Omeni 2017). This is not so much about the Army meeting its match in Boko Haram, as it is about asking a traditional and bureaucratic institution, which has repeatedly used one approach over the years, and has repeatedly found success doing so, to suddenly change its concept of operations (CONOPS) and forget about its traditional military advantages.

A significant challenge for the Nigerian military as a counter-insurgent, therefore, is not just understanding that insurgency constitutes a departure from traditional warfare, but also recalibrating accordingly. Nor is it just the difficulty of learning the differences between COIN and warfighting, *per se*. The challenge in question is a more primitive one, not even unique to the Nigeria case. The problem here is unlearning decades of a successful approach and trusting in this new approach. Even though its written doctrinal manuals still smell fresh from the printing press (with officers meant to be commanding units, shortly in the COIN theatre, still not having read the thing). Even though this approach is fraught with untraditional recommendations; and, even though this approach – COIN – holds no guarantee for success against insurgent warfare. This is the challenge. It is a challenge which, as US Army Lt Colonel (retd) John Nagl puts it, requires unlearning to eat soup with a spoon and, instead, 'learning to eat soup with a knife' (2005). In practice, this is much easier said than done.

Nevertheless, how does one even go about attempting this task? How does a military reinvent itself: its doctrine, its culture, its institutions, and, crucially, its entire CONOPS? Moreover, how does it do so, *in situ*, such that these adjustments actually help it win an ongoing war?

On paper, the start point to making this adjustment, for the Nigerian Army was a switch, aimed at changing its fighting approach, from (responsive) offensive doctrine to the Manoeuvrist Approach to War (MAW) since the 1990s (Nigerian Army 2009). Insofar as much as been made of this switch to MAW within the Nigerian Army (Omeni 2017, 50, 97, 105–109), it is worth taking a closer look at what the manoeuvrist approach entails within the debate frame of the COIN challenge.

The manoeuvrist as a better counter-insurgent

As opposed to traditional attritional warfare, MAW is a tactical fighting doctrine that adopts a more indirect approach, that emphasizes positional elements and effects over firepower, and that uses a mix of kinetic and non-kinetic activity to deter the enemy and achieve objectives. This approach approximates a better approach to countering insurgent warfare, than attritional warfare, which is the more traditional approach to degrading a threat and which is 'aimed at "the reduction of effectiveness of a force by the loss of personnel and matériel"' (Kiszely 1998, 36). MAW's supposed effectiveness is because of the approach's non-kinetic thought process around problem-solving: as much in war as in operations other than war. Major General John Kiszely MC provides further insight around how such an approach that de-emphasizes kinetics, insofar as it might be the manoeuvrist's preferred option, may well be the better choice in operations other than war, including COIN:

> If the manoeuvrist approach can be applied to all levels of warfare, can it be applied to operations other than war – for example, in peace enforcement, counter insurgency or even peacekeeping? Providing one substitutes the word 'opponent' for 'enemy', there seems to be no reason why this should not be so, since one's opponent in these scenarios has cohesion and a will to resist which can be targeted. This holds true equally at the tactical level: a junior commander, for example, facing a road-block in Bosnia, and permitted by Rules of Engagement to do so, may choose to force his way through; but, equally, he might achieve his aim by distracting his opponents and sneaking round a flank, by jamming their radios, or by getting his superior to threaten sanctions against his opponent's superior. An attritionally-minded commander might naturally select the first course; a commander imbued with a manoeuvrist approach would, I suggest, tend to consider the other options first. (Kiszely 1998, 39)

Other writers make this connection between the manoeuvrist approach and more effective ways to counter insurgent warfare. Lance Crowe, as an example, is more to the point, such as where he alludes to 'counter-guerrilla tactics' being referred to, more formally, as 'manoeuvre warfare' (2011). This is similar to the Nigerian Army's own apparent recognition of the manoeuvrist's advantage in COIN. 'Because the theory of manoeuvrist approach shares a common ancestry with some of the most successful insurgent strategies', the writers of the Nigerian Army's COIN manual argue, 'the military planner educated in this [manoeuvrist] doctrine is more likely to cope with the inherent complexities of COIN' (Nigerian Army 2011, 141).

Codified doctrine is not necessarily practising doctrine, however. And the Nigerian military, despite this codified switch and its own sage words, in practice has long failed to embrace the tenets of manoeuvre warfare over its historical bias towards an ideology of the offensive. Moreover, as has been pointed out regarding the Nigerian military in COIN, 'being a good manoeuvrist does not mean a free pass to being a good counter-insurgent. COIN does fall within the manoeuvrist's skill set; but the navigation of the civilian-military interface, for instance, may well require a lot more [than just an understanding and implementation of manoeuvre warfare]' (Omeni 2017, 107). In other words, so what if the Nigerian Army, eventually, fully embraces manoeuvre warfare concepts within a COIN context? So what if its codified and practiced COIN doctrine is, eventually, synergistic? Shall we, therefore, at that point of synergy, expect to see a quick turnaround and a swift end to the Army's COIN campaign against Boko Haram? Probably not.

The attritionists make their case

Also, whereas there is this suggestion that an outright switch is required, from attritional warfare to manoeuvre warfare, we also must remember that 'in practice, warfare is a balance of manoeuvre and attrition, but opponents tend to place emphasis on one or the other in their approach, depending on where they perceive success to lie' (Kiszely 1998, 36). Even so, the very mention of an attritionist approach as being compatible with COIN is likely to elicit groans from the latter's most ardent apologists who push for an altogether different approach in this war form (Kilcullen 2010a). Too often today, the notion that hearts and minds need winning, and that it is problematic when hearts and minds are *not* being won, dominates the conversation. Even though the history of government forces that have tried this approach shows mixed results at best.

That COIN's doctrine and concepts seem at odds with the success of its practice have not dampened the increasingly established popular narrative that the insurgent is not to be attrited as though he was a traditional foe (G. S. McChrystal 2013). Indeed, rather than themes of kinetic military force – now the domain of 'a rabid minority', in the words of Frank Hoffman (2007) – a different military attitude to an old problem and a move away from attritional warfare is, today within the COIN discourses, frequently propositioned.[3]

Not everyone agrees, of course. Some writers, for instance, acknowledge that use of force, in and of itself in COIN, is problematic, but question whether it is, in fact, possible to conduct COIN operations, without a civilian body count (McFate 2010).

There are more extreme versions of this verdict. Ong Weichong, for instance, argues for the utility of extreme force measures by the counter-insurgent (2009). Weichong references the Sri Lankan military's defeat of the Tamil Tigers insurgent group as a case in point of when force, and pretty much just an emphasis on force, effectively defeated this threat (2009). Indeed, if COIN is meant to remove emphasis from kinetic force and build a population-friendly approach to operations, the Sri Lankan case is an anti-thesis to this approach. US Army Major Niel Smith, for instance, writes that the principles of the Sri Lankan Armed Forces, in defeating the Tamil Tigers' insurgency, 'stand in almost complete opposition to the conceptualisation of counterinsurgency articulated in FM 3–24' (N. Smith 2009). Proponents of the Sri Lankan military approach will, however, argue that whereas it was kinetic, it *did* work (Mehta 2010).

Moreover, other theorists such as Edward Luttwak take this kinetics as counter-insurgency thesis even further outfield with the view that a more effective approach to defeat an insurgency and indeed to defeat 'all insurgencies everywhere' is to 'out-terrorise the insurgents, so that the fear of reprisals outweighs the [citizens'] desire to help the insurgents' (2007). Luttwak (2007) points to Nazi exterminative COIN practices in the Sudetenland, particularly after the assassination of SS-Obergruppenführer Reinhard Heydrich by Czech resistance operatives in 1942, as evidence. Granted that the retaliatory force measures were so extreme in that case, the Nazis never really had to worry about further unrest in the Sudetenland (Luttwak 2007). Even so, it is questionable whether referring to what effectively were mass executions of Czech Jews (MacDonald 1989), as COIN, is not simply stretching the concept too far. David Kilcullen, for one, is scathing in his rebuke of Luttwak, commenting that the latter's suggested methods:

> Are not a prescription for success, but a recipe for disaster. As he [Luttwak] quickly admits, U.S. and Coalition forces would never consider such methods for a moment. And this is just as well, since this approach does not work. The best method we know of, despite its imperfections, has worked in numerous campaigns over several decades, and is the one we are now using: counterinsurgency. I admit (and have argued elsewhere) that classical counterinsurgency needs updating for current conditions. But the Nazis, Syrians, Taliban, Iranians, Saddam Hussein and others all tried brutalising the population, and the evidence is that this simply does not work in the long term. (2007, 3)

In general, however, even critics of COIN tend to adopt a less vigorous defence of attrition and kinetic force emphasis as a pathway to defeating insurgency, than does Luttwak (2007). Montgomery Mcfate, as an example, cautiously examining the thesis around 'less force' in COIN, provides 'a caveat [...] to argue that lethal force by *itself* is ineffective in a counterinsurgency is not to argue that lethal force is unnecessary or should never be used' (2010, 193). Doug Saunders likewise appears unconvinced of COIN. Heavy and prolonged military presence within contested areas, Saunders argues, combined with military personnel overseeing projects and adopting non-military roles, makes COIN look like 'a lot more like old-fashioned colonialism' (2008, 2). Moreover, doctrinal differences in military thinking around countering insurgency might mean that not all Western military personnel necessarily buy into the US COIN model. As one senior French commander observes, 'We do not believe in counterinsurgency […] If you find yourself needing to use counterinsurgency, it means the entire population has become the subject of your war, and you either will have to stay there forever or you have lost' (Saunders 2008, 4).

Other critics, such as US Army Colonel (retd) Gian Gentile argue along similar lines. To Gentile, the dominant narrative on COIN has some practical 'defects' (2008) and that today's emphasis on 'population-centric COIN' is 'restrictive in and of itself' (Civins 2011, 3). Gentile challenges the practicality of winning hearts and minds, a much-discussed approach in COIN, which he views as being untraditional to the military function (Gentile 2008, Gentile 2009, Manea 2010, Civins 2011). Gentile, whom Civins refers to as 'a strong critic of population-centric COIN' (Civins 2011) (Civins 2011, 1), argues, instead, for the continued relevance of 'hard power' in COIN (Civins 2011, 1). Indeed, 'population-centric counterinsurgency', Gentile contends, 'has perverted' conventional warfighting functions (2009, 5). One of Gentile's criticisms is that this approach insinuates the lengthy, indistinct, task of 'nation-building', which demands long-term military presence and runs contrary to Sun Tzu's own advice that ' … speed is the essence of war' (2008, 16).

Simply put, therefore, COIN is not merely capital, time and resource intensive, it is, in the view of Colonel Gentile, extremely so (2008). Furthermore, and at least within the context of militaries in Africa, COIN pressures these forces to meddle in areas where they may not be particularly good at, to begin with (Thom 1999, Herbst 2004).

Winning hearts and minds takes time, is role-intensive and financially costly for state forces

The chapter's analysis so far suggests that the Nigerian military is not alone in attempting (and mostly failing at) this challenging 'switch': from an almost entirely kinetic action set to one that de-emphasizes force, within COIN. Rather, for most armed forces, this switch to untraditional roles in COIN, which seek to defeat insurgencies with minimal and discriminate use of force, has proved problematic. Why? This in part is because, generally speaking, militaries were not built to fight wars that discourage the use of ammunition, that are population-friendly, that are fought within urban centres and that require as few casualties as each situation allows. Still, this often is asked of today's counter-insurgent: however large or small he is, no matter how limited his COIN experience or capabilities. Now, such adaptation may yet be possible, but we must expect it to take time. Government forces, after all, are being asked, first to unlearn several decades of thinking around the traditional military establishment, and second to discount the operational benefits that past experiences may have yielded through the utility of force.

From the contemporary COIN experience, the time required for this paradigm and cultural shift within the military institution can be no less than several operational tours – about three or four years at the most optimistic of estimates – to reach the stabilization phase. It takes time for armies even to understand how they are meant to effectively win hearts and minds, much less translate the tactical gains of winning hearts and minds into operational success. Put another way, at least a few years and possibly even over a decade, may be required for a military to reconfigure itself for this approach to defeating insurgency. And in the interim will be phases where the winning of hearts and minds appears to yield little if any, campaign progress. Indeed, war planners should expect such phases, not just periods of visible progress, to dominate the campaign schedule.

Time, moreover, is not just the only factor here. There also is the reconfiguration process itself, its logistics, the wartime innovation required and the sheer extensity of roles, new admin structures, changes to tactics, and civilian-friendly projects it entails. All this is in addition to the regular task of combat and support operations that troops should traditionally be preoccupied with. This all means that for today's military planner COIN has come to require many lines of operations (LOOs[4]) and sometimes *very* many lines of operations if some theorists' recommendations are to be adopted (Sepp 2005, Kilcullen 2010a). Increasingly, military action to counter insurgency has come to be ever wider in scale and broader in scope. Indeed, the sheer scope and magnitude of COIN is, for most government forces, impractical and has been questioned. Within the theory, moreover, COIN's definition is said to now be 'too broad, as it fails to exclude from its remit any action ostensibly taken to counter an insurgency [...]. Even the effectiveness of such action is irrelevant to the use of the term, as the definition centres on the intent to defeat the enemy rather than the success in doing so' (Ucko 2012, 68). In other words, in theory, so long as the counter-insurgent sticks to COIN's best practices, even if results do not go his way, everyone should be happy. In practice, this notion is absurd; militaries do not just need results, they need them quickly, where possible. What contemporary experience suggests, however, is that COIN has failed to deliver such prompt results. Why then should today's war planners be quick to embrace this operational approach?

Moreover, so far as operations are concerned, the sheer expense (in the areas of human capital, monetary costs, *matériel* and others) associated with COIN makes it hard to coordinate, challenging to fund and likely to be an inefficient military adventure not least in the area of cost relative to achieved objectives (Chin 2012, 283–284). COIN's financial implications, in particular, are worth considering insofar as it is a campaign practicality that a war chest is required. If troops are to fight and win a war, regardless of what side they fight for, there have to be constant cash flows to support the war effort. Current thinking around COIN, which often fails to accommodate the financial costs of COIN, therefore, 'must properly account for the fact that the scope and scale of any counterinsurgency campaign are determined by the means made available for that campaign' (Liedman 2011, 1).

In the case of COIN operations in Nigeria, as an example, the Army's budgetary strain been admitted by its Chief of Budget and Accounts (The Sun 2014). As is to be expected given everything discussed in this section, such financial strain has been caused largely by the escalation, in scope and scale, of the Army's north-east campaign and the additional operational objectives that have increasingly have required funding.

To ignore such budgetary realities and press ahead with ambitious COIN objectives increases the likelihood of campaign derailment. Such derailment could be because military funding dries up, if, as an example, politicians become exasperated that past funding failed to match campaign promises. Moreover, finance, even where present, may seldom be well-accounted for if campaign objectives are too ambitious (which, in COIN, they tend to be) or if the goalpost keeps being moved (which, in COIN, it inevitably will be). In COIN, after all, conventional wisdom contends that wells need to be dug, schools built, medical outreaches established and military engineering projects completed. With limited funding, however, combined with modest (if any) operational experience in this area of warfare, and possible capabilities issues, most armies prosecuting COIN end up being tasked to do too much, with too little. Indeed, for smaller militaries, such as Nigeria's, the shortfall between what is available, and what the organization is tasked with, becomes stark.

More to the previous point, there just does not exist the capacity, for most military forces – Nigeria's included – for the extensity of military tasks suggested by the theories. As an example, not only is today's counter-insurgent expected to take up the policeman's role, he now is supposed also to do a great deal more, if the task of 'winning hearts and minds' is to be achieved. Even where this approach fails to produce readily observable results, the theories seem stubbornly wedded to this idea. Indeed, in today's COIN debate, it is not unusual that government forces are encouraged to build schools, dig wells, hold town hall meetings, fund public projects, support local militias (and vigilantes) and even get politically involved as deal-brokers who mediate between key stakeholders. It has even been said that military forces prosecuting COIN may well need to be prepared to play the role of 'trash-pickers', all in an attempt to win over the local population (Anderson 2010). All of this is on top of the task of protecting the population, policing, creating effective counter-propaganda and hammering the insurgent into submission all at the same time. Now, this all-encompassing approach might constitute palatable advice, *if* it has worked with iron consistency in practice. On the strength of recent operational outcomes, however, the evidence in support of COIN's effectiveness is mixed. Moreover, weighted against the practical downsides of this approach, COIN's viability is called into question even more.

Case study 3: FM 3-24 and COIN operations against insurgents in Iraq and Afghanistan

As an example, since 2001 in Afghanistan, the United States and NATO-ISAF arguably have come as close to COIN as the literature recommends. This should not come entirely as a surprise. US COIN manual, FM 3–24 Counterinsurgency, promulgated in December of 2006 to overwrite existing doctrine underpinning operations in both theatres, has been one of the most influential contemporary publications. The manual serves as a guide: to how COIN should be prosecuted (through the 'winning of hearts and minds'). Perhaps more importantly, however, FM 3–34 offers guidance around how COIN should not be prosecuted (through the use of a stick, rather than a carrot, by troops living with proximate groups of locals). As a codification of the so-called 'Petraeus Doctrine', which some argue, 'changed the U.S. military' (Bergen 2012), FM 3–24 is quite possibly the most influential COIN military manual in general circulation today (Rich and Duyvesteyn 2012). Indeed, so influential has US COIN doctrine been that in Afghanistan it came to practically supersede NATO doctrine, as the COIN campaign matured.[5]

The background to the emergence of this now-dominant doctrinal thought process goes back to Iraq, circa 2006. At the time, the US Army and Marine Corps had to create this entirely new doctrine because the existing doctrine, interim manual FMI 3–07.22, *Counterinsurgency Operations* (US Army 2004) was poorly suited for activity within a civilian population. FMI 3–07.22 was too focused on the kinetic aspects of COIN, did not emphasize jointness, and was written only for the Army, that is, was too operationally narrow in scope (Russell 2011, 7). Put another way, the United States was fighting a war against insurgents and was trying to use the local population as a lever in this war. Yet, the US Army was both poor prepared, poorly coordinated with the Marine Corps at the 'joint' level (so far as COIN was concerned, at least), and did not even have tailored guiding principles (doctrine) for this task (Russell 2011, 7). FM 3–24 was aimed at fixing such concerns. And, in guiding operations in both Iraq and Afghanistan, the hope was that this winning of hearts and minds would yield results and, sooner rather than later, defeat the insurgent threats in both countries.

This new approach to countering insurgent warfare, as Thomas Rid notes, aimed to reshape the military function such that the counter-insurgent now 'competes against the insurgent for the trust and the support of the uncommitted, civilian population. These assumptions have become a core conceptual foundation of today's counterinsurgency debate and doctrine' (Rid 2010, 727). The writers of FM 3–24 are entirely in agreement with this population-friendly approach. Quoting classicist COIN theorist David Galula (2006) at length, the doctrine's writers note:

> To confine soldiers to purely military functions while urgent and vital tasks have to be done, and nobody else is available to undertake them, would be senseless. The soldier must then be prepared to become [...] a social worker, a civil engineer, a school-teacher, a nurse, a boy scout. But only for as long as he cannot be replaced, for it is better to entrust civilian tasks to civilians. (US Army and Marine Corps 2007, 2–9)

For all this adherence by the United States and NATO-ISAF to FM 3–24's advice and its emphasis on a population-centric way of war, can it be said that there is sufficient incentive for this to be the new standard for armies fighting insurgents elsewhere: both now in the future? Results, after all, have been mixed: with gains and losses, setbacks and progress – much like would be expected in any other approach to countering an insurgent threat. Moreover, on the other hand, there are some downsides of this recommended approach to COIN, which should give even its most ardent proponents pause for concern.

To begin with, the cost of the war in Afghanistan for the United States, in terms of workforce, matériel and money, has been staggering (Liedman 2011). Moreover, a similar assessment could be made of the coalition campaign against Al-Qaeda in Iraq (AQI). Notwithstanding this embrace of COIN's operational concepts, both the United States and NATO-ISAF failed in their mission to remove the Taliban threat from Afghanistan, even if the COIN itself was not an outright failure. Yes, the Taliban have since been removed from power, but that was achieved almost two decades ago, in October 2001; the Taliban, however, continues its insurgency. By 2019, Taliban fighters had retaken much of the territory that COIN effort worked so hard, at great cost and for over a decade, to deny them. Yes, too, AQI ended its insurgency in 2006. However, an insurgent threat in Iraq endures over a decade later. This threat is not unconnected to past insurgencies in that theatre, which the United States had invested so much to counter. The Islamic State in Iraq (ISI), after all, which waged an Insurgency in Iraq between 2006 and 2013, emerged from AQI. And ISI elements would later transform into the Islamic State (Daesh), which remains active in parts of Iraq today.

The above reflections are not to argue for a failure of COIN in Iraq and Afghanistan, although that argument can certainly be made and has been debated for years. In 'Why did we lose in Afghanistan?', a blog post for Foreign Policy, Thomas Ricks writes:

> I think our fundamental failure can be identified right on page one, chapter one of *On War* [von Clausewitz' classic text]. 'Force ... is thus the means of war; to impose our will on the enemy is its object. To secure that object we must render the enemy powerless.' We never rendered the enemy powerless. As a consequence, he continued to counter our efforts to build a stable government and security force within Afghanistan while also engaging us directly in combat. (2015)

Even so, we must temper such strong assertions by clinging to the sobering reality that success and failure in COIN, perhaps more so than other war forms, is relative. The Taliban is not defeated in Afghanistan, but they have been shut out from the highest levels of governance since 2001 and have been weakened. Afghanistan is not 100 per cent stabilized, but, relatively speaking, the government is stable. Coalition forces stayed much longer than expected, at a much higher cost, but the Afghan National Army, and Police, now do virtually all of the COIN tasks and have been well-trained. On each point, there is a noticeable compromise, and this seems to be the central lesson in assessing COIN: compromise on all sides, rather than a clear battlefield victory in its classic sense.

And as for doctrine, and the fact that FM 3–24 notwithstanding, results were mixed in Afghanistan? Well, we must expect doctrine to take considerable time to demonstrate theatre-level impact. So, again, the assertion here is not that doctrine is useless. For instance, the writers of FM 3–24 themselves caution that campaign-level changes, which reflect new doctrine, cannot be expected anytime soon if the doctrine is introduced while troops are already *in situ*, that is, during an on-going campaign (US Army and Marine Corps 2007, x).

Notwithstanding such caveats on the expected outcomes of COIN versus the reality, the Iraq and Afghanistan cases highlight the fact that COIN, as it is popularized within the discourses today, and even where it is consistent with the best practices encouraged within the theory, may be no more or less likely to defeat insurgency than other methods. Added to this, COIN and the various themes it entails have some disadvantages, as this chapter's critique of the theory shows. The pros and cons of this operational approach, therefore, not just what the theory promises as its advantages, should inform today's war planner tasked with countering insurgent warfare.

In particular, for the Nigerian military war planner pondering COIN's operational feasibility, there should be some pause to reflect on all of the areas discussed so far. It may be tempting to reproduce verbatim the sage advice within FM 3–24 *Counterinsurgency*, rebrand this as localized COIN doctrine and then, like stone tablets, hand down copies to mid-level and senior officers. Recent history, however, suggests COIN advice should be weighed carefully, based on its heuristic outcomes in practice. After all the jury may still be out on whether this operational approach, to countering insurgent warfare, actually works (Gentile 2008, Porch 2013).

3. COIN Challenges Normative Interpretations of War as a 'See-Saw Model' of Victory or Defeat. However, Popular Expectation Still Views this Category of Conflict Within the Same Frame

With so many questions surrounding COIN's operational viability, do we conclude that government forces tasked with COIN have been asked to win an unwinnable war? No. Counter-insurgencies are not unwinnable. Moreover, even in stressing insurgency's intractability, one must be careful not to suggest that traditional warfare is by any means easy. Conventional warfare 'is complex too [...] But the complexity of insurgency environments seems to be dramatically greater even than in conventional warfare. Counterinsurgency operations, therefore, invoke a higher than "normal" degree of ambiguity' (Kilcullen 2010b, 143–144). What further sets COIN apart, in addition to its operational ambiguity, is its departure from the normative interpretations of victory and defeat in military warfare. More so in today's complex environment, COIN 'challenges the see-saw model of victory and defeat that is central to war as traditionally conceived' (Simpson 2012, 3). Consequently, the defeat of the insurgent 'may assist in, but not translate to' strategic victory for the counter-insurgent 'because the interpretation of the conflict in terms of military metrics may well be a frame to which most audiences do not subscribe' (Simpson 2012, 3).

If it is the case that we must reconfigure our thinking around the concepts of success and failure in COIN, then let us begin by considering the various concerned parties in the Nigeria case and creating interpretative frames for each. To start with, it may be difficult to explain to the millions of north-easterners displaced by Boko Haram and still affected by its insurgency, that the COIN has been successful. Even though there has been considerable progress made by the Nigerian Army since 2011 when what is now the COIN campaign was effectively a task force objective for a brigade-sized unit (Omeni 2017). The presidency, on the other hand, may well choose to politicize the military's gains against Boko Haram – such as prematurely stating that this insurgent is weak or even 'technically defeated' (The BBC 2015c). For civilians elsewhere in the nation, detached from the theatre of operations, this idea of Boko Haram's 'defeat' might be more readily accepted within the conventional confines of the term if the media reports indicate the insurgent is not as active now as he had been in the past. The military itself, as another stakeholder, and tasked with an enduring policing task for months or even years after government declarations of the insurgent's technical defeat, may reflect rather differently on this notion. Likewise, for local militias and vigilantes who were an active part of the COIN and had some funding and purpose in the war, what happens when operations end and yet these individuals – numbering in the hundreds or even thousands – are left economically hopeless yet armed and experienced in killing? Such fighters do not have some regiment to which they can return to resume the military occupation; they are civilians, not ex-soldiers. The notion, however, that these individuals will hand over their guns and go back to normal civilian life is illusory. The same applies to the thousands of former Boko Haram fighters who are left poorly reintegrated into civil society. Such considerations, with so many frames of perception, indicate that, in insurgency, this interpretative frame of 'military victory' is rarely one shared by all audiences. Along these lines, Emile Simpson (2012) makes a valid point; in COIN there seldom is the polarized outcome of victory or defeat in the conventional sense. Rather, the defeat of the insurgent as conflict wears on fades 'as a strategic priority' relative to the stabilization of the insurgent's past and present spheres of influence (Simpson 2012, 3).

In the Nigeria case, however, the public, as much as the military, for the most part, still interpret COIN within the old 'see-saw model' of war whereas a more accurate assessment of progress may be the extent of stabilization achieved since operations began. Now, the military plays a role here, and the process indeed involves some warfighting at its earlier phases. So, however, is not just warfighting, nor is it business as usual for the military organization. Adoption of untraditional roles, an acknowledgement that several stakeholders must participate, the military's ability to embrace CIMIC, and the role of the police, are all crucial to stability. How then should this narrative on war, as the Roman model of battlefield victory or defeat, be reframed in countering insurgency? Three broad steps are outlined below.

Step one: Remove insurgent presence

The first phase of this process would be the lowering of hostilities as much as time, resources and the environment (whether the insurgent is urban, rural or in the bush) would allow. In the Nigeria case, years of warfighting and operations by the Nigerian military, combined with Boko Haram's territory-seeking phase between mid-2014 and early 2015, in which the insurgent may have fatally overreached his overt front, have already led to an approximation of this objective. This, therefore, is not a military phase that is yet to begin; it has been ongoing for years (Omeni 2017). Even as of August 2019, for instance, and since 2017, Boko Haram attacks in north-east Nigeria have, gradually, lowered in scale, and intensity (refer to Figure 7.3). Military fighting of the sort that dominated Harmattan offensives of late 2014 to early 2015 exists mostly on the margins of the conflict today. Yes, Boko Haram still holds territory (as discussed in Chapter 3). Yes, there still is a human security challenge, within millions displaced (as discussed in the Annexe to Chapter 9). Nevertheless, there has been progressive stabilization of many areas.

Achievement of this objective, however, has required, for long periods, escalated military operations. Fierce military fighting and territorial contests have featured. Simultaneously, the Nigerian military has been self-recalibrating to face an enemy that fights on two distinct fronts. The reorganization of the Army's COIN, which facilitated this phase, has been considerable. Changes are identifiable from the divisional level where HQ, 7 Div and HQ, 8 Task Force Div – two additional Army divisions – were created between 2013 and 2016. The Army's reorganization goes all the way down to battalion level, moreover. Several new battle groups formed since 2015. Many of these new task force battalions operate within a 'roving' capacity in forward areas. Airpower has also featured prominently within this phase: to support troops as well as deter strategic relocations and military fighting by Boko Haram (Omeni 2017, 159–164, 190–199).

Due to the scale and nature of such adaptations above, the 'clearing' phases, which tend to see the most warfighting, may well be the closest approximation of conventional war in north-east Nigeria as both sides deployed elements of the Infantry, the Artillery and the Armour. Such periods of heavy military fighting have been the most disruptive to locals' everyday lives (refer to Figure 8.3). These also are the phases that are most likely to be criticized for the military's reliance on kinetics. This heavily militarized phase, however, may well be unavoidable if the Nigerian military is to completely discourage Boko Haram from engaging – leaving guerrilla warfare as the only viable tactic for the enemy.

Step two: Build resilience, through a strong and task-oriented military presence

Even where the insurgent's presence has been cleared or greatly diminished through kinetic operations, resilience must still be built into troubled civilian-populated areas, chiefly through military or police presence. Insurgents are notorious for reoccupying territories from which government forces dislodge them. Even a weakened insurgent is minded, every now and again, to conduct probing offensives. So long as the insurgent can persistently remain a localized low-level threat, he remains a strategic concern within the state's internal security calculations. The object of resilience building by government forces, therefore, is twofold: initially, to help ensure that occurrence of low-intensity hostilities does not disrupt everyday civilian life, and over time, as this COIN task matures, to altogether limit the incidence of enemy ingress into civilian populated areas.

As an example, to redress the problem of high civilian casualties from insurgent attacks, ad hoc healthcare services could firstly be localized, that is, provided *in situ* via military-run outreach operations. Substantive civilian-run medical services at the community level, or transits between hamlets and health facilities in larger secure cities, may otherwise be impractical. Further, military and police teams may need to patrol communities and towns to reassure them. Beyond a patrol presence, however, some interaction with locals is essential. Especially during this phase when trust-building and social normality are being encouraged, troops do not want to appear too menacing and unfriendly. Finally, government forces' coordination and presence at all the key points of ingress and egress in and out of safe spaces should be credible and highly vigilant yet restrained and disciplined. The counter-insurgent's overall posture here is, therefore, more defensive than offensive. Such credibility would rule out massive enemy offensives to recapture civilian centres, yet the defensiveness is meant to deter rather than force the engagement.

If therefore, the previous step of this COIN reframing resembles conventional war due to its heavy military fighting, the second phase sees a lot less fighting, yet potentially a lot more troops deployed, to facilitate artificial security. As an example, specific to the north-east Nigeria COIN, Figure 9.1 illustrates the scale of military deployments in Borno, down to company (COY) level, since 2015. The Army's formation of several new task force battalions comes as part of HQ, 7 Div's greatly expanded COIN – Operation *Lafiya Dole* – since 2015. The deployment of these teams and the sheer area they now cover[6] has been instrumental to fewer attacks since late 2015, compared to 2013 and 2014 for instance (Omeni 2017). More than just a patrol presence, battalions from the newly formed Task Force Brigades have increasingly become a permanent security feature in many communities. These teams interact with locals. Sometimes, for better or for worse, they are even assisted by para-militarized local vigilante groups, known as the civilian joint task force (CJTF) (Omeni 2017). And then there is the Army's Mobile Strike Teams (MSTs) initiatives, part of the Army's relatively new Mobile Brigade Concept (MBC), discussed in the Annexe to Chapter 9. These all contribute to resilience building *in situ*.

Of course, there are caveats to this idea that resilience building by the deployment of task-oriented military units, spread across the north-east conflict theatre, is central to hostilities' lowering. First, not all locals and senior government officials, are sold on the idea that a heavy military presence is necessary for artificial stability. Some local politicians, for instance, have likened the Nigerian military presence to an 'occupation force'.[7] Additionally, and insofar as the deployment of newly formed units is widespread within Borno and its frontier, the military presence is spread thin and does not cover several communities. Borno state and the surrounding areas threatened by Boko Haram is just too vast, geographically, for task force units to be on the ground, or even proximate, to every single Boko Haram attack.

On the surface, therefore, Boko Haram's insistence appears to give the lie to this notion that the Task Force Brigades' approach, and the subsequent Mobile Brigade Concept, is working. However, there is no such thing as a foolproof COIN. Even with widespread troops' deployment and years to understand and counter the insurgent's presence, government forces may indeed succeed in lowering the overall threat. Altogether eliminating insurgent attacks, however, is a considerably more challenging task.

Nevertheless, despite such caveats, and whereas sufficient resilience building remains a challenge in the Nigeria case, the theory behind resilience building – via embedded operations within civilian communities – remains sound. Population-to-troops ratio in COIN has theoretical and practical relevance to the debate on resilience building, as much in the north-east Nigeria conflict (Omeni 2017, 229–230), as elsewhere (Philips 2009, Thiel 2011). The more troops are available, the more military personnel can work within the civ-mil interface and with communities.

Moreover, such resilience building through the integration of battalions at the community level has been employed in more sophisticated forms within other recent instances of COIN. An example of this localized counter-threat within the US-Afghan COIN was the use of 'Village Stability Operations (VSO), a mission requiring US soldiers to live in Afghan villages alongside the locals and partner with Afghan leaders and security forces to secure their homeland and eliminate the Taliban' (Jantzi 2017).

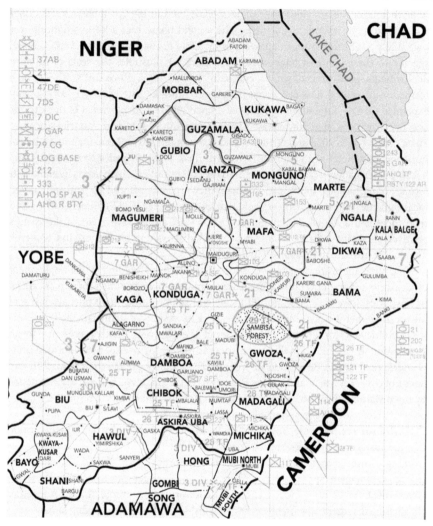

Figure 9.1 Resilience Building via Task Force Battalion Deployments in Borno State (Credit: Author's Sketch (Omeni 2017, 235)).

The VSOs ' … require[d] building partner force capacity in the Afghan military and local police forces while simultaneously improving governance and development at the village level' (2017). The VSO initiative in Afghanistan is a typical example of resilience building via combat and non-combat activities, by mostly combat personnel but with an action set recalibrated for the civilian space.

It should be noted, however, that this idea of the reimagining of the warfighter as a population-friendly individual – seeping tea with locals, taking pictures with children and playing mediator to local disputes – especially when scaled upwards, is a difficult one to implement. Soldiers are not purpose-built for this role. Moreover, such non-kinetic roles may not be feasible before extensive clearing operations have sufficiently degraded the enemy presence. In other words, resilience building of this nature should be expected and planned for as a second or third step into a broader COIN effort, rather than as a first.

As a final point relevant to resilience building, the overall police identity may well be at the periphery of operations over lengthy phases of the COIN campaign. Indeed, the police may rarely be as active as in peacetime, during the warfighting phases of insurgency. It is, nevertheless, vital that the police be at least seen playing some role. Military forces cannot be deployed indefinitely within the public space. When troops eventually leave and return to their barracks, the police must first continue with the stabilization task, resuming, after that, their primary function of policing and community security.

Step three: Stability and the police function

Over the months of resilience building, the local police should have cemented their role in the COIN. This COIN role ideally should be enshrined in police doctrine, which currently is not in the case of Nigeria (Omeni 2017). Still, policing in COIN is not a standalone task. Nor is it as straightforward as deploying police and mobile police (MOPOL) units – as the paramilitary section of the police in Nigeria – to assist COIN effort. Instead, it should come with reforms, training and capacity improvements. Within the Nigeria case, a reframing of the police as a 'service', rather than as a 'force', is all too relevant to a police institution with a badly damaged reputation and a history as a highly coercive appendage of the state against its citizens. Whether or not the police take the lead role in SO, the task must not be underestimated. Nor should it be assumed that stabilization will take months or a few years at the most. This stretch of activity may take several years or even over a decade; that is, it may be even lengthier than the previous phases combined. War planners as well as the government, therefore, must envision this eventuality and come up with a long-term plan, which transcends political administrations and tenures, to stabilize restive areas. Police reform, empowerment, and possibly even rebranding may be crucial within such government plans. The civilian space, after all, is yet to return to normality, if military forces, not the police, provide security. However, as previously highlighted, policing and the police role in COIN is problematic because soldiers are neither trained nor are they particularly keen, to take up the policeman's role. COIN in Nigeria presents a case in point.

Policing duties, within the COIN task, constitute a significant example of a role that the Nigerian Army – as a historically coercive appendage of the state against its own citizens – is poorly suited to fulfil. Indeed, as former British Defence Attaché to Abuja, Col James Hall, notes in-interview, not only is the Army poorly suited for such tasks, its personnel have come to resent being 'policemen' (2012). Notwithstanding these concerning developments for armies deployed within restive areas, war planners are often forced to flood communities with troops to maintain social normality or at least a semblance of it. Local police constabularies are unlikely to defend strategic territory against the insurgent's threat successfully and thus cannot perform the same policing duties during an insurgency that they would in peacetime (Hills 2012). The army, therefore, takes up policing for the same reason it prosecutes such broad lines of operations during COIN: due to necessity. Indeed, whereas many of the tasks the army adopts in COIN 'are best conducted by civilian and humanitarian agencies, the frequent inability of the latter to operate in insecure conditions has and will yet force military troops to assume responsibility for those areas as well, alongside the provision of security' (Ucko 2009, 2).

In the case of Nigeria, capacity issues and a flagrant disregard of police authority by Boko Haram meant that the Army had to assume policing, in its task to counter the north-east insurgency. Indeed, over time, even police stations themselves came under Army protection in affected areas. Police installations, after all, were considerably easier targets for Boko Haram and also sometimes had armouries more vulnerable to looting. Despite the police's lower profile, moreover, some police installations have still been raided or razed to the ground, with police personnel still attacked by Boko Haram, between 2012 and 2016. The police's military section, the Mobile Police, also remained targets. The Mobile Police School at Gwoza, as an example, was attacked and overrun by Boko Haram after multiple attempts in 2014. Even cross-border in Chad, Boko Haram also targeted police stations.[8]

Beyond providing a more accessible pathway to acquiring small arms and ammunition, there is a reason why local police and police installations, tend to be attacked by insurgents over the conflict lifetime. The police play 'a negative role in insurgency because they reproduce the political order that insurgents challenge; their functions usually include regime representation and regulatory activities, so they are targeted' (Hills 2012, 98).

Consequently, the police function tends to be gradually absorbed into troops' COIN roles. This shift in ownership of the policing task, towards the military, is consistent with the gradual marginalization of the police in insurgency. 'In the early days of an insurgency police may attempt to police, but once violence reaches certain levels they either support the insurgents, or they disappear, or they are killed. This is notably [more] so in rural areas where police are rarely present' (Hills 2012, 98).

In the case of Nigeria, and indeed in most cases, whether the Army possesses the capabilities (including the training, anti-riot routines, gear and such) or temperament to assume general policing duties within civilian-populated areas, is debatable. Moreover, there also are workforce issues. To this point, even with several newly formed task force battalions and even with the forming of an additional division at Monguno in 2016 (see Figures 1.1 and 9.1), the Nigerian Army has stretched itself thin by its own admission.

Without providing an exact timetable estimate, the Nigerian Army appears aware of this need to schedule an eventual shift back to regular police functions and the return of civil law as the end goal of stabilization. In 2017 the head of the Nigerian Army (the Chief of the Army Staff), Lt General Tukur Yusuf Buratai acknowledged that progress in the COIN should not be measured by the square miles recovered from Boko Haram or the number of local government areas (LGAs) recaptured by the Army. Lt Gen Buratai observed the need to take a longer-term perspective, in terms of progress made. To this point, he spoke and highlighted the significance of ' ... the reconstruction aspect. We have to see the return of the civil administration [to restive areas], the return of the law and order agencies, the police. This is what we are working at. In terms of military action; militarily; Boko Haram has been defeated' (The BBC 2017b).

Conclusion

Putting together all that has been discussed in this chapter, the scale of the challenge at hand for the counter-insurgent is laid bare. Within this COIN challenge, famously referred to by Colonel Charles Callwell as a 'thankless' task (1996), it seems that there is no shortage of factors that help stack the odds against government forces. Within the Nigeria case, this chapter's narrative suggests that the intractability of the insurgency in north-east Nigeria is not just about Boko Haram's strengths. Rather, the Nigerian military should itself be scrutinized as an institution which, like so many others fighting insurgent warfare, has underperformed against this threat. The problem, however, is not that the kinetic model of war is now irrelevant or even that it has not worked for Nigeria in the past. The problem, rather, is that against today's insurgent, the 'kinetic force as COIN' model is a great deal less likely to defeat this threat. Consequently, the changes required by government forces may be substantive. However, are militaries – is the Nigerian military – ready to embrace the institutional, cultural and operational changes recommended within COIN?

After all, as McChrystal et al. caution regarding the contemporary challenges of larger, more traditional, organizations faced with a 'Proteus' problem – a shape-shifting problem, 'we're not lazier or less intelligent than our parents or grandparents, but what worked for them simply won't do the trick for us now. Understanding and adapting to these factors isn't optional; it will be what differentiates success from failure in the years ahead' (2015, 4). John Nagl in similar vein argues, in *Learning to Eat Soup with a Knife*, that adaptation is not just a vital variable in COIN; it is *the* vital variable (2005). And 'perhaps even more so than being well prepared at the outset' is the ability to adapt, argues Emile Simpson; this is insofar 'as reality often unhinges the best-laid plans' (Simpson 2012, 146).

So, yes, as this volume's analysis indicates, Boko Haram has a resilient organizational structure, competent commanders, a standing army, and has been able to tap into local populations to wage an irregular war. Still, part of the intransigence of the north-east Nigeria conflict, nevertheless, lies in the slow pace of adaptation to insurgent warfare by the Nigerian Army. Therefore, to improve in this war form, the Army may require some soul-searching to figure out why this was the case and what is required.

Along these lines, what does a study of the Nigerian military and its environment tell us about the military's internal function, both real and perceived? How do organizational culture (OC) and historical experience influence the military's perceptions of, and approach to, its internal function? With this function today being both security-focused and predominantly COIN, how have operations been conducted in the north-east against Boko Haram? In what areas have such COIN operations been bottlenecked, and what roles have doctrine and the Army's own institutions played in stifling its practice? In what ways has the Nigerian military counter-adapted against Boko Haram's 'Proteus' attitude and conduct in insurgency? Answers to these questions might make for difficult reading for Nigeria's war planners. However, such considerations, painful as they might be to swallow for this proud institution, must constitute points of reflection for the Nigerian military in COIN.

Annexe to Chapter 9: 2019 Update

Whereas this book's focus is predominantly on insurgency and Boko Haram's specific threat, it has, nevertheless, been useful to explore the counter-insurgency (COIN) challenge in the previous chapter. Chapter 9 employed a mix of theory and practice (local to Nigeria but also via case studies from elsewhere) to illustrate why the Nigerian Army, like most government forces, has struggled against insurgent warfare. Counter-insurgents, however, also get some things right and in so doing, set campaign progress markers. In this regard, so too has the Army in its war against Boko Haram. This Annexe explores campaign progress markers within the Nigerian Army's COIN, between 2017 and 2019. To this end, the Annexe is split into three parts.

The first part discusses COIN operational developments in general. The second part focuses on the humanitarian situation in north-east Nigeria and what the Army has done, as part of the government's broader initiative around displaced persons and the human security challenges caused by Boko Haram's insurgency. Next, the Nigerian Army's Mobile Strike Teams (MST) initiative has emerged as arguably the most crucial operational adaptation within the combat space since operations began in 2011. However, no discussion of this vital battlefield innovation exists within the literature. To this end, the final part of the Annexe is devoted entirely to MSTs. Analysis of the MST initiative will include history and development of mobile warfare doctrine in general. Then, specific to the Nigeria case, the features, deployments, challenges and implications of MSTs for the COIN effort shall be discussed.

1. Military operations to counter Boko Haram's insurgency since 2017

Before July 2015, when Lieutenant General Tukur Yusuf Buratai was appointed Chief of Army Staff (COAS), there was no identifiable and overarching approach – a strategy which superseded theatre-level planning – within the north-east Nigeria COIN. Buratai's tenure brought with it the implementation of a single operational strategy for the various command structures fighting Boko Haram. This strategy, still active as of the time of writing, and continually being developed, is that of Decimate, Dominate and Occupy (DDO). Operations with this new strategic approach that have served to degrade Boko Haram and force it to revert to a more guerrilla-style posture include Op RESCUE FINALE in December 2016, Op DEEP PUNCH in April 2017 and Op RAWAN KADA in July 2017.

Op RADAN KADA, as an example, was primarily prosecuted by the Multinational Joint Task Force (MNJTF) beginning March 2017, which means that during that period, Chadian and Nigérien forces had operational support from the Nigerian Army's divisions, especially 8 Task Force Division at Monguno. At a time when Boko Haram had been trying to establish territory around the borders shared by Borno with Chad and Niger, Op RADAN KAWA commenced along the fringes of the Lake Chad and the areas around the Nigerien-Nigerien border from Gashirgar–Abadam–Arege–Metele up to Kangarwa. An official press release by the Nigerian Army states that its troops, working with Chadian and Nigérien forces as part of the MNJTF security agreement, dislodged Boko Harm from 11 villages along the axis. These include 'Douma, Kilewa, Damara, Abaga, Kilikali Bori, Kalibowa, Karo, Kumaguma, Gashigar, Bogum–Gashigar, Jugula Kura, Giri Jabulam and Menaregi' (Attahiru 2017).

According to Major General Ibrahim Attahiru, of the Nigerian Army who at the time was commanding the theatre effort against Boko Haram but was sacked in December that year (The BBC 2017c), Op RADAN KADA led to scores of Boko Haram casualties. The highly kinetic 'clearing' operation, as the Army refers to them in its lexicon, also saw the recapture of a range of small arms and assault rifles from Boko Haram (Attahiru 2018). Also, by the account of Maj Gen Attahiru, Op DEEP PUNCH led to the deaths of five 'high-profile commanders and many foot soldiers', with several Boko Haram members said to have surrendered within the same operation, due to its effectiveness (Attahiru 2018).

Since the promulgation of the COAS' strategic objective, moreover, and sequel to the operational successes highlighted above over the past three years, there also have been some notable developments in the command structure and deployments of security actors tasked with fighting Boko Haram in 2017. The presence of 8 Task Force Division – the new division created by the Nigerian Army in 2016 and headquartered at Monguno, Borno State – relieved some administrative and operational tasks from 7 Division, which had been tasked with countering Boko Haram since 2013.

The location of 8 Task Force Division further north in Borno additionally enabled faster redeployment of outfield units to remote towns and communities, while its use of minesweeping vehicles, rapid-response units and the creation of several new task-force battalions indicated that the new task force had hit the ground running. The Army also worked with international actors, with the UK being the primary military training partner to Nigeria in 2017, and the only Western country with a significant and ongoing assistance programme. In total, around 22,000 Nigerian military personnel have been trained by British forces between 2015 and 2017.

However, although the Nigerian Army was the spearhead of the COIN operation against Boko Haram in 2017, other security actors also played an instrumental role in securing north-east Nigeria throughout the year. The Mobile Police (MOPOL) – the paramilitary section of the Nigeria Police Force (NPF) – played an increasingly frontline role throughout 2017, with units deployed in Damaturu (Yobe State) and

Maiduguri and Bama (Borno State). Other civilian and paramilitary security groups also assisted the COIN effort throughout the year. On 4 June 2017, the Borno section of the Nigerian Security and Civil Defence Corps (NSCDC) in Borno State announced that 600 of its security operatives had been deployed to protect areas of worship during the holy month of Ramadan.

The vigilante group Civilian Joint Task Force (CJTF) was particularly prominent in the fight against Boko Haram. On 30 June 2017, the Borno chapter of the CJTF revealed that around 680 of its vigilantes had lost their lives in their contribution to the COIN effort against Boko Haram since 2012. A large number of lives lost by this nonstate actor – far more than any other group except the Nigerian Army and Nigerian Police Force, and more than even MOPOL – is indicative of CJTF's frontline role against Boko Haram.

2. The human security challenge

Aside from the constant military threat of attacks from both factions of Boko Haram (al-Barnawi's ISWAP and Shekau's faction), a separate range of socio-economic issues contributed to the human security challenge in north-east Nigeria in 2017. The household fishing economy that sustained the north-eastern areas of the region adjoining Lake Chad remained under Boko Haram's control or influence in 2017, with taxation forcing many fishers – both men and women – to flee to internally displaced persons (IDP) camps further inland. For the fourth consecutive year, farmers were unable to return to their local farming grounds for the planting season due to the conflict. This forced displacement of farmers and fishers further served to erode food security, with the reduced populations and deserted towns encouraging Boko Haram to make more daring raids and stake claims to the abandoned areas. Fighters from the ISWAP (al-Barnawi) faction imposed heavy taxes on occupational fishers around the Marte area up northwards along the border areas into Baga and Doron Baga in particular; as ISWAP was particularly active in those areas (as discussed in Chapter 3). Figure 9.1 indicates the Army presence around this axis. However, Army patrols and units active in this area have been attacked several times by the insurgents, who often wield the numbers within these localized skirmishes.

Even at the IDP camps further South of Borno, however, displaced persons remained at risk, not only from starvation and disease but also from Boko Haram (Shekau faction), which repeatedly attempted to carry out suicide bombings and gun attacks on resident IDPs and humanitarian workers at the camps. This combination of factors created a situation whereby IDPs were insecure in camp, yet unable to return home due to a reduction in viable livelihoods as well as the persistent threat posed by Boko Haram.

Nevertheless, there was some progress regarding the numbers of IDPs in Borno between 2015 and 2017. With the number of new IDPs increasing at a much-reduced rate compared to the previous two years, the government's priority was to ensure that the existing 2.5 million IDPs (housed mainly in Borno State) had the healthcare, food and accommodation required to stabilize the IDP population. These resources were provided in temporary IDP camps, as the Nigerian Army tried in parallel to stabilize the communities from where these groups were displaced. The plan has been for these groups to relocate to their homes, once eventually safe. The practicalities of some IDPs returning home – something unthinkable when Boko Haram contested or controlled much larger tracts of territory between 2014 and 2015 – was explored as part of this plan. Within the first week of the year, the Yobe State government began organizing safety and awareness training for returning IDPs that enabled them to identify IEDs planted by Boko Haram. Such increased hope of displacement reversals was made possible by the Nigerian military's progress in stabilizing some of the areas most affected by the insurgency in the country's north-east. In Borno State, the government earmarked NGN4 billion (US$13 million) for road construction and reconstruction, particularly around Sambisa Forest and border communities who had been controlled by Boko Haram but were subsequently liberated by the Army.

However, the success of the task of caring for this large IDP population – and eventually helping them return home – will depend not only on the Nigerian government but also on strategic partners such as international governmental and non-governmental organizations. In 2017, the US Agency for International Development's Office of Transition Initiatives (USAID OTI) recognized Nigeria as one of the US government's most strategic allies in sub-Saharan Africa and launched the Nigeria Regional Transition Initiative to transition communities back to their homes. Overall, the United States remained one of the largest providers of non-military aid to Nigeria in 2017, but other non-US humanitarian programmes also made essential contributions to the human security landscape in north-east Nigeria throughout the year. In April 2017, the UK launched the North-East Transition to Development Programme (NENTAD), a five-year initiative run by the UK's Department for International Development. The policy's primary goal was to deliver an adequate response to those impacted in the North East geographic zone by providing humanitarian assistance (nutrition and food security), multi-sector support (health, water, shelter and livelihood), efficient crisis response and strengthened government planning. NENTAD also included various implementing organizations, such as the International Committee of the Red Cross and UNICEF. In 2017, Nigeria also became a pilot country for the Global Community Engagement and Resilience Fund, a global public-private partnership that supports local initiatives in strengthening resilience against violent extremist agendas by combining security and development.

The Nigerian government in 2017 also took a more hands-on approach towards working with other international human security programmes by establishing the Presidential Committee on the North East Initiative (PCNI) to address the human security challenge of Boko Haram's insurgency. The PCNI laid the strategic framework for the rebuilding and recovery of the North East region through humanitarian relief, socio-economic stabilization and the return and resettlement of IDPs. The policy also provided a guiding document – known as the Buhari Plan, named after President Muhammadu Buhari – for local or foreign interventions in the region by coordinating the activities of all stakeholders. (Both NENTAD and the USAID OTI programme fall under the Buhari Plan.)

The Nigerian armed forces also engaged in human-security initiatives. For instance, in June 2017, the NAF conducted a medical outreach programme for IDPs in Mainok,

Benishek and Jakana, in Borno State, in which air force personnel provided civilians and IDPs with free health screenings, medicine and eyewear. Also as part of the Nigerian Army's Operation Safe Corridor, repentant ex-Boko Haram fighters were taken through 16 weeks of a de-radicalization programme. The first stage of rehabilitation would consist of ex-fighters on the programme enrolling at a specialist centre in the north-eastern state of Gombe. Following completion of de-radicalization at the centre, ex-fighters would receive the necessary vocational training skills to enable them to earn livelihoods upon reintroduction to society; some of the training skills offered include soap making and farming. The final step of the de-radicalization and re-integration programme would see ex-combatants handed over to the governments in their states of origin. The ultimate goal is to reunite these rehabilitated terrorists with their families, while also providing them with the skills and empowerment to earn a livelihood rather than see insurgency as a viable means of economic sustenance. The first 254 fighters registered by the Army began the programme in the final quarter of 2017 and were due to finish early to mid-January 2018, at which point they would be re-integrated into society.

2017's main conclusion, therefore, was that the conflict in north-east Nigeria was at a stalemate: not unlike what keen observers would point out existed at the end of 2012, during the tenure of JTF ORO. On the one hand, the Nigerian Army has made considerable gains in stabilizing the north-east; the government has temporarily housed IDPs, and other actors such as the CJTF and NGOs have all played roles in improving the region's humanitarian crisis.

On the other hand, Boko Haram remained far from technically defeated, as President Buhari said in December 2015. Indeed, despite shifting to guerrilla warfare and bush war tactics, Boko Haram nevertheless has a standing army with which it continues to contest territory. These periodical territorial thrusts, along with Boko Haram's persistent guerrilla threat, forced a massive deployment of government forces. Here, however, the Nigerian Army has appeared to be one step behind this enemy, over the years. The Army, consequently, made perhaps the most profound combat change in its COIN effort since operations began in June 2011.

This operational adjustment was the introduction of the Army's MST initiative. It could prove to be the most significant step the Army took in 2017 to break its stalemate with Boko Haram. Indeed, not just one of the most noteworthy operational adjustments made in the COIN effort over the past few years, the MST initiative, as I argue in the final section of this Annexe, counts as a wartime innovation for the Nigerian Army. However, before evaluating this positive development in the Army's COIN, let us first discuss some of the most negative aspects of its campaign.

3. A closer look at the Nigerian Army's COIN conduct

Criticisms of the Army's attitude and conduct in COIN operations against Boko Haram

Innovation may not be something that many commentators associate with the Nigerian Army. This, after all, is an organization described as change-averse (Omeni 2017).

Moreover, its institutional attitude and conduct of operations against Boko Haram have been criticized for years now, in both the academic literature and the broader media. For instance, Jon Hill writes that 'Boko Haram has been in a state of perpetual evolution. It has actively embraced innovation and adaptation by constantly changing what it does, where and to whom'. The same writer concludes that the Nigerian military's ability to escalate its COIN towards results is questionable (J. Hill 2014). Likewise, former US Ambassador to Nigeria, John Campbell, suggests the Nigerian Army is less interested in improving its approach to COIN warfare by working with the United States as an equal military partner and more interested in obtaining new hardware and financial contributions within a client-patron relationship that is less helpful for the military institution (News.com 2014). Hill, again, in another damning assessment of the Nigerian military, suggests that 'its efforts to combat these [insurgent] factions are exacerbating the insecurity endured by millions of Nigerians. Their safety is threatened by the attacks carried out by these groups and the counter insurgency operations mounted by security forces' (2012, 24).

Some of these criticisms are well-founded. Whereas it is dubious to assume that millions of Nigerians would be safer without the Army's COIN than otherwise (J. N. Hill 2012, 24, 26), it should not be taken for granted that operations against Boko Haram have been smooth or undeserving of criticism. The Army's calculations around its response to internal threats have, after all, been problematic for their historical overdependence on less than discriminate application of force. Also, the various human rights reports critical of the Army's COIN tactics, including detentions and summary executions, cannot be explained away (Amnesty International 2012, HRW 2012, Amnesty International 2015).

Serious concerns remain around how this institution views force as a tool of coercion against fellow Nigerians, even if they are suspected Boko Haram insurgents. Questions remain too, on its methods – its tactics when dealing with civilians – within the COIN. The Army's Chief of Staff, Lt General Tukur Yusuf Buratai was asked a straight set of answers regarding the extremely coercive methods employed by troops within the COIN. These include wrongly profiling suspects in areas contested by Boko Haram; arbitrary arrests of hundreds, including children; squalid detention facilities within the holding cells of Giwa Barracks, Maiduguri; and over 240 dead in Army detention between January and July of 2017 and secretly buried afterwards. There were also allegations that the Army, via its engagement with civilian militias (the CJTF), effectively uses children as young as 12 years old, albeit indirectly, in COIN 'support roles' (The BBC 2017b). Indeed, these allegations were so serious that, during the Obama Administration, the United States at a point took a step back as Nigeria's strategic military partner and pulled away from supporting the COIN military effort in certain areas (The BBC 2017b).

Lt General Buratai denied that the Nigerian Army employed children in its COIN, noting that 'there is no way the Nigerian Army would pick a child and get him employed to serve any way'. Such tactics, the head of the Army noted, would breach both International Humanitarian Law and the Law of Armed Conflict. Nevertheless, Lt Gen Buratai had no substantive answers to the impact that these allegations, if true, would have on trust-building within the Army's COIN effort (The BBC 2017b). Nor was there a substantive response to accusations that the Nigerian Army had effectively relinquished COIN's best practices for a heavy stick. Despite these denials, which probably were to be expected by the Army, the mere fact that allegations on this scale exist, and that they have not had a vigorous and evidence-based rebuttal from the Army, is problematic. Not just from a humanitarian perspective, moreover: these attitudes are damaging for the Army's COIN profile, suggesting an organization that is running out of ideas and defaulting to a colonial-era tactic of mass detentions as COIN. Such allegations of coercive tactics, especially if true, could provide Boko Haram leverage for recruitment.

4. With its reputation, is the Nigerian Army capable, or even interested, in innovating in war?

Even aside from such allegations of poor conduct, other operational concerns remain, within the Army itself, around challenges that negatively impact the COIN effort. To this point, there are so many field problems with operations – in logistics, in the living conditions and welfare of deployed troops, in availability and maintenance of equipment and platforms, in sometimes unreasonable demands from Army Headquarters to field units, the list goes on – it is a feat in itself that the Army's campaign has made current gains.

In adopting such critical views, however, a counter-argument should be made that, despite its failures, the Nigerian Army in countering Boko Haram's insurgency, has, nevertheless, improved its operations. To the above point, the case could be made that the Army has adapted its operations, in many aspects, for this form of war. Nor do such adaptations all sit within the frame of new equipment and hardware, more troops, and changes in tactics. There have been both tactical and operational developments in more intelligent applications of force, just as there has been progress in civil-military cooperation (CIMIC) that de-emphasizes kinetic operations. Some of these adjustments, furthermore, have been driven by innovation within and outside the field (Omeni 2017). This Annex builds on this adaptation narrative, showing how, via its MST initiative, the Nigerian Army continues to innovate into 2019, albeit this time within the combat space.

5. The concept of military innovation

Military innovation, as Peter Rosen defines it, is 'a change that forces one of the primary combat arms of service to change its concepts of operation and its relation to the other combat arms, and to abandon or downgrade traditional missions. Such innovations involve a new way of war … ' (1988, 134). Moreover:

> A common theme that runs through the literature on military innovation is the fact that innovation must necessarily have battlefield impact. It is not sufficient for an idea to exist on paper; there must be a demonstration of old tasks conducted in new ways or new challenges surmounted via untraditional methods. Innovation

does not mean battlefield defeat of the enemy; though it suggests different approaches to battlefield activities. In this regard, technology can, but is not necessary to, facilitate battlefield innovation (Omeni 2017, 171).

Along these lines, this final section of the Annexe does not aim to argue that MSTs, as an innovation, will lead to Boko Haram's defeat. I will show, however, that MSTs, introduce a balance of speed, manoeuvrability and firepower that the Nigerian Army till date, has lacked. This balance means that MSTs can respond to, and engage credible Boko Haram threats, further away, and at a higher pace than has been achieved so far in the theatre of operations. In order words, MSTs promote the conduct of old tasks in new ways. They employ new doctrine based on a unique entry of Standard Operating Procedures (SOPs) within the Army's revised capstone manual from 2017. Moreover, MSTs Techniques, Tactics and Procedures (TTPs) are, likewise, consistent with this idea of untraditional ways of organizing, deploying, supporting and engaging with fighting units.

Consequently, I shall argue that if they can overcome specific operational challenges, MSTs can prove instrumental: first, to a more effective north-east COIN campaign by the Nigerian Army, and second, to the Army's development of its manoeuvre warfare doctrine. To the above point, MSTs could be a game changer, not just for the Army's combat function in the north-east theatre but even so far as mobile warfare is concerned in this part of the world. This is a bold assertion. So, before proceeding to discuss MSTs within the Nigerian Army's Mobile Brigade Concept (MBC), it is worth providing a bit of background to what the concept itself is and how its progenitor doctrine and practice emerged and developed to the point where it has seen use within modern warfare environments – including against insurgent groups, even in urban contexts.

6. An abridged history of the development of mobile warfare

A significant technological innovation, with a near-immediate effect on warfare, was the invention of the internal combustion engine, in the later years of the nineteenth century. Advances to the design eventually led to its use in the automobile, which entered mass production by the early 1900s. Shortly after technology led to automobiles, they were converted to fighting land machines, which changed the conduct of war. The Great War (1914–1918) was the first major conflict to phase out cavalry and mounted troops ordered into horse regiments. The Great Powers instead deployed motorized infantry units, at scale, for the first time in modern operations (Guderian 1999).

Development of armour in the interwar period further influenced the pace of advancement of mobile or manoeuvre warfare (Guderian 1999). The Second World War (1939–1945) accelerated the development of this concept even further. Germany is of particular interest here, due to the speed and scale of the concept's development within the *Heer*, the German Army. The effects of German operational innovation within the armour space shaped the army's *Bewegungskrieg* (manoeuvre warfare) doctrine of the period. This was evidenced in the Manstein Plan that swiftly led to Germany's defeat of France in a few short weeks between May and June 1940 (Lemay

2010). Innovation in *Bewegungskrieg* was also observable in Field Marshall Erwin Rommel's North Africa campaign for the Germans, such as in his deployment of motorized units in support of the armour, for rapid attacks (Fraser 1993). Rommel's innovative manoeuvre tactics in North Africa built on his previous use of related tactics (albeit using light infantry) during his command in the First World War.[1] Such uses of highly mobile units of infantry and armour, working in combined arms would later come to be known as *Blitzkrieg* (lightning war).[2] Rommel's adventure in North Africa and the Manstein Plan's implementation during the Fall of France are perhaps the earliest archetypes of this technique, employed at scale.

During the Cold War, mobile warfare did not see much use at scale, and its development was modest amongst Major Powers. There were, nevertheless some instances within the Third World context. In Indonesia, as an example, the Mobile Brigade Korps (BRIMOB) was established and employed against communist guerrillas: during the operation in West Kalimantan and also the East Timor Operations (1965 and 1975, respectively).

However, where warfare in the post-Cold War era scaled downwards into asymmetric campaigns against terrorists and insurgent groups, another form of mobile warfare emerged. This involved use of reinforced fire units conveyed in APCs and Mine Resistant Ambush Protected Vehicles (MRAP) to pursue adversaries using firepower, mobility and air support. Units that employed this concept were denoted Mobile Strike Force (MSF).

An early instance of the employment of MSF was Russian forces' swift entry into Kosovo in 1999 in wheeled *Bronetransportyor* (BTR) type vehicles. Indeed, the speed of Russian ingress and the mobility of Russian MSTs using wheeled armour and light infantry in combined arms appeared to pique Western military interests. In the West, not long after, British Royal Marines successfully employed MSF, such as in Operation JACANA in Afghanistan (2002). The Sri Lankan Army also applied a variation of the concept in 2009 to help end the country's war against the Liberation Tigers of Tamil Eelam (LTTE). Conspicuously missing from this narrative, however, is the United States, so far, at least.

During the first Gulf War (1990–1991), brigade combat teams (BCTs), the most fundamental deployable unit of manoeuvre in the United States' army, were still a largely underdeveloped concept. Heavier armoured units or light armoured units were the US Army's preferred manoeuvre options, without much to fill the middle gap. By 2003's campaign against AQI in Iraq, however, US Mobile Strike Forces in Fallujah served to dispel the myth that armour could not be employed within a manoeuvre context in urban spaces. Moreover, notwithstanding setbacks in their induction and deployment (Freedberg Jr. 2003), US Army Stryker Mobile Brigades by that time had gradually come into their own. Stryker Mobile Brigades provide a balance of fire, armour, speed and manoeuvrability and in so doing have filled a decades-long gap in US strategic forces' capabilities: between high-intensity operations typically undertaken by 'heavy forces' and classic low-intensity operations typically undertaken by 'heavy forces' (Vick et al. 2002, 6–8). By this period, and certainly by the latter half of the 2000s, it could, therefore, be said that the MSF concept had gained traction within many military operations.

7. Innovating in war: The Nigerian Army's MST initiative within operation LAFIYA DOLE (OLD)

The Nigerian Army inaugurated a variation of this mobile warfare concept with the introduction of MSTs in the Operation LAFIYA DOLE (OLD) theatre, Borno State, in July 2017. Part of the Army's MBC, MSTs constitute reinforced company-strength subunits equipped with MRAPs, APCs and the necessary fire support and logistics to engage in independent operations. The idea of establishing MSTs came with the MBC initiated by Army Headquarters (AHQ). The aim? Conserve force while dominating the entire theatre (Nigerian Army 2017). With the MSTs now operational, AHQ was able to draw down units and fully implement the Army's ORBAT 2016. More to this point, MSTs were to help the Amy maintain operational momentum on the one hand and, on the other, were to contribute to the expected tactical momentum of lighter forces in the north-east theatre.

To fulfil this task, MSTs are highly mobile troops given Special Forces training to conduct special operations that keep the Main Supply Route (MSR) clear of interference by Boko Haram, within the Theatre of Operations. MSTs capabilities enable them to traverse rugged cross-country terrain, cover longer distances and pursue the insurgents deep into the forest – destroying their camps and logistic dumps along the way. This is achieved by dominance through aggressive mobility, manoeuvre and firepower.

Key strengths of the MST tend to be (the skill and specializations of its) personnel composition, its lean command structure, the experience and support options brought to bear by the MST leader (MSTL), and the hardware and communications capabilities of the unit (Nigerian Army 2017). These strengths create a balance of mobility, communications, firepower and deployment speed. These strengths, moreover, enable MST coordination and integration with other support assets: both in and out of a combined arms frame. The MST strengths also facilitate deployment speed and make available response capabilities, in terms of equipment (including some tactical assets such as UAVs not typically employed by regular units of the same size), manpower, experience (brought by the MSTL and his staff), expertise (including the special forces training requirement for MST troops) and communications options. All these translate to a fighting force suited to chase down, defend against and otherwise engage a wide range of mobile threats that may otherwise escape heavier and less-mobile units or lighter units with inferior firepower capabilities. However, what exactly is the make-up of an MST, which makes it such an essential asset in COIN operations against mobile threats?

An MST at its core is a more substantive compound of the quick reaction force (QRF), used for decades by armies to respond to security situations still developing and without a full military response *in situ*. Each of the two subteams within an MST can undertake missions independently – which means that MSTs generally have many organizational features of a battalion, including an officer commanding (OC) typically at the rank of Major or Captain (Nigerian Army 2017). An MST, nevertheless, can be fully mobilized, with both subteams working combined to contain more significant threats.

The command task will see the OC take charge of an MST unit composed of 7 x 153 soldiers. Such MST troops, at least for the original three MSTs within Sector 1 of 7 Div's Area of Responsibility (AOR), have been drawn from forces already deployed to the affected sectors. The purpose here is that troops, within their new MST postings, experience a faster acclimatization process. Moreover, as MSTs require some specialized training, deployed troops typically undergo a two-week tactics training programme at the Nigerian Army Special Forces School (NASFS), Buni Yadi (Nigerian Army 2017).

For the initial three MSTs, designated MST 1, 2 and 3, the AOR was collectively around the areas of Maiduguri, Bama, Banki, Dikwa, Gamboru, Damboa and Biu. More specifically, MST 1 in Sector 1 (the AOR of 7 Division of the Nigerian Army) covers Maiduguri – Bama – Banki junction. MST 2, Sector 1, covers the Maiduguri – Dikwa – Gamboru axis and MST 3, Sector 1 covers Maiduguri – Damboa – Biu axis. Each MST has an operational base, which means that the base location has a heavier presence of troops with land mobility assets. The operational bases for MST 1, 2 and 3 are at Bama, Dikwa and Damboa, respectively.

In 2017, Sector 3 (the AOR of 8 Task Force Division of the Nigerian Army, headquartered at Monguno, Northern Borno) was directed to create a fourth MST. This MST, MST 4, became operational late August 2017, after its troops commenced training at NASFS. MST 4's operational base is stationed at Gubio. And its AOR is the Gubio–Kareto–Damask–Kanama axis. Subsequent MSTs would be deployed to other axes, to achieve objectives discussed across the remainder of this Annexe. MST troops require completion of training at NASFS, before becoming operational. This training requirement also applies to Nigerian Army Mechanical and Electronics Engineers (NAEME) troops inducted to the theatre within an MST support capacity. Shortly, I shall highlight why NAEME, as well as the Army's engineers and supply and transport personnel, play such vital roles within the MST task.

8. Mobile strike teams (MST) logistics: Features and main challenges

In this section, I shall devote time to discussing the practical, real-life challenges faced by MSTs within the north-east Nigeria COIN effort. All too often, the literature tends to focus so much on what a particular approach can yield if it works, that too little time is spent analysing why in practice performance tends to be different (and, sometimes, quite markedly so) to expectations on paper. Along these lines, insofar as MSTs have operational potential within the Nigerian Army's COIN, it is, nevertheless, essential to understand (1) that they do not quite work as effectively in practice and (2) why this is the case.

Within Op LAFIYA DOLE (OLD), the designation for the Nigerian Army operation to defeat Boko Haram, there are a total of 48 MSTs, at least one for each of the 16 forward operating bases (FOBs) that helped fill the gaps left by de-inducted and disbanded units. Therefore, unlike the five mobile brigades also inducted and since operational in the theatre, the MSTs, both on paper and in practice, are even more manoeuvrable and responsive to proximate insurgent threats. On paper, each MST, to this end, is to be equipped with gun trucks, recce vehicles, APCs, logistics vehicles, an ambulance, water tanker, fuel bowser, Tracked Combat Vehicles (TCVs) and even Unmanned Aerial Vehicle (UAV, known pejoratively as 'Drones'). As of present, the mobility assets of each of the inducted MSTs include two Spartan APCs, one Typhoon MRAP, two Cobra APCs, at least two gun trucks and the required logistics and support vehicles. MSTs also have attached to them, a mix of 'A' and 'B' vehicles for adequate mobility, firepower and force protection to undertake limited operations within the AOR of the associated Mobile Brigade (MB), to which the MST is attached.

These capabilities indicate that so far as that highly sought-after balance of speed, mobility and firepower is concerned, MSTs should be considered – indeed, they are considered at Echelons Above Brigade (EAB) in the Nigerian Army – the tip of the troop's combat spear. These units, after all, were envisioned as being able to strike almost as hard as a regular combat battalion yet be more mobile and streamlined than even a regular platoon (Nigerian Army 2017).

In practice, however, logistics challenges – in terms of spare parts, training, repairs speed and necessary workforce to maintain the entire complement of MSTs platforms – mean that MSTs are not as effective as Army war planners would like. Moreover, a shortage of support options and logistics vehicles within MSTs contribute to operational inefficiencies that limit battlefield capabilities. Water-based fuel bowsers, as an example, and even fully provisioned ambulances for medical services have proved to be in short supply for MSTs. This means that on-paper capabilities do not match the real-life performance of MSTs within OLD. Theatre Command, nevertheless, has acknowledged challenges.

Such acknowledgements notwithstanding, what the rest of this analysis will show is the extent of real-life problems faced by MSTs, has limited their field performance. To begin with, whereas the Administrative and Logistics Strategy for OLD is 'Motivation' and 'Provisioning', so far as the latter is concerned, there certainly are real-life problems faced within the logistics space, for NAEME as a support component of MSTs. Not that logistics challenges of this nature are anything new within the Army establishment. NAEME has had to contend with such challenges for decades. As an example, asked point blank what one of the main challenges were for Nigerian Army mobile units fighting Boko Haram, Brigadier General C.D. Nengite, Pioneer Directing Staff at the Army War College Nigeria (AWCN) once told me, in one word: 'logistics' (2012). Let us explore this idea further. With mobile assets, various categories of armoured and non-armoured vehicles, and motorized platforms at the core of the MST function, it is little wonder that NAEME and its logistics challenge is inextricable from the question around MST's real-life bottlenecks.

Historically, for NAEME, workshops as far back as Lagos (such as One Base Workshop, Yaba) have often been tasked with repairs of platforms towed rearward from theatres much, much, further away. On paper, this problem should not exist for MSTs (in general, moreover, not just those deployed within OLD). After all, in addition to 6x Engineering Soldiers (Explosive Ordnance Disposal, EOD team), MSTs are also composed of an experienced complement of six NAEME soldiers. The latter, moreover, form part of the MST's Main Repair Group (MRG) within its organizational structure. Further, a Repair and Recovery Task Force (RRTF) deployed within a support capacity in the north-east COIN effort supplements the task of the Forward

Repair Team (FRT), which aims to repair MST assets, *in situ*, promptly. Where such repairs are not possible, the vehicle or equipment is recovered rearwards to a higher NAEME workshop facility. Such facilities aim to strike a balance between repair and maintenance capabilities and reactivation of damaged assets back to their field roles. In practice, however, insufficiently skilled workforce, lack of necessary spare parts and inadequate recovery/mobile workshop equipment mean that NAEME, RRTF and FRT tasks are often problematic and not completed adequately if at all.

Also, without a significant forward presence of NAEME, the limited number of support personnel *in situ* affects the speed at which platforms can be inducted into the theatre, including for use by MSTs. For instance, regular pre-delivery inspection and pre-procurement tests and trials of platforms may not be as thorough as in the Corp's peacetime role (although this too, is to be expected). On paper, at the brigade level within NAEME, speedy repairs are facilitated by affiliated brigade workshop which is split into a Main Repair Group (MRG) and a Forward Repair Group (FRG) in order to facilitate repairs as far forward as possible. In practice, however, the same challenges that affect both RRFT and FRT are also scaled up to the MRG and FRG.

Another issue, moreover, so far as repairs are concerned, whether on-site or at the rearward base, is that of standardization, or the lack thereof. Since parts across 'A' and 'B' vehicles, as an example, are not standardized to inventory, parts are not always interchangeable and compatible; this makes repairs and even routine maintenance problematic. Moreover, NAEME's training school, the Nigerian Army School of Electrical and Mechanical Engineering (NASEME) does not always have the training manuals required for its teaching staff: to learn, to integrate into the school curriculum where necessary and then train on to technicians and visiting students as required.

A final operational challenge for NAEME is along organizational lines. This issue regards what, for some time now, has been NAEME's exclusion from operations planning and, correspondingly, the fact that NAEME repair and recovery plans are not incorporated into Nigerian Army operations planning at and higher than Echelons Above Brigade (EAB). MSTs, more to this point, are deployed without NAEME's foreknowledge of equipment inventory, workshop requirements, support and maintenance needs, and possible logistics and repairs tasks *in situ*. Consequently, should NAEME support personnel be deployed to site, or even where they are required to repair assets towed rearwards within a workshop setting, such personnel may struggle. Whereas such workshops and personnel may ultimately take the blame for repair failures, shoddy repairs, unacceptably lengthy repair lead times and such; as this section's analysis of NAEME's challenges highlights, it is not quite so simple in practice.

NAEME is not the only corps faced with a logistics challenge that affects MST performance. The Nigerian Army Corps of Supply and Transport (NACST) is tasked with provision and operation of mechanical transport for the Army's units as well as provision and distributing of combat supplies, ammunition, petrol, oil and lubricants (collectively known as POL in Army lexicon), industrial gas, and food supplies and rations to MSTs active in the north-east. However, like NAEME and the Nigerian Army Engineers Corps (NAE), NACST's logistics and supply role for MSTs in OLD also faces challenges. Such mainly logistical challenges mean that a gap exists between what is necessary and what actually is available for MSTs, in terms of operational performance. An additional issue of note is security-based. Specifically, movement of logistics items by road has sometimes proved problematic due to the possibility of attack en route to MSTs' operational bases, from Forward Logistics Bases (FLB). Even where routes are secure, logistics again is an issue. Numbers of vehicles as well as admin and logistics personnel in practice may not match the numbers on paper required for smooth logistics and transfer activity. This has meant that such human and *matériel* resources are often earmarked for future deliveries rather than speedily delivered as and when due.

Equipment, transport and maintenance logistics are not the only issues of note, moreover. MSTs, as of initially at least, also had a staffing and office personnel availability challenge. Concerning the operational command of existing MSTs within LAFIYA DOLE, as an example, relatively low numbers of officers at the rank of Major at SO2 (OF-3) and Lt Colonel at SO1 (OF-4) available to take up command within MSTs means that officers at Captain rank at SO3 (OF-2), and no higher than Major, had commanded some MSTs. By mid-2017, as an example, only one of the three operational MSTs (MST 4 was yet to be operational) was fully staffed with the highest-ranked officers designated for the required tasks being in place. Nevertheless, to redress this, requests were put into AHQ Department of Military Secretary (Dept of MS), such that at least two additional Majors were posted in the theatre, to command MSTs.

A final note on the MSTs logistical challenges is that some of them appear to be self-inflicted, via poor planning and design. As an example, MSTs' Armoured Fighting vehicles (AFV) and gun trucks were to be fitted with Anti-Aircraft (AA) guns as of December 2017. This, however, is an unusual requirement that may introduce more problems than it solves. First, because the enemy being chased, in Boko Haram, has no aircraft capabilities (beyond the use of non-armed consumer UAVs for limited recce). However, the time and costs required to refit a vehicle with AA capabilities, the serviceability of the AA gun platform and the long-term maintenance issues associated with such platforms are all problems (and quite possibly unnecessary ones) with which MSTs' MRGs may now have to contend. Second, vehicles fitted with AA guns are considerably heavier than their counterparts without guns. This reduces speed, mobility and manoeuvrability. All of these, for the task at hand, are capabilities being sacrificed for something far less valuable (anti-aircraft options) given the context of the enemy. Third, the more parts and fittings a platform possesses, the more failure points it has and, by definition, the more likely is to fail (compared to a similar platform with fewer fittings). Having AFVs and gun trucks fitted with AA guns increases the possible points of failure over the platform's lifetime. Moreover, short-term, this unnecessarily adds to MRG's logistics and maintenance tasks *in situ*. AA guns may well give MSTs added capabilities, yet a question worth asking here is capabilities for what, and at what cost?

9. MSTs: Tactical objectives and innovations

Despite challenges, however, MSTs have proved so useful since induction in 2017 that their deployment has expanded. Part of the MSTs success story is the achievement of their primary operational objective: the denial of BHTs Main Supply Routes (MSRs) via ambushes and patrols. This has been implemented via (1) quick strike tactical operations, (2) tactics that secure and protect land routes, (3) the roving defence of surrounding communities within the AOR and (4) vigilance against the proximate BHT threat. MSTs also employ tactics embedded years into the Army via prior learning and mentoring in 2015. The patron organization here was South Africa-based Private Mercenary and Security Contractor (PMSC) group, Specialized Tasks, Training, Equipment and Protection International (STTEP). At the time, the details of STTEP's mentorship and training role made fewer headlines than the fact that 'mercenaries' were present in north-east Nigeria (Varin 2016). However, the patron-client relationship between STTEP and the Nigerian Army in 2015 fostered particular skills and tactics that MSTs are effectively employing today.

More to this point, some bush and flat terrain tactics employed by MSTs today were earlier absorbed by the Army from STTEP units embedded within the Nigerian Army in 2015. One such tactic is that of 'relentless pursuit', which involves 'mimicking Boko Haram's hit-and-run tactics with non-stop assaults. Once the insurgents were on the run and their likely route established, members of the strike force would be helicoptered into land ahead of them to cut off their likely escape routes, gradually exhausting them' (Freeman 2015). MSTs have taken this tactic of relentless pursuit a step further by (a) co-opting air support and informing air component command and staff at a designated number of hours before the requirement of air support and air liaison (b) coordinating with positioned observation posts using signals and communications equipment. The MST leader (MSTL) also coordinates with supporting outfield battalions from the Army's task force brigades that have been gradually made operational within the AORs of 7 Div and 8 TF Div later, since 2015.

Additionally, a central part of MSTs Standard Operating Procedures (SOPs) are the two areas of 'fighting patrol planning' and the 'conduct of deliberate and hasty ambush' (Nigerian Army 2017). The former provides the Army with superior counter-ambush advantages, whereas the latter integrates better ambush and hasty-attack tactics into MSTs. Tactics such as these deter mobile Boko Haram units attempting to move in numbers. Such adaptations, moreover, also have a force-multiplier effect on MST operations in the theatre, effectively helping the Nigerian Army dominate the theatre further down the engagement ladder in combat, ambush and counter-ambush scenarios where Boko Haram hitherto had proved more competitive.

MSTs introduction, and the associated force-multiplier effect, is in part the reason why Boko Haram's ability to conduct large-scale attacks, and then seemingly disappear as it did in the past, has been limited since 2017. Further, MSTs' theatre-level impact within OLD builds upon the little-discussed, yet operations-critical theme of wartime innovation within the Nigerian Army's COIN. Yet, campaign markers suggest this theme has nevertheless been identifiable since *c.* 2013 (Omeni 2017).

10. Conclusion

There is a range of concerns around the Nigerian Army's conduct in COIN. So much so, that human rights issues, along with the Army's poor operational performance, tends to dominate the academic and media conversation on the COIN. Campaign negatives, after all, like most negative news, generate more chatter than the otherwise unremarkable yet essential progress made out of view. However, within a campaign setting, there also are positives, which, in general, do not get emphasized within the discourses. The MBC and MSTs are one such positive in the conduct of COIN operations by the Nigerian Army since 2017.

Whereas even fully operational MSTs are not an encompassing solution to Boko Haram's mobile threat, these strike teams can, nevertheless, lend the Army a combination of fire and mobility unprecedented at formation level in its institution. Indeed, MSTs have now enabled the Army to match Boko Haram for speed at a time when the insurgent has begun to claw back momentum.

Should MSTs be enabled to achieve their full potential, this could be not just the future of mobile warfare in the Nigerian Army; MSTs could serve as a model for operations in Nigeria and, within the Peace Support Operations (PSO) space outside of it, in sub-Saharan Africa. Against land threats that are mobile, evasive and problematic for traditional military formations to counter, MSTs fill a capabilities gap within the Nigerian Army's ORBAT. First, however, there are issues related to maintenance, logistics, repairs and support, to be redressed.

So, revisiting the order of events: if Boko Haram is an enemy that is mobile and refuses to engage, and the Nigerian Army hopes to match or exceed this enemy's balance of mobility, speed and firepower, then MSTs may well be a significant asset in this space. Yet MSTs themselves face their challenges, which primarily are logistical, repair, maintenance and support related. An added issue is that NAEME and the other combat support branches, which should be helping the MSTs with such issues, are, themselves faced with challenges. From the preceding, how is NAEME meant to play an unimpeachable support function for MSTs, and the COIN campaign in general, if the corps itself is blighted with a range of challenges?

As the sceptic philosopher Sextus Empericus once observed in his classic writings, 'Nor does the non-expert teach the non-expert, any more than the blind can lead the blind' (2000, Book III, 259). Therefore, if NAEME is to reliably help MSTs achieve their full potential by redressing these issues, then the corps' own strategic concerns, along with the tactical and operational concerns of its support units deployed to the theatre of operations, need to be taken more seriously. Such units, insofar as redressing their concerns can have force-multiplier effects, should no longer be viewed by Echelons Above Brigade as a side note to operations against Boko Haram.

Conclusion: So, Why Has the Nigerian Army Struggled Against Boko Haram?

Frustrated at his enemy's refusal to fight in open warfare, King Darius of Persia sent Idanthyrsus, the Scythian king, a message. 'Why on earth, strange man, do you keep running away?' asked Darius, seeking an end to the endless avoidance of battle. If you think yourself strong enough to oppose me, stand up and fight [...] or, if you admit you are too weak, [...] send earth and water to your master, as a sign of your submission and come to a conference'.

'Persian,' Idanthyrsus replied, [...] 'There is nothing unusual in what I have been doing [...] unless for good reason – we shall continue to avoid a battle. This is my reply to your challenge; and as for your being my master, I acknowledge no masters but Zeus from whom I sprang and Hestia, the Scythian queen'. And so it was that the Scythian cavalry continued to avoid the Persian infantry and persisted with vexing night raids.

– Herodotus, The Histories

False positives

So, why do traditional militaries struggle against insurgent warfare; or, conversely, why is the insurgent, small and as under-resourced as he is, so successful at frustrating resource-heavy government forces, who in addition to being more numerous, possess strategic superiority? Armies often rush into the task of countering insurgency – optimistic that the poorly armed and under-resourced irregulars would capitulate in short order. Government forces, after all, have in their favour sophisticated operational concepts, well-rehearsed tactics and plans, and traditional military advantages. The insurgent's army, conversely, is often neither deep enough nor versed in military warfare in the same manner as government forces.

Moreover, early victories by state forces – aerial bombings, grounds offensives and such – tend to disperse the threat of insurgency artificially and suggest an imminent end to operations. Indeed, for traditionalists, early gains against the insurgent appear to vindicate an ideology of the offensive and confidence in the tried and tested utility of force. Such early results, however, tend to be false positives. They suggest, by the sheer evidence of the shock and awe effect of initial offensives, that the end has been reached; or that, at the least, it is imminent. In insurgency, however, the enemy's predilection for avoidance at the early stages of the conflict should not be confused with his cowardice, and it certainly must not be confused with his defeat or its imminence. Today's insurgent, much like the Scythians of antiquity described by Greek historian Herodotus (2003, 282–283), tends to avoid the engagement against a more powerful enemy, until such a time as it suits him. Time is the key word here. It is left to government forces not to misdiagnose the threat initially but also to understand that the insurgent and his campaign will, over time, evolve, and so must they. At some point, for the insurgent, criminality and a criminal element might well be the emphasis; at another, hostilities might pivot to military fighting. At other times, guerrilla warfare may be preponderant to his calculus of war. Indeed, during some phases, the insurgent may intentionally lie dormant, leading to a stalemate or at least the sense of one. Government forces must not believe, during such periods, the most believable outcome – that rebel forces capitulated after only the opening salvo, and that the war is over. History, after all, indicates that government forces fighting insurgents tend to do so for much longer than expected.

Premature optimism

In 2003, President George Bush gave a poorly conceived 'mission accomplished' speech on 1 May, on the aircraft carrier, USS Abraham Lincoln (CBS News 2003). Sixteen years on, as of August 2019, Iraq is still fighting remnants of an insurgency despite multiple defeats of Daesh (the Islamic State) till date. Daesh sleeper cells remain active in at least three Iraqi provinces (Salahaddin, Nineveh and Anbar) as of July 2019. Moreover, the United States retains strategic commitments in Iraq. Part of this troops' presence is traceable all the way back to the fallout of the initial US-led Invasion of Iraq in 2003. Ergo, the notion that even now it is 'mission accomplished' in Iraq, if that mission ever was long-term stable peace, is debatable.

The United States does not have a monopoly on such premature optimism. At the start of Nigeria's civil war (1967–1970), Army Headquarters was confident that Biafra's rebellion would be defeated in a month, within four phases of operations (Atofarati 1992). However, the civil war entered a fourth calendar year before Biafra eventually surrendered. Decades later as the Army dismantled Boko Haram's threat in July 2009, the General Officer Commanding, 3 Division of the Nigerian Army, Major General Saleh Maina, would say similar words to President Bush, 'the mission has been accomplished' (D. Smith 2009a). The Army assumed that Abu Shekau, Yusuf's deputy, had been killed. The Army's task force viewed Boko Haram's threat as neutralized, and its mandate complete, after soldiers stormed the group's mosque in Maiduguri. About a decade later, however, despite the Army's largest mobilization since the civil war, Boko Haram continues to wage its insurgency, and the military's mission is still not accomplished. Indeed, the head of the Nigerian Army, Lieutenant General Yusuf Tukur Buratai, admitted in July 2017 to the 'resilience of insurgency'. Buratai observed that whereas the Army has degraded Boko Haram after years of COIN operations, the group remains active in some areas: that it has not been eliminated (The BBC 2017b).

Such premature statements around insurgency's faded threat, when in reality such conflicts are in their embryonic stages, aligns with the histories, theory and practice of this war form. Caution, therefore, must be exercised by the counter-insurgent who feels he has dealt a significant blow to the insurgent and that operations are all but over. Too many times have government forces declared defeat of an insurgency, only for conflict to drag on for years.

Despite its operations experience, the Nigerian military does not have a mature COIN culture

As insurgency leaves its embryonic stages, gains momentum, and begins to mature, government forces, which at one point dominated and assumed victory to be a foregone conclusion, start to struggle. Facing a population-centred threat, these forces realize they cannot as often deploy their most sophisticated platforms, destructive ordnance or most powerful armoured units. Today more than in the past, military action within the civilian space, whether to counter insurgency or contain civil unrest, is under scrutiny. As a recent New York Times video report on the Nigerian Army's heavy-handedness demonstrates, state forces' actions within the civilian space can today be recorded or even broadcast in real time, leading to a damning verdict in the court of public opinion (Koettl et al. 2018). Blundering troops are now watched not just by human rights NGOs but also the citizen-reporter empowered by Internet-ready personal devices and the real-time broadcasting power of new media and social media.

Over time, this reality (some version of it, at least) sets in for war planners: indiscriminate force, in today's world more often than not causes operational problems, even if the tactic initially seemed a good idea. So, as absurd as this might sound to traditionalists, in COIN, taking off sunglasses and smiling to take selfies with locals; hosting community town hall meetings, complete with eager photo-ops amongst community heads; and navigating the civ-mil interface, may accelerate the progress of operations faster than the latest equipment, military hardware or use of force. Whether facing riotous behaviour or trying to flush out insurgents within communities suspected to be sympathetic, citizens today cannot be flogged, bullied, detained or, worse, killed as a pathway to success. A softer approach, a rejection of the cult of the offensive, must take over the modern counter-insurgent's violent instincts. This is not just about winning hearts and minds; it also is about not looking bad in front of a camera lens that troops cannot see, set to post a video feed that could go viral – ending careers and possibly a lot worse.

Consequently, state forces tasked with countering insurgency today are often pressured to conduct their task with discriminate force. 'Courageous restraint' as one British Army colonel interviewed called it, could mean that even when resorting to force is justifiable, troops stay disciplined and self-restrained (Hall 2012). The question is whether they will, in practice. Let us remember that, historically speaking, violence rather than restraint was what soldiers were trained for. Moreover, the Nigerian Army was built and equipped to plan and fight a conventional war against a similar sized armed force, with comparable capabilities. The Army's capstone doctrine and culture centres around this idea of planning and operationalizing for a traditional adversary, against whom conventional capabilities can be manoeuvred at scale and overwhelming firepower can be brought to be bear.

The Nigerian military, as a result, does not have a COIN culture. Instead, the Army's thinking, its organization, its doctrine, its learning environment and indeed a breakdown of its year-on-year military spending, suggest a strong pivot towards warfighting and conventional warfare: an ideology of the offensive as opposed to one created from the ground-up for counter-insurgency (COIN) (Omeni 2017).

For such reasons, despite massive troop mobilization, the Army's progress has been slow in its north-east campaign; its forces, for the most part, have been mobilized as they would have been against a conventional enemy. Indeed, neither the Army's Order of Battle in 2011 (ORBAT 2011) nor its optimistic assumptions around how far that ORBAT would take it against 'contemporary threats', were indicative of an institution with the culture, doctrine, planning and organization for COIN. Not surprisingly, therefore, the Nigerian Army, much like armies tasked with COIN elsewhere, in the first several months of campaigning fought a highly infantry-centric war with little resemblance to all the talk of COIN's 'best practices' in the theories (Sepp 2005).

Now, over the years as the Army's campaign has matured. Extensive recalibration for the broad lines of operations (LOOs) required for COIN has been ongoing (Omeni 2017). Likewise, some extent of innovation in the crucible of war has been identifiable since 2013 (Omeni 2017). Even the MSTs since 2017 are further proof of such wartime innovation by the Army (see Annexe to Chapter 9). These adaptations, however, take time to translate into tactical momentum against Boko Haram. Moreover, they will take even longer to be entrenched within the Army as its COIN culture matures.

The traditional state military is change-averse. This is not a COIN-specific problem; it is institutional

Being so successful against various adversaries over the years, the Nigerian Army was a learning organization only on paper. How much would one if to learn if the same standing operating procedures appear to always work just fine? In practice, therefore, arms acquisition rather than any substantive attempt to change its CONOPS against internal threats seemed to be the Army's pathway to improving in war. Now, against Boko Haram, the tried-and-tested method of superior firepower was employed. When that failed, the Army was stuck in an uncomfortable space; it might have wanted to change, but was not quite sure how, because it had never had to – not even against Biafra rebels in the civil war (its most stringent test before Boko Haram). Without any substantive and methodical plan for change, and with decades of institutional inertia holding back innovation and adaptation, the COIN effort, for years, struggled.

An emergent question here is why it takes government forces so long to change, so long to build tactical momentum (on the strength of that change), and even longer to entrench COIN's best practices within their culture? One possible reason is that the traditional military institution is bureaucratic and top-heavy. Such traits stifle quick decision-making and rapid implementation of plans. Moreover, because militaries tend to be traditionalist by nature – which is one way of saying that they are change-averse, sometimes deaf to field signals and generally inflexible – there is, therefore, the need for the traditional military institution to first recognize the threat of insurgency for what it is and then begin the recalibration process. This recalibration process takes much time, however. Thus, in the interim, poorly equipped and inexperienced armies overwhelmed by COIN (and the scale of learning and unlearning it requires) may require other ways to build tactical momentum. Otherwise, the war might be lost before the process of change and COIN capacity building is even half complete.

In the case of the Nigerian Army's campaign against Boko Haram, the previously highlighted use of private military security contractors (PMSCs) circa 2015 was one such interim approach to building tactical momentum. In March of that year, scores of security contractors from 'South Africa and the former Soviet Union' – so-called 'mercenaries' – were hired by the Nigerian government ' ... in a last-ditch effort to counter the Boko Haram insurgency before the presidential elections' (Varin 2018, 144). As Caroline Varin points out, 'STTEP chairman Eeben Barlow confirmed that his company was subcontracted in mid-December 2014 and began deployment in January 2015' (2018, 150). The aim here was to ' ... train [the Nigerian Army as] a mobile strike force with its own organic air support, intelligence, communications, logistics, and other relevant combat support elements ... ' (Varin 2018, 150). Part of STTEP's assistive task in Nigeria, the Army was, therefore, 'schooling Nigeria's largely traditional army in "unconventional mobile warfare"' (Freeman 2015).

In any event, such measures should be seen as a stop-gap effort at best. If the Nigerian Army is to defeat Boko Haram at the long game, then substantive changes to its attitudes and organization, its doctrine and its war conduct – its tactics and operations – need to underpin its COIN culture. Moreover, hiring PMSCs to perform a set of tasks is not the same as building the institutional capacity and changing attitudes such that you can then perform that task yourself. That being said, the military may also need to concede that it cannot conduct all the tasks required in COIN on its own. COIN, particularly as security is stabilized in later phases, may need community policing, reconstruction, rebuilding, rehabilitation and reform. Not all of these are tasks that armies expect to perform over the long term.

The military dilemma: Boko Haram's insurgency requires a force response, yet cannot be solved by force

Militaries are minded to employ force to solve security problems. However, a common answer floated within the discourses around why Nigeria's military has failed to end

Boko Haram's insurgency is that the underpinning issues are non-military, and so cannot be solved by military force. Northern Nigeria's political and socio-economic problems, this argument goes, must be fixed, if the insurgency is to go away. Military intervention, therefore, is not the answer, going by this established popular narrative. 'This problem cannot be solved by force,' said Muhammad Sa'ad Abubakar, the Sultan of Sokoto and the spiritual head of Nigerian's 80 million Muslims; 'what we need is dialogue' (Rice and Wallis 2012). This is identical to the views of the Catholic Archbishop of Abuja, John Onaiyekan that, 'the use of military force by the Federal Government will not solve the challenges posed by Boko Haram terrorists [...] the use of force to solve a problem has never worked in any part of the world' (The Will 2016).

Specific criticisms of the Nigerian Army's role in COIN point to the 'hopelessness hanging over' the institution and suggest that there is 'no solution to Boko Haram from Nigeria's army' (Whitehead 2015). Daniel Brett, the economic and political analyst for Huffington Post, takes this thesis further still. For Brett, the '[Nigerian] military is the problem, not the solution' to Boko Haram's threat. Brett is convinced that 'due to ineptitude, corruption and indiscriminate violence, the [Nigerian] military is one of the causes of the insurgency' and argues that 'giving funds and resources to the Nigerian armed forces risks exacerbating the problem' (2014). Such views are consistent with longstanding commentary on the Nigerian military as a discredited and incompetent institution. Going by this established popular narrative, it almost seems as though the Nigerian government, rather than send in the 'discredited' Army against Boko Haram, should starve it of 'funds and resources' while seeking a bloodless outcome and self-medicating to redress long-standing governance failures in the north-east.

As humane as this might all sound, what this book has shown is that Boko Haram has metastasized into a formidable military outfit that is intent and demonstrably capable of making territorial gains. Without the Army's intervention and resilience building through its task force brigades since 2015, Boko Haram's orbit would have increased considerably.[1] Furthermore, the Nigerian authorities are up against a threat that considerably outmatches the Nigerian Police Force. This makes the military the last line of defence against an enemy that Western forces have refused to engage on the ground, even though Boko Haram has consistently been one of the top three perpetrator groups in the world in terms of human cost. The combination of these facts, added to the aggressive nature of Boko Haram's idea system discussed in Chapter 1, gives the lie to the notion that the Nigerian military should sit at the margins of the conversation around Boko Haram's threat.

Certainly, war, as an army's occupation, should be a policy option of last resort. Moreover, the war object should always be to hold peace-seeking congress eventually. A good military strategy often does not seek to annihilate an enemy's forces; strategy should stop shy of such extreme bloodshed with the hopes that the enemy would either seek terms or be minded to accept their offering. Such expectations should be no different in the north-east Nigeria conflict. Analyses across this volume, however, reveal the extreme nature of Boko Haram's war calculus. To make good on its threat of jihad, Boko Haram is willing to spill blood, is uninterested in strategic negotiations (prisoner exchanges should not be confused with strategic dialogue), and is ready to exploit a range of force-multipliers – many of which are unavailable to the Nigerian Army. From the preceding, it becomes critical not to misjudge this enemy, the nature of his war object, or the existential threat he poses. Moreover, we must be sceptical of this emerging idealism that military warfare does not, in fact, solve the problem of enemies armed and on a killing spree. As von Clausewitz cautions:

> Kind-hearted people might, of course, think there was some ingenious way disarm or defeat an enemy without too much bloodshed, and might imagine that this is the true goal of the art of war. Pleasant as it sounds, it is a fallacy that must be exposed: war is such a dangerous business that mistakes that come from kindness are the very worst. The maximum use of force is in no way incompatible with the simultaneous use of the intellect. If one side uses force without compunction, undeterred by the bloodshed it involves, while the other side refrains, the first will gain the upper hand [...] This is how the matter must be seen. It would be futile – even wrong – to try to shut one's eyes to what war really is from sheer distress at its brutality (1976, 75–76).

Boko Haram's insurgency is underpinned by a campaign intent on causing as many casualties, at every opportunity, as is possible. To facilitate its objective, the group, on the one hand, has fought a bush war that employs guerrilla tactics and war avoidance; yet, on the other, Boko Haram has also fought, with some success, a conventional war that employs elements of the Infantry, Armour and the Artillery. Nigeria is not faced with an enemy that might – future tense – pose a credible military. This is the present; Boko Haram's military already *is* operational. The solution to this military problem, therefore, cannot shy away from the technicalities of operational and tactical warfare.

Certainly, it is true that socio-political and economic reform, not military force, must redress the underpinnings of Boko Haram's insurgency in the long term. However, it also is true that (1) the Nigerian military was not sent to fix the underpinnings of the conflict; it was mandated to counter an ongoing and escalating armed insurgency. This distinction is critical, yet often overlooked. (2) Without some semblance of artificial security brought about by a COIN campaign, governance, government structures, socio-political reform and, indeed, civilian society cannot function during insurgency as constitutionally required. Von Clausewitz famously observes that 'war is not merely an act of policy but a true political instrument, a continuation of political intercourse, carried on with other means' (1976, 87). Here, however, we must, irreverent as this might sound to Clausewitzian thinking, consider the reversal: that COIN is not just a continuation of policy on the battlefield, but that policy and politics should, as a post-operational necessity, form a continuation of the military effort even where successful. In order words, war is the short-term fix and political reform, the long-term. By definition, there can be no long-term if short-term problems are unsolved. Moreover, even where overlap exists between these two functions (which, in COIN, it must), it is as problematic to ignore the military solution as it is to downplay the role of politics and reform in countering insurgency via a stabilizing effect.

Nevertheless, there is an order of events, which serves as a reminder that COIN, despite the role of government, is still a form of war. It involves soldiers with guns, officers who command them, a General Staff whose strategies lead the deployment of these officers, and everything else that war planning and warfighting entail. We cannot skip the predominantly physical nature of war and focus on the cerebral nature of policy, because the former might now need to precede the latter (Simpson 2012, 243–244).

Final notes

As a final note, in considering insurgency as an armed threat and war (COIN) as a necessary initial response, we also should consider the following caveat. COIN, unlike the historical pitched engagement, must reflect 'courageous restraint', on the part of government forces, due to the conflict's population-centred nature (Hall 2012). Despite their strategic superiority, these forces cannot, like the insurgent's, shed moral compulsion and fight a war of attrition. Government forces must show restraint: in the calculus of coercion and the application of force. Without such restraint, COIN is more likely to resemble attritional warfare and less likely to be accepted by the very population whose ultimate protection must be the object of war. In today's climate where armies are increasingly expected to fight and achieve objectives with minimal casualties, this, perhaps, is the greatest COIN lesson for the Nigerian Army.

Notes

Chapter 1

1 *Sunnah*: The social traditions, jurisprudence and longstanding practices of the *ummah* (Islamic community).
2 Walker (2012), Loimeier (2012) and Umar (2012) credible writers in their right, all present slightly different versions of events.
3 The Al-Muntada mosque at Dorayi quarters, Kano, was where Adam was assassinated on the morning of Friday 13 April 2007.
4 Fatwa: issue-specific Islamic legal pronouncements made by an expert in religious law, otherwise known as a mufti.
5 Yusuf was not the first firebrand cleric, nor was he the first to launch polemics against the established Islamic order. In particular, the Sufi Brotherhoods, influential within the Muslim establishment in northern Nigeria, had been accused of bid'ah in the past (Loimeier 1997).
6 Even in sections of Nigerian society that follow Islamic law and are not secular, the influence of Westernization remains undeniable.
7 As at late 2011, a total of forty-one Islamic associations, which Amoda (2011) notes reflect 'an institutional portrait of Islamic intellectualism', make up the DCCN. The full listing of the organizations is from DCCN (2009).

Chapter 2

1 A popular mode of transport in northern Nigeria, also referred to, in that part of the country, as *Achaba*. *Achaba*, motorcycle riders, constitute an entire class of semi-regulated social work.
2 Please refer to the appendix at the end of Omeni (2017) for interview sources.
3 Much of what the Chief Superintedant of Police (CSP) and I discussed in Maiduguri is corroborated by Umar's account in his excellent essay, 'The Popular Discourses of Salafi Radicalism and Salafi Counter-radicalism in Nigeria: A Case Study of Boko Haram' (Umar 2012).
4 In November 2016, the Army's chief of staff, Lt. General Tukur Buratai remarked that up to 60 per cent of Boko Haram members were not Nigerian (News Agency of Nigeria 2016).
5 Ali Modu Sherrif, at time of writing, is now a senator for Borno Central.
6 Also known as the Islamic State (IS), the Islamic State of Iraq and Syria (ISIS) and the Islamic State of Iraq and the Levant (ISIL).
7 See, for instance, Abdulkareem Mohammed's excellent text, *The Paradox of Boko Haram* (2010); also, another recommended essay is that by Muhammad Sani Umar (2012).

8 See the excerpts of conversations that Sheikh Ja'afar Adam had with Yusuf, around this subject, highlighted in this chapter (2).
9 A statement by Boko Haram in August 2009 confirmed this alignment with Al-Qaeda's jihadist idea system: 'Boko Haram is just a version of the Al-Qaeda which we align with and respect. We support Osama bin Laden; we shall carry out his command in Nigeria until the country is totally Islamised which is according to the wish of Allah' (Vanguard 2009).
10 For a dedicated account of the Nigerian military and its operations against Boko Haram, refer to Omeni (2017).

Chapter 3

1 As far back as 2012, the same individual, 'Habibu Yusuf (AKA Asalafi)', was listed as being number two, only behind Shekau in Boko Haram's shura, within the Nigerian Army's 'Most Wanted' schema for Boko Haram. Please refer to Table 7.1.

Chapter 4

1 See, for instance, Mohammed, Abdulkareem. 2010. *The Paradox of Boko Haram*. Edited by Mohammed Haruna. Nigeria: Moving Image Limited; Hill, J.N.C. 2014. Boko Haram, the Chibok Abductions and Nigeria's Counterterrorism Strategy. Post, Combating Terrorism Center at West Point. Accessed 6 May 2016. http://bit .ly/1STmN9E; Solomon, Hussein. 2012. 'Counter-Terrorism in Nigeria: Responding to Boko Haram'. *The RUSI Journal* 157 (4): 1–11; Comolli, Virginia. 2015. *Boko Haram: Nigeria's Islamist Insurgency*. London: C. Hurst & Co. (Publishers) Ltd; Comolli, Virginia, and Kate Robertson. 2015b. *Boko Haram (ISWAP) and ISIS: two of a kind?* Terrorism Research and Analysis Consortium (TRAC); Walker, Andrew. 2016. '*Eat the Heart of the Infidel*': *The Harrowing of Nigeria and the Rise of Boko Haram*. London: C. Hurst & Co. (Publishers) Ltd; Onuoha, Freedom C. 2010. 'The Islamist Challenge: Nigeria's Boko Haram Crisis Explained'. *African Security Review* 19 (2): 54–67; Umar, Muhammad Sani. 2012. 'The Popular Discourses of Salafi Radicalism and Salafi Counter-Radicalism in Nigeria: A Case Study of Boko Haram'. *Journal of Religion in Africa* 42 (2): 118–144; Loimeier, Roman. 2012. Boko Haram: The Development of a Militant Religious Movement in Nigeria'. *Africa Spectrum* 47 (2–3): 137–155.
2 See, for instance, Matfess (2017b).
3 See, for instance, Brett (2014); Whitehead (2015); The Will (2016); Rice and Wallis (2012).
4 Chapter 9 dedicates a whole section to this idea of insurgency as a departure from the Roman war model.
5 An air sortie is an air mission, typically conducted from defensive positions.
6 Please refer to Figure 1.1, Chapter 1, for a map of Nigeria showing these locations.
7 Typical of the duties of some of the far north formations deployed by the Nigerian Army.

8   Over the course of the campaign against Boko Haram, 7 Div has come to be more active than 3 Div, its sister div, in COIN operations.
9   Please refer to Figure 4.1 for a map of 7 Div's units' deployments, relative to Sambisa. Figure 9.1 also shows that map but within a much wider context of 7 Div's entire Area of Responsibility (AOR).
10 Chapter 7 discusses Boko Haram's mobile offensives, including its use of 'swarming' tactics.
11 Chapters 7 discusses this theme of Boko Haram's overt front, and its sophistication, in depth.
12 See, for instance, Higazi (2013a); Walker (2016); Comolli (2015); Varin (2016); Udounwa (2013).

Chapter 5

1   These historical linkages between Nigeria and Cameroon extend down to the extreme south-south areas of both countries, all the way down to the Bakassi Peninsula, ownership of which, for a long time, was disputed by both countries (Enaikele, Olutayo and Aluko 2009). However, it is in the north where shared ethnic identity is of particular relevance to insurgency.
2   These were called provinces. Since 2008, however, they have been called regions, hence the designation used in this book. In total, there are ten regions in Cameroon. Two of these are shared with Nigeria's northeast and five regions in total share land borders with Nigeria.
3   This in part is why the Hadeja-Nguru Wetlands in Yobe (highlighted earlier in Chapter 4), due to its natural tactical barrier features, holds potentiality for strong defence, should Boko Haram choose to challenge that axis.
4   The Republican Guard (French: *Garde Nationale du Niger*) fall under the Nigérien interior ministry and have not, nor are they likely to be, deployed within a joint role in the regular army's COIN operations.
5   See, for instance, Schehl (2016); Hinshaw (2013); Udounwa (2013); and Comolli (2015, 90, 102).

Chapter 6

1   In developing this model, I build on the existing model by Mercy Corps (2016), as well as on research by my PhD supervisor, Professor Funmi Olonisakin.
2   Almajirai: plural of almajiri. Rather than use of the plural tense (alamjirai) however, almajiri is often used to denote the phenomenon's plurality.
3   I also further explore the role of MAMs, within Boko Haram's insurgency, in Chapter 9.
4   See, for instance, Okonta and Douglas (2003); Isichei (1987); Mohammed (2010); Adesoji (2011); and Obi and Rustad (2011).
5   Chapter 9 further discusses this idea of resilience building through the formation several new formed task force battalions, deployed by the Nigerian Army since 2015.
6   Such units made this study possible.

Chapter 7

1   As discussed in the book introduction, Chapter 7 is a much-revised version of Omeni (2018b). The particular areas revised and rewritten for this volume are detailed in the Introduction.

2   The Nigerian Army's Mobile Strike Teams initiative is discussed in the Annex to Chapter 9.

3   Data obtained from Nigeria Security Tracker, by John Campbell at the Council on Foreign Relations (Campbell 2019).

4   Ibid.

5   Ibid.

6   As evidenced in the Army's ever-expanding wire diagram for Boko Haram's organizational structure. This diagram, as of the time of writing, had over 240 HVTs, commanders, Shura members and persons of interest.

7   Please refer to the Annex to Chapter 9 for more operational information on this phase of the Nigerian Army's COIN effort. I discuss both Op DEEP PUNCH and Op RAWAN KADA in some more detail there.

8   For a detailed examination of the Joint Intelligence Preparation of the Operational Environment (JIPOE) methodology, including what it means, how it was employed within Operation Restore Order by the Nigerian military's Joint Task Force in Maiduguri, and what the implications of its use were for the COIN effort, please see: Omeni (2017, 6, 124, 136–137, 146, 152, 158–159).

9   JTF ORO was the task force operation mandated to defeat Boko Haram between 2011 and 2013. See: Omeni (2017) for an analysis of this operation

10   On rare occasions, there have been instances of Boko Haram employing amputees as fighters during raids. One such individual was part of Boko Haram's motorized infantry offensive against Giwa Barracks in March 2014.

11   Also, Achaba; local name for motorcycle.

12   I am most grateful to Paul B. Rich for drawing my attention to this point.

13   I discuss the battle of Konduga elsewhere; see: Omeni (2017).

14   An armed force's ORBAT relates to its hierarchical organization of command structure, combat readiness (and disposition) of forces, battle-ready equipment and platforms, formations, and their strengths.

15   It could be argued that few aspects of air power have advanced as fast as the surface-to-air aspect.

16   Air Commodore Sampson is being succeeded in November 2016 by Air Commodore J. J. Stringer. However, as of time of writing, Air Cdre Sampson's next appointment was next to be announced. So I have listed him in his last command.

17   Also referred to as the Islamic State in the Levant (ISIL), the Islamic State of Iraq and Syria (ISIS) or the Islamic State (IS).

18   For more details on both side of the airpower debate, see: Pape (2014, 1997b, 1997a); Watts (1997); Warden (1997).

19   I focus in some detail on the airman's role within Nigerian military COIN. See, for instance, Omeni (2017, 190–199).

20   Ibid.

21   The TCCs are part of the regional multinational joint task force (MN-JTF), headquartered in the Chadian capital of N'Djamena, but commanded by a Nigerian Army officer of two-star rank (Major General and equivalent). As of 2017, the TCCs

include brigade or battalion-sized contingents from Nigeria, Chad, Cameroon and Niger. Benin also pledged to contribute a small complete of ground forces, in 2016.

22   Especially considering that the northern region was unaffected during the Civil War of Nigeria.
23   Refer, for instance, to Mackinlay (2012) and also Reno (2012).
24   The Liberation Tigers of Tamil Eelam (LTTE) in Sri Lanka is one of the more notable examples of an insurgent movement that deployed air assets as a counter-threat against state forces. This, however, is the exception, not the norm. Not even Daesh has air capabilities.

Chapter 8

1   As discussed in the book introduction, Chapter 8 is a much-revised version of Omeni (2018).
2   Refer to Figure 1.1 for a map of Nigeria, showing the relative locations of Abuja (FCT) and Borno.
3   Uses data from the Global Terrorism Index (Institute for Economics and Peace 2015).
4   Ibid.
5   Please refer to the notes for Chapter 2; they provide a brief outline of innovation (bid'ah) in Islam.
6   Controversial practices such as *Taqiyya* (methodology) and *Istishhadia* originate the larger Shia ideology (Moghadam 2011, 11–12). However, these practices themselves are considered innovation, even amongst Shiite scholars.
7   See map of Boko Haram's territory at its peak in 2015, at Chandler (2015).
8   For Biafra, guerrilla warfare was not a viable concept of operations (CONOPS) because strategic territory needed to be defended and administered to preserve the integrity of the short-lived rebel republic. A regular standing army was formed for this task and much of Biafra's statecraft centred around the armaments, training, equipment and sustenance for that army. The army, after all, was the biggest obstacle between Biafra and the reabsorption of the Eastern region into Nigeria. Biafra's insistence on military fighting, therefore, was a function of the most practicable concept of operations, given the war object. A covert front prosecuting a guerrilla war could not have achieved this war object (territorial defence). If the engagement is refused, as guerrillas tend to do when faced with a massive enemy offensive, then territory is lost. In this sense, it became unrealistic, by the time that Federal forces began offensives to reabsorb Eastern territory, for Biafra's army to become guerrillas. As the commander of the Biafran army, Alexander Madiebo, remarks on this particular point:

I do not want to be drawn into a lengthy discussion on guerrilla warfare [...] those who say we should have changed to guerrilla warfare when we appeared to be failing in the conventional way ... [It] was rather too late and no longer possible at that stage [...]. If, when the Nigerians attacked us on the 6th of July, 1967, we had not offered any resistance but rather allowed the enemy to go anywhere he wanted [effectively to control territory], normal life would have continued in Biafra, and the setting would have been perfect for a very effective guerrilla warfare soon afterwards. (1980, 107)

Chapter 9

1   For a volume focused entirely on the Nigerian military and its COIN plans and operations against Boko Haram between 2011 and 2017, see Omeni (2017).

2   In locating the Centre of Gravity (COG) 'in a conventional fight', US Army Command and General Staff College (CGSC) students 'many times identified an enemy's most powerful corps or armored division as the Operational CoG that must be defeated in order for U.S. forces to be successful' (Martin 2010, 1). Whereas in counterinsurgency exercises, 'the CoG was usually identified as 'the will of the people', in fact 'many instructors stifled debate by insinuating there was no alternative' (Martin 2010, 1).

3   See, for instance, Carruthers (1995); Eland (2013); Iqbal (2011); Mortenson and Relin, (2008); Nagl (2005); Kilcullen (2010a). Perhaps also of note is that Mortensen's *Three Cups of Tea* thesis has been called into serious question; see: John Krakauer's *Three Cups of Deceit* (2011).

4   Alternatively, Lines of Action (LoAs), using Nigerian military lexicon.

5   Paul B. Rich and Isabelle Duyvesteyn, for instance, contend that 'while intended specifically for the [US] Army and Marine Corps it [FM 3–24] now holds such stature that in practice it overrides NATO counterinsurgency doctrine, which should inform the NATO operations in Afghanistan' (2012, 14).

6   See Figure 9.1 for the area in question and a breakdown of the Task Force Brigades' deployment.

7   I highlight this earlier in Chapter 8. Also, see: Scan News (2014).

8   See, for instance, Olukayode (2016); Caulderwood (2015); News Wire NGR (2015); CNN (2016); Premium Times (2014a); The Guardian (2012).

Annexe

1   These tactics were earlier documented in Rommel's highly regarded classic text on military tactics, Infanterie greift an (Infantry Attacks), first published 1937 (Rommel 2012).

2   This term, Blitzkrieg, was first used in 1935 and was popularized within the Western military, media and academic settings both during and after the Second World War, though not in Germany or in the Wehrmacht (the Armed forces of Nazi Germany).

Conclusion

1   I write about the Nigerian Army's Task Force Brigades in more detail elsewhere. Refer to Omeni (2017, 173, 176, 185, 233, 248–249, 253).

Bibliography

Abubakar, Yusufu Mahmud. 2012. 'Author's interview with Yusuf Abubakar Mamud, Research Fellow and Islamic Scholar at the Office of the Deputy Commandant, at the National Defence College (Former War College).' Abuja.

Adeoye, Aderemi. 2012. 'Author's interview with JTF ORO Police Component Commander and Chief Superintendent of Police (CSP), Aderemi Adeoye.' Maiduguri.

Adesoji, Abimbola O. 2011. 'Between Maitatsine and Boko Haram: Islamic Fundamentalism and the Response of the Nigerian State.' *Africa Today* 57 (4): 98–119.

AFP. 2016. *Boko Haram leader Shekau promises to continue fight in new video.* 8 August. Accessed 8 August 2016. http://bit.ly/2b37std.

Africa Confidential. 2012. 'Boko Haram Looks to Mali.' 30 November. https://bit. ly/2D0eB9s.

Agbiboa, Daniel Egiegba. 2013. 'Why Boko Haram Exists: The Relative Deprivation Perspective.' *African Conflict and Peacebuilding Review* (ACPR) 3 (1): 144–157.

Aghedo, Iro. 2015. 'Nigeria's Boko Haram: From Guerrilla Strategy to Conventional War?' *The Round Table: The Commonwealth Journal of International Affairs* 104 (4): 515–516. doi: 10.1080/00358533.2015.1063839.

Ahmed. 2012. 'Author's interview with DSS Borno state director, and head of the JTF ORO DSS Component, Ahmed.' Maiduguri.

Ahmed, Abdul-Azim. 2017. *Why do Muslims call the Islamic State 'Khawarij'?* 23 July. Accessed 25 February 2019. https://bit.ly/2tzVm13.

Ajala, Adekunle. 1983. 'The Nature of African Boundaries.' *Africa Spectrum* (Institute of African Affairs at GIGA) 18 (2): 177–189. http://bit.ly/2bkCziq.

Al Jazeera. 2015b. *Chad troops enter Nigeria to fight Boko Haram: First ground offensive launched by Chad against Nigerian rebels in bordering town of Gambaru after days of air-strikes.* 3 February. Accessed 23 September 2016. http://bit.ly/1KqwGqP.

Al Jazeera. 2010. *Nigeria killings caught on video.* 9 February. Accessed 7 August 2016. http://bit.ly/2bbOSeP.

Alabi-Isama, Godwin. 2013. *The Tragedy of Victory: On-the-Spot Account of the Nigeria-Biafra War in the Atlantic Theatre.* Ibadan, Nigeria: Spectrum Books.

al-Akiti, Shaykh Muhammad Afifi. 2005. *Defending the Transgressed by Censuring the Reckless against the Killing of Civilians (Mudāfiʿ al-Maẓlūm bi-Radd al-Muhāmilʿalā Qitāl Man Lā Yuqātil).* UK: Aqsa Press. Accessed 3 October 2016. http://bit. ly/2dIaYhW.

Al-Tamimi, Aymenn Jawad. 2018. *The Islamic State West Africa Province vs. Abu Bakr Shekau: Full text, translation and analysis.* 15 August. Accessed 13 February 2019. https://bit.ly/2GHkz1o.

Amnesty International. 2012. *NIGERIA: Trapped in the Cycle of Violence.* London: Amnesty International, 88. Accessed 9 May 2016. http://bit.ly/1WiJ2f5.

Amnesty International. 2015. *Stars on their Shoulders. Blood on Their hands. War Crimes Committed by the Nigerian Military.* London: Amnesty International, 133. Accessed 9 May 2016. http://bit.ly/1FU5aCa.

Amoda, John. 2011. *Appraisal of Da'wah Coordination Council of Nigeria, DCCN: The 'Boko Haram' tragedy*. 20 September. Accessed 3 December 2016. http://bit.ly/2glnb4W.

Anderson, Gary. 2010. 'Counterinsurgency vs. Counterterrorism: A Civilian's View.' *Small Wars Journal* https://smallwarsjournal.com/jrnl/art/counterinsurgency-vs-counterterrorism.

Armstrong, Hannah. 2014. 'The In Amenas Attack in the Context of Southern Algeria's Growing Social Unrest.' *Combating Terrorism Center at Westpoint (CTC) Sentinel* 14–16. https://ctc.usma.edu/app/uploads/2014/02/CTCSentinel-Vol7Iss2.pdf.

Asadu, Chinedu. 2018. *Report: Boko Haram factional leader killed by own associates*. 14 September. Accessed 13 February 2019. https://bit.ly/2N27oZZ.

Asari, Dokubo. 2012. *Dokubo Asari: Boko Haram, Goodluck Jonathan and Me*. 23 August. Accessed 18 July 2017. http://bit.ly/2utBsa1.

Atofarati, Abubakar A. 1992. 'The Nigerian Civil War: Causes, Strategies and Lessons Learnt.' US Marine Command and Staff College. Command and Staff Course (CSC) 1992, Marine Corps University Command and Staff College.

Attahiru, Ibrahim. 2017. *Gen Attahiru provides updates on counterinsurgency operations*. June. Accessed 19 March 2019. https://bit.ly/2UOfVTu.

Attahiru, Ibrahim. 2018. *We Eliminate[d] 5 top Boko Haram Commanders, neutralize 70 terrorists in special Op-Gen. Attahiru*. Accessed 19 March 2019. https://bit.ly/2ObV2Px.

Baca, Michael W. 2015. *As attacks on Boko Haram Mount, where might they hide?* 11 March. Accessed 16 August 2016. http://bit.ly/2aWKFj8.

Bamalli, Zahrau, Abdulkarim Sabo Mohammed, Hasanah Mohd Ghazali, and Roselina Karim. 2014. 'Baobab Tree (Adansonia digitata L) Parts: Nutrition, Applications in Food and Uses in Ethno-medicine – A Review.' *Annals of Nutritional Disorders & Therapy* (Austin Publishing Group) 1 (3): 1–9. Accessed 20 August 2016. http://bit.ly/2bEz2tn.

Barker, Chris, and Emma A. Jane. 2016. *Cultural Studies: Theory and Practice*. London: SAGE Publications LTD.

Bayo, General Alberto. 1963. *150 Questions for a Guerrilla*. Denver, CO: Cypress.

Bello, Sarkin-Yaki. 2012. 'Author's interview with Maj. Gen Sarkin-Yaki Bello. National Coordinator Counter-Terrorism at the Office of the National Security Advisor (ONSA).' Abuja.

Bergen, Peter. 2012. *How Petraeus changed the U.S. military*. 11 November. Accessed 19 April 2015. http://cnn.it/1yFT0gB.

Bishop, Patrick. 2004. *The bomber will always get through, be he ETA or al-Qaeda*. 12 March. Accessed 6 October 2016. http://bit.ly/2duZ1Fq.

Blair, David. 2015a. *Boko Haram is now a mini-Islamic State, with its own territory*. 28 January. Accessed 18 July 2015. http://bit.ly/1BNybOK.

Boot, Max. 2013. *Invisible Armies: An Epic History of Guerrilla Warfare from Ancient Times to the Present*. New York: Liveright Publishing Corporation.

Braun, David Maxwell. 2010. *Lake Chad to be fully protected as international wetlands*. 2 February. Accessed 26 August 2016. http://bit.ly/2bkQGU9.

Brett, Daniel. 2014. *Boko Haram: Military is the problem, not the solution*. 15 August. Accessed 2 August 2017. http://bit.ly/2wmNv6d.

Brown, Larissa. 2016. *British warplanes are attacked by ISIS forces on the ground: Militants fire surface-to-air missiles at RAF jets dropping bombs over Syria and Iraq*. 23 September. Accessed 24 September 2016. http://dailym.ai/2cXUlsv.

Bull, Stephen, and Steve Noon. 2007. *World War II Jungle Warfare Tactics*. Oxford, UK: Osprey Publishing.

Buratai, Lieutenant General Tukur Yusuf. 2016. *Chief of Army Staff's Speaking Notes on the Topic: Challenges and Priorities for Combatting Boko Haram Terrorists Delivered at Atlantic Council*. Washington, D.C.: Atlantic Council. http://bit.ly/2cqzLxX.

Butt, Tahir Mehmood. 2012. 'Social and Political Role of Madrassa: Perspectives of Religious Leaders in Pakistan.' *South Asian Studies* 27 (2): 387–407. http://bit.ly/2bS1O96.

Byman, Daniel A., and Matthew C. Waxman. 2000. 'Kosovo and the Great Air Power Debate.' *International Security* 24 (4): 5–38. Accessed 18 August 2016. http://bit.ly/2aWMBXR.

Byman, Daniel. 2009. 'Do Targeted Killings Work?' *Foreign Policy.* 14 July. https://bit.ly/2SXCza6.

Callwell, Charles. 1996. *Small Wars: Their Principles and Practice*. 3rd New edition of Revised ed. Nebraska: University of Nebraska.

Campbell, John. 2019. *Nigeria Security Tracker*. 20 March. Accessed 20 March 2019. https://on.cfr.org/2Jhc9MQ.

Carruthers, Susan. 1995. *Winning Hearts and Minds: British Governments, the Media and Colonial Counter-insurgency, 1944–60*. Leicester: Leicester University Press.

Caulderwood, Kathleen. 2015. *Boko Haram update: Female suicide attack, police station bombing herald more violence ahead of Nigeria elections*. 12 February. Accessed 18 October 2016. http://bit.ly/2doVLZz.

CBS News. 2003. '*Mission Accomplished*' *Whodunit*. 29 October. Accessed 15 April 2017. http://cbsn.ws/2pC4tKv.

Central Intelligence Agency. 2015. *Africa: Niger*. Accessed 22 August 2016. http://bit.ly/1wuDM8G.

Chandler, Adam. 2015. *The Islamic State of Boko Haram?* 9 March. Accessed 10 August 2017. http://theatln.tc/2vTyxaK.

Chayes, Sarah. 2015. *Thieves of State: Why Corruption Threatens Global Security*. New York: W. W. Norton & Company Inc.

Chin, Warren. 2012. 'From Belfast to Lashkar Gar via Basra: British Counterinsurgency Today.' In *The Routledge Handbook of Insurgency and Counterinsurgency*, edited by Paul Rich and Isabelle Duyvesteyn, 276–285. Abingdon, Oxon: Routledge.

Civins, Braden. 2011. 'A Civilian's Comprehensive Critique of the U.S. Army/Marine Corps Counterinsurgency Field Manual … In 5–6 Pages.' *Small Wars Journal* 3.

CNN. 2016. *Boko Haram Fast Facts*. 17 October. Accessed 18 October 2016. http://cnn.it/1QxBvGd.

Collier, Paul, and Anke Hoeffler. 2001. *Greed and Grievance in Civil War*. World Bank. http://bit.ly/2qSNaZ1.

Comolli, Virginia. 2015. *Boko Haram: Nigeria's Islamist Insurgency*. London: C. Hurst & Co. (Publishers) Ltd.

Comolli, Virginia, and Kate Robertson. 2015b. *Boko Haram (ISWAP) and ISIS: two of a kind?* Terrorism Research and Analysis Consortium (TRAC). http://bit.ly/1HKTGzN.

Corte, Luis de la, and Andrea Giménez-Salinas. 2009. 'Suicide Terrorism as a Tool of Insurgency Campaigns: Functions, Risk Factors, and Countermeasures.' *Perspectives on Terrorism* 3 (1). http://bit.ly/2dsld3Y.

Crisis Group. 2010. *Northern Nigeria: Background to Conflict*. Brussels, Belgium: International Crisis Group.

Cross, J. P. 2008. *Jungle Warfare: Experiences and Encounters.* Barnsley, South Yorkshire:
Pen & Sword Military.

Crowe, Lance. 2011. *Asymmetric warfare in counterinsurgency.* 4 October. Accessed 20 July
2015. http://bit.ly/15ovNAR.

Curtis, Mark. 2004. *Unpeople: Britain's Secret Human Rights Abuses.* London: Vintage.

Daily Trust. 2012. *The Occupation of Northern Nigeria.* 12 October. http://bit.ly/2oFeNBG.

Danjibo, Nathaniel D. 2010. *Islamic Fundamentalism and Sectarian Violence: The
'Maitatsine' and 'Boko Haram' Crises in Northern Nigeria.* Peace and Conflict Studies
Programme, Institute of African Studies. Ibadan: University of Ibadan. Accessed
2 August 2016. http://bit.ly/2adHemD.

Danmadami, Musa. 2012. 'Authors interview with the JTF ORO Assistant Chief of Staff,
Operations (ACoS G3), at the JTF ORO HQ.' Maiduguri, Borno.

Dasuki, Sambo. 2015. *Nigeria's Security: Insurgency, Elections and Coordinating Responses
to Multiple Threats.* Africa Programme Transcript. London: Chatham House. http://bit.
ly/2bpvehg.

David, Ojochenemi, Lucky E. Asuelime, and Hakeem Onapajo. 2015. *Boko Haram: The
Socio-Economic Drivers.* Cham: Springer International Publishing AG.

DCCN. 2009. *The Boko Haram Tragedy: Frequently Asked Questions; Responses to 26
of the most commonly asked questions regarding the Boko Haram crisis and tragedy'.
Da'wah Coordination Council of Nigeria (DCCN).* Minna, Niger State, Nigeria: Da'wah
Coordination Council of Nigeria, DCCN.

de Tocqueville, Alexis. 1840. *Democracy in America: Part the Second, The Social Influence
of Democracy.* Translated by Henry Reeve. New York: J. & H. G. Langley. Accessed
22 March 2019.

Deep, Alex. 2015. 'Hybrid War: Old Concept, New Techniques.' *Small Wars Journal* 1–4.
http://bit.ly/2xzKxvP.

Dempsey, Joseph. 2015. *Joseph Dempsey: Boko Haram's armoured fighting vehicles.*
18 February. Accessed 4 July 2016. http://bit.ly/1AS8gFX.

Diintayda, Dadkayga & Dalkayga (Somalia). 2010. *What is Khawarij? Who are the
Khawarji? (abridged from the book: The 'Wahhabi' Myth).* 9 December. Accessed
25 February 2019. https://bit.ly/2SWUum6.

Dixon, Norman F. 1979. *On the Psychology of Military Incompetence.* London: Futura
Publications.

Don Van Natta, Jr. 2003. *Big Bang Theory: The terror industry fields its ultimate weapon.* 24
August. Accessed 3 October 2016. http://nyti.ms/2dE0uMX.

Doucet, Lyse. 2016. *Iraq violence: Did IS use new type of bomb for deadliest attack?* 28 July.
Accessed 6 August 2016. http://bbc.in/2auw60z.

Dzikansky, Mordecai, Gil Kleiman, and Robert Slater. 2012. *Terrorist Suicide Bombings:
Attack Interdiction, Mitigation, and Response.* Boca Raton, FL: CRC Press, Taylor and
Francis Group.

Eland, Ivan. 2013. *The Failure of Counterinsurgency: Why Hearts and Minds Are Seldom
Won.* Santa Barbara: Praeger Publishers.

Empiricus, Sextus. 2000. *Outlines of Scepticism.* Translated by J Annas and J Barnes.
Cambridge: Cambridge University Press.

Enaikele, M.D, A.O Olutayo, and T.K.O Aluko. 2009. 'France Diplomacy and
Conspiratorial Role in Nigeria-Cameroon Border Dispute.' *The Nigerian Army
Quarterly Journal* 5 (2): 228–244.

Falola, Toyin. 2001. *Violence in Nigeria: The Crisis of Religious Politics and Secular
Ideologies (Rochester Studies in African History and the Diaspora).* Rochester:
University of Rochester Press.

Falola, Toyin, and Ann Genova. 2009. *Historical Dictionary of Nigeria (Historical Dictionaries of Africa)*. Plymouth, UK: Scarecrow Press, Inc.

Farrell, Theo. 2010. 'Improving in War: Military Adaptation and the British in Helmand Province, Afghanistan, 2006–2009.' *Journal of Strategic Studies* 33 (4): 567–594. Accessed 19 May 2016. doi:10.1080/01402390.2010.489712.

Feldman, Noah. 2006. *Islam, terror and the Second Nuclear Age*. 29 October. Accessed 3 October 2016. http://nyti.ms/2cW8TII.

Mathias, Grégor, 2011. *Galula in Algeria: Counterinsurgency. Practice versus Theory*. Westport, Connecticut, United States: Praeger Publishers.

Fick, Maggie. 2016. *Boko Haram dispute with Isis bursts into the open*. 5 August. Accessed 6 August 2016. http://on.ft.com/2aG7XaE.

Forest, James J. F. 2012. *Confronting the Terrorism of Boko Haram in Nigeria*. JSOU Report 12–5, Strategic Studies Department, Joint Special Operations University, Tampa Point Boulevard, Florida: The JSOU Press MacDill Air Force Base.

Fraser, David. 1993. *Knight's Cross: A Life of Field Marshal Erwin Rommel*. New York: HarperCollins Publishers.

Freedberg Jr., Sydney J. 2003. *Army's lightweight Stryker brigade to get tested in Iraq*. 10 October. Accessed 25 March 2019. https://bit.ly/2CDUYDp.

Freeman, Colin. 2015. *South African mercenaries' secret war on Boko Haram*. 10 May. Accessed 8 January 2019. https://bit.ly/2KISypX.

Freeman, Colin, Martin Henderson, and Mark Oliver. 2014. *Isis, Boko Haram and other affiliates' strongholds across Africa and Asia*. 12 June. Accessed 18 July 2015. http://bit.ly/1kwa0bd.

Fuglestad, Finn. 1983. *A History of Niger 1850–1960*. Cambridge: Cambridge University Press.

Galula, David. 2006. *Counterinsurgency Warfare: Theory and Practice*. Edited by John Nagl. Westport: Praeger Security International.

Geels, Jolijn. 2006. *Niger: The Bradt Travel Guide*. Chalfont St Peter, Bucks, England: Bradt Travel Guides.

Gentile, Gian. 2008. 'A (Slightly) Better War: A Narrative and Its Defects.' *World Affairs Journal*.

Gentile, Gian. 2009. 'A Strategy of Tactics: Population-centric COIN and the Army.' *US Army War College Quarterly* 39 (3): 5.

Géré, François. 2007. 'Suicide Operations: Between War and Terrorism.' In *The History of Terrorism From Antiquity to Al Qaeda*, edited by Gerard Chaliand and Arnaud Blin, translated by Edward Schneider, Kathryn Pulver and Jesse Browner, 363–397. London, England: University of California Press, Ltd.

Google Maps. 2017. 'Sambisa Forest Reserve.' *Google Maps*. 1 October. Accessed 18 August 2017. http://bit.ly/2b3XYsw.

Greene, Robert. 2007. *The 33 Strategies Of War*. London: Profile Books Ltd.

Greene, Robert. 2000. *The 48 Laws Of Power*. London: Profile Books.

Griswold, Eliza. 2014. *Why fear Boko Haram*. 28 April. Accessed 27 August 2016. http://slate.me/1tWUHAf.

Guderian, Heinz. 1999. *Achtung Panzer!: The Development of Tank Warfare*. Translated by Christopher Duffy. London: Cassell Military.

Guevara, Ernesto Che. 1968. *Guerrilla Warfare*. Petit Collection, French ed. Edited by François Maspero. Paris: Oeuvres.

Hall, James, interview by Akali Omeni. 2012. *Interview with British Army Defence Attache to Nigeria, Colonel James Hall*, Abuja (September).

2014. 'Boko Haram and its Muslim Critics: Observations from Yobe State.' In *Boko Haram: Islamism, politics, security and the state in Nigeria*, by Johannes Harnischfeger, edited by Marc-Antoine Pérouse de Montclos, 33–62. Leiden, Netherlands: African Studies Centre.

Herbst, Jeffrey. 2004. 'African Militaries and Rebellion: The Political Economy of Threat and Combat Effectiveness.' *Journal of Peace Research* 41 (3): 357–369.

Herodotus. 2003. *The Histories*. London: Penguin Books.

Higazi, Adam. 2013a. 'Insurgency and Counter-Insurgency in North-East Nigeria.' Sciences Po | Centre De Recherches Internationales, 1–5. http://bit.ly/2aKf0OG.

Higazi, Adam. 2013b. 'The origins and transformation of the Boko Haram insurgency in northern Nigeria - published in French translation as: Les origines et la transformation de l'insurrection de Boko Haram dans le nord du Nigeria.' *Forthcoming in French in Politique Africaine in a special issue on the Sahel.*

Hill, J.N.C. 2014. *Boko Haram, the Chibok Abductions and Nigeria's Counterterrorism Strategy*. Post, Combating Terrorism Center at West Point. Accessed 6 May 2016. http://bit.ly/1STmN9E.

Hill, Jonathan N. C. 2012. *Nigeria Since Independence: Forever Fragile?* Basingstoke, Hampshire: Palgrave MacMillan.

Hill, Jonathan N.C. 2010. *Sufism in Northern Nigeria: Force for counter-radicalization?* Monograph, Strategic Studies Institute, Carlisle, Pennsylvania: US Army. http://bit.ly/2bNClS4.

Hills, Alice. 2012. 'Insurgency, Counterinsurgency and Policing.' In *The Routledge Handbook of Insurgency and Counterinsurgency*, edited by Paul B. Rich and Isabelle Duvesteyn, 98–108. Abingdon, Oxon: Routledge.

Hinshaw, Drew. 2013. *Timbuktu training site shows terrorists' reach | Nigerians flooded to al Qaeda-linked camp in Mali*, Locals *Say, drilling with shoulder-Fired Arms*. 1 February. Accessed 26 August 2016. http://on.wsj.com/2c1WAuX.

Hinshaw, Drew, and Joe Parkinson. 2016. *The kidnapped boys of Boko Haram*. 12 August. Accessed 13 August 2016. http://on.wsj.com/2bnVcnu.

Hiribarren, Vincent. 2016. *A History of Borno: Trans-Saharan African Empire to Failing Nigerian State*. London: C Hurst & Co Publishers Ltd.

Höchner, Hannah, interview by Akali Omeni. 2013. *Almajiri interview, based on interviewee's fieldwork with these youth in northern Nigeria* Quaker's Friend's House. Euston, London.

Höchner, Hannah. 2014. *Rejoinder to 'why fear Boko Haram'*. 11 June. Accessed 27 August 2016. http://bit.ly/2bpWQ2I.

Höchner, Hannah. 2015. 'Traditional Qur'anic students (almajirai) in Nigeria: Fair game for unfair accusations?' In *Boko Haram: Islamism, Politics, Security, and the State in Nigeria*, edited by Marc-Antoine Pérouse de Montclos, 63–84. Leiden: African Studies Centre. http://bit.ly/1nChRIA.

Hoffman, Frank. 2008. *Conflict in the 21st Century: The Rise of Hybrid War*. Arlington, Virginia: Potomac Institute for Policy Studies. http://bit.ly/1phKnCf.

Hoffman, Frank. 2007. 'Neo Classical Counter Insurgency.' *Parameters* 71–72.

Home Office. 2011. *Prevent Strategy*. Government, Home Office, UK Government, London, UK: Home Office, 116. Accessed 22 August 2016. http://bit.ly/1At8sIA.

HRW. 2012. *Spiraling Violence Boko Haram Attacks and Security Force Abuses in Nigeria*. Human Rights Watch, Washington, D.C.: Human Rights Watch. Accessed 14 May 2016. http://bit.ly/1Xr0Vrr.

Iaccino, Ludovica. 2016. *Could Ansaru leader Mamman Nur be the man behind Boko Haram split?* 12 August. Accessed 10 January 2019. https://bit.ly/2Frjryf.

Idris, Hamza, and Ibrahim Sawab. 2018. *Factional Boko Haram leader Mamman Nur killed by own fighters.* 14 September. Accessed 10 January 2018. https://bit.ly/2Rlm1wC.

Idris, Hamza, and Ronald Mutum. 2018. *Why Boko Haram is attacking military formations in N/East.* 27 November. Accessed 11 February 2019. https://bit.ly/2E41nsQ.

Idris, Hamza, and Uthman Abubakar. 2019. *Military prepares massive operation to retake Baga, others.* 6 January. Accessed 10 January 2019. https://bit.ly/2SMWUzN.

Igata, Francis. 2016. 'Boko Haram: Sambisa Forest as big as Enugu State – Buratai.' *Vanguard.* 17 March. Accessed 18 August 2016. http://bit.ly/2bAb4zY.

Ihsanic intelligence. n.d. *The Hijacked Caravan: Refuting Suicide Bombings as Martyrdom Operations in Contemporary Jihad Strategy.* Monograph, Ihsanic intelligence, 26. Accessed 25February 2017. http://bit.ly/1px0gmH.

IISS. 2015. *The Military Balance 2015.* Abingdon, Oxon: Routledge Journals, Taylor & Francis.

Institute for Economics and Peace. 2015. *2015 Global Terrorism Index.* New York: Institute for Economics and Peace. Accessed 14 May 2016. http://bit.ly/1SUWVvg.

International Crisis Group. 2014. *Curbing Violence in Nigeria (II): The Boko Haram Insurgency.* Africa Report #216. Brussels, Belgium: International Crisis Group.

Iqbal, Murtaza. 2011. *The Real Counterinsurgency, Winning Hearts and Repairing Minds: Lessons in Vietnam, Iraq and Afghanistan.* Saarbrücken, Germany: Lambert Academic Publishing.

Isa, Garba A. 2009. *Sheikh Ja'afar Adam: Martyrdom at dawn.* 19 March. Accessed 23 July 2017. http://bit.ly/2tRoDBP.

Isichei, Elizabeth. 1987. 'The Maitatsine Risings in Nigeria 1980–85: A Revolt of the Disinherited.' *Journal of Religion in Africa* 17 (3): 194–208.

Jantzi, Jennifer. 2017. 'Book Review - American Spartan: The Promise, The Mission, and the Betrayal of Special Forces Major Jim Gant.' *Small Wars Journal* 13 (4). http://bit.ly/2pyGrQA.

Johnson, Patrick, and Anoop Sarbahi. 2016. 'The Impact of U.S. Drone Strikes on Terrorism in Pakistan and Afghanistan.' *International Studies Quarterly* 60: 203–219. https://bit.ly/2CedRNb.

Jordan, Jenna. 2014. 'Attacking the Leader, Missing the Mark: Why Terrorist Groups Survive Decapitation Strikes.' *International Security* 38 (4): 7–38.

Joscelyn, Thomas. 2015. *Analysis: Osama bin Laden's son praises al Qaeda's branches in new message.* 17 August. Accessed 6 August 2016. http://bit.ly/1TPyT5S.

JTFC. 2012. *Operational Report - Joint Task Force Commander (JTFC) Briefing at HQ, JTF ORO.* Brief. Maiduguri: Nigerian Army.

Kayode, Bodunrin. 2014. *Inside Nigeria's Sambisa forest, the Boko Haram hideout where kidnapped school girls are believed to be held.* 29 April. Accessed 18 August 2016. http://bit.ly/2bEdGiF.

Keen, David. 2012. 'Greed and Grievance in Civil War.' *International Affairs* 88 (4): 757–777.

Kilcullen, David. 2010a. *Counterinsurgency.* New York: Oxford University Press.

Kilcullen, David. 2007. 'Edward Luttwak's "Counterinsurgency Malpractice".' *Small Wars Journal* https://smallwarsjournal.com/blog/edward-luttwaks-counterinsurgency-malpractice.

Kilcullen, David. 2010b. 'Intelligence.' In *Understanding Counterinsurgency: Doctrine, Operations, and Challenges,* edited by Thomas Rid and Thomas Keaney, 141–159. Abingdon, Oxon: Routledge.

Kilcullen, David. 2009. *The Accidental Guerrilla: Fighting Small Wars in the Midst of a Big One*. Oxford: Oxford University Press.

Kiszely, Major General John. 1998. 'The meaning of manoeuvre.' *The RUSI Journal* 143 (6): 36–40. Accessed 15 March 2019. doi:10.1080/03071849808446326.

Koettl, Christoph, Emmanuel Akinwotu, Malachy Browne, Natalie Reneau, Ainara Tiefenthäler, David Botti, and Whitney Hurst. 2018. *How an Elite Nigerian Army unit killed dozens of protesters*. 17 December. Accessed 08 January 2019. https://nyti.ms/2THthzZ.

Kolenda, Christopher D. 2013. *The Counterinsurgency Challenge: A Parable of Leadership and Decision Making in Modern Conflict*. Mechanisburg, PA: Stackpole Books.

Krakauer, John. 2011. *Three Cups of Deceit: How Greg Mortenson, Humanitarian Hero, Lost His Way*. New York: Random House.

Lange, Dierk. 2010. 'An Introduction to the History of Kanem-Borno: The Prologue of the Diwan.' *Borno Museum Society Newsletter* 76 (84): 79–103.

Lemay, Benoît. 2010. *Erich Von Manstein: Hitler's Master Strategist*. Newbury, Berkshire: Casemate.

Liedman, Sean. 2011. 'Don't Break the Bank with COIN: Re-setting U.S. Defense Strategy After Iraq and Afghanistan.' Cambridge, MA: Weatherhead Center For International Affairs, Harvard University.

Loimeier, Roman. 2012. 'Boko Haram: The Development of a Militant Religious Movement in Nigeria.' *Africa Spectrum* 47 (2–3): 137–155.

Loimeier, Roman. 1997. *Islamic Reform and Political Change in Northern Nigeria (Islam and Society in Africa)*. Evanston: Northwestern University Press.

Londoño, Ernesto. 2014. *U.S. deploys 80 troops to Chad to help find kidnapped Nigerian schoolgirls*. 21 May. Accessed 25 August 2016. http://wapo.st/2unaz8v.

Luttwak, Edward. 2007. 'Dead End: Counterinsurgency Warfare as Military Malpractice.' *Harper's Magazine*, February: 33–42.

MacDonald, Callum. 1989. *The Killing of SS Obergruppenführer Reinhard Heydrich 27 May 1942*. London: Macmillan.

MacEachern, Scott. 2018. *Searching for Boko Haram: A History of Violence in Central Africa*. Oxford: Oxford University Press.

Mackinlay, John. 2012. *The Insurgent Archipelago: From Mao to Bin Laden*. New York: Columbia University Press.

Maclean, Ruth, and Isaac Abrak. 2018. *Boko Haram kept one Dapchi girl who refused to deny her Christianity*. 24 March. Accessed 13 February 2019. https://bit.ly/2INEbzp.

Madiebo, Alexander A. 1980. *The Nigerian Revolution and the Biafran War*. Enugu, Nigeria: Fourth Dimension Publishing Co., Ltd.

Mahmood, Omar S. 2018. *Is Islamic State in West Africa becoming more hardline?* 28 November. Accessed 13 February 2019. https://bit.ly/2TWBkd9.

Manea, Octavian. 2010. 'Thinking Critically about COIN and Creatively about Strategy and War: An Interview with Colonel Gian Gentile.' *Small Wars Journal* https://smallwarsjournal.com/jrnl/art/thinking-critically-about-coin-and-creatively-about-strategy-and-war.

Marama, Ndahi. 2014. *41 Boko Haram members beheaded in Biu*. 1 November. Accessed 26 May 2017. http://bit.ly/2rXxEts.

Martin, Grant M. 2010. 'COIN, Complexity, and Full-Spectrum Warfare: Is it possible to have Center of Gravity given all the Fog and Friction?' Accessed 31 March 2012. http://smallwarsjournal.com/blog/journal/docs-temp/591-martin.pdf.

Maslow, Abraham H. 1966. *The Psychology of Science*. New York: Harper & Row.

Massalaki, Abdoulaye. 2015. *Niger troops and Chad air force fight off Boko Haram attack.* 6 February. Accessed 23 September 2016. http://reut.rs/2cXRePr.

Massalaki, Abdoulaye, and Richard Valdmanis. 2012. *Niger seeks joint southern border patrols to bar Boko Haram.* 7 October. Accessed 22 August 2016. http://bit.ly/2bum7Jp.

Matfess, Hilary. 2017. *The anatomy of a suicide mission.* 10 August. Accessed 10 August 2017. http://bit.ly/2vTbOwp.

Matfess, Hilary. 2017. *Women and the War on Boko Haram: Wives, Weapons, Witnesses.* London: Zed Books.

McChrystal, General Stanley A. 2013. *The Evolution of Joint Special Operations Command and the Pursuit of Al Qaeda in Iraq: A Conversation with General Stanley McChrystal.* Washington, D.C.: The Brookings Institution. Accessed 15 March 2019. https://brook. gs/2dWeGk9.

McChrystal, General Stanley, Tantum Collins, David Silverman, and Chris Fussell. 2015. *Team of Teams: New Rules of Engagement for a Complex World.* UK: Portfolio Penguin.

McFate, Montgomery. 2010. 'Culture.' In *Understanding Counterinsurgency: Doctrine, Operations and Challenges*, edited by Thomas Rid and Thomas Keaney, 189–204. Abingdon, Oxon: Routledge.

Mearsheimer, John J. 2001. *The Tragedy of Great Power Politics.* New York: W. W. Norton & Company.

Mehta, Maj. Gen. Ashok. 2010. *Sri Lanka's Ethnic Conflict: How Eelam War IV Was Won.* Manekshaw Paper 22 A, New Delhi: Centre for Land Warfare Studies. Accessed 29 March 2019. http://bit.ly/1AY3Jk5.

Mekhennet, Souad, and Greg Miller. 2016. *He's the son of Osama bin Laden's bombmaker. Then ISIS wanted him as one of their own.* 5 August. Accessed 6 August 2016. http://wapo.st/2b0c3cF.

Mercy Corps. 2016. 'Motivations and Empty Promises': *Voices of Former Boko Haram Combatants and Nigerian Youth.* April. http://bit.ly/2bqUGRH.

Middlemas, Keith, and John Barnes. 1969. *Baldwin: A Biography.* London: Weidenfeld and Nicolson.

Moghadam, Assaf. 2011. *The Globalization of Martyrdom: Al Qaeda, Salafi Jihad, and the Diffusion of Suicide Attacks.* Baltimore: Johns Hopkins University Press.

Mohammed, Abdulkareem. 2010. *The Paradox of Boko Haram.* Edited by Mohammed Haruna. Nigeria: Moving Image Limited.

Montclos, Marc-Antoine Pérouse de. 2014. 'Boko Haram and Politics: From Insurgency to Terrorism.' In *Boko Haram: Islamism, politics, security and the state in Nigeria*, edited by Marc-Antoine Pérouse de Montclos, 135–157. Leiden, Netherlands: African Studies Centre.

Mortenson, Greg, and David Relin. 2008. *Three Cups of Tea.* London: Penguin.

Mutum, Ronald. 2015. *Military intercepts B/Haram drugs, logistics suppliers.* 9 September. Accessed 14 August 2016. http://bit.ly/2aVzGTa.

Nagl, John A. 2005. *Learning to Eat Soup with a Knife: Counterinsurgency Lessons from Malaya and Vietnam.* Chicago: University of Chicago Press.

National Bureau of Statistics. 2012. *National Baseline Youth Survey.* Abuja: NBS. http://bit.ly/2bc2fut.

National Population Commission. 2010. *2006 Population and Housing Census | priority Table Volume IV | Population Distribution By Age and Sex (State & Local Government Areas).* Census Data, Abuja: Federal Government of Nigeria. http://bit.ly/2bitIM3.

NATO-ISAF. 2009. *ISAF Commander's Counterinsurgency Guidance.* ISAF Headquarters: NATO-ISAF. Accessed 10 August 2016. http://bit.ly/2bffAXG.

Neba, Aaron Suh. 1987. *Modern Geography of the Republic of Cameroon*. Cameroon: Neba Publishers.

Nengite, D. I. O. 2012. *Author's interview with NA Colonel Nengite, at Marda Barracks, Lagos. I am grateful to the colonel for his insightful views across the various other informal interactions we had'*. Lagos: Nigerian Army.

Neumann, Peter R., and M. L. R. Smith. 2005. 'Strategic Terrorism: The Framework and its Fallacies.' *Journal of Strategic Studies* (Routledge, Taylor and Francis Group) 28 (4): 571–595. Accessed 13 June 2016. doi:10.1080/01402390500300923.

News Agency of Nigeria. 2016. *60% of Boko Haram now not Nigerians, Buratai says*. 16 November. Accessed 2 December 2016. http://bit.ly/2fOV1mo.

News Wire NGR. 2015. *B'Haram Attack Police Station, 23 Killed, More Than 100 Injured*. Read more http://newswirengr.com/2015/06/15/bharam-attack-police-station-23-killed-more-than-100-injured/. 15 June. Accessed 18 October 2016. http://bit.ly/2dZ0svO.

News.com. 2014. *US spy plane photos reveal 'groups of girls' believed to be those kidnapped by Boko Haram from a Nigerian boarding school*. 6 August. Accessed 7 August 2014. http://bit.ly/1lDh9rT.

Ngarmbassa, Moumine. 2015. *Suspected Boko Haram suicide bombers kill 27 in Chad capital*. 15 June. Accessed 16 August 2016. http://reut.rs/2bdaxm5.

Ngbea, Gabriel Terwase, and Hilary Chukwuka Achunike. 2014. 'Poverty in Northern Nigeria.' *Asian Journal of Humanities and Social Studies* 2 (2): 266–272.

Ngoh, Victor Julius. 1996. *History of Cameroon since 1800*. Limbé: Presbook.

Nigerian Army. 2009. *G/G3/001 Nigerian Army Doctrine*. Abuja: Army HQ.

Nigerian Army. 2011. *G/G3/10, The Nigerian Army in Military Operations Other than War Volume 4A, Counter Insurgency Operations*. Abuja: Army HQ.

Nigerian Army. 2016. *Nigerian Army inducts combat motorbike battalion into battle*. 28 February. Accessed 19 August 2016. http://bit.ly/2b5Kq2x.

Nigerian Army. 2017. *Standing Operating Procedures for Mobile Strike Teams*. Abuja: Nigerian Army.

Nigerian Conservation Foundation. 2001. *Sambisa Game Reserve*. Accessed 18 August 2016. http://bit.ly/2bElz7w.

Njeuma, Martin Z. 2012. *Fulani Hegemony in Yola (Old Adamawa) 1809–1902*. Yaoundé, Cameroon: Langaa RPCIG.

NSRP. 2017. *How an improved understanding of drug use can contribute to peace and stability in Nigeria*. Nigeria Stability and Reconciliation Programme. http://bit.ly/2qcNt2b.

Nwaubani, Adaobi Tricia. 2017. *Letter from Africa: Freed Boko Haram 'wives' return to captors*. 26 July. Accessed 26 July 2017. http://bbc.in/2uYMTqf.

Nye, Joseph S. 2004. *Soft Power: The Means to Success in World Politics*. New York: Public Affairs.

Obi, Cyril, and Siri Aas Rustad,. 2011. *Oil and Insurgency in the Niger Delta: Managing the Complex Politics of Petroviolence (Africa Now)*. New York: Zed Books.

Odunsi, Wale. 2016. *Troops ambush Boko Haram, recovers hard drugs, anti-aircraft gun, GPMGs [PHOTOS]*. 14 July. Accessed 14 August 2016. http://bit.ly/2aLx39q.

Ogundele, K. 2011. *Boko Haram: Why we struck, by taskforce commander*. 7 December. Accessed 21 August 2013. http://bit.ly/2nkVk8d.

Okonta, Ike, and Oronto Douglas. 2003. *Where Vultures Feast: Shell Human Rights, and Oil*. London: Verso Books.

Olalekan, Elegbede Isa, Li-Hammed Morufat Abimbola, Matemilola Saheed, and Omosanya Azeezah Damilola. 2014. 'Wetland Resources of Nigeria: Case Study of the

Hadejia-Nguru Wetlands.' *Poultry, Fisheries & Wildlife Sciences* (Poultry, Fisheries & Wildlife Sciences) 2 (123). doi: 10.4172/2375-446X.1000123.

Oliver, Haneef James. 2005. *The 'Wahhabi Myth': Dispelling prevalent Fallacies and the Ficticious Link with Bin Laden*. Bloomington, Indiana: Trafford Publishing.

Olonisakin, 'Funmi. 2004. 'Children and Armed Conflict.' In *West Africa's Security Challenge: Building Peace in a Troubled Region*, edited by Adekeye Adebajo and Ismail Rashid, 245–261. Boulder, Colorado: Lynne Rienner Publishers, Inc.

Olukayode, Michael. 2016. *Boko Haram Militia attacks police station in Northeast Nigeria*. 8 June. Accessed 18 October 2016. http://bloom.bg/2eeCyOV.

Omeni, Akali. 2018. 'Boko Haram's Covert Front.' *Journal of African Conflicts and Peace Studies* 4 (1). doi:https://doi.org/10.5038/2325-484X.4.1.1101.

Omeni, Akali. 2018b. 'Boko Haram's Increasingly Sophisticated Military Threat.' *Small Wars and Insurgencies* 29 (5–6): 886–915. doi:https://doi.org/10.1080/09592318.2018. 1519299.

Omeni, Akali. 2017. *Counter-insurgency in Nigeria: The Military and Operations against Boko Haram, 2011-17*. Abingdon, Oxon: Routledge.

Omeni, Akali. 2015. 'The Almajiri in Northern Nigeria: Militancy, Perceptions, Challenges, and State Policies.' *African Conflict & Peacebuilding Review* 5 (2): 128–142. http://bit.ly/2aiQTHk.

Omoigui, Nowa. 2015. *Nigerian Civil War File: Federal Nigerian Army blunders of the Nigerian Civil War - Part 2*. 8 April. Accessed 31 October 2016. http://bit.ly/2dTZ14c.

ONSA. 2012. *Some Characteristics of 'Boko Haram' Terrorist Group and the Way Forward by Major Gneral Sarkin-Yaki Bello - Coord CT Dept - ONSA*. Abuja: ONSA.

Onuoha, Freedom. 2014. 'Boko Haram and the evolving Salafi Jihadist threat.' In *Boko Haram: Islamism, politics, security and the state in Nigeria*, edited by Marc-Antoine Pérouse de Montclos, 151–192. Leiden, Netherlands: African Studies Centre.

Oxford Islamic Studies Online. n.d. *Gumi, Shaykh Abubakar*. Accessed 31 May 2018. http://www.oxfordislamicstudies.com/article/opr/t125/e754.

Paden, John. 2002. *Islam and Democratic Federalism in Nigeria*. Africa Program. Washington, D.C.: Center for Strategic and International Studies, 1–10. http://bit. ly/2aNSUwL.

Paden, John N. 2008. *Faith and Politics in Nigeria: Nigeria as a Pivotal State in the Muslim World*. Washington, D.C.: United States Institute of Peace Press.

Pape, Robert A. 2014. *Bombing to Win: Air Power and Coercion in War*. Ithaca, NY: Cornell University Press.

Pape, Robert A. 1997b. 'The Air Force Strikes Back: A Reply to Barry Watts and John Warden.' *Security Studies* 7 (2): 191–214. doi:10.1080/09636419708429346.

Pape, Robert A. 1997a. 'The Limits of Precision-Guided Air Power.' *Security Studies* 7 (2): 93–114. doi:http://dx.doi.org/10.1080/09636419708429343.

Patterson, Katy. 2012. *Seven Environments*. Chapel Hill: University of North Carolina at Chapel Hill, 1–5. Accessed 16 August 2016. http://unc.live/2aS80kQ.

Perrett, Bryan, and General Sir Walter KCB CBE DSO Walker. 1990. *Canopy of War: Jungle Warfare, from the Earliest Days of Forest Fighting to the Battlefields of Vietnam*. Somerset, UK: Patrick Stephens Ltd.

Perrett, Bryan, and Walter Walker. 2015. *Jungle Warfare: From the Earliest Days of Forest Fighting to the Battlefields of Vietnam*. Barnsley, South Yorkshire: Pen & Sword Military.

Philips, Michael M. 2009. *Stalemate*. 23 May. Accessed 20 July 2015. http://on.wsj. com/1xa4H8M.

Porch, Douglas. 2013. *Counterinsurgency: Exposing the Myths of the New Way of War.* Cambridge: Cambridge University Press.

Power, Samantha. 2007. *NY Times Book Review: FM 3-24.* 29 July. Accessed 23 October 2016. http://nyti.ms/2dA9htj.

Premium Times. 2014a. *Boko Haram on rampage in Gombe, attacks police station.* 4 November. Accessed 18 October 2016. http://bit.ly/2eeCQoN.

Premium Times. 2016b. *Boko Haram's Shekau, group's new leader, al-Barnawi, in war of words.* 5 August. Accessed 7 August 2016. http://bit.ly/2b0Re3H.

Rapoport, Yossef, and Shahab Ahmed. 2010. *Ibn Taymiyya and His Times (Studies in Islamic Philosophy).* Karachi: Oxford University Press.

Reno, William. 2012. 'Insurgent movements in Africa.' In *The Routledge Handbook of Insurgency and Counterinsurgency,* edited by Paul B. Rich and Isabelle Duyvesteyn, 157–171. Abingdon, Oxon: Routledge.

Rice, Xan. 2012. *Changing face of Nigeria's Boko Haram.* 22 May. Accessed 28 July 2016. http://on.ft.com/2akoBfY.

Rice, Xan, and William Wallis. 2012. *Pressure in Nigeria for Boko Haram talks.* 6 April. Accessed 2 August 2017. http://on.ft.com/2u16dQ9.

Rich, Paul B., and Isabelle Duyvesteyn. 2012. *The Routledge Handbook of Insurgency and Counterinsurgency.* Abingdon, Oxon: Routledge.

Ricks, Thomas E. 2015. *A challenge from Gourley: 'Why did we lose in Afghanistan?' in 500 words or less.* 4 February. Accessed 29 March 2019. https://bit.ly/2YzFsSj.

Ricks, Thomas E. 2009. *The Gamble: General David Petraeus and the American Military Adventure in Iraq, 2006-2008.* New York: The Penguin Press.

Rid, Thomas. 2010. 'The Nineteenth Century Origins of Counterinsurgency Doctrine.' *Journal of Strategic Studies* 33 (5): 725–758.

Rigasa, Yakubu Muhammad. 2008. *Finding The Killers of Sheikh Ja'afar Adam.* 28 April. Accessed 23 July 2017. http://bit.ly/2uoLh6t.

Roblin, Sebastian. 2016. *Nigeria's Tiny, Low-Tech Alpha Jets Have Flown in Brutal Wars Across Africa | Now the former training jets are blasting Boko Haram.* 28 July. Accessed 15 September 2016. http://bit.ly/2d0vUbJ.

Rommel, Erwin. 2012. *Infantry Attacks.* Barnsley: Frontline Books, an Imprint of Pen & Sword Books Limited.

Rosen, Stephen Peter. 1988. 'New Ways of War: Understanding Military Innovation.' *International Security* 13 (1): 134–168. doi:10.2307/2538898.

Russell, James. 2011. *Innovation, Transformation and War: Counterinsurgency Operations in Anbar and Ninewa Provinces, Iraq, 2005-2007.* Stanford, CA: Stanford University Press.

Sahara Reporters. 2018. *Boko Haram Leader Mamman Nur 'Killed by His Closest Lieutenants' for releasing Dapchi girls.* 14 September. Accessed 13 February 2019. https://bit.ly/2NmEbw0.

Sahara Reporters. 2016c. *Boko Haram: Abubakar Shekau reappears again after ISIS named his successor, claims he was deceived.* 5 August. Accessed 5 August 2016. http://bit.ly/2azCfM7.

Sahara Reporters. 2016b. *New Boko Haram Leader, al-Barnawi, accuses Abubakar Shekau of killing fellow Muslims, living in luxury.* 5 August. Accessed 5 August 2016. http://bit.ly/2aYGDq4.

Salkida, Ahmad. 2018. *Boko Haram released video showing 'gunned down aircraft,' drone and other military assets in Sambisa.* 14 01. Accessed 10 January 2019. https://bit.ly/2RExVkQ.

Salkida, Ahmad. 2017. *Shekau's faction of Boko Haram claims credit for Maiduguri attack.* 6 June. Accessed 10 January 2019. https://bit.ly/2FncM8W.

Salkida, Ahmad. 2019b. *Special report: Why troops are losing ground to ISWAP.* 02 January. Accessed 10 January 2019. https://bit.ly/2Fn9NMU.

Saunders, Doug. 2008. *Afghanistan: Colonialism or Counterinsurgency? Americans bring Afghans their new 60-year plan.* 31 May. Accessed 21 July 2015. http://bit.ly/1ljIP4H.

Scan News. 2014. *Nyako claims that the Nigerian Army in Adamawa is an occupation force.* 19 April. Accessed 4 April 2017. http://bit.ly/2oF3auG.

Schehl, Matthew L. 2016. *U.S. Marines prep West African allies to fight ISIS, Boko Haram, al-Qaida.* 3 March. Accessed 27 August 2016. http://bit.ly/2bIyceo.

Schmid, Alex P., ed. 2011. *The Routledge Handbook of Terrorism Research.* Abingdon, Oxon: Routledge.

Schneider, James. 2015b. *Boko Haram: fearsome yet reliant on exploited children.* 22 July. Accessed 16 August 2016. http://bit.ly/1JCeTft.

Schneider, James. 2015a. *Inside Boko Haram.* 22 July. Accessed 16 August 2016. http://bit.ly/1N6JBRh.

Schweitzer, Yoram, and Sean London. 2009. 'Assaf Moghadam: The Globalization of Martyrdom: Al Qaeda, Salafi Jihad, and the Diffusion of Suicide Attacks.' *Democracy and Security* 5 (3): 320–321. doi:http://dx.doi.org/10.1080/17419160903249044.

Sepp, Kalev. 2005. 'Best Practices in Counterinsurgency.' *Military Review* 8–12.

Simpson, Emile. 2012. *War From The Ground Up: Twenty-First Century Combat as Politics.* London: C. Hurst & Co. (Publishers) Ltd.

Smith, David. 2009b. *Inquiry call after Nigerian sect leader dies in custody.* 31 July. Accessed 4 August 2016. http://bit.ly/2aTYoGQ.

Smith, David. 2009a. *Nigerian forces storm militant Islamist mosque.* 30 July. Accessed 11 September 2016. http://bit.ly/1SWmcaz.

Smith, Niel. 2009. 'Sri Lanka's disconcerting COIN strategy for defeating the LTTE.' *Small Wars Journal.*

Snyder, Jack. 1984. *The Ideology of the Offensive: Military Decision Making and the Disasters of 1914.* New York: Cornell University Press.

Solomon, Hussein. 2015. *Terrorism and Counter-Terrorism in Africa: Fighting Insurgency from Al Shabaab, Ansar Dine and Boko Haram (New Security Challenges).* Edited by Stuart Croft. Basingstoke, Hampshire: Palgrave Macmillan.

Stewart, Frances. 2008. 'Horizontal Inequalities and Conflict: An Introduction and some Hypotheses.' In *Horizontal Inequalities and Conflict: Understanding Group Violence in Multiethnic Societies,* edited by Frances Stewart, 3–24. New York: Palgrave Macmillan.

Stewart, Frances. 2009. 'Horizontal inequalities as a Cause of Conflict.' *Bradford Development Lecture.* Bradford: University of Bradford. 1–55. Accessed 22 March 2019. https://bit.ly/2EpkCxa.

The BBC. 2011b. *Abuja attack: Car bomb hits Nigeria UN building.* 27 August. Accessed 2 October 2016. http://bbc.in/2dHmeqJ.

The BBC. 2016e. *Boko Haram in Nigeria: Abu Musab al-Barnawi named as new leader.* 3 August. Accessed 6 August 2016. http://bbc.in/2au7Jzu.

The BBC. 2016d. *Boko Haram in Nigeria: Split emerges over leadership.* 4 August. Accessed 5 August 2016b. http://bbc.in/2aA5NsB.

The BBC. 2017b. *Buratai: Boko Haram defeated but 'not eliminated'.* 4 July. Accessed 5 July 2017. http://bbc.in/2uriUo6.

The BBC. 2014b. *Chibok abductions in Nigeria: 'More than 230 seized'.* 21 April. Accessed 6 May 2016. http://bbc.in/1gN0Vtw.

The BBC. 2017. '*Jihad pills' found by Dutch and Italian police*. 10 May. Accessed 24 May 2017. http://bbc.in/2qWYBzv.

The BBC. 2015a. *New Boko Haram attack on Nigerian city of Maiduguri*. 1 February. Accessed 18 July 2015. http://bbc.in/1wRrBAw.

The BBC. 2015c. *Nigeria Boko Haram: Militants 'technically defeated' - Buhari*. 24 December. Accessed May 14, 2016. http://bbc.in/1JxcuDT.

The BBC. 2009. *Nigeria row over militant killing*. 31 July. Accessed 30 March 2017. http://bbc.in/2ojhJnE.

The BBC. 2017c. *Nigeria's anti-Boko Haram general Attahiru Ibrahim sacked*. 7 December. Accessed 19 March 2019. https://bbc.in/2TOxwy6.

The BBC. 2011c. *Nigeria's Boko Haram Islamists 'bombed Abuja police HQ'*. 17 June. Accessed 2 October 2016. http://bbc.in/2djPtxN.

The BBC. 2014. *Nigeria's Boko Haram leader Abubakar Shekau in profile*. 9 May. Accessed 10 January 2019. https://bbc.in/2AEXB7g.

The Economist. 2004. *Suicide terrorism: Martyrdom and Murder*. 8 January. Accessed 5 October 2016. http://econ.st/2dJUNgm.

The Economist. 2005. *The bomber will always get through*. 6 October. Accessed 5 October 2016. http://econ.st/2dwV6Y4.

The Guardian. 2010. *More than 700 inmates escape during attack on Nigerian prison*. 8 September. Accessed 29 July 2016. http://bit.ly/2aNT8Ri.

The Guardian. 2012. *Nigerian police station bombed in 'Boko Haram' attack*. 25 January. Accessed 18 October 2016. http://bit.ly/2eiYRo8.

The Sun. 2014. *Army lacks funds to fight insurgents — Finance Chief*. 21 May. Accessed 21 July 2015. http://bit.ly/1CBrrTT.

The Will. 2016. *Military action won't solve militancy, Boko Haram*. 27 September. Accessed 2 August 2017. http://bit.ly/2u19fnt.

Thiel, Joshua. 2011. 'COIN Manpower Ratios: Debunking the 10 to 1 Ratio and Surges.' *Small Wars Journal*. https://smallwarsjournal.com/jrnl/art/coin-manpower-ratios-debunking-the-10-to-1-ratio-and-surges.

Thom, William G. 1999. 'Congo-Zaire's 1996-97 Civil War in the Context of Evolving Patterns of Military Conflict in Africa in the Era of Independence.' *The Journal of Conflict Studies* 19 (2).

Thompson, Caitlin. 2011. *When half the country is off limits*. 31 January. Accessed 4April 2017. http://to.pbs.org/2nG4JaJ.

Thompson, Loren B. 2016. *The U.S. Air Force's incoherent plan to replace the A-10 Warthog*. 22 July. Accessed 24 September 2016. http://bit.ly/2cKT8BJ.

Thurston, Alexander. 2018. *Boko Haram: The History of an African Jihadist Movement (Princeton Studies in Muslim Politics)*. New Jersey: Princeton University Press.

Today. 2015. *Boko Haram: Nigeria Airforce conducts 1,448 air sorties in 4 months*. 28 October. Accessed 23 September 2016. http://bit.ly/2ctiEzx.

Trigg, Jonathan. 2016. *The Defeat of the Luftwaffe: The Eastern Front 1941–45, A Strategy for Disaster*. Stroud, Gloucestershire: Amberley Publishing.

Tse-Tung, Mao. 1967. 'Introducing The Communist.' In *Selected Works, Vol. II*, by Mao Tse Tung, 292. Foreign Languages Press. Accessed 9 August 2016. http://bit.ly/1FX84Xt.

Tse-tung, Mao. 2007. *On Guerrilla Warfare*. Illinois: BN Publishing.

Tse-tung, Mao. 1967. 'Problems of War and Strategy.' In *Selected Works, Vol. II*, by Mao Tse-Tung, 225. Foreign Languages Press. Accessed 1 September 2016. http://bit.ly/1FX84Xt.

Tse-tung, Mao. 1927. 'Vanguard of the Revolution (Translated)'. Accessed 1 August 2016. http://bit.ly/2bF0TOj.

Tuamanjong, Emmanuel, and Drew Hinshaw. 2016. *Chad soldiers to fight Boko Haram in Cameroon | Move draws the Central African Nation into regional conflict against Islamic militants.* 16 January. Accessed 17 August 2016. http://on.wsj.com/2bsN7cI.

Tzu, Sun. 2003. *Art of War.* Translated by Ralph D. Sawyer. Philadelphia: Running Press.

Ucko, David H. 2009. *The New Counterinsurgency Era: Transforming the U.S. Military for Modern Wars.* Washington, D.C.: Georgetown University Press.

Ucko, David H. 2012. 'Whither Counterinsurgency: The rise and fall of a divisive concept'. In *The Routledge Handbook of Insurgency and Counterinsurgency*, edited by Paul B. Rich and Isabelle Duyvesteyn, 67–79. Abingdon, Oxon: Routledge.

Udounwa, Colonel Solomon Effiong. 2013. *Boko Haram: Developing New Strategies to Combat Terrorism in Nigeria.* Masters of Strategic Studies Degree. Carlisle, PA: United States Army War College. http://bit.ly/2bbY0yQ.

Umar, Muhammad Sani. 2012. 'The Popular Discourses of Salafi Radicalism and Salafi Counter-radicalism in Nigeria: A Case Study of Boko Haram'. *Journal of Religion in Africa* 42 (2): 118–144. doi:10.1163/15700666-12341224.

Umoru, Henry, Joseph Erunke, and Levinus Nwabughiogu. 2014. *I'll have a home in Cameroon if … – Lamido Adamawa.* 26 March. Accessed 24 August 2016. http://bit.ly/2c60lB7.

US Army and Marine Corps. 2007. *Field Manual No. 3–24: Counterinsurgency.* Washington, D.C.: Marine Corps Warfighting Publishing.

US Army. 2004. *FMI 3-7.22 Counterinsurgency Operations.* Washington, D.C.: Department of the Army.

US Department of the Treasury. 2015. *Treasury sanctions senior Boko Haram leaders.* 1 January. Accessed 13 February 2019. https://bit.ly/2UWlgru.

Van Creveld, Martin. 1994. 'The Future of Low-intensity War'. In *War*, edited by Lawrence Freedman, 355–357. Oxford: Oxford University Press.

Van Creveld, Martin. 1991. *The Transformation of War.* New York: The Free Press, A Division of Simon & Schuster Inc.

Vanguard. 2009. *Boko Haram resurrects, declares total Jihad.* 14 August. Accessed 3 December 2016. http://bit.ly/2gMnZAv.

Vanguard. 2017. *Boko Haram terrorists kill 11 soldiers in Borno attacks.* 21 April. Accessed 21 April 2017. http://bit.ly/2p42eTp.

Vanguard. 2011. *Boko Haram: Yusuf had only 4,000 followers in 2009, Army tells court.* 8 December. Accessed 4 August 2016. http://bit.ly/1wyfbxd.

Vanguard. 2011b. *How Nur, Shekau run Boko Haram.* 3 September. Accessed 13 June 2019. https://bit.ly/2VOTMoR.

Vanguard. 2016d. *Saving Lake Chad from extinction.* 18 August. Accessed 26 August 2016. http://bit.ly/2bTmJc5.

Varin, Caroline. 2016. *Boko Haram and the War on Terror.* Santa Barbara, California: Praeger.

Varin, Caroline. 2018. 'Turning the tides of war: The impact of private'. *African Security Review* 27 (2): 144–157. doi:0.1080/10246029.2018.1489863.

Venter, Al. 2015. *Biafra's War 1967–1970: A Tribal Conflict in Nigeria That Left a Million Dead.* Solihull, West Midlands: Helion & Company Limited.

Vick, Alan, David Orletsky, Bruce Pirnie, and Seth Jones. 2002. *The Stryker Brigade Combat Team: Rethinking Strategic Responsiveness and Assessing Deployment Options.*

United States Air Force Report, Santa Monica, CA: RAND. Accessed 25 March 2019.
    https://bit.ly/2CBVlhU.

von Clausewitz, Carl. 1976. *On War*. Indexed digital version. Edited by Michael Howard.
    Translated by
Peter Paret. Princeton, New Jersey: Princeton University Press.

Walker, Andrew. 2009. *Brutal reality of Nigeria killing*. 31 July. Accessed 30 March 2017.
    http://bbc.in/2nnujkN.

Walker, Andrew. 2016. '*Eat the Heart of the Infidel*': *The Harrowing of Nigeria and the Rise
    of Boko Haram*. London: C. Hurst & Co. (Publishers) Ltd.

Walker, Andrew. 2012. *What Is Boko Haram?* Special Report, Washington, D.C.: United
    States Institute of Peace.

Walker, Andrew. 2016b. *Will Nigeria's divided Boko Haram be more or less dangerous*.
    5 August. Accessed 5 August 2016. http://bbc.in/2az1OeP.

Warden, John. 1997. 'Success in modern war: A response to Robert Pape's bombing
    to win.' *Security Studies* 7 (2): 172–190. doi:http://dx.doi.org/10.1080/096
    36419708429345.

Warner, Jason, and Hilary Matfess. 2017. *Exploding Stereotypes: The Unexpected
    Operational and Demographic Characteristics of Boko Haram's Suicide Bombers*.
    New York: Combating Terrorism Center at West Point. http://bit.ly/2vTuo7v.

Watts, Barry D. 1997. 'Ignoring reality: Problems of theory and evidence
    in security studies.' *Security Studies* 7 (2): 115–171. doi:http://dx.doi.
    org/10.1080/09636419708429344.

Weichong, Ong. 2009. 'Military Defeat of the Tamil Tigers: From Velvet Glove to Iron Fist.'
    RSIS Commentaries https://www.rsis.edu.sg/rsis-publication/idss/1208-military-defeat-
    of-the-tamil-t/#.XSnXHS2ZPFM.

Weiss, Caleb. 2016. *Ansar Dine's branch in southern Mali releases first video*. 18 May.
    Accessed 27 August 2016. http://bit.ly/1OLRtgL.

Whitehead, Eleanor. 2015. *No solution to Boko Haram from Nigeria's army*. 23 February.
    Accessed 2 August 2017. http://bit.ly/2ho9aYZ.

Wiktorowicz, Quintan. 2005. 'A Genealogy of Radical Islam.' *Studies in Conflict and
    Terrorism* 28 (1): 75–97.

Windrem, Robert. 2014. *While world watches ISIS, Boko Haram declares its own caliphate
    in Nigeria*. 12 September. Accessed 4 October 2016. http://nbcnews.to/YLzcaR.

Zedalis, Debra D. 2004. *Female Suicide Bombers*. Carlisle, PA: Strategic Studies Institute,
    U.S. Army War College.

Zenko, Micah. 2012. *Ask the Experts: Do Targeted Killings Work?* Washington, D.C.:
    Council of Foreign Relations. Accessed 10 March 2019. https://on.cfr.org/2SXdqfE.

Zenn, Jacob. 2014. 'Leadership Analysis of Boko Haram and Ansaru in Nigeria.'
    Combating Terrorism Center at Westpoint (CTC) Sentinel 7 (2): 23–29. https://bit.
    ly/2TACt8U.

Index